2005 Bankruptcy Reform Legislation with Analysis

by Hon. William Houston Brown and Lawrence R. Ahern III

- Topical examination and analysis of the Bankruptcy Abuse Prevention and Consumer Protection Act of 2005
- Checklists of new duties for debtors, debtors' attorneys, trustees, and creditors
- Charts summarizing Code changes
- Effective dates of significance to practitioners
- Text of new and significantly amended Code sections — in red-line form

2005 Bankruptcy Reform Legislation with Analysis

Commentary and Highlighted Text of the
United States Bankruptcy Code
as Amended by the
Bankruptcy Abuse Prevention and Consumer Protection Act
of 2005
Public Law 109-8

by

Hon. William Houston Brown
United States Bankruptcy Judge
Western District of Tennessee

and

Lawrence R. Ahern III
Greenebaum Doll & McDonald PLLC
Nashville, Tennessee

Copyright is not claimed as to any part of the original work prepared by a United
States Government officer or employee as part of that person's official duties.

For authorization to photocopy, please contact the Copyright Clearance Center at
222 Rosewood Drive, Danvers, MA 01923, USA (978) 750-8400; fax (978) 646-
8600 or West's Copyright Services at 610 Opperman Drive, Eagan, MN 55123, fax
(651) 687-5526. Please outline the specific material involved, the number of
copies you wish to distribute and the purpose or format of the use.

Thomson West have created this publication to provide you with accurate and
authoritative information concerning the subject matter covered. However, this
publication was not necessarily prepared by persons licensed to practice law in a
particular jurisdiction. Thomson West is not engaged in rendering legal or other
professional advice, and this publication is not a substitute for the advice of an
attorney. If you require legal or other expert advice, you should seek the services
of a competent attorney or other professional.

THOMSON
—✦—™
WEST

© 2005 Thomson/West

ISBN: 0-314-95281-0

Publisher
Cheryl J. Giraulo

Team Coordinators
Peter D. Sullivan
John Bloomquist

Publication Editors
Gavin Phillips, J.D.
Cheryl Bergstrom, J.D.
Mary A. Raha
Thomas I. Parry

Composition Specialist
Thomas M. Jones

Editorial Staff
Brian D. Bobbie
Colleen R. Courtade, Esq.
Philip A. Felman, Esq.
Richard Gallagher, Esq.
Thomas F. Hess
Shirley K. Iannone
Elaine Keller-Petryk
Zach Kuvizic
Jose Muriel
I. Jeannine Sims
David Tamber, Esq.
Stephen P. Tarolli, Esq.
Michael J. Yaworsky, Esq.

ABOUT THE AUTHORS

HONORABLE WILLIAM HOUSTON BROWN

Honorable William Houston Brown is a U.S. bankruptcy judge for the Western District of Tennessee, sitting primarily in Memphis. He also has been designated to sit in the Middle District of Tennessee, the Southern District of Florida, the Eastern District of Michigan and the Western District of Kentucky. Judge Brown served a four-year term on the Bankruptcy Appellate Panel for the Sixth Circuit from 1999 through 2002. After graduating first in his class, he received his law degree and was elected to the Order of Coif at the University of Tennessee College of Law. Judge Brown is a member of the American Bankruptcy Institute and the American College of Bankruptcy and is also the author of several other Thomson/West publications, including *Bankruptcy Exemption Manual*, *Debtor and Creditor Relations* (Vols 9-11, West's Legal Forms), *Debtor-Creditor Law and Practice* (Vol. 16, Tennessee Practice Series), *Bankruptcy Courts* (Vols 6-6B, West's Federal Forms). He is also is an editor for *Norton Bankruptcy Law Adviser* and a contributing editor to *Norton Bankruptcy Law and Practice, 2d*.

LAWRENCE R. AHERN III

Lawrence R. Ahern III practices bankruptcy and commercial law, with a practice based in Nashville, and is Member-in-Charge of the Nashville and Atlanta offices of Greenebaum Doll & McDonald PLLC. He is a graduate of Vanderbilt University Law School, where he has served as Adjunct Professor of Law, teaching Secured Transactions, since 1998. Mr. Ahern serves on the Advisory Board of the St. John's Bankruptcy LL.M. program and was Visiting Professor at Cumberland School of Law, Fall 2002, teaching Secured Transactions and Banking. He is a Fellow of the American College of Bankruptcy. Certified since 1994 as a business bankruptcy specialist by the American Board of Certification, he since has been named Director and Secretary of the ABC. Mr. Ahern's other affiliations include the American Bankruptcy Institute (Director). He is admitted to practice law in all Tennessee state courts, all federal courts in Tennessee and the Eastern District of Michigan, the Third and Sixth Circuit Courts of Appeals and the U.S. Supreme Court, He is also the author of several other Thomson/West publications, including *Bankruptcy Procedure Manual*, *Bankruptcy Exemption Manual*, *Commercial Transactions* (Vols 12-15, West's Legal Forms), *Bankruptcy Courts* (Vols 6-6B, West's Federal Forms), *Debtor and Creditor Relations* (Vols 9-11, West's Legal Forms) and *Debtor-Creditor Law and Practice* (Vol. 16, Tennessee Practice Series).

DEDICATION

We dedicate this publication to the United States Bankruptcy Judges who, with the assistance of experienced members of the bankruptcy bar, will make the changes found in these amendments work in the real world of debtors and creditors.

IN THIS VOLUME:

COMMENTARY ON AMENDED CODE

D. Other Asset Protection Issues Under the 2005 Code

    1. Section 548(e)

    2. New Exemption Timing Issues

XIII. Changes of Primary Interest to Parties in Business Cases

    A. Small Business Cases

        1. Introduction

        2. "Small Business" Defined

        3. Reporting Requirements

        4. Initial Interview

        5. New Duties in Small Business Cases

        6. Exclusivity, Disclosure, and Confirmation

    B. Health Care Cases

        1. Patient Records

        2. Patient Transfer

        3. New Administrative Expense Claim

        4. Patient Care Ombudsman

        5. Restriction on Transfer of Assets by Non-Profit Entities

        6. Relief from Stay for Department of Health and Human Services

    C. Cross-Border Cases

        1. Introduction

        2. Commencement of Chapter 15 Case

        3. Administrative Issues

    D. Other Case Administration Issues

        1. Introduction

        2. Status Conferences

I. INTRODUCTION AND SCOPE OF COMMENTARY

On April 20, 2005, the President signed the Bankruptcy Abuse Prevention and Consumer Protection Act of 2005 ("BAPCPA"), Public Law 109-8, 119 Stat. 23, which makes the most substantial changes to the Bankruptcy Code since its enactment in 1978. The principal purpose of this publication is to highlight and briefly comment upon the significant changes to the former Bankruptcy Code. As to some sections of the amended Code, we will suggest how the amendments may be interpreted while in discussing other sections we will pose some of the questions that will remain unanswered until court decisions provide some guidance. Not all of the amendments are consistent with other amended sections, leaving open for interpretation how they may be applied, and we attempt to point out those inconsistencies. It is not the purpose of this publication to explore in depth each change to the Code, and the focus will be upon the consumer and commercial changes in the Code that will be applicable to cases filed in the United States. Since the predominant changes made by BAPCPA are directed to consumer bankruptcies, the bulk of this commentary is so directed. The cross-border insolvency provisions found in chapter 15 of the amended Code and the financial transaction changes made in the Bankruptcy and other titles of the United States Code will be described generally but not commented upon in depth, since those are of more limited interest in the typical bankruptcy case. That is not to say that those new financial provisions are unimportant; rather, the focus of this analysis of the 2005 bankruptcy legislation is on the changes made in the consumer and domestic commercial sections of the Bankruptcy Code.

Throughout the commentary references to the Bankruptcy Code prior to its 2005 amendments will be to the former Code ("former Code §"); references to the Bankruptcy Abuse Prevention and Consumer Protection Act of 2005 will be to BAPCPA ("BAPCPA §"); references to the Bankruptcy Code as amended by BAPCPA will be to the 2005 Code ("2005 Code § or 11 U.S.C.A. §"); and references to other titles of the United States Code as amended by BAPCPA will be to that title and section (e.g., "18 U.S.C.A. §").

We begin this commentary with a review of the effective dates of the various amendments, then some checklists of the new duties imposed by the 2005 Code. The organization of the substantive commentary is by bankruptcy subject matter divided into four groups: the consumer or individual debtor changes, identifying the significant changes in each chapter of the 2005 Code; the changes in various Code topics that will apply to all or most bankruptcy cases, arranged in a basic topical order; the changes to exemptions and exclusions from the bankruptcy estate with commentary on asset protection under the 2005 Code; and the commercial bankruptcy changes. As we discuss amendments to the Bankruptcy Code, we will reference the amended 2005 Code by pointing to the highlighted version of the 2005 Code, found in the second part of this publication. The highlighted 2005 Code shows the actual changes by BAPCPA as follows: new language is in italics and language deleted from the former Code is shown by strikethrough. The changes in titles 11, 18, and 28 are included but the amendments made by BAPCPA to other titles are not included, since the focus of this publication is on bankruptcy amendments.

This highlighted Code hopefully will be useful to the bankruptcy bar and judiciary, since those amendments that are not effective immediately upon enactment leave the bench and bar with two Bankruptcy Codes to contend with for quite some time. Not only will the pre-2005 Code apply for most cases and proceedings filed in the next six months, it will continue to apply to many cases and proceedings that remain in the courts beyond that six months. Timing of filings and events within cases may determine which version of the Code controls. Notice should be taken that there are technical errors within some of the amendments, causing incorrect numbering in places. There will, no doubt, be a technical amendments bill that will be considered by Congress in the near future; therefore, caution must be taken in looking at the numbering for subsections in the attached highlighted Code to see if numbering changes as technical amendments may be made.

II. EFFECTIVE DATES OF THE AMENDMENTS

GENERAL EFFECTIVE DATE: October 17, 2005
(180 days from enactment by President's signing on April 20, 2005)

A. ENACTMENT DATE

The United States Senate passed BAPCPA on March 10, 2005, and the House of Representatives passed the Act without amendment on April 14, 2005, sending it to the President. President Bush signed the Act into law on April 20, 2005; thus that is the enactment date that triggers the various effective dates.

B. GENERAL DATE 180 DAYS FROM ENACTMENT

Although several specific provisions of BAPCPA are effective immediately upon enactment or at other times specified, the bulk of BAPCPA's amendments and additions to the former Code are effective in cases filed 180 days after enactment. The 180 days from the President's signing would be October 17, 2005. BAPCPA § 1501 provides:

> Except as otherwise provided in this Act, this Act and the amendments made by this Act shall take effect 180 days after the date of enactment of this Act.
>
> (1) Except as otherwise provided in this Act and paragraph (2), the amendments made by this Act shall not apply with respect to cases commenced under title 11, United States Code, before the effective date of this Act.
>
> (2) the amendments made by sections 308, 322, and 330 shall apply with respect to cases commenced under title 11, United States Code, on or after the date of the enactment of this Act.

As paragraph (1) indicates, the bulk of the amendments do not apply in pending bankruptcy cases or pending proceedings within cases; rather, they will apply in those cases initially filed 180 or more days later. There are other effective dates spread throughout BAPCPA that apply to government agencies, including the Executive Office of United States Trustees, but this publication will not address most of those dates since they are of limited immediate interest to practitioners. The exceptions to the 180-day effectiveness that are of most interest to those engaged in bankruptcy practice are noted below.

11

Lease Rejection Timeline

```
(1)----------------------- >(2)--------------->(3) - - - - - >
      (first 120 days)          (90 more days)
(1)                            (2)                    (3)
    Timeline                   Extension          Additional
    Starts with                After First        Extensions
    Filing of                  120 Days           Only With
    Petition                   Only For           Landlord's
    ("Order for                "Cause" and        Consent
    Relief")                   90-day
                               Maximum
```

The sections of the 2005 Code that apply immediately upon enactment, on or after April 20, 2005, are as follows:

2005 Code § 522(o), as provided by BAPCPA § 308, reduces the homestead exemption to the extent that value is attributable to any portion of nonexempt property that the debtor disposed of within 10 years of filing bankruptcy, if the disposition was made with intent to hinder, delay, or defraud creditors. See discussion of the new § 522(o) and its related §§ 522(p) and (q) in the exemption discussion.

2005 Code § 522 (p), as provided by BAPCPA § 322, generally places a $125,000 cap on the homestead acquired within 1,215 days (approximately 3.3 years) of filing bankruptcy. 2005 Code § 522(q) extends that $125,000 cap to situations involving a felony criminal conviction or other violations specified in the section. See the discussions of those new sections and their exceptions in the exemption discussion.

2005 Code § 727(a)(12), § 1141(d), § 1228(f), and § 1328(h), as provided by BAPCPA § 330, delay the granting of a discharge when it appears that Code § 522(q) may be applicable. See discussion of those amendments in the discharge and exemption discussions.

In addition to these provisions that are specifically identified in BAPCPA § 1501(2), there are others that are effective upon enactment, according to specific BAPCPA sections:

Code § 104(b) adds several sections to its list for which dollar amounts are adjusted in 3-year intervals.

Changes to §§ 363, 541, and 1129 concerning the rules for nonprofit property sales are effective immediately, subject to the court considering in a confirmation hearing the effect of those rules on a party whose rights in the property had previously been established.

Code §1222(a)(2) and § 1231(b), as provided in BAPCPA § 1003, are effective in all cases on the date of enactment, but specifically would not apply retroactively to title 11 cases commenced before the enactment. New § 1222(a)(2) generally requires the payment of priority claims, except for a claim owed to a governmental unit that arose from the disposition of a farm asset, and amended § 1231(b) replaces former language with "any governmental unit." See discussion of these provisions under the chapter 12 discussion.

Code § 547(i), as specified in BAPCPA § 1213, provides that in the event that the trustee successfully avoids a preferential transfer made by the debtor between

90 days and one year prior to bankruptcy to a creditor that is not an insider, but the transfer is for the benefit of an insider, the transfer is avoided only as to the creditor that is an insider. This amendment "shall apply to any case that is pending or commenced on or after the date of enactment"; thus this retroactive amendment reaches to those cases in which avoidance proceedings are pending upon enactment.

BAPCPA § 1223 adds 28 temporary bankruptcy judgeships in various districts, effective upon enactment, by amendment to 28 U.S.C.A. § 152. Of course, the filling of these new judgeships by the circuit courts depends upon funding of the new positions, and the judgeships approved do not represent the most current list as requested by the Judicial Conference of the United States Courts.

Code § 303(b)(1), as specified in BAPCPA § 1234, provides that a creditor may not commence an involuntary chapter 7 or chapter 11 case if the debtor's liability on a claim or the amount of the claim is contingent or is the subject of a bona fide dispute. This amendment "shall take effect on the date of the enactment of this Act and shall apply with respect to cases commenced under title 11 of the United States Code before, on, and after such date," again, a retroactive amendment. See discussion of these amendments under involuntary bankruptcy.

Sections 507(a)(4) and (5) make changes in the amount of employee priority claims, increasing the amounts to $10,000.

Section 1104(e) requires the U.S. trustee to move for a chapter 11 trustee appointment if it appears that current corporate management participated in fraud, dishonesty, or criminal conduct in the management of the debtor.

Section 1114(l) provides for reinstatement of retiree benefits that the chapter 11 debtor may have modified in the 180-days preceding filing.

Section 1334(e) of title 28 is amended to give the district court jurisdiction over all claims or causes of action that involve construction or rules governing 11 U.S.C.A. §327.

28 U.S.C.A. § 1930 changes the filing fees for chapter 7, 11, and 13 cases and makes changes in the U.S. trustee system fund. Section 1930(f) institutes an in forma pauperis category under which chapter 7 filing fees may be waived for those debtors well below an official poverty income level. See the fee discussion.

Current Monthly Income (gross before required
      deductions and no averaging required for
      6 months since salary stable)   8,000.00
Plus: Contributions to family expenses from
      debtor's mother   950.00

      Total Family Income   **8,950.00**

Expense Deductions:

    IRS National Standard for a 4-person family (food,
        housekeeping supplies, apparel, personal care),
        based on gross monthly income (assume IRS amount
        is less than actual expenses and
        lesser amount is used)   1,564.00

    5% increase in food and apparel(assuming documented)   59.25

    IRS Local Standard for housing and utilities in
        Memphis, Shelby County, TN (amount is $1,354.00
        which is reduced by the debtor's actual
        mortgage payment of $ 1,138.09)   215.91

    IRS Regional Standard for transportation:
        (debtor's actual car note is less than IRS ownership
        cost of $475, so no ownership cost is deducted here)
        Operating costs   197.00

Debtor's Other Actual Expenses:

    Actual deductions for taxes and social security
        (assume these are the correct withholding amounts) 1,500.00
    Property taxes on home   225.00
    Health insurance for debtor, spouse and child   260.00
    Debtor's retirement deduction for 401K plan   475.00
    Documented expenses for disabled mother's care
        (Assume part-time nursing care is needed)   1,800.00
    Child's private school ($1,500 annual cap)   125.00
    Mortgage principal and interest due over 60 months
        and divided by 60   1,138.09
    Car debt divided by 60   250.00
    Furniture debt divided by 60   25.00
    Priority income tax debt divided by 60   33.33
    Priority real property tax debt divided by 60   25.00
        (these priority amounts would be more with interest)
    Amount required to cure mortgage arrearage over 60 months 72.00
        (assume this would be correct with interest)
    Assumed chapter 13 administrative expenses(based on
        secured and priority payments and 100%
        of unsecured in a plan and assume this
        is below the 10% cap)   211.31

Net Current Monthly Income for Means Test $ 774.11

Chapter 12, the family farmer and now also a family fisherman chapter, is made a permanent part of the Bankruptcy Code, effective July 1, 2005. Pending the enactment of BAPCPA, Congress had temporarily extended chapter 12 several times. This July 1 date is the expiration date for the most recent temporary extension of chapter 12.

Section 523(a)(19)(B), concerning securities fraud, is effective retroactively until July 30, 2002, the date of enactment of the Sarbanes-Oxley Act.

The reach-back period of § 548(a) and (b) is changed from one to two years, effective one year following enactment.

New reporting requirements for small business debtors will become effective 60 days following the promulgation of the new reporting forms.

There are other effective dates spread throughout BAPCPA that apply to government agencies, including the Executive Office of United States Trustees, but this publication will not address those dates since they are of limited immediate interest to practitioners.

III. CHECKLIST OF NEW DUTIES FOR DEBTOR

❑ **Rule 9011 Verification**

BAPCPA § 319 expresses the "sense of Congress" that Federal Rule of Bankruptcy Procedure 9011 should be modified to include the requirement that all documents, including schedules, whether signed or unsigned, that are submitted to the court or to a trustee by a debtor who is acting pro se or who is represented by an attorney should not be submitted until the debtor and the debtor's attorney have made "reasonable inquiry to verify that the information contained in such document is—(1) well grounded in fact; and (2) warranted by existing law or a good faith argument for the extension, modification, or reversal of existing law." While Congress does not normally establish procedural rules, this expression of congressional intent will no doubt receive the attention of the Rules Committee of the Judicial Conference of the United States and will affect the manner in which Bankruptcy Rule 9011 is interpreted. Basically, this expression by Congress puts an emphasis upon the debtor's responsibility to verify the factual accuracy and legal basis for everything contained in bankruptcy schedules and other documents. This general "sense of Congress" expression is in addition to the specific amendments to 11 U.S.C.A. § 707 that impose the Rule 9011 standard for the certification by a debtor's attorney about the need for filing under chapter 7 and that the filing is both accurate and not an abuse. See the discussion of those amendments under the chapter 7 discussion.

❑ **Prebankruptcy Credit Briefing**

Section 109(h) requires, with limited exceptions, all individual debtors to obtain within 180 days of filing bankruptcy an individual or group briefing from an approved nonprofit budget and credit counseling agency, and the briefing must, at a minimum, have "outlined the opportunities for available credit counseling and assisted such individual in performing a related budget analysis." Unless an exception applies, as a condition to filing bankruptcy, the debtor must file with the court a certificate from the agency describing the services offered, and, if a debt repayment plan was created, the debtor must file that plan. See the later discussion of this requirement and its exceptions.

❑ **File Tax Returns**

Section 521(e) requires the chapter 7 and 13 debtor to give to the trustee, prior to the meeting of creditors, a copy of the most recent year's federal tax return and to give a copy to any creditor requesting it. A transcript may be provided instead of the return. Failure to provide the return requires dismissal of the case unless the debtor can show that failure is due to circumstances beyond the debtor's control. See discussion of tax return requirements under chapters 7 and 13 and under conversion or dismissal of cases.

In addition, chapter 13 debtors must file all required tax returns (state, federal, or local) prior to the meeting of creditors, and the trustee may delay that meeting only for 120 days to permit the filings. See discussion of this in chapter 13. Section 521(j) provides that, during any case of an individual debtor, if the taxing authority so requests and upon the debtor's failure to file postpetition returns, the court shall dismiss or convert the case, whichever is in the best interests of the creditors and the estate.

In a chapter 7, 11, or 13 case of an individual debtor, upon request by the court, the U.S. trustee (and presumably bankruptcy administrator), or a party in interest, the debtor shall file a copy of all federal tax returns due while the case is pending, and in chapter 13 these returns must be filed annually.

❑ **Debtor Education**

Prior to receiving a discharge, the individual debtor must complete a personal financial management course. See 11 U.S.C.A. § 727(a)(11) and the discussion of debtor education.

❑ **Schedules**

In addition to the typical schedules accompanying a petition, the debtor must file a certificate by the debtor's attorney or a petition preparer that the debtor has been given the extensive notice required by § 342(b); a copy of all payment advices from the debtor's employer showing payments to the debtor within the prior 60 days; a statement of net monthly income, itemized to show how it was calculated (note that while different terminology is used, this may be the same as the current monthly income, after allowable deductions, that is the basis for a means test analysis); and a statement of reasonably anticipated increases in income or expenditures over the next 12 months.

Failure to complete and file all required schedules within 45 days of filing shall result in dismissal of the case, unless the debtor, trustee, or a party in interest successfully moves for an extension, which cannot exceed another 45 days.

❑ **Compliance with Chapter 7 Statement of Intention**

Within 30 days of the meeting of creditors, the chapter 7 debtor must perform the stated intention of surrender, redemption, or reaffirmation, and the failure to do so will result in stay relief. See the discussion of automatic stay. Also, § 521(a)(6) provides that a chapter 7 debtor may not retain possession of purchase-money collateral beyond 45 days from the meeting of creditors without redeeming the collateral or reaffirming the debt. Failure here also results in stay relief. The difference in the 30 and 45 days will create confusion.

❏ **Education Retirement Account**

If the debtor has an interest in an education individual retirement account or a qualified state tuition program, the debtor must disclose that interest at the time of filing the schedules. See the discussion of these accounts in exemptions and exclusions from the estate.

❏ **Preserve Automatic Stay**

If the debtor has filed previously, the filings may trigger termination of the automatic stay or prevent the stay from taking effect. To preserve the stay, or to activate it, in a subsequent filing, the debtor will need to take quick steps and carry a burden of proof. The debtor must disclose and notice a landlord who has obtained a prebankruptcy judgment, and for property subject to bailment or lease, any prebankruptcy defaults are retained as effective. For these and other reasons, familiarity with the changes in the automatic stay, discussed later, is essential.

❏ **Identification Document**

If the U.S. trustee or case trustee (and presumably bankruptcy administrator) requests it, the debtor must provide a document establishing identity, such as driver's license or passport.

IV. CHECKLIST OF NEW DUTIES OF DEBTOR'S ATTORNEY

❏ **Rule 9011 Verification**

BAPCPA § 319 of the Act states the "sense of Congress" that Federal Rule of Bankruptcy Procedure 9011 should be modified to include the requirement that all documents, including schedules, whether signed or unsigned, that are submitted to the court or to a trustee by a debtor represented by an attorney should not be submitted until the attorney has made "reasonable inquiry to verify that the information contained in such document is—(1) well grounded in fact; and (2) warranted by existing law or a good faith argument for the extension, modification, or reversal of existing law."

Basically, this expression by Congress puts an emphasis upon the responsibility of the debtor's attorney to verify the factual accuracy and legal basis for everything contained in bankruptcy schedules and other documents. This general "sense of Congress" expression is in addition to the specific amendments to 11 U.S.C.A. § 707 that place the Rule 9011 standard on the certification by a debtor's attorney about the need for filing under chapter 7 and that the filing is both accurate and not an abuse. See the discussion of those amendments under the chapter 7 discussion. Sanctions may be awarded under § 707(b)(4). What remains to be seen in practice is the extent to which the attorney for the debtor is held liable, under a Rule 9011 application, for inaccuracies in the debtor's schedules. The congressional expression is that there must be a reasonable inquiry.

❏ **Debt Relief Agency**

Under the definition of debt relief agency in §101(12A) and assisted person under §101(3), an attorney providing bankruptcy assistance to a consumer debtor is a debt relief agency and must comply with the strict restrictions and disclosure requirements for such agencies found in §§ 526, 527, and 528. See the discussion of debt relief agency.

❑ **Enforce New Debtor Requirements and Notice to Debtor**

In order to effectively represent consumer debtors under the amended Code, the debtor's attorney must assure that the debtor carries out all of the new and former duties. A part of what the debtor must file is a certification from the debtor's attorney that the debtor has been provided with the specific notice required by § 342(b).

❑ **Means Test Calculation**

As will be seen, the means test is complex, and most consumer debtors will require the assistance of an attorney in calculating whether that test applies. BAPCPA amends 18 U.S.C.A. § 2075 to state that the bankruptcy rules shall prescribe a form for the statement of monthly income required by § 707(b)(2)(C). The Judicial Conference's Rules Committee is already meeting to recommend changes in the rules and forms in order to comply with BAPCPA.

❑ **Awareness of Code Changes**

Obviously, in order to effectively represent consumer debtors, an attorney must be familiar with the many changes in consumer bankruptcy law.

V. CHECKLISTS OF NEW DUTIES FOR TRUSTEES

A. NEW CHAPTER 7 TRUSTEE DUTIES

❑ **Domestic Support Creditors**

The chapter 7 trustee has an expanded duty under Code § 704(a)(10) and (c)(10) to advise a domestic support creditor in writing of the existence of and right to use support enforcement and collection agencies and to provide notice of such a claim to those agencies. Also, the trustee must provide notice to the domestic support creditor and the support collection agencies of the debtor's chapter 7 discharge, any reaffirmations, any debts excepted from discharge under §§ 523(a)(2), (4), or (14A), and current address information about the debtor and the debtor's employer. Similar changes would be made in the chapter 11 trustee's duties found in section 1106, the chapter 12 trustee's duties under section 1202, and the chapter 13 trustee's duties under section 1302.

❑ **Employee Benefit Plans**

Under § 704(a)(11), the chapter 7 trustee must continue to perform the duties of a employee benefit plan administrator, if the debtor was serving at the time of filing bankruptcy as a plan administrator, as that term is defined under ERISA.

❑ **Health Care Business**

If the debtor is in the health care business, the chapter 7 trustee must use "all reasonable and best efforts" to transfer any patients of such a business being closed to another such business in the physical vicinity that provides substantially similar services with a reasonable quality of care. Obviously, in those few such cases, the trustee is given a duty of investigating the availability of and quality of similar health care businesses and seeing that patients are properly transferred.

❏ **Uniform Final Reports**

By amendment to 28 U.S.C.A. § 589b, as a part of the emphasis on improving bankruptcy data, the final reports required of trustees must be uniform, and the Attorney General is required to issue rules for those forms.

B. NEW CHAPTER 11 TRUSTEE DUTIES

Since a chapter 11 debtor in possession has most of the duties of a trustee, and there is no change to Code § 1107, a debtor in possession would have the following new duties as well. (Some will be problematic for individual chapter 11 debtors. For example, the duties owed to domestic support creditors will require the debtor in possession to provide personal information.)

❏ **Domestic Support Creditors**

The chapter 11 trustee has an expanded duty under amended Code § 1106(a)(8) and (c) to advise a domestic support creditor of support enforcement and collection agencies in the same manner as chapter 7 trustees. See those duties above under the chapter 7 trustee, and see Code §§ 1106(a)(8) and (c).

❏ **Employee Benefit Plans**

Under 2005 Code § 1106(a)(1), the chapter 11 trustee's duties incorporate § 704(a)(11); thus, like the chapter 7 trustee, a trustee in chapter 11 must continue to perform the duties of an employee benefit plan administrator, if the debtor was serving as a plan administrator at the time of the bankruptcy filing, as that term is defined under ERISA.

❏ **Health Care Business**

Under 2005 Code § 1106(a)(1), the chapter 11 trustee's duties incorporate § 704(a)(12); thus if the debtor is in the health care business, the chapter 11 trustee must use "all reasonable and best efforts" to transfer any patients of such a business being closed to another such business in the physical vicinity that provides substantially similar services with reasonable quality of care. Obviously, in those few such cases, the trustee is given a duty of investigating the availability of and quality of similar health care businesses and seeing that patients are properly transferred.

❏ **Uniform Final Reports**

By amendment to 28 U.S.C.A. § 589b, as a part of the emphasis on improving bankruptcy data, the final reports required of trustees must be uniform, and the Attorney General is required to issue rules for those forms.

C. NEW CHAPTER 12 AND 13 TRUSTEE DUTIES

❏ **Domestic Support Creditors**

The chapter 12 and 13 trustees have the expanded duties under 2005 Code § 1202(b)(6) and (c) and § 1302(b)(6) and (d) to advise a domestic support creditor of support enforcement and collection agencies in the same manner as chapter 7 trustees. See those duties above under the chapter 7 trustee, and see Code §§1202 (b)(6) and (c); 1302(b)(6) and (d).

❑ **Uniform Final Reports**

By amendment to 28 U.S.C.A. § 589b, as a part of the emphasis on improving bankruptcy data, the final reports required of trustees must be uniform, and the Attorney General is required to issue rules for those forms.

VI. CHECKLIST OF NEW DUTIES FOR CREDITORS

Although the focus of BAPCPA and of the publicity surrounding it has been upon changes impacting consumer debtors, there are changes that impose new responsibilities on creditors. The principal new creditor duties are:

❑ **Domestic Support Creditors**

In cases under chapters 7, 11, 12, or 13 that include creditors holding domestic support claims, any other creditors in the case that hold a claim that was excepted from discharge under §523(a)(2), (4), or (14A), or that was reaffirmed, have a duty to provide the last known address of the debtor upon request from the domestic support creditor. Creditors fulfilling this duty have a protection from liability for the disclosure. See 11 U.S.C.A. §§ 704(b)(2); 1106(c)(2); 1202(c)(2); and 1302(d)(2).

❑ **Filing Abuse Motions—Rule 9011**

New § 707(b)(5) gives the court discretion on its own initiative or on motion of a party in interest to award the debtor reasonable costs and attorney's fees in contesting a § 707(b) motion that is not granted by the court, but there are strict limitations on this possibility. The creditor filing a motion to dismiss for abuse has some duty to comply with Rule 9011 standards in filing the motion. See discussion of this section under the discussion of chapter 7.

VII. CHECKLIST OF NEW DUTIES FOR U.S. TRUSTEE AND BANKRUPTCY ADMINISTRATOR

❑ **Statement of Abuse**

By an addition to Code § 704(b), which formerly addressed only the duties of the chapter 7 trustee, the U.S. trustee or bankruptcy administrator must file a statement of whether a case would be presumed abusive within 10 days of the § 341 meeting. Within five days of receiving the statement, the clerk of the court "shall provide a copy of the statement to all creditors," and, within 30 days of the § 341 meeting, the U.S. trustee or bankruptcy administrator must file a § 707(b) motion based upon abuse or a statement of why the case is not presumed abusive even though the debtor's current monthly income:

...is not less than–

(A) in the case of a debtor in a household of 1 person, the median family income of the applicable State for 1 earner; or

(B) in the case of a debtor in a household of 2 or more individuals, the highest median family income of the applicable State for a family of the same number or fewer individuals.

11 U.S.C.A. § 704(b)(2)

❑ Chapter 13 Administrative Expense

Section 107 of the Act requires the Director of the Executive Office for the United States Trustees to issue within 180 days of enactment "schedules of reasonable and necessary administrative expenses of administering a chapter 13 plan for each judicial district of the United States." The stated purpose for this directive is the implementation of the newly amended Code § 707(b), that is the means test, to aid in the calculation of current income for that test by knowing what the administrative costs in chapter 13 would be.

❑ Debtor Education

Section 105 of BAPCPA requires the Director of the Executive Office for United States Trustees "to consult with a wide range of individuals who are experts in the field of debtor education," including chapter 13 trustees, to develop a financial management curriculum and materials to educate individual debtors. Six judicial districts would be chosen to test the effectiveness of that curriculum and the financial management training materials, to be tested over an 18-month period beginning no later than 270 days after enactment. The Director will report to Congress the results of the testing within three months of its conclusion. Notwithstanding this study, a chapter 7 or 13 debtor's requirement to obtain financial education as a precondition to discharge is effective 180 days from enactment.

❑ Household Goods Definition

Section 313(b) of the Act states that the Director of the Executive Office of United States Trustees is to submit a report to the Judiciary Committees of the House and Senate within two years of enactment, with the report to contain findings concerning the utilization of the new definition for household goods under § 522(f), including findings of the impact on debtors. That report may contain recommendations for any changes in § 522(f).

VIII. "SENSE OF CONGRESS" STATEMENTS

In some sections of BAPCPA, Congress expressed its "sense" about changes in the procedural rules and in other aspects of bankruptcy procedure. These "sense of Congress" statements are not a part of the enacted amendments to the Bankruptcy Code, but they have importance in the way that the amendments will be interpreted and applied since they supply a form of legislative history and rationale.

❑ Rule 9011

BAPCPA § 319 expresses the "sense of Congress" that Federal Rule of Bankruptcy Procedure 9011 should be modified to include the requirement that all documents, including schedules, whether signed or unsigned, that are submitted to the court or to a trustee by a debtor who is acting pro se or who is represented by an attorney should not be submitted until the debtor and the debtor's attorney have made "reasonable inquiry to verify that the information contained in such document is—(1) well grounded in fact; and (2) warranted by existing law or a good faith argument for the extension, modification, or reversal of existing law."

❑ **IRS Standards**

BAPCPA § 103 expresses the "sense of Congress" that the Internal Revenue Service Standard guidelines for repayment plans may be adjusted "by the Secretary of the Treasury as needed to accommodate their use for § 707(b) means testing purposes." Within two years of enactment, the Executive Office for the United States Trustees is to report to Congress on its "findings regarding the utilization of Internal Revenue Service Standards for determining" the § 707(b) monthly expenses and the impact of those standards on debtors and the bankruptcy court.

❑ **Debtor Education**

Congress expresses a sense that states should develop personal finance curricula for elementary and secondary schools.

❑ **Creditworthiness**

A "sense of Congress" is also expressed that the Board of Governors of the Federal Reserve System shall conduct a study of the consumer credit industry practices of soliciting and extending credit and report within 12 months on its findings.

❑ **Data**

In conjunction with the part of BAPCPA that addresses the improvement of bankruptcy data and statistics, Congress expressed its sense that national policy should be that all bankruptcy data be maintained by the clerks in electronic form, subject to appropriate privacy concerns. A single set of data definitions and forms should be established, and this may require changes in the electronic filing methods currently being used by the bankruptcy courts.

IX. NEW DEFINITIONS—11 U.S.C.A. §101

Code § 101 is amended to add several new definitions:

Section 101(3) defines "assisted person" in bankruptcy, a term that applies only to consumer debtors with nonexempt property below $150,000 in value.

Section 101(4A) defines "bankruptcy assistance" as the providing of goods or services related to a title 11 bankruptcy case to an "assisted person"; thus "bankruptcy assistance" only comes into play in regard to consumer debtors.

Section 101(7A) defines "commercial fishing operation" and § 101(7B) defines "commercial fishing vessel." See the discussion of chapter 12.

Section 101(10A) defines "current monthly income." See discussion of that definition in chapter 7's discussion of the means test.

Section 101(12A) defines "debt relief agency" to mean "any person who provides any bankruptcy assistance to an assisted person" or "who is a bankruptcy petition preparer under section 110," but the definition excludes some specific persons or entities. The exclusions include creditors who are assisting the consumer debtor in a debt restructuring effort and depository institutions or credit unions as well as employees of "debt relief agencies" or tax-exempt nonprofit organizations. Since "debt relief agency" is linked to "bankruptcy assistance" and an "assisted person," the bankruptcy debtor being assisted must be a consumer debtor. If an attorney, for example, is giving bankruptcy assistance to a consumer debtor, that attorney is a "debt relief agency," but if an attorney is giving bankruptcy assistance to a corporate or other nonconsumer debtor, that attorney is not a "debt relief agency." The definition of "debt relief agency" is linked to a new Code § 526 that provides restrictions on such agencies. See the discussion under debt relief agencies.

§ 101(13A) is added to define "debtor's principal residence," as:

(A) a residential structure, including incidental property, without regard to whether that structure is attached to real property; and

(B) includes an individual condominium or cooperative unit, a mobile or manufactured home, or trailer.

§ 101(14) is amended to exclude investment banker from the definition of "disinterested person."

§ 101(14A) defines "domestic support obligation," a term that replaces alimony, maintenance, or support in §§ 523(a)(5) and (15) and in other areas of the Code. See the discussion of domestic support obligation.

§ 101(18)'s definition of "family farmer" is changed by an increase in the debt limit for that chapter. See the discussion of chapter 12.

§ 101(19A) and (B) define "family fisherman," a term that is discussed in chapter 12.

§ 101(22) defines "financial participant." See the discussion of the new title 15.

§ 101(23) and (24) modify the definitions of "foreign proceeding" and "foreign representative." See the discussion of the new title 15.

§ 101(25) modifies the definition of "forward contract."

§ 101(27A) defines "health care business."

§ 101(27B) is added to define "incidental property" as meaning:

with respect to a debtor's principal residence—

(A) property commonly conveyed with a principal residence in the area where the real property is located;

(B) all easements, rights, appurtenances, fixtures, rents, royalties, mineral rights, oil or gas rights or profits, water rights, escrow funds, or insurance proceeds; and

(C) all replacements or additions.

§ 101(38A) defines "master netting agreement," and §101(38B) defines "master netting agreement participant."

§ 101(39A), defines "median family income," which:

means for any year—

(A) the median family income both calculated and reported by the Bureau of the Census in the then most recent year; and

(B) if not so calculated and reported in the then current year, adjusted annually after such most recent year until the next year in which median family income is both calculated and reported by the Bureau of the Census, to reflect the percentage change in the Consumer Price Index for All Urban Consumers during the period of years occurring after such most recent year and before such current year.

§ 101(41A) is added to define "personally identifiable information."

§ 101(47) modifies the definition of "repurchase agreement."

§ 101(48A) defines "securities self regulatory organization."

§ 101(51D) modifies the definition of "small business debtor."

§ 101(53B) modifies the definition of "swap agreement."

§ 101(54) modifies the definition of "transfer."

X. CHANGES FOR CONSUMER AND INDIVIDUAL BANKRUPTCY CASES

A. CHAPTER 7

1. CONVERSION

Code § 706(c) is amended to permit conversion to chapter 12 or 13 with the "consent" of the debtor. The former section required: "The court may not convert a case under this chapter to a case under chapter 12 or 13 of this title unless the debtor requests such conversion." This change is a part of the "Needs-Based Bankruptcy" referred to in Title I of BAPCPA.

2. ABUSE

Code § 707(b)(1) is amended to permit the case trustee, bankruptcy administrator, and any party in interest, with some standing restrictions, to move for dismissal of an individual's chapter 7 case, and the amendment reduces substantial abuse to "an abuse," while imposing a means test to presume an abuse when a debtor's current monthly income exceeds a formula amount, as described in the addition to 2005 Code § 707(b)(2)(A). As an alternative to dismissal for abuse, with the debtor's consent, the case may be converted to chapter 11 or 13.

We discuss the means test next, but if the presumption of abuse that arises under that test does not apply in a particular chapter 7 case, or if the presumption arises but is sufficiently rebutted, 11 U.S.C.A. § 707(b)(3) states that the court shall consider whether the petition was otherwise filed in bad faith or whether the totality of circumstances involving the debtor's financial situation demonstrates an abuse. In the totality of circumstances examination, that section directs that the court consider "whether the debtor seeks to reject a personal services contract and the financial need for such rejection as sought by the debtor."

3. STANDING

Standing to file abuse motions is found first in the general language of § 707(b)(1), giving the U.S. trustee, bankruptcy administrator, or any party in interest standing to file a motion to dismiss a consumer debtor's chapter 7 case. The court may initiate the dismissal on its own motion. Using the current monthly income of the debtor, it is multiplied by 12. If that total is equal to or less than the median family income of the debtor's domicile state for a similar size family, only the court, U.S. trustee, or bankruptcy administrator may bring a motion under § 707(b)'s general abuse standard. 11 U.S.C.A. § 707(b)(6). Here, the income of the debtor's spouse is used only if it is a joint case.

If the combined current monthly income of the debtor and the spouse, when mulitipled by 12, is equal to or less than the same median family income, the § 707(b)(2) presumption of abuse test does not apply at all. Only if the debtor and spouse are separated, and the debtor so certifies under penalty of perjury, is the spouse's income excluded for this part of the standing test, even if only one of them files bankruptcy. 11 U.S.C.A. § 707(b)(7)(B). This is an odd concept of standing, using combined current monthly income of both spouses even though only one files bankruptcy to test whether the current monthly income under the means test can apply to presume abuse. It is especially odd in light of the fact that the definition of current monthly income excludes the income of the other spouse unless they both file for bankruptcy relief. The obvious question is why should the court consider the spouse's income at all under the current monthly income definition.

4. THE MEANS TEST

This test is the heart of what has been called "need-based" bankruptcy reform, the concept being that an individual with primarily consumer debts will be permitted to file for chapter 7 relief only if that chapter's relief is warranted, based upon an analysis of whether the debtor can repay a scheduled amount or percentage to unsecured creditors. In its most basic expression, a presumption of abuse is created if the debtor's current monthly income, after reductions as described below, when multiplied by 60 (for the maximum number of months of a chapter 13 plan) is not less than the lesser of either $10,000 or 25% of the debtor's nonpriority unsecured creditors (or $6,000, whichever of the 25% or $6,000 is greater). As a minimum expression, therefore, if the debtor can repay out of adjusted current monthly income $100 monthly to unsecured creditors over 60 months, then the debtor has presumptively failed the means test. Using the $10,000 standard, if it is the lesser measure, if the debtor could pay $166.67 per month to nonpriority, unsecured creditors over 60 months, the presumption of abuse exits. Once the presumption of abuse is created under this formula, unless the debtor rebuts the presumption with documented special circumstances or expenses, the case will be dismissed unless the debtor consents to a conversion (presumably to chapter 13, although in an appropriate case it could be to chapter 11 or 12).

This, however, is its most basic expression and that is not a complete explanation of § 707(b)(2)'s means test. The complete test follows this track:

a. The court may not consider in its abuse analysis the debtor's past or continued charitable contributions to charitable entities as defined in § 548(d)(4). 11 U.S.C.A. § 707(b)(1).

b. The presumption is triggered by the current monthly income times 60 being no less than the lesser of 25% of the nonpriority unsecured creditors (or $6,000 if greater than the 25%) or $10,000. 11 U.S.C.A. § 707(b)(2)(A)(i)(I) and (II).

c. "Current monthly income" is a defined term in § 101(10A), meaning a six-month average of the monthly income from all sources, whether taxable or not, and including both spouses if it is a joint case. The six-month period ends on the last calendar day of the month immediately preceding the filing (or a later date determined by the court if the debtor does not file the § 521(a)(1)(B)(ii) statement of current monthly income), and the calculation of current monthly income includes any amounts paid by others for the debtor's household expenses. The definition excludes, however, some income, as discussed below.

As suggested in the standing discussion, a question that exists under this definition is whether the income of the debtor's spouse should be considered at all in an abuse analysis unless it is a joint case. Under former law, the income of the debtor's spouse was often a part of a substantial abuse analysis, even though only one debtor filed for bankruptcy relief. The fact that the definition looks to the spouse's income only for joint cases will perhaps permit some individual consumer debtors to qualify for chapter 7 relief if they do not file jointly with their spouse.

Another question posed by this definition is related to debtors who may not have income in each of the six months used to average income. For example, if the debtor had been unemployed for three months out of that period but had then obtained employment with substantial income, a less than actual current monthly income would result, permitting some debtors to pass the means test while having the actual ability to pay the minimum amount to unsecured creditors. This defined method for calculating current monthly income diminishes the court's discretionary authority, although the court may still find actual abuse under § 707(b)(1).

d. Current monthly income excludes any social security benefits, payments to victims of war crimes or victims of crimes against humanity, and payments to victims of international or domestic terrorism. 11 U.S.C.A. § 101(10A).

The exclusion of these benefits, most commonly social security benefits, would automatically permit a debtor whose sole income was from those benefits to pass the means test. Many such debtors may be currently filing for chapter 13 relief in an effort to save houses or other collateral, but those debtors remain viable candidates for chapter 7 relief under the means test.

e. The definition of current monthly income does not specify if it means gross income or net income after tax and other withholding deductions. While on one hand it makes no sense to look to gross income since an employed debtor is obviously obligated to withhold taxes, social security, and medicare payments, it may be argued that Congress intended to begin with gross income. This conclusion may be reached by the congressional adoption of the Internal Revenue Service Standards for allowable expense deductions from current monthly income. If one examines the Internal Revenue Manual, which will be referred to later, and which is available on WestLaw in its Library FTX-IRM, the IRS's allowable expense overview explains that the Service examines whether a taxpayer's tax withholdings are correct and allows only the correct deductions for those expenses. This method is not specified in §707(b)(2)'s lengthy explanation of use of the IRS Standards. There is no mention of taxes, social security, or other required withholdings. It is suggested that it is unnecessarily time-consuming for everyone involved to require debtors to ignore their required withholding in starting their current monthly income calculation, since most debtors would not be expected to withhold excessively. It makes more practical sense to begin the current monthly income calculation with income less the required withholdings and permit the trustee or other parties in interest to question whether those withholdings are correct. It remains to be seen whether those creating a form for this calculation will adopt an efficient approach to this calculation.

f. If the current monthly income does not reach the lesser of $10,000 or 25% of nonpriority unsecured creditors (or $6,000 if greater than the 25%), the debtor's expenses should not need to be examined. Under the standing test found in §707(b)(7), if the joint current monthly income of the debtor and spouse falls below the applicable median income, no one can file a motion to dismiss based on the means test, but the judge, U.S. trustee, or bankruptcy administrator could file a motion based upon actual abuse. Many consumer debtors with minimal income will continue to qualify for chapter 7 relief without extensive financial analysis; however, a question exists as to how much paperwork such debtors may need to complete. If a debtor's income under the current monthly income definition does not trigger the means test, will such debtors need to complete the expense portion of the forms? Will attorneys for debtors feel that they are obligated under a broader Rule 9011 standard to complete forms that are nevertheless unnecessary? These questions become real ones in light of the requirement of § 707(b)(2)(C) that the debtor's § 521 schedule of current income and expenses include a statement of the current monthly income and the debtor's calculation of whether a presumption of abuse exists, and it must "show how each such amount is calculated." Does this mean expense calculations even if unnecessary?

g. The practical answer to this may again be in § 707(b)(6) and (7)'s provisions on standing to file abuse motions. If the debtor's current monthly income, or, in a joint case, both spouses' total current monthly income, does not exceed the median income for a household of like numbers multiplied by 12, only the judge, U.S. trustee, or bankruptcy administrator may file a § 707(b) general abuse motion. Moreover, no one may file the motion under § 707(b)(2), the means testing presumptive abuse, when the combined total current monthly income of the debtor and the debtor's spouse does not exceed the median income for a household of like numbers multiplied by 12. 11 U.S.C.A. § 707(b)(7). The median income numbers are taken from U.S. Census Bureau tables for each state, based upon the number of persons in the household. The most recent tables are from 1999 and will need adjustment for cost of living increases, based on the Consumer Price Index. See definition of median family income at 11 U.S.C.A. § 101(39A).

h. Assuming that the debtor is subject to the means test, once the average current monthly income is calculated, § 707(b)(2)(A)(ii) provides a list of expenses that may be deducted in arriving at the net current monthly income for means testing purposes. The allowed expenses begin with those defined under both the national and local standards established by the Internal Revenue Service. BAPCPA § 103 expresses the "sense of Congress" that the Internal Revenue Service Standard guidelines for repayment plans may be adjusted "by the Secretary of the Treasury as needed to accommodate their use for § 707(b) means testing purposes." Within two years of enactment, the Executive Office for the United States Trustees is to report to Congress on its "findings regarding the utilization of Internal Revenue Service Standards for determining" the § 707(b) monthly expenses and the impact of those Standards on debtors and the bankruptcy court. This study and report is apparently a reaction to criticism by some that the IRS Standards are not appropriate for bankruptcy means testing purposes.

Pending such a study and any future amendments to the test or adjustments to the Standards by the Secretary of Treasury, the IRS national standards will govern such items as food, clothing, personal items, housekeeping supplies, and entertainment, while the local standards govern housing, utility, and transportation costs. Those IRS standards are found at www.irs.gov and are on Westlaw as a part of the Internal Revenue Manual at Westlaw's library FTX-IRM.

That Manual summarizes the Standards as follows:

Internal Revenue Manual

Part 5—Collecting Process

5.15.1.7—Allowable Expense Overview (05-01-2004)

(1) Allowable expenses include those expenses that meet the necessary expense test. The necessary expense test is defined as expenses that are necessary to provide for a taxpayer's and his or her family's health and welfare and/or production of income. The expenses must be reasonable. The total necessary expenses establish the minimum a taxpayer and family needs to live.

(2) There are three types of necessary expenses:
- National Standards
- Local Standards
- Other Expenses

(3) National Standards: These establish standards for reasonable amounts for five necessary expenses. Four of them come from the Bureau of Labor Statistics (BLS) Consumer Expenditure Survey: food, housekeeping supplies, apparel and services, and personal care products and services. The fifth category, miscellaneous, is a discretionary amount established by the Service. It is $100 for one person and $25 for each additional person in the taxpayer's household.

All five standards are included in one total national standard expense.

(4) Local Standards: These establish standards for two necessary expenses: housing and transportation. Taxpayers will be allowed the local standard or the amount actually paid, whichever is less.

    (a.) Housing—Standards are established for each county within a state. When deciding if a deviation is appropriate, consider the cost of moving to a new residence; the increased cost of transportation to work and school that will result from moving to lower-cost housing and the tax consequences. The tax consequence is the difference between the benefit the taxpayer currently derives from the interest and property tax deductions on Schedule A to the benefit the taxpayer would derive without the same or adjusted expense.

    (b.) Transportation—The transportation standards consist of nationwide figures for loan or lease payments referred to as ownership cost, and additional amounts for operating costs broken down by Census Region and Metropolitan Statistical Area. Operating costs were derived from BLS data. If a taxpayer has a car payment, the allowable ownership cost added to the allowable operating cost equals the allowable transportation expense. If a taxpayer has no car payment only the operating cost portion of the transportation standard is used to figure the allowable transportation expense. Under ownership costs, separate caps are provided for the first car and second car. If the taxpayer does not own a car a standard public transportation amount is allowed.

(5) Other—Other expenses may be allowed if they meet the necessary expense test. The amount allowed must be reasonable considering the taxpayer's individual facts and circumstances.

(6) Conditional expenses. These expenses do not meet the necessary expenses test. However, they are allowable if the tax liability, including projected accruals, can be fully paid within five years.

(7) National local expense standards are guidelines. If it is determined a standard amount is inadequate to provide for a specific taxpayer's basic living expenses, allow a deviation. Require the taxpayer to provide reasonable substantiation and document the case file.

(8) Generally, the total number of persons allowed for national standard expenses should be the same as those allowed as dependents on the taxpayer's current year income tax return. Verify exemptions claimed on taxpayer's income tax return meet the dependency requirements of the IRC. There may be reasonable exceptions. Fully document the reasons for any exceptions. For example, foster children or children for whom adoption is pending.

(9) A deviation from the local standard is not allowed merely because it is inconvenient for the taxpayer to dispose of valued assets.

(10) Revenue officers should consider the length of the payments. Although it may be appropriate to allow for payments made on the secured debts that meet the necessary expense test, if the debt will be fully repaid in one year only allow those payments for one year.

5.15.1.8—National Standards (05-01-2004)

(1) National standards include the following expenses:

(a.) Apparel and services. Includes shoes and clothing, laundry and dry cleaning, and shoe repair.

(b.) Food. Includes all meals, home and away.

(c.) Housekeeping supplies. Includes laundry and cleaning supplies; other household products such as cleaning and toilet tissue, paper towels and napkins; lawn and garden supplies; postage and stationary; and other miscellaneous household supplies.

(d.) Personal care products and services. Includes hair care products, haircuts and beautician services, oral hygiene products and articles, shaving needs, cosmetics, perfume, bath preparations, deodorants, feminine hygiene products, electric personal care appliances, personal care services, and repair of personal care appliances. (e.) Miscellaneous. A discretionary allowance of $100 for one person and $25 for each additional person in a taxpayer's family.

(2) Allow taxpayers the total national standard amount for their income level.
Example: The taxpayer's expenses are: housekeeping supplies—$150, clothing—$150, food—$600, miscellaneous—$400 (Total Expenses—$1,300). The taxpayer is allowed the national standard of $1,100.

(3) A taxpayer that claims more than the total allowed by the national standards must substantiate and justify each separate expense of the total national standard amounts.
Example: A taxpayer may claim a higher food expense than allowed. Justification would be based on prescribed or required dietary needs.

5.15.1.9—Local Standards (05-01-2004)

(1) Local standards include the following expenses:

(a.) Housing and Utilities. The utilities include gas, electricity, water, fuel, oil, bottled gas, trash and garbage collection, wood and other fuels, septic cleaning, and telephone. Housing expenses include: mortgage or rent, property taxes, interest, parking, necessary maintenance and repair, homeowner's or renter's insurance, homeowner dues and condominium fees. Usually, this is considered necessary only for the place of residence. Any other housing expenses should be allowed only if, based on a taxpayer's individual facts and circumstances, disallowance will cause the taxpayer economic hardship.

(b.) Transportation. Vehicle insurance, vehicle payment (lease or purchase), maintenance, fuel, state and local registration, required inspection, parking fees, tolls, driver's license, public transportation. Transportation costs not required to produce income or ensure the health and welfare of the family are not considered necessary. Consider availability of public transportation if car payments (purchase or lease) will prevent the tax liability from being paid in part or full. Public transportation costs could be an option if it does not significantly increase commuting time and inconvenience the taxpayer.

If the taxpayer has no car payment, or no car, question how the taxpayer travels to and from work, grocer, medical care, etc. The taxpayer is only allowed the operating cost or the cost of transportation.

5.15.1.10—Other Expenses (05-01-2004)

(1) Other expenses may be considered if they meet the necessary expense test—they must provide for the health and welfare of the taxpayer and/or his or her family or they must be for the production of income. This is determined based on the facts and circumstances of each case.

(2) If other expenses are determined to be necessary and, therefore allowable, document the reasons for the decision in your history.

(3) The amount allowed for necessary or conditional expenses depends on the taxpayer's ability to fully pay the liability within five years and on the taxpayer's individual facts and circumstances. If the liability can be paid within 5 years, it may be appropriate to allow the taxpayer the excessive necessary and conditional expenses. If the taxpayer cannot pay within 5 years, it may be appropriate to allow the taxpayer the excessive necessary and conditional expenses for up to one year in order to modify or eliminate the expense.

As these explanations indicate, there is quite a bit of discretion permitted to IRS collection officers in applying these standards, and it remains to be seen how this discretion will carry over to the courts, as well as to those who devise forms for calculation of the means testing while using these standards.

The Manual and its examples indicate that the Service permits only the lower amount between the taxpayer's actual expenses or the standard allowance. Will this lesser standard be controlling in the means test? There is no answer found in the Code amendments, but it may be argued that the Code's reference to the IRS Standards mandates the use of all the criteria and calculation methods used by IRS.

IRS has published national standard tables based upon the number of persons in the household and upon gross monthly income. So now, the debtor and counsel must go back to gross income for the expense calculations. These standards include food, housekeeping supplies, apparel and services, personal care products and services, and miscellaneous. When there are more than four persons in the household, the standards permit an additional amount per person.

The published state standards provide housing and utilities expenses that are allowable by each state, and the regional standards are for transportation ownership or public transportation costs, as well as for transportation operating expenses. These regional standards are based upon the following regions: Northwest, Midwest, South, and West, and within each region there are Metropolitan Statistical Areas to account for the larger urban areas where transportation expenses are expected to be higher.

All of the IRS standards are found at www.irs.gov.

i. In addition to these standard costs, the actual monthly expenses of the debtor and dependents for the Other Necessary Expense category issued by IRS are allowable. These expenses specifically include reasonably necessary health and disability insurance as well as health saving account expenses for the debtor and dependents. The calculation of actual monthly expenses does not include the debtor's ongoing monthly debt payments since those payments are brought into the formula later. If the debtor or dependents have monthly expenses for protection from family violence, as identified in the Family Violence Prevention and Services Act or other federal law, those expenses, to the extent reasonably necessary, are deductible under §707(b)(2)(A)(ii)(I). If there are such expenses, the court is required to keep those expenses confidential. This would be problematic since the court does not create the calculation; rather, the debtor and debtor's counsel supply those numbers. Does this mean that part of such debtor's expenses would be filed under seal? How would the trustee and other parties in interest know of this expense? How would the court test reasonableness of the amount without a hearing? How would the hearing be kept confidential?

If the debtor could establish that it is reasonable and necessary, an additional allowance of monthly expenses for food and clothing up to 5% of the IRS national standards is allowable. 11 U.S.C.A. § 707(b)(2)(A)(ii)(I). Of course, if contested, it would be the debtor's burden to establish that the increased amount was reasonable and necessary, but since the debtor and debtor's counsel prepare the expense calculation to start the process, the choice is theirs to enhance this amount up to the 5% maximum.

j. After deducting the above standard and actual expenses, § 707(b)(2)(A)(ii)(II) permits the debtor to deduct continuing actual expenses for the reasonable and necessary care and support of an elderly, chronically ill, or disabled household member or such a member of the debtor's immediate family. Immediate family is defined to include parents, grandparents, siblings, children and grandchildren of the debtor, the debtor's spouse, or debtor's dependents. This allowance depends upon the debtor actually paying those expenses and the inability of the supported person to pay those expenses. In a contested scenario, the court would be called upon to make factual findings of reasonableness and necessity as well as the inability of the supported person to pay for the expenses, a hearing that may involve persons that would otherwise have no connection with the bankruptcy case or court. There are obvious privacy issues as to those persons that are not addressed in the Code's amendment.

k. In addition to the above expenses, assuming that the debtor is otherwise eligible to file under chapter 13 by its debt limits under §109(e), the debtor may deduct the actual administrative expenses of a chapter 13 plan in the debtor's judicial district, up to a maximum of 10% of projected chapter 13 plan payments. This deduction is intended to calculate the cost of the debtor being in chapter 13 rather than chapter 7, but the calculation does not specifically include any allowance for the attorney's fees of the debtor in chapter 13. In many judicial districts, the fees charged by attorneys for chapter 13 filings are higher than for chapter 7, and those fees are often paid through the plan. Does this 10% allowance permit the debtor to include attorney's fees in that percentage if the chapter 13 trustee's administrative expenses are less than the 10%?

Note also that this deduction is based upon the projected chapter 13 payments that would require the debtor and counsel to make all of the assumptions of what would be required in arriving at plan payments for a plan that is not filed. This obviously will require chapter 7 attorneys to be familiar with the chapter 13 practice in their district.

l. Next, the debtor may deduct actual expenses for each dependent's and minor child's private or public elementary or secondary education expense, up to a maximum of $1,500 per year per child. The debtor must provide documentation of these expenses and a detailed explanation of why the expenses are reasonable and necessary. In addition, the debtor must explain why these education expenses are not already accounted for in the IRS national, local, or other standards described above.

m. If the debtor can establish the need for it, monthly expenses may include an allowance for housing and utilities in excess of the IRS local housing and utilities standards. Here, the debtor must establish that the home energy costs are actual and that they are reasonable and necessary.

n. After deduction of all expenses under the standards and actual tests, the debtor deducts an average monthly payment of each secured debt, calculated as follows: The total of all contractually due amounts for each of the 60 months following filing of the petition, plus any additional payments that would be required in a chapter 13 plan (curing arrearages) to maintain the debtor's primary residence, motor vehicle, or other collateral necessary for the support of the debtor and dependents would be divided by 60, and this 1/60th amount would be deducted from current monthly income.

Many questions are unanswered in this calculation, including: If the debtor only has 12 payments remaining on a secured debt, such as for furniture, is the total of those payments divided by 60? Obviously, for a home mortgage that will continue beyond the 60 months, you only use the total payments due contractually within the 60 months, but many secured debts will have less than 60 months remaining. For home mortgages that include escrows for insurance and taxes, does the calculation include those escrows or only principal and interest? This calculation is not the same as the one that would be required to arrive at a chapter 13 plan payment, so it is not a true indicator of what the debtor's actual net income would be in a chapter 13. For example, a 1/60th payment to a car lender under this calculation may be much less than the adequate protection payment that would be required to that creditor in a chapter 13, especially where the car is older and secures a relatively high balance. The point is that if this means test is intended to measure the debtor's ability to repay creditors in a chapter 13, the 1/60 division of secured debt may falsely indicate an ability to pay unsecured creditors. Moreover, as will be seen in discussion of chapter 13, the length of a chapter 13 debtor's plan is dependent upon a median income test, so using a 1/60 division is not necessarily indicative of the period of time a particular debtor would pay on secured or unsecured debt in chapter 13.

o. The debtor's expenses for all priority claims, including taxes, child support, and alimony claims, would be totaled and divided by 60, again arriving at a 1/60th expense deducted from current monthly income. There are some of the same problems with the 1/60 division as seen in the prior discussion. In chapter 13, a priority creditor might not be willing to accept payments over a 60-month period, nor may this term be required of a particular chapter 13 debtor under the median income test for length of plans.

p. Assuming that we began with net income after required wage deductions, we are now finally at the debtor's net current monthly income. If the calculation must begin with gross income, the appropriate amount of tax and other required deductions from gross wages must be entered at some stage to arrive at net current monthly income. Abuse is presumptively established if the net when multiplied by 60 exceeds the lesser of 25% (or $6,000 if greater than the 25%) or $10,000 numbers described above.

q. A debtor may attempt to demonstrate a special circumstance that would rebut the presumption, but that is permitted only by such circumstances as a serious medical condition or a call to active military duty, and then the debtor must document the increased expenses and provide a detailed explanation, under oath as to accuracy, of the special circumstances. A showing of such circumstances and increased expenses still must bring the net current monthly income below the lesser of 25% (or $6,000) or $10,000 numbers. See 11 U.S.C.A. § 707(b)(2)(B).

r. Code § 707(b)(2)(D) states that no form of means testing shall be applied to dismiss a chapter 7 case filed by a disabled veteran, as defined in 38 U.S.C.A. § 3741(1), if that veteran's indebtedness occurred primarily during a period of active duty or while performing a homeland defense activity. If it is disputed whether a disabled veteran qualifies for this exemption from the means testing, the bankruptcy court would need to make factual findings about the time period for the origination of the indebtedness and whether the debtor's military or homeland defense activity occurred during the time period. A finding adverse to the veteran would then result in the application of the means test. A question, therefore, is whether such a disabled veteran must complete the means testing calculation, as all chapter 7 debtors are obligated to do, as a part of the original bankruptcy schedules. See 11 U.S.C.A. § 521(a)(1)(B)(v)'s requirement that the debtor file a statement of monthly net income, "itemized to show how the amount is calculated." Section 727(b)(2)(C) requires that all chapter 7 debtors include in this statement the calculation of whether a presumption of abuse arises. Such a presumption would not arise for qualified disabled veterans under § 727(b)(2)(D), but there appears to be an inconsistency between the duty called for by debtors in their § 521 scheduling. It is unclear why the latter section refers to "monthly net income," rather than "current monthly income," but they surely must be the same thing.

5. CENSUS BUREAU MEDIAN INCOME TABLES

In the Appendix, we have included the Census Bureau Median Income Tables since these tables are not easily found on the Census Bureau website. An extract may also be found at the American Bankruptcy Institute website, abiworld.org, through its link covering the 2005 legislation. It is assumed that the Executive Office of United States Trustees or other agencies will publish the median income tables, along with relevant IRS Standard tables in an easily accessed format.

6. MEANS TEST EXAMPLE

BAPCPA § 1232 amends 28 U.S.C.A. § 2075 to provide that the Bankruptcy Rules shall prescribe a form to be used for the calculation that must be made by the debtor under § 707(b)(2)(C). This section is the one referring to the debtor's requirement to file a calculation of current monthly income, showing whether a presumption of abuse exists.

The following example merely illustrates how the various subsections of § 707(b) would be applied.

MEANS TEST EXAMPLE

Assumptions: This example is based upon a chapter 7 debtor who files individually but is married with one minor child, age 10, who is in a private school due to learning disabilities. The private school costs $1,000 a month. The debtor's disabled mother lives in this home and contributes her social security income of $950 to the family's household expenses. The debtor's spouse is unemployed. The debtor and spouse own their home, valued at $225,000 with a mortgage debt of $200,000 and with monthly principal and interest payments of $1,138.09. The debtor is delinquent on the mortgage for three months due to paying medical expenses for his mother. The debtor wants to attempt reaffirmation with the mortgage creditor. There is no escrow on the taxes and insurance, and the debtor is delinquent on 2004 real property taxes in the amount of $1,500. The debtor owns one vehicle, with a balance of $15,000 and monthly payments of $375, and the debtor has one other secured debt for furniture with a balance of $1,500 and monthly payments of $150. The debtor is employed with a gross monthly salary of $8,000, and employment has been stable for one year, with no variation in income over the prior 6 months. The debtor has unsecured debts of $40,000 and a delinquent income tax debt that would be a priority claim for $2,000. The debtor lives in Memphis, Tennessee, which is in the South Region for IRS Standards, and the amount of the household income exceeds the median income for a comparable size family in Tennessee under the Census Bureau tables; thus, the debtor is subject to the means test.

D. Other Effective Dates of Significance to Practitioners

July 1, 2005	Chapter 12 permanent in Code
July 30, 2002, Sarbanes-Oxley Enactment	§523(a)(19)(B), securities fraud
One year after enactment	§548(a) & (b), reach-back changed from 1 to 2 years
60 days after promulgation of reporting forms	Chapter 11 small business debtor reporting requirements

The amount of unsecured debt is $40,000 to be used to test means to pay and 25% of that debt is $10,000, which is greater than the $6,000 part of the test and the same as the other $10,000 part of the test. Since the debtor's net current monthly income $774.11 x 60 = more than $10,000, this debtor would "fail" the means test.

Note that this $774.11 is not the amount that this debtor would be required to pay to unsecured creditors in a chapter 13 plan, since a plan may require substantially more to the secured creditors in order to cure arrearages, provide insurance, or otherwise satisfy the creditors and plan confirmation requirements. The disposable income test for chapter 13 does not necessarily produce the same number as net current monthly income under the means test.

Also note that spreading the mortgage arrearage over 60 months for the means test is not what the lender would require in a chapter 7 to permit the debtor to reaffirm. Typically, such lenders require the mortgage to be current prior to reaffirmation.

The following assumptions illustrate just some of the possible changes in the means test result:

- Assuming that the debtor has no vehicle insurance and such insurance would be required in a chapter 13 plan, would the debtor be able to deduct this insurance cost for the means test? Section 707(b)(2)(A)(iii)(II) says so. Therefore, if the insurance would cost $250 monthly because of the debtor's prior accidents, the net current income would come down to $524.11, still a "failing" result.

- Assume that the debtor needs disability insurance, not supplied by his employer. The IRS Standards and § 707(b)(2)(A)(ii)(I) would permit this, potentially reducing the net income.
- Assume that the debtor established a health savings account through his employer. This would be deductible under § 707(b)(2)(A)(ii)(I).
- Assuming that the debtor had regularly made and continues to make charitable deductions of approximately 10% of his net salary, § 707(b)(1) says that cannot be considered in an abuse dismissal; therefore, the contributions must be deductible, just as they would be in chapter 13. That alone would take the debtor's net to $124.11, which would permit this debtor to "pass" the means test. ($124.11 x 60 = $7446.60, which is less than the lesser of 25% of the unsecured debt or $10,000).
- Assume that the debtor's utility costs were unusually high due to the lack of proper insulation in the home. Section 707(b)(2)(A)(ii)(V) would permit an increased deduction above the IRS Standard if it is documented that it is reasonable and necessary. How can the court say it is unreasonable if it is the actual utility cost?
- The monthly cost shown in the example for the furniture debt would be higher if the debt matures in 12 months, assuming that § 707(b)(2)(A)(iii) was interpreted to mean that only the contractual term could be used as the basis of the calculation; however, part (iii) also says that the monthly payments contractually due within 60 months are divided by 60. Would such creditors accept payments spread over 60 months in a chapter 13 plan? No, but that does not seem to be a factor in the means testing.
- The same issue as above would arise for the car lender, if the term of that contract is less than 60 months. Amendments to chapter 13 prevent this debtor from modifying the car loan if the car was purchased within 910 days of bankruptcy. Assume this car was purchased 12 months before bankruptcy, and assume the actual car note was $650 a month. Could that actual amount be used in the deduction, even though for the South region, the IRS ownership allowable cost is $475? If the IRS guideline that permits the lesser of actual or Standard cost is followed for the means test, the debtor would be limited to a deduction of $475, but in a chapter 13 case, the debtor would be required to pay the full $650. The means test in such an instance would give a false result compared to an actual chapter 13 plan.
- This debtor could perhaps demonstrate a special circumstance due to supporting his disabled mother, if the debtor could show the need for additional expenses. See § 707(b)(2)(B).
- Assume that this debtor had borrowed $10,000 from his retirement account and was repaying this loan through employee deductions. In a chapter 13, such a loan could not be modified. Could the debtor deduct those loan payments for the means test? If a secured debt, it would be deducted but spread over 60 months. If the debt matured in less than 60 months, should not the actual monthly payment be deductible? If not, again a false result occurs compared to what would occur in chapter 13.

There are as many factual scenarios as there are potential debtors, and how the means test plays out in actual practice remains to be seen, but its results clearly do not equate to what may be required of the same debtor in a chapter 13 plan. It is entirely possible that a debtor may be forced into a chapter 13 plan due to failing the means test and then be unable to obtain confirmation of a plan.

7. RULE 9011 AND ABUSE

a. For Benefit of a Trustee

If a chapter 7 trustee files a motion for dismissal of a chapter 7 case on the basis of abuse, under either the actual abuse or the means-testing presumptive abuse standard, and if the court finds abusive cause for dismissal of the case, 11 U.S.C.A. § 707(b)(4)(A) directs that a Rule 9011 standard be applied. The court then must determine whether the debtor's attorney violated the Rule. If so, the sanction of reimbursement of the trustee's reasonable costs in prosecuting the § 707(b) motion, including the trustee's reasonable attorney's fees, may be ordered against the debtor's attorney.

b. Civil Penalty

Separate from the trustee's potential recovery for a Rule 9011 violation, 11 U.S.C.A. § 707(b)(4)(B) provides that the court may award a civil penalty against the debtor's attorney under Rule 9011. The court, on its own initiative or on motion of a party in interest, may assess such a penalty to be payable to the case trustee, U.S. trustee, or bankruptcy administrator, if a Rule 9011 violation is found.

c. Certification by Debtor's Attorney

The signature of the debtor's attorney on the petition or any pleading constitutes a certification that the attorney has "performed a reasonable investigation into the circumstances that gave rise to the petition, pleading, or written motion," and that the attorney determined that the petition or other pleading is "well grounded in fact" and warranted under the law, and that the petition or pleading is not an abuse under § 707(b)(1). See 11 U.S.C.A. § 707(b)(4)(C). This is a broad certification by the debtor's attorney, one seemingly requiring some level of inquiry into why the debtor needs to file for chapter 7 relief. The certification that the petition is not an abuse is broadly worded to include that it is not an abuse under either the general bad faith or the means-testing standard. A separate certification is called for by § 707(b)(4)(D): "The signature of an attorney on the petition shall constitute a certification that the attorney has no knowledge after an inquiry that the information in the schedules filed with such petition is incorrect." Thus the debtor's attorney is certifying both that the debtor has good cause to file for chapter 7 relief and that the attorney has no knowledge of incorrect information in the schedules.

Many questions arise under these certification rules. How much inquiry must the attorney make into the reasons for the bankruptcy filing and to what extent must the attorney inquire into accuracy? An obvious question is how willing attorneys are going to be to make this certification and how rigidly the Rule 9011 implications will be applied. Other questions are how this requirement for attorneys will impact the fees that they will charge for chapter 7 work and how the broad certification will impact their professional liability insurance coverage and rates.

d. Fees to Debtor

Section 707(b)(5) does permit the court to award reasonable costs, including reasonable attorney's fees to the debtor under a limited circumstance when a motion for abuse dismissal is filed and not granted. First, the court may on its own initiative or on motion of a party in interest (which likely would always be the debtor) again apply a Rule 9011 standard to see if the party filing a § 707(b) motion violated that Rule. The possibility of an award to the debtor does not apply when the motion is filed by a case trustee, U.S. trustee, or bankruptcy administrator, but it does apply when the motion is filed by another party in interest, such as a creditor. If the court finds that the filing party's position violated Rule 9011 or that the attorney who filed the motion did so "solely for the purpose of coercing a debtor into waiving a right guaranteed to the debtor under this title," the court may make the award, but a small business with an aggregate claim of less than $1,000 is exempt from such a penalty. A small business for this purpose is defined as one that has fewer than 25 full-time employees and is engaged in a commercial or business activity. 11 U.S.C.A. § 707(b)(5)(B) and (C).

This possible award to the debtor for creditor abuse seems hollow in reality. First, the door is open for a small business creditor to abuse the process with no penalty, but the larger issue is how the debtor could ever prove the requirements for an award. Note that the statute requires the court to find that the party who filed the motion violated Rule 9011 based upon the "position" of that party. We are talking about a § 707(b) motion that would be filed by the creditor under a statute that exposes virtually all chapter 7 debtors to an abuse and means testing analysis, so how could a creditor's legal position in filing the motion be in violation of Rule 9011? As to the second part of the statute concerning possible violation by the creditor's attorney, that requires a showing that the motion was filed "solely" for the purpose of coercing the debtor to forego some guaranteed title 11 right. Again, the motion being addressed is only the § 707(b) motion, and all chapter 7 debtors are potentially subject to that motion. How could the creditor's filing of such a motion be construed as an effort to coerce the debtor to give up a right not to have a § 707(b) motion filed? It is unlikely that this possible remedy for creditor abuse will see success for debtors.

e. U.S. Trustee and Bankruptcy Administrator Responsibility

By an addition to 11 U.S.C.A. § 704(b), which currently addresses the duties of the chapter 7 trustee, the United States trustee or bankruptcy administrator must file a statement of whether a case would be presumed abusive within 10 days of the § 341 meeting. Within five days of receiving the statement, the clerk of the court "shall provide a copy of the statement to all creditors." Within 30 days of the § 341 meeting, the United States trustee or bankruptcy administrator must file a § 707(b) motion based upon abuse or a statement of why the case is not presumed abusive even though the debtor's current monthly income:

is not less than—

(A) in the case of a debtor in a household of 1 person, the median family income of the applicable State for 1 earner; or

(B) in the case of a debtor in a household of 2 or more individuals, the highest median family income of the applicable State for a family of the same number or fewer individuals.

In addition to the notices described above, Code § 342's notice provisions are amended by adding subsection (d) to require further notice from the clerk to creditors in each chapter 7 case where abuse is presumed under the means test:

(d) In a case under chapter 7 of this title in which the debtor is an individual and in which the presumption of abuse arises under section 707(b), the clerk shall give written notice to all creditors not later than 10 days after the date of the filing of the petition that the presumption of abuse has arisen.

This clerk's notice must be based upon what the debtor's required calculation shows at the time of filing, since the clerk at this point would not have the benefit of the analysis by the U.S. trustee or bankruptcy administrator. See the notice discussion for additional comments about the clerk's notice.

f. Crime Victim Dismissal

Section 707(c) is added to provide for dismissal upon motion of a victim of a crime of violence or drug-trafficking crime, and when the debtor has been convicted of such a crime, unless it is shown by a preponderance of evidence that the chapter 7 bankruptcy "is necessary to satisfy the claim of a domestic support obligation." See the discussion of domestic support obligations.

8. TAX RETURNS

Under § 521(e)(2)(A)(i), a chapter 7 debtor must give to the trustee the most recent tax year's return or transcript no later than seven days before the meeting of creditors, and a copy must be given to creditors that request it. At the request of the court or a party in interest, the debtor is required to file tax returns or transcripts for tax periods ending while the case is pending. The latter requirement is insignificant in most chapter 7 cases since most move through the system to discharge quickly within a few months.

B. INDIVIDUAL CHAPTER 11 CASES

Individual chapter 11 debtors must comply with the § 521 duties. See discussion of those duties under debtor duties. Chapter 11 individual debtors have the same rights to exemptions as other debtors; therefore, the new exclusions from the bankruptcy estate and new exemptions affect these debtors. See those discussions under exclusions from the estate and exemptions. Changes in discharge exceptions and denial of discharge may affect individual chapter 11 debtors, and those discussions will address the extent to which chapter 11 is impacted.

As noted under the Checklist of New Duties for the Chapter 11 Trustee, if the debtor remains in possession, that debtor in possession will have the new trustee duties, including complying with the domestic relations creditor noticing requirements found in 11 U.S.C.A. § 1106(c).

Among the new grounds for dismissal or conversion of a chapter 11 case is § 1112(b)(4)(P), which provides that the debtor's failure to pay a domestic support obligation that arose postbankruptcy is cause. Many individual chapter 11 cases have been filed for a purpose of adjusting alimony or support obligations, and the changes in the Code concerning domestic support obligations and their nondischargeability will decrease the likelihood of success of such filings. See the discussions of domestic support obligations. Other changes in § 1112 will be discussed in the business bankruptcy sections of this commentary.

Property of the estate for an individual debtor will now include all property described in §541 that the debtor acquires after filing the case, as well as the debtor's earnings until the case is closed, dismissed, or converted. 11 U.S.C.A. §1115.

Confirmation requirements for chapter 11 plans are amended by a new § 1129(a)(14) providing that "if the debtor is required by a judicial or administrative order, or by statute, to pay a domestic support obligation, the debtor has paid all amounts payable under such order or such statute for such obligation that first become payable after the date of the filing of the petition." In other words, the individual debtor may not obtain confirmation unless postpetition domestic support obligations are paid in full.

An additional confirmation requirement found in 11 U.S.C.A. § 1129(a)(15) affects only individual chapter 11 debtors. In those cases where the holder of an allowed unsecured claim objects to confirmation, either the value of property distributed in the plan to the objecting unsecured creditor must be no less than the value of that unsecured claim or else the value of all property distributed under the plan must be no less than the projected disposable income of the debtor for the longer of a five-year period or the period for which the plan provides for payments. This establishes a disposable income test for individual chapter 11 debtors, specifically using the definition of disposable income found in 11 U.S.C.A. 1325(b)(2), and a presumptive minimum five-year plan would be the standard.

Confirmation of an individual debtor's plan will not have the effect of discharging debts until the completion of all plan payments, under 11 U.S.C.A. § 1141(d)(5)(A), except that the court may grant a discharge prior to plan completion under subpart (B). Such an early discharge is conditioned upon a lack of practical ability to modify the confirmed plan and the distribution of all property under the plan to be no less than unsecured creditors would have received in a chapter 7 liquidation.

Under 11 U.S.C.A. § 1141(d)(5)(C), the court must delay granting any discharge if there is "reasonable cause to believe" that the new exemption § 522(q) applies to this individual debtor. This is the exemption section that caps the homestead exemption at $125,000 under the circumstances described in that section. See the discussion of this section under exemptions.

C. CHAPTER 12

1. PERMANENT CHAPTER

Chapter 12 is made a permanent part of the Bankruptcy Code, effective July 1, 2005. Pending the enactment of BAPCPA, Congress had temporarily extended Chapter 12. This July 1 date is the expiration date for the most recent temporary extension of Chapter 12.

2. FAMILY FISHERMAN

Chapter 12 relief is extended to include family fishermen, a new term defined in Code §101(19A) to include individuals "engaged in a commercial fishing operation," or corporations and partnerships engaged in such fishing, provided they are more than 50% owned by a family conducting the business. The debt limit for family fishermen is $1.5 million and at least 80% of the noncontingent, liquidated debts (excluding the debt for the principal residence of the individuals) must arise out of the commercial fishing operation.

3. DEBT LIMIT INCREASE FOR FAMILY FARMER

The debt limit for family farmer is increased, however, from $1.5 million to $3,237,000, and the percentage of debt that must be attributed to the farming operation drops from 80% to 50%; therefore, more family farmers than family fishermen will qualify for chapter 12 relief under the debt restrictions. The debt limits are subject to periodic adjustment by amendment to 11 U.S.C.A. § 104(b). Family farmers are also given a longer look-back for purposes of determining whether 50% of the debt arose from the farming, now looking back to the second and third year prior to filing bankruptcy.

4. DISMISSAL OF CASE

Section 1208(c)(10) is amended to add as cause for dismissal of a chapter 12 case the "failure of the debtor to pay any domestic support obligation that first becomes payable after the date of the filing of the petition."

5. PLAN CONTENTS

Chapter 12 plan contents are changed by amendment to § 1222(a)(4):

> [N]otwithstanding any other provision of this section, a plan may provide for less than full payment of all amounts owed for a claim entitled to priority under section 507(a)(1)(B) only if the plan provides that all of the debtor's projected disposable income for a 5-year period beginning on the date that the first payment is due under the plan will be applied to make payments under the plan.

This latter reference to new § 507(a)(1)(B) would apply to domestic support obligations that are assigned to a governmental unit, meaning that a plan might propose to pay less than 100% of such assigned claims only if disposable income is committed for a full five years.

Section 1222(b)(11) is added to the effect that chapter 12 plans would be permitted to "provide for the payment of interest accruing after the date of the filing of the petition on unsecured claims that are nondischargeable under section 1228(a), except that such interest may be paid only to the extent that the debtor has disposable income available to pay such interest after making provision for full payment of all allowed claims." This means that a plan may provide for payment of interest on such debts as nondischargeable student loans but only if there is excess disposable income for that purpose.

Code § 1222(a)(2) is amended to provide for full payment of § 507 priority claims, unless the claimant agrees to a different treatment of the claim. An exception to this provision would be created for claims owed to a governmental unit as a result of the sale, transfer, exchange, or other disposition of a farm asset used in the debtor's farming operation. Any such governmental claim would be treated as an unsecured claim, not entitled to priority, if and only if the debtor receives a discharge. The specific provision states that a plan may:

> (2) provide for the full payment, in deferred cash payments, of all claims entitled to priority under section 507, unless—
>> (A) the claim is a claim owed to a governmental unit that arises as a result the sale, transfer, exchange, or other disposition of any farm asset used in the debtor's farming operation, in which case the claim shall be treated as an unsecured claim that is not entitled to priority under section 507, but the debt shall be treated in such manner only if the debtor receives a discharge; or

     (B) the holder of a particular claim agrees to a different treatment of that claim;

BAPCPA § 1003 makes this change effective in all cases filed after the enactment, but it specifically does not apply retroactively to title 11 cases filed before the enactment. The effect of this provision is that §1222(a)(2) will apply to new cases filed after enactment, but it would not apply to cases begun under another chapter and then converted to chapter 12.

6. DISPOSABLE INCOME

If the trustee or an unsecured creditor objects to confirmation, thus triggering a disposable income application, § 1225(b)(1)(C) is added to provide an alternative method of determining the minimal distributions to unsecured creditors under the plan by looking to the value of the property to be distributed for a three-year period or such longer period as the court approves. This three-year period begins with the first distribution date under the proposed plan rather than looking back in time, and the total property to be distributed must be no less than the debtor's disposable income for that same time period.

The definition of disposable income would be expanded to include in § 1225(b)(2)(A) "or for a domestic support obligation that first becomes payable after the date of the filing of the petition," meaning that ongoing postpetition domestic support obligations would be excluded from the debtor's disposable income.

7. CONFIRMATION

Plan confirmation in chapter 12 would have the additional requirement that "the debtor has paid all amounts that are required to be paid under a domestic support obligation and that first become payable after the date of the filing of the petition if the debtor is required by a judicial or administrative order, or by statute, to pay such domestic support obligation." This is found in a new § 1225(a)(7).

8. MODIFICATION OF PLAN

Section 1229 is amended to prohibit attempts to modify a confirmed plan to increase the amount of any payment that is due under the plan before the proposed modification becomes effective, and this prohibition is applicable even if the debtor had an increase in disposable income, unless the debtor requested an increase in payments. In the final plan year, no one but the debtor may seek an increase in plan payments if it would leave the debtor with insufficient funds to continue the farming operation after completion of the plan.

9. DISCHARGE

A precondition to discharge after confirmation of a chapter 12 plan is found in an addition to § 1228(a) by adding "and in the case of a debtor who is required by a judicial or administrative order, or by statute, to pay a domestic support obligation, after such debtor certifies that all amounts payable under such order or such statute that are due on or before the date of the certification (including amounts due before the petition was filed, but only to the extent provided for by the plan) have been paid" after the former language "... completion by the debtor of all payments under the plan." The gist of this addition is that a chapter 12 debtor must certify the payment in full of domestic support obligations or that the confirmed plan provides for payment of prebankruptcy domestic support obligations.

D. CHAPTER 13

There are extensive changes in chapter 13 from amendments found throughout BAPCPA, affecting plan contents, timing of confirmation, exceptions from discharge, and the length of the plan term, as well as other areas of chapter 13 practice.

1. CONVERSION OR DISMISSAL

Section 1307(c)(11) is amended to add as cause for dismissal or conversion of a chapter 13 case the "failure of the debtor to pay any domestic support obligation that first becomes payable after the date of the filing of the petition." The same amendment is made in chapter 12. See the discussion of domestic support obligation.

Section 1307(e) requires the court to either dismiss or convert the case upon the failure of the debtor to file a tax return as required under new § 1308, to be discussed below. A party in interest or the U.S. trustee may move for dismissal or conversion, and the court "shall" dismiss or convert the case, "whichever is in the best interest of the creditors and the estate." Note that the best-interest analysis does not include consideration of the debtor's personal interest.

2. PLAN CONTENTS

Chapter 13 plans contents are changed by the following new § 1322(a)(4):

> [N]otwithstanding any other provision of this section, a plan may provide for less than full payment of all amounts owed for a claim entitled to priority under section 507(a)(1)(B) only if the plan provides that all of the debtor's projected disposable income for a 5-year period beginning on the date that the first payment is due under the plan will be applied to make payments under the plan.

This latter reference to new § 507(a)(1)(B) applies to domestic support obligations that are assigned to a governmental unit, meaning that such claims may be paid less than 100% if disposable income is dedicated to the plan for a full five years.

Former § 1322(b)(10) is redesignated as (11) and a new § 1322(b)(10) is added to the effect that chapter 13 plans would be permitted to "provide for the payment of interest accruing after the date of the filing of the petition on unsecured claims that are nondischargeable under section 1328(a), except that such interest may be paid only to the extent that the debtor has disposable income available to pay such interest after making provision for full payment of all allowed claims." An example of this would be that a debtor could propose to pay interest on a nondischargeable student loan and that would be permissible if the debtor had remaining disposable income for that purpose and so long as the debtor's plan otherwise proposed to pay other claims in full. Since the requirement is to pay other allowed claims in full, it is doubtful that many chapter 13 debtors will have excess disposable income for payment of such interest.

A plan may not propose any material alteration in a loan by the debtor from a pension, profit-sharing, stock bonus, or other tax-sheltered employee plans. New § 362(b)(19) excludes repayment of these types of loans from the automatic stay, and new § 1322(f) refers to this automatic stay exception for a description of the loans that may not be materially altered. In other words, the debtor's chapter 13 plan must propose continuation of the terms of such a loan, and the amount needed to repay those loans is specifically excluded from disposable income.

3. LENGTH OF PLAN

Code § 1322(d) is amended to substitute the following:

(d)(1) If the current monthly income of the debtor and the debtor's spouse combined, when multiplied by 12, is not less than—

(A) in the case of a debtor in a household of 1 person, the median family income of the applicable State for 1 earner;

(B) in the case of a debtor in a household of 2, 3, or 4 individuals, the highest median family income of the applicable State for a family of the same number or fewer individuals; or

(C) in the case of a debtor in a household exceeding 4 individuals, the highest median family income of the applicable State for a family of 4 or fewer individuals, plus $525 per month for each individual in excess of 4,

the plan may not provide for payments over a period that is longer than 5 years.

(2) If the current monthly income of the debtor and the debtor's spouse combined, when multiplied by 12, is less than—

(A) in the case of a debtor in a household of 1 person, the median family income of the applicable State for 1 earner;

(B) in the case of a debtor in a household of 2, 3, or 4 individuals, the highest median family income of the applicable State for a family of the same number or fewer individuals; or

(C) in the case of a debtor in a household exceeding 4 individuals, the highest median family income of the applicable State for a family of 4 or fewer individuals, plus $525 per month for each individual in excess of 4,

the plan may not provide for payments over a period that is longer than 3 years, unless the court, for cause, approves a longer period, but the court may not approve a period that is longer than 5 years.

In this reduced form of means testing, therefore, whether a chapter 13 debtor's plan must last for three or five years is determined by current monthly income measured against the median income for a family of like size.

Concurrent with this change, §1325(b)(1)(B) is amended to substitute "applicable commitment period" for the "three-year period" in the former Code, and the term "applicable commitment period" is defined in a new subsection (4), again measuring the debtor's current monthly income against median income and using the same language as seen in §1322(d).

Section 1329(c) is amended to substitute "the applicable commitment period under section 1325(b)(1)(B)" for "three years."

4. FILING TAX RETURNS

A new § 1308 requires the chapter 13 debtor to file all necessary tax returns (federal, state, or local) that are required under nonbankruptcy law for the four years preceding the bankruptcy filing, and these must be filed no later than the § 341 meeting. If the returns are not filed by that date, the chapter 13 trustee may delay the meeting of creditors for a "reasonable time" to permit the debtor to file any unfiled returns, but this additional time is limited to either the last date that the return is due under nonbankruptcy extensions or 120 days after the first date set for the § 341 meeting. The debtor may move for time in addition to this, provided that the debtor can demonstrate by a preponderance of evidence that the untimely filing is beyond the debtor's control, but the court's discretion is limited by allowing only an additional 30 days or the nonbankruptcy extension period that is applicable.

Moreover, a plan may not be confirmed until the debtor has filed all tax returns required by § 1308. See 11 U.S.C.A. § 1325(a)(9).

These requirements are in addition to § 521(e) and (f)'s requirements for chapter 13 debtors to give the most recent prebankruptcy tax returns to the trustee no later than seven days prior to the meeting of creditors and to file all returns that become due during the pendency of the case.

5. CONFIRMATION HEARING DATE

Code § 1324 is amended to add a subpart (b):

(b) The hearing on confirmation of the plan may be held not earlier than 20 days and not later than 45 days after the date of the meeting of creditors under section 341(a), unless the court determines that it would be in the best interests of the creditors and the estate to hold such hearing at an earlier date and there is no objection to such earlier date.

Note that the court's discretion to permit an earlier confirmation hearing is dependent on the lack of any objection to the earlier date.

6. PLAN CONFIRMATION

Code § 1325(a) is amended to add subsection (7) providing that confirmation of a plan is dependent upon whether "the action of the debtor in filing the petition was in good faith." Whether this addition of a good faith requirement in the commencement of the case will present conflicts with the reality that the debtor may have been forced into chapter 13 by dismissal of a chapter 7 case based upon abuse under the means test remains to be seen.

Code §1325(a)(5)(B)(i) is amended to provide that the holder of a secured claim retains its lien until the earlier of payment in full of the contractual obligation under nonbankruptcy law or the granting of a discharge under §1328. Moreover, if the chapter 13 case is dismissed or converted to another chapter prior to completion of the plan, the creditor's lien is retained to the extent recognized by the applicable nonbankruptcy law. The effect of these amendments is to prevent the chapter 13 debtor from paying the secured claim as provided in the plan and obtaining a release of the creditor's lien prior to obtaining a chapter 13 discharge. These provisions are consistent with the changes made to § 348(f)(1)(C).

Code § 348(f)(1) is amended by changing subpart (B) to provide that valuations in chapter 13 shall apply in converted cases only if the case is converted to chapter 11 or 12, but chapter 13 valuations shall not apply when the case is converted to chapter 7. Subpart 348(f)(1)(C) is added to control the claims of secured creditors when the chapter 13 case is converted.

The effect of these changes to § 348(f) is to require the secured creditor's claim, as determined under nonbankruptcy law, to be paid in full if the case is converted to chapter 7 from chapter 13. Therefore, regardless of any valuation placed on the collateral, assuming it is possible in view of the amendments to § 1325(a), the claim and lien are retained in full upon such a conversion. The debtor could not, for example, take advantage of redeeming the collateral in the case converted to chapter 7 based upon a reduced value. Also, the prebankruptcy default is restored in effect upon conversion unless that default has been cured in full while the case was in chapter 13.

Section 1325(a)(5)(B) is also amended to add subsection (iii):
(iii) if—
    (I) property to be distributed pursuant to this subsection is in the form of periodic payments, such payments shall be in equal monthly amounts; and
    (II) the holder of the claim is secured by personal property, the amount of such payments shall not be less than an amount sufficient to provide to the holder of such claim adequate protection during the period of the plan;

These additions require that chapter 13 plans must provide for payment to secured claims in equal monthly periodic payments that equal at least an amount sufficient to provide the secured creditor with adequate protection. Will these provisions disrupt the practical administration of chapter 13 plans under current law? They will if they are interpreted to mean that all secured creditors must be paid in equal monthly payments, beginning promptly after filing. For example, current practice in many districts is to permit payment of the arrearages on home mortgages prior to beginning payment of automobile debts. If the automobile creditor must be paid in equal monthly payments and those payments must provide adequate protection throughout the plan, doesn't that mean that such creditors cannot be delayed in receiving payment? If the debtor's monthly income is not sufficient to cure the home mortgage arrearage while making ongoing mortgage payments and making monthly payments to all other secured creditors, either the plan will not be feasible or the debtor must make an election on which collateral will be retained.

Section 1325(a) is further amended to add at the end a provision that § 506 does not apply in determining a secured claim, for purposes of § 1325(a)(5), if the creditor has a purchase-money security interest in a motor vehicle purchased by the debtor for the debtor's personal use within 910 days before the filing of the bankruptcy or if the debtor has purchased other purchase-money collateral within one year of the filing. The Code uses the definition of "motor vehicle" found in 49 U.S.C.A. § 30102. The 910 days is approximately 2 1/2 years. Of course, there will be factual scenarios where the chapter 13 debtor will have purchased a motor vehicle not for the debtor's personal use, in which event the prohibition against using § 506 would not control. The effect of this amendment is to prohibit the strip-down of purchase-money secured claims that are covered by the amendment, thus requiring their full payment under the contract terms. It is interesting that the same "personal use" restriction is not found in the reference to non-vehicle purchase-money collateral; therefore, it appears that any non-vehicle collateral purchased within one year of the bankruptcy and secured by a purchase-money security interest would be subject to full payment of the contract price in chapter 13, even if it were not for purely personal use. Does this mean, for example, that a business chapter 13 debtor purchased non-vehicle collateral for business use, it would not be subject to strip-down in value? It would appear so.

Plan confirmation in chapter 13 will have the additional requirement that "the debtor has paid all amounts that are required to be paid under a domestic support obligation and that first become payable after the date of the filing of the petition if the debtor is required by a judicial or administrative order, or by statute, to pay such domestic support obligation." This is a new § 1325(a)(8).

7. DISPOSABLE INCOME

Code § 1325(b)(1)(A) is amended to require that the disposable income dedicated to the plan must be paid to unsecured creditors. The former § 1325(b)(2), defining disposable income, is struck and in its place inserted:

(2) For purposes of this subsection, the term "disposable income" means current monthly income received by the debtor (other than child support payments, foster care payments, or disability payments for a dependent child made in accordance with applicable nonbankruptcy law to the extent reasonably necessary to be expended for such child) less amounts reasonably necessary to be expended—

(A)(i) for the maintenance or support of the debtor or a dependent of the debtor, or for a domestic support obligation, that first becomes payable after the date the petition is filed; and

(ii) for charitable contributions (that meet the definition of 'charitable contribution' under section 548(d)(3) to a qualified religious or charitable entity or organization (as defined in section 548(d)(4)) in an amount not to exceed 15 percent of gross income of the debtor for the year in which the contributions are made; and

(B) if the debtor is engaged in business, for the payment of expenditures necessary for the continuation, preservation, and operation of such business.

(3) Amounts reasonably necessary to be expended under paragraph (2) shall be determined in accordance with subparagraphs (A) and (B) of section 707(b)(2), if the debtor has current monthly income, when multiplied by 12, greater than—

(A) in the case of a debtor in a household of 1 person, the median family income of the applicable State for 1 earner;

(B) in the case of a debtor in a household of 2, 3, or 4 individuals, the highest median family income of the applicable State for a family of the same number or fewer individuals; or

(C) in the case of a debtor in a household exceeding 4 individuals, the highest median family income of the applicable State for a family of 4 or fewer individuals, plus $525 per month for each individual in excess of 4.

As BAPCPA refers to these additions, they represent a form of the means test applicable in chapter 13. The monetary cap is subject to the periodic adjustment provided by amended 11 U.S.C.A. § 104(b).

Withholdings for deferred compensation plans as well as for repayment of loans from such plans are not disposable income for purposes of § 1325(b)(2). See also the discussion of the exclusion from the bankruptcy estate of such withholdings under the amendment to § 541(b)(7) and the amendment of § 362(b)(19).

Section 1325(b)(2) is amended to exclude from disposable income in a chapter 13 any amounts needed for the maintenance or support of the debtor or debtor's dependents or for a domestic support obligation that first becomes payable after the filing of the bankruptcy petition. Also excluded are any child support, foster care payments, or disability payments received by the debtor for a dependent child if those payments are made under nonbankruptcy law.

The charitable contribution exception from disposable income, up to 15% of the debtor's gross income, continues to exist in the amended Code.

8. PLAN PAYMENTS

Section 1326(a) is amended to replace the current section completely with the requirement that, unless the court orders otherwise, the debtor must begin plan payments no later than 30 days after the earlier of filing the plan or the order for relief. The plan payments must be paid to the trustee in the amount as proposed in the plan, but the debtor must pay directly to the lessor of personal property the amount of the lease that becomes due after the bankruptcy filing pending plan confirmation, and the amount payable to the trustee can be reduced by the lease payments, provided proof is given to the trustee.

Pending confirmation, the debtor must pay adequate protection payments to the holders of purchase-money claims that are secured by personal property, at least to the extent of that portion of the obligation that comes due after the bankruptcy filing, again reducing the payments to the trustee in that amount paid to such creditors, provided that proof of payment is given to the trustee.

The court may, after notice and hearing, increase or reduce the amount of the payments required to lessors and secured creditors, pending confirmation.

Unless a practical solution is found, the payments directly to lessors and secured creditors will create administrative problems. How would such payments be accounted for and would those creditors be required to amend their claims to reflect the payments received from the debtor? How will the debtor deal with disputes about the amount of the claim when the trustee does not have records of payments made and is not the disburser of those payments?

9. INSURANCE

By amendment to § 1326(a)(4):

> Not later than 60 days after the date of filing of a case under this chapter, a debtor retaining possession of personal property subject to a lease or securing a claim attributable in whole or in part to the purchase price of such property shall provide the lessor or secured creditor reasonable evidence of the maintenance of any required insurance coverage with respect to the use or ownership of such property and continue to do so for so long as the debtor retains possession of such property.

The current practice in some districts of requiring proof of insurance or otherwise forced placing insurance in the plan for the benefit of the vehicle creditor is adopted and expanded to other secured creditors.

10. CHAPTER 7 TRUSTEE'S CLAIM

If a chapter 7 trustee has been allowed compensation due to conversion or dismissal of a chapter 7 case under §707(b), any unpaid portion will be paid in the subsequent chapter 13 case. The payment shall be monthly with a cap depending upon the amount of other unsecured claims in the case.

11. DISCHARGE

A precondition to discharge is found in an addition to § 1328(a), adding the following:

> [I]in the case of a debtor who is required by a judicial or administrative order, or by statute, to pay a domestic support obligation, after such debtor certifies that all amounts payable under such order or such statute that are due on or

before the date of the certification (including amounts due before the petition was filed, but only to the extent provided for by the plan) have been paid.

The gist of this addition is that a chapter 13 debtor must certify the payment in full of domestic support obligations or that the confirmed plan provides for payment of prebankruptcy domestic support obligations.

For chapter 13 debtors, § 1328(f) is added to provide that the court may not grant a discharge under that chapter if the debtor has received a chapter 7, 11, or 12 discharge in a prior case filed within four years preceding the filing of the current chapter 13 case or, if the debtor has received a chapter 13 discharge, in a case filed within two years of the current case filing.

The chapter 13 discharge that may be granted upon completion of plan payments is changed and more restricted by the substitution of a new § 1328(a), excepting from the discharge those debts:

(1) provided for under section 1322(b)(5);

(2) of the kind specified in section 507(a)(8)(C) or in paragraph (1)(B), (1)(C), (2), (3), (4), (5), (8), or (9) of section 523(a);

(3) for restitution, or a criminal fine, included in a sentence on the debtor's conviction of a crime; or

(4) for restitution, or damages, awarded in a civil action against the debtor as a result of willful or malicious injury by the debtor that caused personal injury to an individual or the death of an individual.

As a result of this replacement, all debts that are excepted from discharge under § 523(a)(1)(B) and (C), (2), (3), (4), (5), (8), and (9) are now excepted from the chapter 13 discharge. The reference to §507(a)(8)(C) brings within the exception those taxes that the debtor was responsible for collecting or withholding. Also, any damages or restitution resulting from a willful or malicious injury that caused personal injury or death would be excepted from discharge. Note that this subsection uses "willful or malicious," rather than § 523(a)(6)'s requirement of "willful and malicious." Does this mean that the chapter 13 discharge is even more limited than a possible discharge under chapter 7? That would seem to be likely, since "or" is broader than "and."

The court may not grant a chapter 13 debtor a discharge until the debtor has completed an "instructional course concerning personal financial management" as those courses are defined in § 111. See the discussion of Credit Briefing and Debtor Education.

In addition, the court may not grant a discharge if it appears that the new § 522(q)(1) applies to the debtor or if any action is pending where the debtor may be found guilty of a felony as described in § 522(q)(1)(A) or liable for a debt as described in § 522(q)(1)(B).

12. MODIFICATION OF PLAN AFTER CONFIRMATION

Code § 1329(a) is amended by adding subsection (4) to the end, providing that a chapter 13 debtor's plan may be modified to reduce payments that might otherwise be required in order to permit the purchase of health insurance for the debtor and dependents without such insurance coverage, provided that the expenses are reasonable and necessary and that the amount of insurance and the cost of the premium are in line with coverage previously held or with coverage for similarly situated persons. Moreover, the debtor cannot double up this expense: If disposable income has already been reduced for health insurance, the new purchase cannot increase that prior deduction. Proof that the debtor purchased the health insurance can be demanded.

It is odd that permitting purchase of health insurance is found in the postconfirmation modification section. Surely a debtor would be permitted to purchase such insurance and deduct it from disposable income rather than waiting until after confirmation to do so.

XI. CHANGES IN CODE SECTIONS THAT APPLY TO ALL CHAPTERS

A. ADMINISTRATIVE EXPENSE

Section 503(b)(1)(A) is amended to add a new subsection (A)(ii) allowing administrative expenses for the wages and benefits awarded by a judicial proceeding or an NLRB proceeding. Subsection 503(b)(1)(D) is added to make it clear that a governmental unit does not need to file a request for payment of expenses related to taxes in order to be allowed an administrative expense for those taxes and related fines or penalties.

Section 503(b)(7) is added concerning nonresidential real property lease previously assumed but then rejected.

Section 503(b)(8) is added to permit administrative expenses for the actual and necessary costs related to closing a health care business.

Section 503(b)(9) adds an administrative expense for the value of goods received by the debtor within 20 days of the filing of the case where the goods were sold to the debtor in the ordinary course of the debtor's business.

Section 503(c) is added to restrict the allowance of administrative claims and severance payments for insiders of the debtor.

See the discussion of these additions to § 503 in the business section of this publication.

B. APPEALS

28 U.S.C.A. § 158(d) is amended to provide that the court of appeals has jurisdiction for all final orders of a bankruptcy court and may take an appeal directly if the bankruptcy court, district court, or bankruptcy appellate panel, on the lower court's own motion or on the motion of a party to the judgment, certifies that the bankruptcy court's final order involves a question of law on which there is no controlling decision in that circuit or that the issue involves one of public importance or that an immediate appeal is otherwise necessary.

C. ATTORNEYS AND OTHER PROFESSIONALS

28 U.S.C.A. § 1334 is amended to substitute a new subsection (e) giving the district court exclusive jurisdiction over not only all property of the debtor and of the bankruptcy estate but over "all claims or causes of action that involve construction of section 327" of the Bankruptcy Code, as well as "rules relating to disclosure requirements under section 327." This amendment takes effect upon enactment as to all cases filed after that date.

Section 504 of title 11 dealing with sharing of compensation is amended by adding a new subsection (c):

(c) This section shall not apply with respect to sharing, or agreeing to share, compensation with a bona fide public service attorney referral program that operates in accordance with non-Federal law regulating attorney referral services and with rules of professional responsibility applicable to attorney acceptance of referrals.

In compensating professional persons, the court may consider whether that person is board certified "or otherwise has demonstrated skill and experience in the bankruptcy field." 11 U.S.C.A. § 330(a)(3)(E).

By amendment to § 330(a)(7), a trustee's compensation must be calculated on a commission basis as described in § 326, while other professionals may be paid on an hourly basis, a fixed fee, or percentage fee basis when they are employed under § 328. See 11 U.S.C.A. § 328(a).

See other discussions concerning professionals in the business section.

D. AUDITS

The U.S. trustee or bankruptcy administrator will be responsible for conducting random audits of 0.4% of chapter 7 and 13 cases with the purpose of determining the accuracy, veracity, and completeness of petitions and schedules. The debtor's failure to cooperate in such an audit is grounds for revocation of discharge under § 727(d)(4), and the debtor generally has a duty to cooperate. 11 U.S.C.A. § 521(a)(2)(C).

E. AUTOMATIC STAY

1. DOMESTIC RELATIONS EXCEPTION

Several changes are made to automatic stay provisions in § 362 that will impact domestic support creditors. Under the exceptions to the automatic stay, a new § 362(b)(2) replaces the current subsection (2), expanding the current provision to except from the stay:

(A) of the commencement or continuation of a civil action or proceeding—
(i) for the establishment of paternity;
(ii) for the establishment or modification of an order for domestic support obligations;
(iii) concerning child custody or visitation;
(iv) for the dissolution of a marriage, except to the extent that such proceeding seeks to determine the division of property that is property of the estate; or
(v) regarding domestic violence;
(B) of the collection of a domestic support obligation from property that is not property of the estate;
(C) with respect to the withholding of income that is property of the estate or property of the debtor for payment of a domestic support obligation under a judicial or administrative order or a statute;
(D) of the withholding, suspension, or restriction of a driver's license, a professional or occupational license, or a recreational license, under State law, as specified in section 466(a)(16) of the Social Security Act;

(E) of the reporting of overdue support owed by a parent to any consumer reporting agency as specified in section 466(a)(7) of the Social Security Act;

(F) of the interception of a tax refund, as specified in sections 464 and 466(a)(3) of the Social Security Act or under an analogous State law; or

(G) of the enforcement of a medical obligation, as specified under title IV of the Social Security Act;

11 U.S.C.A. § 362(b)(2).

2. PENSION LOAN REPAYMENT EXCEPTION

Section 362(b)(19) excepts from the stay the continuing withholding from the debtor's wages and the collection of loan amounts due as a result of the debtor's borrowing from employer-sponsored pension, profit-sharing, stock bonus, or other plans recognized by the IRS as tax-exempt. This exception goes in hand with the recognition in chapter 13 that such loan repayment withholdings are not disposable income and with the prohibition against a chapter 13 debtor materially modifying such loan terms.

3. IN REM ENFORCEMENT EXCEPTION

A new subsection 362(b)(20) is added to exclude from the automatic stay actions to enforce liens or security interests following entry of an in rem order described in the the new § 362(d)(4), unless the debtor in the subsequent bankruptcy case successfully reinstates the automatic stay under the provisions of (d)(4).

Code § 362(d)(4) is added to provide that, as to real property, if the court finds that the bankruptcy case was filed as part of a "scheme to delay, hinder, and defraud creditors," either by the transfer of all or part of an interest in the realty without the secured creditor's consent or by multiple bankruptcy filings that affect the realty (presumably stopping foreclosure actions, for example), the court may grant in rem relief from the automatic stay. That is, the relief from the stay would have a binding effect in any other bankruptcy case that might be filed within two years of the entry of the order, provided that the order was also recorded in compliance with state real estate noticing laws. A debtor in a subsequent case who may be affected by this in rem order could move for relief from the order to reinstate a stay, provided that the debtor must show a change of circumstances since entry of the order or other good cause. The subsection specifically provides that federal, state, or local governmental units must accept a certified copy of the in rem order for "indexing and recording."

4. INELIGIBLE FILING EXCEPTION

A new subsection 362(b)(21) excludes from the automatic stay any action taken to enforce a lien or security interest if the debtor is ineligible to file bankruptcy under § 109(g) or if the case was filed in violation of a bankruptcy court order prohibiting the debtor from being a debtor under title 11. Presumably, these provisions would mean that the stay does not come into effect, even though the court only later determined that the debtor was not eligible to file, but this creates a problem if the court finds that the debtor was in fact eligible to file.

5. EVICTION EXCEPTIONS

A new subsection (b)(22) excludes from the stay, except for a new subsection 362(l), the "continuation of any eviction, unlawful detainer action, or similar proceeding by a lessor" of residential property where a prebankruptcy judgment for possession has been obtained against the tenant/debtor, and new subsection (b)(23) excludes from the stay, except as provided in new subsection 362(m), an "eviction action that seeks possession of the residential property in which the debtor resides as a tenant," if the eviction is based on "endangerment of such property or the illegal use of controlled substances on such property," but here the landlord must file with the court a "certification under penalty of perjury." The landlord's certification must assert that an eviction proceeding has begun or that the necessary endangerment or illegal use has occurred within 30 days of the bankruptcy filing.

The new subsection § 362(l) provides that the exception for the landlord in § 362(b)(22) shall be delayed for 30 days, that is, the stay would be in effect for that time, if the debtor files with the bankruptcy petition a certification under penalty of perjury that there are circumstances recognized by applicable nonbankruptcy law that would permit the debtor to cure "the entire monetary default that gave rise to the judgment for possession," and the debtor must deposit with the clerk of the court sufficient money to pay any rent becoming due during that 30-day period. Assuming the debtor does all of this, the stay would be in effect until the court ordered otherwise, but if the landlord objected to the certification, a hearing must be held within 10 days of the objection.

Subsection 362(m) is similar but requires the debtor to object within 15 days of the landlord's certification that the tenancy is endangering the property or that the tenant is conducting the described illegal activity. A hearing must be held within 10 days of the debtor's objection, and the debtor has the burden of satisfying the court that the conditions complained of by the landlord have been remedied in order to keep the stay in effect.

6. TRANSFER EXCEPTION

A new subsection 362(b)(24) excludes from the stay "any transfer that is not avoidable under section 544 and that is not avoidable under section 549."

7. EFFECT OF PRIOR FILINGS

Section 362(c) is amended to add subsections (3) and (4), which broadly restrict application of the stay when the debtor has previously filed bankruptcy within one year of the current case. If the individual debtor has been in a single or joint chapter 7, 11, or 13 case, whether filed or merely pending, within one year of filing the current case and that prior case was dismissed (unless it was dismissed and the current case filed as a result of § 707(b)), the automatic stay with respect to any action taken against the debtor as well as the debtor's property or lease "shall terminate with respect to the debtor on the 30th day" after filing the current case. A party in interest may move to keep the stay in effect, only if a motion is filed within the 30 days and if the moving party shows that the current case was filed in good faith.

There is a presumption that the current case was filed in bad faith if the prior case was dismissed due to the debtor's failure to file required documents or otherwise comply with a court order or if the debtor failed in the first case to pay adequate protection ordered by the court or otherwise perform plan terms and if there has not been a substantial change in circumstances and no reason to believe the debtor will carry the current case through to discharge.

If the debtor filed two cases within the one-year period following dismissal of a case within that term, the automatic stay does not go into effect with the third filing. On request of a party in interest, the court "shall promptly enter an order confirming that no stay is in effect." Presumably this would require the court to verify without the benefit of a hearing that the request for such an order was based upon correct facts. Another party in interest may still try to put the stay into effect by filing a motion within 30 days of the bankruptcy filing, again with the burden of showing that the latest filing was in good faith and again having to overcome any presumption of bad faith.

8. EFFECT OF STATEMENT OF INTENT

Former § 362(h) is redesignated as (k) and a new subsection (h) is added to provide that, consistent with the amendment to § 521(a)(2), if the individual debtor does not timely file the statement of intention as to leased property or secured personal property or does not redeem or reaffirm as to that personalty within the 30 days from the first meeting of creditors or does not timely assume an unexpired lease, the automatic stay terminates as to that property. Note that new subsection (h) refers to § 521(a)(2) for the time within which the debtor must carry out the statement of intent. Section 521(a)(2) reduced the time for the debtor to carry out those choices to 30 days. However, a new subsection 521(a)(6) retains 45 days as the trigger for automatic termination of the stay when the debtor fails to act on the statement of intent as to purchase-money collateral. This difference will no doubt cause confusion and some litigation.

There is a savings clause in § 362(h)(1)(B): If the secured creditor does not agree to the reaffirmation proposed by the debtor, the stay does not automatically terminate; presumably, the creditor would then have to move for stay relief. Section 362(h)(2) provides that subparagraph (1)'s termination of the stay does not apply if the court finds on the trustee's motion that the property has value for the bankruptcy estate. The court may order adequate protection to the secured creditor and surrender of the collateral to the trustee, and, if the court does not grant the trustee's motion, which must be filed before the expiration of the § 521(a)(2) time for the debtor to file a statement of intent and to carry out that statement (a maximum total of 60 days from the meeting of creditors), the automatic stay terminates upon conclusion of the hearing on the trustee's motion. This would seem to say that termination is automatic and not requiring an order, but no doubt orders will be requested.

9. TERMINATION IN 60 DAYS

Section 362(e) is amended and renumbered to add a new subsection (2):

(2) Notwithstanding paragraph (1), in a case under chapter 7, 11, or 13 in which the debtor is an individual, the stay under subsection (a) shall terminate on the date that is 60 days after a request is made by a party in interest under subsection (d), unless—

(A) a final decision is rendered by the court during the 60-day period beginning on the date of the request; or

(B) such 60-day period is extended—

(i) by agreement of all parties in interest; or

(ii) by the court for such specific period of time as the court finds is required for good cause, as described in findings made by the court.

10. EFFECT OF DEBT REPAYMENT PLAN

If a prior chapter 7, 11, or 13 case was dismissed due to the debtor entering into a debt repayment plan, then no presumption of bad faith is created by the prior dismissal. 11 U.S.C.A. § 362(i).

11. WILLFUL VIOLATIONS

By amendment to § 362(k)(2), if a violation of the automatic stay, even though willful, was made by a creditor who in good faith believed that the debtor's prior case was dismissed due to the conditions specified in § 362(h), any recovery by the debtor is limited to actual damages. This would appear to greatly limit those situations in which courts have previously awarded punitive damages or other incidental damages.

12. TAX PROCEEDINGS

A new proceeding stay is found in § 362(a)(8), staying tax court proceedings concerning a corporate debtor's liability for a taxable period that the bankruptcy court may determine or concerning the tax liability of an individual debtor for a taxable period ending before the date of the order for relief.

13. SECURITIES REGULATION EXCEPTION

Section 362(b)(25) excepts from the stay the commencement or continuation of an investigation or action by a securities regulatory agency.

14. TAX REFUND SETOFF

An exception from the stay is added in § 362(b)(26) to permit setoff under applicable nonbankruptcy law of an income tax refund by a governmental unit as to a taxable period ending before the order for relief against a tax liability for a period ending before the order for relief, unless nonbankruptcy law does not permit it.

15. NETTING AGREEMENT SETOFF

Section 362(b)(27) recognizes an exception for a setoff by a master netting agreement participant.

16. SOCIAL SECURITY ACT EXCEPTION

The stay does not apply to the Secretary of Health and Human Services for the purpose of excluding the debtor's participation in Medicare or other federal health care programs. 11 U.S.C.A. § 362(b)(28).

F. CONVERSION OR DISMISSAL OF CASE

See the discussions of each chapter for new causes for conversion or dismissal of cases, with the principal one being abuse under amended § 707. In addition to these chapter-specific causes, 11 U.S.C.A. § 521 provides cause in all cases based upon the debtor's failure to file required tax returns. First, § 521(e)(2) requires the chapter 7 or 13 debtor to provide the trustee a copy of the most recent year's federal income tax return (or a transcript of that return) at least seven days before the meeting of creditors. If a creditor requests a copy, it must be provided to that creditor as well, and if the debtor fails to comply, the "court shall dismiss the case unless the debtor demonstrates that the failure... is due to circumstances beyond the control of the debtor." Moreover, in a duplicative statement, § 521(e)(2)(C) states that if the debtor fails to provide a copy to a requesting creditor at the same time as provided to the trustee, the court shall dismiss the case, again unless the debtor shows that the failure is beyond the debtor's control. Neither of these dismissal clauses mentions notice and hearing, but since the debtor is to be given an opportunity to show that circumstances were beyond the debtor's control, a hearing opportunity must exist.

As a second tax-related provision, § 521(j)(1) provides that, in addition to any other provision in the Code, "if the debtor fails to file a tax return that becomes due after the commencement of the case or to properly obtain an extension of the due date of such return, the taxing authority may request that the court enter an order converting or dismissing the case." Subparagraph (2) then provides that if the debtor does not file the required return or obtain an extension from the taxing authority within 90 days after the authority's request, the court "shall convert or dismiss the case, whichever is in the best interests of creditors and the estate." This must mean that the debtor has an automatic 90-day window to comply with the taxing authority's request for filing postpetition returns, but note that the ultimate decision to convert or dismiss does not mention that the court should consider the debtor's interests.

Section 315 of BAPCPA requires the Administrative Office of the United States Court to establish, within 180 days of enactment, procedures to safeguard the confidentiality of any tax information that is required to be provided under these increases in the debtor's duties. Within 540 days of enactment, the Administrative Office is to submit a report to Congress of the effectiveness of these procedures as well as any proposals for changes in legislation necessary to protect the confidentiality of tax information.

Another cause for dismissal of a case that is common to all chapters for individual debtors is the debtor's failure to pay postpetition domestic support obligations. See the discussion of domestic support obligations.

G. CREDIT BRIEFING AND DEBTOR EDUCATION

1. PREBANKRUPTCY CREDIT BRIEFING

Code § 109 is amended by adding subsection (h) to generally preclude an individual debtor from filing for bankruptcy before a briefing has been obtained from an approved nonprofit budget and credit counseling service within 180 days prior to filing. A list of service providers that have been approved by the U.S. trustee or bankruptcy administrator must be maintained by the clerk, and an exception exists for debtors in districts where the U.S. trustee or bankruptcy administrator has determined that nonprofit counseling services cannot provide adequate services. A debtor also could seek a court determination that this briefing was not possible due to exigent circumstances or that it was unavailable within five days of the debtor's request for the service. In the event of such a pre-filing waiver, that debtor would be required to obtain the services within 30 days of filing for bankruptcy, and the court could extend that time for cause but for no more than an additional 15 days.

The briefing requirements could be waived by the court after notice and hearing for a debtor who "is unable to complete those requirements because of an incapacity, disability, or active military duty in a military combat zone." "Incapacity" and "disability" are specifically defined for the purposes of such a waiver.

The debtor's duties under new Code § 521(b) would include producing a certificate of receipt of the credit counseling agency services and any debt repayment plan developed by the service.

In what will produce some confusion, the statute uses the term "briefing" in § 109(h)(1), describing the required prebankruptcy task as "an individual or group briefing (including a briefing conducted by telephone or the Internet) that outlined the opportunities for available credit counseling and assisted such individual in performing a related budget analysis." This seems to require less than full-blown "counseling," since the briefing must advise the debtor about "available credit counseling," but the briefing must "assist" the debtor in "performing" a budget analysis. To add to the confusion, in § 109(h)(3)(A), the Code uses the term "credit counseling services" concerning possible waiver of the requirement. Is there a difference between credit briefing and counseling? There would appear to be, but the extent to which the required briefing must reach true counseling is unknown.

2. DEBTOR EDUCATION

By an addition to Code § 727(a)(11) and to § 1328(g), a debtor would be unable to obtain a discharge in chapter 7 or 13 until completing a newly required personal financial management course, unless such a course is not available as unavailability is described in new § 109(h). The personal financial management course is in addition to the prebankruptcy budget and credit briefing discussed above. It is described in a new Code § 111, which also describes the nonprofit budget and credit counseling agencies.

3. EFFECT OF DEBT REPAYMENT PLAN

Some relief is given to the debtor who files one case that is then dismissed due to the creation of a debt repayment plan, for example one arranged through a credit counseling service. In a subsequent filing, the automatic stay's termination shall not be based upon a presumption of that second filing being in bad faith, since Code § 362 is amended by adding subsection (i):

(i) If a case commenced under chapter 7, 11, or 13 is dismissed due to the creation of a debt repayment plan, for purposes of subsection (c)(3), any subsequent case commenced by the debtor under any such chapter shall not be presumed to be filed not in good faith.

H. CREDITOR'S MEETING REPRESENTATIVE

By an amendment to § 341(c), a corporate partnership or LLC creditor may appear at the meeting of creditors by a representative who is not an attorney.

I. CLAIMS

Code § 502 is amended to add subsection (k) at the end, providing for the potential reduction of a creditor's claim by no more than 20%. The conditions precedent to such a reduction are restrictive, however, suggesting that there will be few opportunities to actually make such a reduction. First, the reduction only applies to claims "based in whole on an unsecured consumer debt." Second, the claim to be reduced would be one filed by a creditor who "unreasonably refused to negotiate a reasonable alternative repayment schedule" that was negotiated on behalf of the debtor by a budget and credit counseling agency. This is the type of agency that the debtor is generally required to consult with prior to filing bankruptcy. Note that the critical words are "unreasonably refused." Third, this section would only apply to unsecured debts that would be dischargeable; if any part of the debt would be nondischargeable, no reduction would be required. Finally, the debtor has the burden of proving "by clear and convincing evidence" that the creditor unreasonably refused to even "consider the debtor's proposal." This burden of proof requiring a showing of the creditor's lack of consideration is extremely heavy.

See the later discussion of the effect of amendment to §506(a)(2), which provides that, for chapter 7 and 13 cases, the value of personal property securing an allowed claim shall be determined based on replacement value as of the date of filing bankruptcy without deducting for the costs of sale or marketing. For consumer personal property, the replacement value is retail, based on the age and condition of the property.

J. CRIMES

BAPCPA § 203 includes an amendment to 18 U.S.C.A. § 158(d) that requires the bankruptcy courts' development of "procedures for referring any case that may contain a materially fraudulent statement in a bankruptcy schedule to" the United States attorneys and agents of the FBI.

By amendment to 18 U.S.C.A. § 157, filing a fraudulent involuntary petition may be bankruptcy fraud. See the discussion of involuntary bankruptcy.

K. DATA

Amendments to 28 U.S.C.A.§ 159 and 589b place emphasis upon the improvement of bankruptcy statistics and data. As a part of this, uniform forms for final reports of the trustees in all cases must be developed.

L. DEBTOR'S CHOICES UNDER § 521

Code § 521(a) is amended to add subsection (6) providing that the individual debtor's choices as to collateral do not include retention of personal property that is secured by an allowed purchase money claim, either entirely or partially. When such a claim exists, if the debtor wishes to retain the collateral, the debtor must either redeem the personal property or enter into a reaffirmation agreement within 45 days of the first meeting of creditors; otherwise, the automatic stay terminates with respect to that collateral, and the property is no longer property of the bankruptcy estate, unless the court, upon motion of the case trustee, finds that the property has value for the estate. The trustee's motion must be filed within the 45 days, and, if granted, the order may provide for adequate protection to the secured creditor and for surrender of the property by the debtor to the trustee. This 45 days is longer than the 30 days that the debtor now has under § 521(a)(2)(B) to carry out the statement of intent by redeeming, surrendering, or reaffirming, but it is the same maximum time that the amended Code gives the debtor to possess purchase-money collateral without redeeming or reaffirming. Section 521(a)(2)(C) is amended to clarify that the debtor's or trustee's rights to the collateral are affected by new subsection 362(h), which provides that the automatic stay terminates when the debtor does not timely carry out one of the three choices.

Note that § 521(a)(2) is amended to delete "consumer," meaning that the debtor's duties concerning filing and complying with a statement of intent for collateral apply to all individual debtors, not merely those who have consumer debts.

Section 521(d) is added to provide that if the debtor fails to timely take the action concerning a statement of intent with respect to property that is leased or subject to a bailment or property that is subject to a security interest that is not voidable under §§ 522(f), 544, 545, 547, 548, or 549, then nothing in the Bankruptcy Code prevents the operation of a default provision in the lease, bailment, or security instrument. Such a default provision may include insolvency or a title 11 bankruptcy filing.

M. DEBT RELIEF AGENCY

A new definition for "debt relief agency" is found in § 101(12A), as are related definitions for "assisted person" and "bankruptcy assistance" found in § 101. Essentially, these terms all become relevant in the consumer bankruptcy filings since an "assisted person" is defined as a consumer debtor with less than $150,000 in nonexempt assets. Attorneys who provide bankruptcy assistance to such debtors fall within the definition of a "debt relief agency" and will be subject to the restrictions and disclosure requirements placed upon those agencies by new Code §§ 526, 527, and 528.

The restrictions in § 526 include potential voiding of any contract for services that does not comply fully with the new Code section requirements; the potential liability in the amount of fees paid plus reasonable attorney's fees if the debt relief agency intentionally or negligently fails to comply with the new Code section requirements or with the Federal Rules of Bankruptcy Procedure; the enforcement of the new requirements by some designated state official; and injunctive relief and civil penalties for violations of these new requirements.

The new disclosures mandated by § 527 include providing the assisted consumer debtor with the information set out in the prebankruptcy notice requirement of § 342(b)(1), and, in addition to this notice, § 527(a)(2) requires specific, clear, and conspicuous written notice to the consumer debtor within three business days of the first date of services that all information provided in a bankruptcy petition must be complete, accurate, and truthful; that all assets and liabilities, with the replacement value of assets, must be stated; that current monthly income and disposable income in a chapter 13 must be stated; and that failure to provide such information can result in dismissal of a case and other sanctions, including a criminal sanction.

In a clear and conspicuous single document that is separate from any other documents, the consumer debtor must be provided with the information as specified in § 527(b).

Underlying the responsibility for accuracy by the consumer debtor and anyone assisting the debtor, § 527(c) requires that the debtor be given information to assist in valuing assets, completing the list of creditors and what they are owed, and how to determine exempt assets and their value under a replacement value approach.

A debt relief agency must maintain for two years a copy of all notices given to the debtor as required by § 527(a).

New Code § 528 provides specific requirements for debt relief agencies. Under these requirements, the consumer debtor's attorney or other person providing bankruptcy assistance must execute a written contract with the debtor within five days of providing the first assistance and prior to the bankruptcy filing. All advertisements by such attorneys or assistance providers must disclose that the services are bankruptcy services, an attempt to reduce the advertisements that refer only to such things as debt restructuring or foreclosure prevention. The advertisement must contain a clear statement that this is a bankruptcy debt relief agency.

These debt relief agency requirements that apply to consumer debtor's attorneys raise issues of how they will relate to the Code's other references to Rule 9011 and the attorney certifications implicit in signing the petition and other pleadings. If an attorney represents both consumer debtors and creditors in different cases, there is an obvious question of the impact that will result for that attorney to be required to disclose or advertise that he or she assists debtors in obtaining bankruptcy relief.

N. DISCHARGE AND EXCEPTIONS FROM DISCHARGE

1. TIME BETWEEN DISCHARGES

Section 727(a)(8) is changed to make the time between chapter 7 discharges or discharges granted under § 1141 eight years rather than the current six years.

For chapter 13 debtors, § 1328(f) is added to provide that the court may not grant a discharge under that chapter if the debtor has received a chapter 7, 11, or 12 discharge in a prior case filed within four years preceding the filing of the current chapter 13 case or if the debtor has received a chapter 13 discharge in a case filed within two years of the current case filing.

2. DELAY IN GRANTING DISCHARGE

Section 727(a) is amended to add a new subsection (11), providing that the court should not grant a discharge when the debtor has failed to complete the instructional course in personal financial management as described in § 109(h)(4). See the discussion of debtor education.

Section 727(a) is also amended to add a new subsection (12) providing that the court should not grant a discharge when it finds that there is "reasonable cause to believe" either that the new § 522(q)(1) applies or that there is a pending proceeding in which the debtor may be found guilty of a felony or liable for damages under the new § 522(q)(1)(A) or (B).

A similar change is made to chapter 11 by adding § 1141(d)(C); to chapter 12 by adding § 1228(f); and to chapter 13 by adding § 1328(h).

3. REVOCATION OF DISCHARGE

Section 727(d)(4) adds a cause to revoke a discharge when the debtor has failed to satisfactorily explain a material misstatement made in reference to an audit that is randomly required in 28 U.S.C.A. § 586(f) or when the debtor has failed to make available for inspection any of the debtor's accounts, papers, or financial records that are requested for audit purposes.

4. LUXURY GOODS AND ADVANCES EXCEPTION

Section 523(a)(2)(C) is amended to change the amount of luxury goods from the current $1,225 to $500 and change the 60-day measuring period for their acquisition to 90 days, and other changes are made in the replaced subsection to eliminate possible exceptions for goods acquired for the support and maintenance of dependents of the debtor and the current "open end credit" provision. Cash advances under an open end credit plan are changed from the current $1,225 to $750 and the current 60-day measuring period is expanded to 70 days.

5. DOMESTIC SUPPORT EXCEPTIONS

There are significant changes to both §§ 523(a)(5) and (15) that are discussed in detail under the Domestic Support Obligations.

6. STUDENT LOAN EXCEPTION

The exception from discharge for education benefits is expanded, with § 523(a)(8) amended to except from discharge, absent an undue hardship showing, of any educational benefit debt or loan without regard to whether it was a debt to a profit-making entity, government entity, or to a government guaranteed creditor.

7. LOANS FOR TAXES EXCEPTION

A new exception from discharge is added for debts "incurred to pay a tax to a governmental unit, other than the United States, that would be nondischargeable under paragraph (1)." 11 U.S.C.A. § 523(a)(14A). Thus, if the debtor borrows money for the purpose of paying a state or local tax, that debt would be nondischargeable provided that the underlying tax is also nondischargeable under § 523(a)(1). The new exception does not include debts incurred for the payment of taxes owing to the United States.

8. ELECTION LAW PENALTY EXCEPTION

New § 523(a)(14B) excepts from discharge fines or penalties imposed under federal election laws.

9. PRISONER EXCEPTION

Section 523(a)(17) is amended to clarify that it applies only to fees imposed on prisoners by a court.

10. PENSION LOAN EXCEPTION

Section 523(a)(18) is added to except from discharge all debts for loans from pension, profit-sharing, stock bonus, or other tax-sheltered plans, but the fact that the loan is excepted from discharge is not to be construed to mean the one owed has a claim or a debt. This is peculiar since it runs counter to the general concept of the definitions of a debt and claim; moreover, § 523(a) begins with the precept that only debts are excepted from discharge. This conflict in terms and concepts will no doubt be the subject of litigation.

11. CHAPTER 13 EXCEPTIONS

Significant increases in the types of debts excepted from discharge are made in the amendments. See the discussion under chapter 13.

O. DISCHARGE INJUNCTION

Code § 524 is amended by adding subsections (i) and (j) at the end, with (i) making it a violation of the discharge injunction for a creditor to "willfully fail" to "credit payments received under" a confirmed plan under any chapter of the Code, with exceptions from that rule when plan confirmation is revoked, the plan is in default or plan payments have not been received in accordance with the confirmed plan's provisions, and the violation is only triggered "if the act of the creditor... to credit payments... caused material injury to the debtor." It may be difficult in most cases, especially chapter 13 cases, for a debtor to show a "material injury." What such an injury must be is not defined by this amendment.

New subsection (j) provides a specific exception from the discharge injunction found in § 524(a)(2), which "operates as an injunction against the commencement or continuation of" collection from the debtor personally. This exception would permit a creditor secured by the debtor's principal residence to seek and obtain from the debtor "periodic payments associated with a valid security interest in lieu of pursuit of in rem relief to enforce the lien." In other words, the home mortgage creditor could pursue with the debtor continued payments rather than foreclose. There is no cross reference here to the amended reaffirmation provisions found in § 524(c). It is uncertain whether subsection (j) is intended to permit retention of a home without reaffirming the secured debt, but that result could occur, notwithstanding the amendment of § 722 to give a chapter 7 debtor only the choices of surrender, redemption, or reaffirmation. See the discussion of that amendment under the debtor's § 521 choices and redemption.

Note also that subsection (j)(2) says that the creditor's actions must be in the ordinary course of business between the debtor and creditor. It is difficult to imagine that consumer debtors have an ordinary course of business that would include negotiating with their mortgage lender about continued payments in lieu of foreclosure.

P. DOMESTIC SUPPORT OBLIGATIONS AND CHANGES IN §§ 523(A)(5) AND (15)

In the place of former Code § 523(a)(5), the amended section will simply provide that "a domestic support obligation" is excepted from discharge. Since that new term is not defined in the exception itself, reference to the definition of that obligation must be found in the new § 101(14A):

> "[D]omestic support obligation" means a debt that accrues before, on, or after the date of the order for relief in a case under this title, including interest that accrues on that debt as provided under applicable nonbankruptcy law notwithstanding any other provision of this title, that is—
> (A) owed to or recoverable by—

(i) a spouse, former spouse, or child of the debtor or such child's parent, legal guardian, or responsible relative; or

(ii) a governmental unit;

(B) in the nature of alimony, maintenance, or support (including assistance provided by a governmental unit) of such spouse, former spouse, or child of the debtor or such child's parent, without regard to whether such debt is expressly so designated;

(C) established or subject to establishment before, on, or after the date of the order for relief in a case under this title, by reason of applicable provisions of—

(i) a separation agreement, divorce decree, or property settlement agreement;

(ii) an order of a court of record; or

(iii) a determination made in accordance with applicable nonbankruptcy law by a governmental unit; and

(D) not assigned to a nongovernmental entity, unless that obligation is assigned voluntarily by the spouse, former spouse, child of the debtor, or such child's parent, legal guardian, or responsible relative for the purpose of collecting the debt.

As will be seen in other amendments, this term "domestic support obligation" appears throughout the Code and replaces current references to support, maintenance, and alimony. The definition of "domestic support obligation" seems to give § 523(a)(5) a broader scope because the definition of "domestic support obligation" includes postbankruptcy accruals and because the new definition changes the treatment of assigned debts.

First, the definition includes debts that accrue before or after the commencement of the case. This on its face should not expand the exception from discharge of these debts since § 523 generally covers only prebankruptcy debts. For example, a chapter 7 discharge only discharges "debts that arose before the date of the order for relief." 11 U.S.C.A. § 727(b). It is likely that the reference to postbankruptcy accruals of these debts, "including interest that accrues," is intended to address the changes made in the confirmation of plans and obtaining of discharges that are preconditioned upon payment of postpetition domestic support obligations. Those changes are discussed under chapters 12 and 13.

The definition continues to refer to debts "in the nature of alimony, maintenance, or support" but that reference now specifically includes "assistance provided by a governmental unit," which, of course, can be either local, state, or federal. Tied to this expansion is the alternative requirement that the debt either be "owed to or recoverable by a spouse, former spouse, or child of the debtor" or by "a governmental unit." Thus any doubt that might exist under the former statute that a debt held by a governmental unit but one never owing to or recoverable by the spouse or child might be dischargeable is erased. Debts owing to or recoverable by the governmental unit that provided support assistance would be excepted from discharge even if the spouse or child who received that assistance could not recover the debt individually.

Another significant change is that the order, agreement, or determination creating the obligation could be one in existence prior to or coming into existence after the filing of the bankruptcy case. Again, this is not so much an expansion of the actual exception from discharge as a complement to the changes made to the automatic stay that will more broadly permit continuations of domestic relations actions in nonbankruptcy courts. Those automatic stay changes are discussed under that topic.

Former § 523(a)(15) would be changed completely by deletion of its subpart (A) and (B) defenses to nondischargeability. The new § 523(a)(15) would simply read:

>   (15) to a spouse, former spouse, or child of the debtor and not of the kind described in paragraph (5) that is incurred by the debtor in the course of a divorce or separation or in connection with a separation agreement, divorce decree or other order of a court of record or a determination made in accordance with State or territorial law by a governmental unit.

Thus the reach of subsection (15) may be to all domestic support obligations that are not alimony, maintenance, or support in nature and without the benefit to the debtor of the current ability-to-pay or balancing tests. Essentially, the combination of amended §§ 523(a)(5) and (15) would be to exclude from discharge all marital and domestic relations obligations, whether support in nature, property division, or hold-harmless, provided that they were incurred in the course of a divorce or separation or established in connection with a separation agreement, divorce decree, or other order of a court of record or a determination made in accordance with state or territorial law by a governmental unit. The only window in this broad reach of the exceptions may be that the amendment of § 523(a)(15) seems to limit it to debts to a spouse, former spouse, or a child of the debtor, but it would appear that only those parties would ever have a domestic relations-type claim under this section. Governmental support assistance agencies are covered by § 523(a)(5) and would not appear to be within the reach of § 523(a)(15).

The former § 523(a)(5) permits the discharge of support-type debts that have been assigned to nongovernmental entities. See 11 U.S.C.A. § 523(a)(5)(A). The new definition of domestic support obligations that is incorporated by reference into the amended § 523(a)(5) would recognize the nondischargeability of these debts that had been voluntarily assigned to a nongovernmental entity by the spouse, former spouse, a child, or other person responsible for the child, for the purposes of collection of the debt.

An extremely significant change would be made to the timing requirements for filing complaints under §§ 523(a)(5) and (15). Formerly, complaints under § 523(a)(5) could be filed "at any time" while complaints under § 523(a)(15) had to be filed within 60 days of the first date set for the meeting of creditors. This requirement for § 523(a)(15) rested upon § 523(c), which included (a)(15) in its list of subsections for which the debtor automatically received a discharge in the absence of a timely complaint. Subsection (c) is amended to delete subsection (15) from this list. This would mean that complaints under (a)(15) could be filed at any time, just like those for (a)(5), and the debtor's discharge would automatically exclude both (a)(5) and (a)(15) debts from the discharge unless a complaint for determination is filed. With the expansion of both §§ 523(a)(5) and (15), the question may be asked when the filing of a complaint could result in a discharge of these debts.

Another change that impacts these types of debts is found in the amendment to § 522(c) concerning the continued liability of exempt property after discharge for debts covered by amended § 523(a)(5). See discussion of that change under exemptions.

The priority of domestic support obligations goes to the top of the list in an amendment to § 507(a)(1). See that discussion under priority.

An amendment to the preference section is made to protect domestic support transfers from avoidance. See the discussion under preferences.

An amendment to § 522(f)(1)(A) incorporates the new § 523(a)(5) into the type of judicial lien that is not avoidable by the debtor. See lien avoidance.

Within 270 days following enactment, the Comptroller General must conduct a study of the feasibility, costs, and effectiveness of requiring all bankruptcy trustees to provide to offices of child support enforcement information about debtors in bankruptcy who may be obligated for child support. See the trustees' duties to such offices and to support creditors under new trustee's duties.

Q. FEES

BAPCPA § 325 increases the filing fee for chapter 7 cases to $200 and reduces the fee for chapter 13 cases to $150. Chapter 11 filing fees are increased to $1,000. The percentage upon which U.S. trustee fees are calculated is increased, and increased filing fees are dedicated to payment of the salaries and benefits for the additional bankruptcy judges provided for in BAPCPA § 1223, with any remainder going into the Treasury.

In forma pauperis is recognized in an amendment to 28 U.S.C.A. § 1930(f), thus permitting the bankruptcy court to waive filing fees in appropriate cases.

R. INVOLUNTARY BANKRUPTCY

Code § 303(b)(1) is amended to provide that a creditor may not commence an involuntary chapter 7 or chapter 11 case if the debtor's liability on a claim or the amount of the claim is contingent or is the subject of a bona fide dispute. This amendment "shall take effect on the date of the enactment of this Act and shall apply with respect to cases commenced under title 11 of the United States Code before, on, and after such date." Former provisions of the Code made a creditor ineligible to seek involuntary relief if the claim is contingent as to liability or the subject of a bona fide dispute. The amendment would extend this to include disputes as to the amount of the claim. Section 303(h)(1) of the Code is amended accordingly to provide that relief shall be granted against an objecting debtor only if the debtor is not paying debts as they become due, unless the debts are subject to a bona fide dispute as to liability or amount.

A new subsection 303(l) is added to provide that if the involuntary petition is against an individual and the petition contains a "false, fictitious or fraudulent statement," and if the court dismisses the petition, the court shall seal all records of the case upon motion of the debtor. The court may prohibit consumer-reporting agencies from reporting anything concerning such a dismissed involuntary case. Finally, the court may expunge the record under this section. In line with this change, 18 U.S.C.A. §157 is amended to include fraudulent involuntary bankruptcy in the bankruptcy fraud described under § 157(3).

S. LIEN AVOIDANCE

The debtor's ability to avoid judicial liens found in § 522(f)(1)(A) is reduced by the deletion of most of that former section. It reads instead that a judicial lien could be avoided, "other than a judicial lien that secures a debt of a kind specified in section 523(a)(5)." Therefore, any judicial lien securing a domestic support obligation would be protected from avoidance.

Such obligations would also be fully protected from a trustee's avoidance under the preference statute. Section 547(c)(7)'s former exception from preference avoidance is changed to read: "to the extent such transfer was a bona fide payment of a debt for a domestic support obligation."

Section 522(f)(4)(A) is added to adopt a definition of "household goods" for purposes of nonpossesssory, nonpurchase-money lien avoidance under § 522(f)(1)(B). Section 313(b) of the Act states that the Director of the Executive Office of the U.S. Trustee is to submit a report to the Judiciary Committees of the House and Senate within two years of enactment, with the report to contain findings concerning the utilization of this definition under § 522(f), including findings of the impact on debtors. That report may contain recommendations for any changes in § 522(f).

T. NOTICES

Code § 342(b) is amended to more specifically describe the prebankruptcy notice that the clerk of court is to give to individual debtors under any chapter of title 11. Among other things, this notice alerts the debtor to possible bankruptcy crimes.

Section 342 is also amended by the addition of subsection (c)(2), (e), (f), and (g), which concern the address and noticing that must be given to creditors based upon the address that may have been supplied to the debtor by the creditor prior to bankruptcy.

Within 10 days of the filing of an individual's chapter 7 petition in which a presumption of abuse arises under § 707(b), the clerk is required to notice creditors that the presumption exists. This is problematic, since this 10 days is before the time that the U.S. trustee or bankruptcy administrator will have completed its abuse analysis; therefore, the clerk may only act upon the debtor's own calculation admitting that a presumption of abuse exists. If the debtor is going to admit that, one may fairly question why that debtor would file chapter 7 anyway. It is unknown at this point what effect the clerk's notice will serve.

There are other notice requirements discussed under other topics.

U. PETITION PREPARERS

Code § 110 is substantially amended to specify the notices that must be given by non-attorney bankruptcy petition preparers and to more tightly regulate the fees that may be charged by them. The Supreme Court is given specific authority to promulgate rules "setting a maximum allowable fee chargeable by a bankruptcy petition preparer," and the preparer must notify the debtor of that maximum fee as well as of the fact that the preparer is not an attorney. Such a preparer may not give legal advice. The bankruptcy court may order the turnover of excess fees over the value of services provided, and a debtor may exempt any excess fees recovered. Specific injunctive authority is modified, and treble damages are authorized.

V. PREFERENCES AND FRAUDULENT TRANSFERS

1. PREFERENCES

Section 547 is amended in several important ways. First, §547(c)(2) is amended to reduce the requirements for a transfer to be in the ordinary course of business. Now, that exception will be satisfied by the transfer being a payment made in the ordinary course of both the debtor and transferee *or* being a payment made according to ordinary business terms. The transfer still must be one for a debt incurred in the ordinary course of both the debtor and transferee.

Section 547(c)(3)(B) changes the time for perfection to 30 days from 20 days.

Code § 547(c)(7) is amended to simply exclude from the trustee's avoidance power a transfer "to the extent such transfer was a bona fide payment of a debt for a domestic support obligation."

Section 547(c)(9) sets $5,000 as the threshold for the trustee to initiate preference avoidance for the transfer of nonconsumer debts, and this is an aggregate amount. The consumer threshold remains at $600.

Code § 547(h) is also added to prohibit the trustee's avoidance of a transfer that was "made as a part of an alternative repayment schedule between the debtor and any creditor of the debtor created by an approved nonprofit budget and credit counseling agency." This refers to the credit briefing that the debtor is generally required to seek prior to filing bankruptcy.

An addition of § 547(c)(i) provides that, in the event that the trustee successfully avoids a transfer made by the debtor between 90 days and one year prior to bankruptcy to a creditor who is not an insider, but the transfer is for the benefit of a creditor who is an insider, the transfer is avoided only as to the creditor that is an insider. This amendment "shall apply to any case that is pending or commenced on or after the date of enactment," including those in which avoidance proceedings are pending. This is a further legislative attempt to limit the effect of the *DePrizio* decision, *Levit v. Ingersoll Rand Financial Corp.*, 874 F.2d 1186, 19 Bankr. Ct. Dec. (CRR) 574, 22 Collier Bankr. Cas. 2d (MB) 36, 11 Employee Benefits Cas. (BNA) 1323, Bankr. L. Rep. (CCH) P 72910 (7th Cir. 1989) (disapproved of by, In re Arundel Housing Components, Inc., 126 B.R. 216, 21 Bankr. Ct. Dec. (CRR) 959, Bankr. L. Rep. (CCH) P 73922 (Bankr. D. Md. 1991)), and the majority of decisions from courts that have followed it.

2. Fraudulent Conveyances

The trustee's reach-back period is extended to insiders and the period is extended from one to two years. 11 U.S.C.A. § 548(a) and (b). The change to two years is not effective until April 20, 2006, one year after the enactment.

Section 548(e) is added concerning self-settled trusts. See the discussion under exclusions and exemptions.

W. PRIORITY

Section 507(a) is amended to move domestic support obligations to the first priority of § 507(a)(1), with subsection (C) giving the trustee a superpriority for payment of administrative expenses but only to the extent that the trustee administers assets that benefit domestic support claimants. This first priority includes domestic support claims that have been assigned to a governmental unit, unless the assignment was done voluntarily for the purpose of collection.

The priority for wage claims is increased to $10,000, as are the claims for contributions to employee benefit plans, but the priority amount for grain producers and fishermen is reduced to $4,000. Under §507(a)(7), the priority amount for deposits is reduced to $1,800.

Under §507(a)(8), the tax priority now recognizes that the 240-day tax assessment period is tolled for any period of time that the automatic stay was in effect under title 11, plus an additional 90 days. This priority will have an effect on the nondischargeability of taxes that depend upon §507(a)(8). See 11 U.S.C.A. § 523(a)(1).

A new tenth priority is added to § 507(a)(10) for personal injury and death claims "resulting from the operation of a motor vehicle or vessel if such operation was unlawful because the debtor was intoxicated from using alcohol, a drug, or another substance."

X. PROTECTION OF INFORMATION AND IDENTITY

Several additions to the Code attempt to protect personally identifiable information about debtors and their minor children. Section 363(b)(1) is amended to add a restriction on the trustee's ability to sell property of the estate if it might include personally identifiable information about individuals who are not debtors but were connected to the debtor in some business transaction or otherwise. In line with this, and notwithstanding a sale of property of the estate by a trustee or debtor in possession, § 363 is amended by inserting a new subsection (o) to preserve claims and defenses in a consumer credit transaction or contract if it is one subject to the Truth in Lending Act or other defined consumer credit transaction. Note that this insertion of (o) does not replace the existing subsection (o), which deals with the trustee's burden of proof. That subsection is renumbered subsection (p).

Section 101(41A) is added to define "personally identifiable information," a term that will broadly include names, addresses, telephone numbers, birth dates, and social security numbers.

A new Code § 332 provides for a consumer privacy ombudsman to be appointed by the U.S. trustee or bankruptcy administrator upon a court order when required for a hearing under the amended § 363(b)(1)(B). That ombudsman would assist the court by providing information concerning any personally identifiable information that might be involved in a sale of property of the bankruptcy estate. The ombudsman may be compensated from the estate as a professional by amendment to § 330(a)(1).

A new Code § 112 provides that if a debtor is required to furnish information about a minor child, for example in the schedules of expenses, the debtor may only be required to disclose the name of such a child in a nonpublic record, and the court and court officers shall not disclose the child's name. It is not clear how the debtor would protect a child's name without that document being filed under seal.

Code § 107(c) is added to authorize the court to protect an individual from disclosure of information that might expose that individual to identity theft or other unlawful injury. How this authority will fit with the debtor's requirements to file tax returns that are available to creditors upon request is not clear, and the Administrative Office of U.S. Courts is directed to prepare regulations for protection of the debtor concerning tax returns. However, there is much information in tax returns beyond the name and social security number that may disclose potentially damaging information about taxpayers/debtors, and, prior to the issuance of these regulations, it is unclear how they will be effective.

Code § 342(c) is amended to require that notices to creditors give only the last four digits of the debtor's social security number, except where a creditor is being added to schedules, in which event that creditor shall be provided with the full social security number.

Y. REAFFIRMATION

Code § 524 is amended to add a new subsection (k) at the end specifically setting out disclosures that must be in the reaffirmation agreements referred to in § 524(c). The written disclosures include an explanation about rescinding the agreement and the obligations incurred by a reaffirmation, and specific contents for such agreements are established. A national form, in conformity with the expanded disclosure requirements, will be developed by the Administrative Office of the U.S. Courts. The new disclosures established by § 524(k) are specifically not applicable to reaffirmations with a credit union as defined by the Federal Reserve Act.

BAPCPA also amends title 18 of the Code to designate the United States attorneys and the FBI as responsible for investigating and addressing abusive reaffirmation practices as well as materially fraudulent statements made in bankruptcy schedules.

The Comptroller General is directed by BAPCA § 205 to conduct a study of reaffirmation practices and report to Congress within 18 months of enactment any recommendations for legislation needed to address abusive or coercive tactics.

Z. REDEMPTION

Section 722 is amended to specify that redemption of personal property in chapter 7 requires payment of the allowed secured claim in full at the time of the redemption. This is intended to preclude redemptions by installment payments.

AA. REPEAT FILINGS

By several amendments, discouragement of repeat filings by debtors is seen. See the discussion under automatic stay for changes in the effect of the stay, termination of the stay, or failure of the stay to be triggered.

BB. TAXES

In addition to the changes in exceptions from discharge for taxes and the broad requirements to file tax returns, BAPCA makes other changes that affect tax obligations. See the discussion of some of the tax issues under the business section of this publication.

CC. UTILITIES

Section 366(c) is added to specify what the term "assurance of payment" means and what forms of assurance are required. In what will make a significant difference in negotiations between the debtor and utility providers, including in chapter 11 cases, § 366(c)(1)(B) specifically states that "an administrative priority shall not constitute an assurance of payment."

DD. VALUATIONS

Section 506(a) is amended to add a subsection (2):

(2) If the debtor is an individual in a case under chapter 7 or 13, such value with respect to personal property securing an allowed claim shall be determined based on the replacement value of such property as of the date of the filing of the petition without deduction for costs of sale or marketing. With respect to property acquired for personal, family, or household purposes, replacement value shall mean the price a retail merchant would charge for property of that kind considering the age and condition of the property at the time value is determined.

This amendment overturns those opinions that had permitted valuations based upon wholesale valuations, including the Supreme Court's *Rash* decision, by requiring retail values to be used in chapters 7 and 13, at least as to property acquired by the debtor for personal, family, or household use. However, the retail value is to take into account the age and condition of the property at the time of the value determination.

EE. VENUE

Venue for recovery by a trustee of a consumer debt is changed to require that if the amount is less than $15,000 the suit must be in the district where the defendant resides. If the suit is against a noninsider and on a nonconsumer debt and for less than $10,000, again it must be filed in the district where the defendant resides.

XII. NEW EXEMPTIONS, EXCLUSIONS, AND ASSET PROTECTION

A. HOMESTEAD AND EXEMPTION CHOICES

BAPCPA amends § 522(b), renumbering it, and new subsection (3)(A)'s timing for exemption choice strikes the reference to the 180-day period and substitutes "730 days," including the following phrase at the end of the section: "or if the debtor's domicile has not been located at a single State for such 730-day period, the place in which the debtor's domicile was located for 180 days immediately preceding the 730-day period or for a longer portion of such 180-day period than in any other place." This would mean that a debtor who moved from state to state within the 730 days prior to bankruptcy would be forced to use the exemptions in that state where the debtor had been domiciled prior to the 730-day period. Presumably, this is an effort to prevent persons taking advantage of favorable state exemptions by moving within two years before bankruptcy, but, of course, there will be instances where the moving was without any bad motive and where the debtor might actually benefit by returning to the prior domiciliary state's exemptions. For example, if the debtor had been domiciled in Florida, with its unlimited homestead up until 750 days ago (more than two years) and then moved to a state with poor exemptions, the debtor might time a bankruptcy filing to take advantage of the Florida exemptions.

The Act further amends renumbered section 522(b)(3) by adding a new section at the end: "If the effect of the domiciliary requirement under subsection (A) is to render the debtor ineligible for any exemption, the debtor may elect to exempt property that is specified under subsection (d)." That is, such a debtor would have the federal bankruptcy exemptions as a fall-back choice. It is not completely clear when the federal exemptions would be triggered and that may depend upon whether the state in which the debtor was domiciled for most of the 180 days immediately preceding the 730-day period had specific rules governing its exemptions that prevented the debtor from using that state's exemptions.

Renumbered section 522(b)(3)(A) states:

> (A) subject to subsections (o) and (p) any property that is exempt under Federal law, other than subsection (d) of this section, or State or local law that is applicable on the date of the filing of the petition at the place in which the debtor's domicile has been located for the 730 days immediately preceding the date of the filing of the petition or if the debtor's domicile has not been located at a single State for such 730-day period, the place in which the debtor's domicile was located for 180 days immediately preceding the 730-day period or for a longer portion of such 180-day period than in any other place.

The effect of the "subject to subsection (o) and (p)" language is to restrict the homestead under those subsections even if the debtor's homestead choice is limited by the debtor's domiciliary state having opted out of the bankruptcy exemptions. This is a significant limitation on the opt-out clause that was a crucial part of the 1978 Code's exemption provisions.

Whether claimed under federal bankruptcy law or applicable state law, the homestead can now be capped by the addition of subsections 522(o), (p), and (q):

> (o) For purposes of subsection (b)(3)(A), and notwithstanding subsection (a), the value of an interest in—
>> (1) real or personal property that the debtor or a dependent of the debtor uses as a residence;
>> (2) a cooperative that owns property that the debtor or a dependent of the debtor uses as a residence;
>> (3) a burial plot for the debtor or a dependent of the debtor; or
>> (4) real or personal property that the debtor or a dependent of the debtor claims as a homestead;
>
> shall be reduced to the extent that such value is attributable to any portion of any property that the debtor disposed of in the 10-year period ending on the date of the filing of the petition with the intent to hinder, delay, or defraud a creditor and that the debtor could not exempt, or that portion that the debtor could not exempt, under subsection (b), if on such date the debtor had held the property so disposed of.

New subsections (p) and (q) are added to the end of § 522, limiting the amount of the homestead that was acquired within 1,215 days of filing bankruptcy:

> (p)(1) Except as provided in paragraph (2) of this subsection and sections 544 and 548, as a result of electing under subsection (b)(3)(A) to exempt property under State or local law, a debtor may not exempt any amount of interest that was acquired by the debtor during the 1215-day period preced-

ing the date of the filing of the petition that exceeds in the aggregate $125,000 in value in—

(A) real or personal property that the debtor or a dependent of the debtor uses as a residence;

(B) a cooperative that owns property that the debtor or a dependent of the debtor uses as a residence;

(C) a burial plot for the debtor or a dependent of the debtor; or

(D) real or personal property that the debtor or dependent of the debtor claims as a homestead.

(2)(A) The limitation under paragraph (1) shall not apply to an exemption claimed under subsection (b)(3)(A) by a family farmer for the principal residence of such farmer.

(B) For purposes of paragraph (1), any amount of such interest does not include any interest transferred from a debtor's previous principal residence (which was acquired prior to the beginning of such 1215-day period) into the debtor's current principal residence, if the debtor's previous and current residences are located in the same State.

New sections 522(o), (p), and (q) are effective immediately upon enactment, that is, the date the President signed the legislation, April 20, 2005. Subsection (q) provides:

(q)(1) As a result of electing under subsection (b)(3)(A) to exempt property under State or local law, a debtor may not exempt any amount of an interest in property described in subparagraphs (A), (B), (C), and (D) of subsection (p)(1) which exceeds in the aggregate $125,000 if—

(A) the court determines, after notice and a hearing, that the debtor has been convicted of a felony (as defined in section 3156 of title 18), which under the circumstances, demonstrates that the filing of the case was an abuse of the provisions of this title; or

(B) the debtor owes a debt arising from—

(i) any violation of the Federal securities laws (as defined in section 3(a)(47) of the Securities Exchange Act of 1934), any State securities laws, or any regulation or order issued under Federal securities laws or State securities laws;

(ii) fraud, deceit, or manipulation in a fiduciary capacity or in connection with the purchase or sale of any security registered under section 12 or 15(d) of the Securities Exchange Act of 1934 or under section 6 of the Securities Act of 1933;

(iii) any civil remedy under section 1964 of title 18; or

(iv) any criminal act, intentional tort, or willful or reckless misconduct that caused serious physical injury or death to another individual in the preceding 5 years.

(2) Paragraph (1) shall not apply to the extent the amount of an interest in property described in subparagraphs (A), (B), (C), and (D) of subsection (p)(1) is reasonably necessary for the support of the debtor and any dependent of the debtor.

The dollar amounts in new subsections (p) and (q) are subject to adjustment as are other monetary amounts in the Code.

These amendments to the Code alter the debtor's choices of exemptions to be used, but to the extent that these amendments do not modify the states' rights to determine which exemptions are used in bankruptcy, the debtor's choice is still restricted by the provision found in amended § 522(b)(1) and (2) known as the "opt out."

B. EXCLUSIONS FROM THE ESTATE

BAPCPA makes significant changes in what is excluded from the bankruptcy estate by amendments to § 541(b) and in what may be exempt from the bankruptcy estate by additions to § 522(d). In addition, there would be changes in the automatic stay and exceptions from discharge concerning some exempt assets.

As to exclusions from the bankruptcy estate, § 541(b) is amended to protect certain education savings by renumbering current subsection (5) to (9) and adding the following subsections:

(5) funds placed in an education individual retirement account (as defined in section 530(b)(1) of the Internal Revenue Code of 1986) not later than 365 days before the date of the filing of the petition in a case under this title, but—

(A) only if the designated beneficiary of such account was a child, stepchild, grandchild, or stepgrandchild of the debtor for the taxable year for which funds were placed in such account;

(B) only to the extent that such funds—

(i) are not pledged or promised to any entity in connection with any extension of credit; and

(ii) are not excess contributions (as described in section 4973(e) of the Internal Revenue Code of 1986); and

(C) in the case of funds placed in all such accounts having the same designated beneficiary not earlier than 720 days nor later than 365 days before such date, only so much of such funds as does not exceed $5,000;

(6) funds used to purchase a tuition credit or certificate or contributed to an account in accordance with section 529(b)(1)(A) of the Internal Revenue Code of 1986 under a qualified State tuition program (as defined in section 529(b)(1) of such Code) not later than 365 days before the date of the filing of the petition in a case under this title, but—

(A) only if the designated beneficiary of the amounts paid or contributed to such tuition program was a child, stepchild, grandchild, or stepgrandchild of the debtor for the taxable year for which funds were paid or contributed;

(B) with respect to the aggregate amount paid or contributed to such program having the same designated beneficiary, only so much of such amount as does not exceed the total contributions permitted under section 529(b)(7) of such Code with respect to such beneficiary, as adjusted beginning on the date of the filing of the petition in a case under this title by the annual increase or decrease (rounded to the nearest tenth of 1 percent) in the education expenditure category of the Consumer Price Index prepared by the Department of Labor; and

(C) in the case of funds paid or contributed to such program having the same designated beneficiary not earlier than 720 days nor later than 365 days before such date, only so much of such funds as does not exceed $5,000.

Moreover, a new subsection (e) is added to the end of section 541:

(e) In determining whether any of the relationships specified in paragraph (5)(A) or (6)(A) of subsection (b) exists, a legally adopted child of an individual (and a child who is a member of an individual's household, if placed with such individual by an authorized placement agency for legal adoption by such individual), or a foster child of an individual (if such child has as the child's principal place of abode the home of the debtor and is a member of the debtor's household) shall be treated as a child of such individual by blood.

The debtor would have a new duty under new subsection 521(c), related to these education individual retirement accounts:

(c) In addition to meeting the requirements under subsection (a), a debtor shall file with the court a record of any interest that a debtor has in an education individual retirement account (as defined in section 530(b)(1) of the Internal Revenue Code of 1986) or under a qualified State tuition program (as defined in section 529(b)(1) of such Code).

Section 541(b) is further expanded to exclude from the bankruptcy estate

(7) any amount—

(A) withheld by an employer from the wages of employees for payment as contributions—

(i) to—

(I) an employee benefit plan that is subject to title I of the Employee Retirement Income Security Act of 1974 or under an employee benefit plan which is a governmental plan under section 414(d) of the Internal Revenue Code of 1986;

(II) a deferred compensation plan under section 457 of the Internal Revenue Code of 1986; or

(III) a tax-deferred annuity under section 403(b) of the Internal Revenue Code of 1986;

except that such amount under this subparagraph shall not constitute disposable income as defined in section 1325(b)(2); or

(ii) to a health insurance plan regulated by State law whether or not subject to such title; or

(B) received by an employer from employees for payment as contributions—

(i) to—

(I) an employee benefit plan that is subject to title I of the Employee Retirement Income Security Act of 1974 or under an employee benefit plan which is a governmental plan under section 414(d) of the Internal Revenue Code of 1986;

(II) a deferred compensation plan under section 457 of the Internal Revenue Code of 1986;

or

(III) a tax deferred annuity under section 403(b) of the Internal Revenue Code of 1986; except that such amount under this subparagraph shall not constitute disposable income, as defined in section 1325(b)(2); or

(ii) to a health insurance plan regulated by State law whether or not subject to such title;

The exclusions include ERISA employee benefit plans and others types of benefit plans or tax-sheltered trusts or plans referred to in the following Internal Revenue Code sections:

- IRC § 530(b)(1)— "Coverdell" education savings accounts, "meaning a trust created or organized in the United States exclusively for the purpose of paying the qualified education expenses of an individual who is the designated beneficiary of the trust," with qualifications for the trust defined in that statute.
- IRC § 529(b)(1)—a "qualified tuition program," meaning "a program established and maintained by a State or agency or instrumentality thereof or by 1 or more eligible educational institutions," under which tuition credits may be purchased for a beneficiary, as defined in that statute.
- IRC § 414(d)—a "governmental plan" for retirement established and maintained by the United States, any state or political subdivision of a state.
- IRC § 457—an "eligible deferred compensation plan" established and maintained by an eligible employer, as defined in that statute.

- IRC § 403(b)—a "qualified annuity plan" purchased for an employee by the employer described in IRC § 501(c)(3), which generally includes religious, charitable, scientific, public safety, literary, or educational corporations and organizations.

Section 541(b)(8) is another new exclusion from the estate for pawned property, excluding:

> any interest of the debtor in property where the debtor pledged or sold tangible personal property (other than securities or written or printed evidences of indebtedness or title) as collateral for a loan or advance of money given by a person licensed under law to make such loans or advances, where—
>
> (A) the tangible personal property is in the possession of the pledgee or transferee;
>
> (B) the debtor has no obligation to repay the money, redeem the collateral, or buy back the property at a stipulated price; and
>
> (C) neither the debtor nor the trustee have exercised any right to redeem provided under the contract or State law, in a timely manner as provided under State law and section 108(b);

These new exclusions become effective 180 days following enactment; that is, on October 17, 2005.

C. EXEMPTIONS

As to exemptions, BAPCPA amends the following Code sections:

Section 522(b) is renumbered, with the new § 522(b)(3)(A) providing that:

> (A) subject to subsections (o) and (p) any property that is exempt under Federal law, other than subsection (d) of this section, or State or local law that is applicable on the date of the filing of the petition at the place in which the debtor's domicile has been located for the 730 days immediately preceding the date of the filing of the petition or if the debtor's domicile has not been located at a single State for such 730-day period, the place in which the debtor's domicile was located for 180 days immediately preceding the 730-day period or for a longer portion of such 180-day period than in any other place;

Section 522(b)(3)(C) is added to permit exemption, notwithstanding a state's opt out from federal bankruptcy exemptions, of "(C) retirement funds to the extent that those funds are in a fund or account that is exempt from taxation under section 401, 403, 408, 408A, 414, 457, or 501(a) of the Internal Revenue Code of 1986." The following would be added to § 522(b):

> (4) For purposes of paragraph (3)(C) and subsection (d)(12), the following shall apply:
>
> (A) If the retirement funds are in a retirement fund that has received a favorable determination under section 7805 of the Internal Revenue Code of 1986, and that determination is in effect as of the date of the filing of the petition in a case under this title, those funds shall be presumed to be exempt from the estate.
>
> (B) If the retirement funds are in a retirement fund that has not received a favorable determination under such section 7805, those funds are exempt from the estate if the debtor demonstrates that—
>
> (i) no prior determination to the contrary has been made by a court or the Internal Revenue Service; and
>
> (ii)(I) the retirement fund is in substantial compliance with the applicable requirements of the Internal Revenue Code of 1986; or

(II) the retirement fund fails to be in substantial compliance with the applicable requirements of the Internal Revenue Code of 1986 and the debtor is not materially responsible for that failure.

(C) A direct transfer of retirement funds from 1 fund or account that is exempt from taxation under section 401, 403, 408, 408A, 414, 457, or 501(a) of the Internal Revenue Code of 1986, under section 401(a)(31) of the Internal Revenue Code of 1986, or otherwise, shall not cease to qualify for exemption under paragraph (3)(C) or subsection (d)(12) by reason of such direct transfer.

(D)(i) Any distribution that qualifies as an eligible rollover distribution within the meaning of section 402(c) of the Internal Revenue Code of 1986 or that is described in clause (ii) shall not cease to qualify for exemption under paragraph (3)(C) or subsection (d)(12) by reason of such distribution.

(ii) A distribution described in this clause is an amount that—

(I) has been distributed from a fund or account that is exempt from taxation under section 401, 403, 408, 408A, 414, 457, or 501(a) of the Internal Revenue Code of 1986; and

(II) to the extent allowed by law, is deposited in such a fund or account not later than 60 days after the distribution of such amount;

In addition, in the event that a debtor may and does choose the federal bankruptcy exemptions of § 522(d), the following new subsection (12) would be added at the end of § 522(d):

(12) Retirement funds to the extent that those funds are in a fund or account that is exempt from taxation under section 401, 403, 408, 408A, 414, 457, or 501(a) of the Internal Revenue Code of 1986.

Thus, under either the opt-out state or the federal exemptions, the retirement funds described in those Internal Revenue Code sections would be exempt. As described in those sections, they refer to the following types of retirement funds:

- IRC § 401—a qualified pension, profit-sharing, and stock bonus plan created under a trust established by an employer for the exclusive benefit of employees or beneficiaries.
- IRC § 403—qualified annuity plans that are established by an employer for an employee under IRC § 404(a)(2) or § 501(o)(3).
- IRC § 408—individual retirement accounts (IRA), meaning "a trust created or organized in the United States for the exclusive benefit of an individual or his beneficiaries," provided that the trust meets the requirements of that statute.
- IRC §408A—a "Roth" IRA.
- IRC § 414—other retirement plans for controlled groups of employees, including predecessor employers, partnerships or propietorships, governments and churches.
- IRC § 457—eligible deferred compensation plans established and maintained by eligible employers.
- IRC § 501(a)—retirement plans established and maintained by defined tax-exempt organizations.

As a part of these additions to the exemptions, the automatic stay has a new exception, by adding § 362(b)(19):

(19) under subsection (a), of withholding of income from a debtor's wages and collection of amounts withheld, under the debtor's agreement authorizing that withholding and collection for the benefit of a pension, profit-sharing, stock bonus, or other plan established under section 401, 403, 408, 408A, 414, 457, or 501(c) of the Internal Revenue Code of 1986, that is sponsored by the

employer of the debtor, or an affiliate, successor, or predecessor of such employer—

(A) to the extent that the amounts withheld and collected are used solely for payments relating to a loan from a plan under section 408(b)(1) of the Employee Retirement Income Security Act of 1974 or is subject to section 72(p) of the Internal Revenue Code of 1986; or

(B) a loan from a thrift savings plan permitted under subchapter III of chapter 84 of title 5, that satisfies the requirements of section 8433(g) of such title;

but nothing in this paragraph may be construed to provide that any loan made under a governmental plan under section 414(d), or a contract or account under section 403(b), of the Internal Revenue Code of 1986 constitutes a claim or a debt under this title;

Further, a new exception from discharge is inserted in § 523(a). The Act refers to this new section as (18), replacing the former § 523(a)(18), which was struck as a part of the amendments to domestic support obligations:

(18) owed to a pension, profit-sharing, stock bonus, or other plan established under section 401, 403, 408, 408A, 414, 457, or 501(c) of the Internal Revenue Code of 1986, under—

(A) a loan permitted under section 408(b)(1) of the Employee Retirement Income Security Act of 1974, or subject to section 72(p) of the Internal Revenue Code of 1986; or

(B) a loan from a thrift savings plan permitted under subchapter III of chapter 84 of title 5, that satisfies the requirements of section 8433(g) of such title;

but nothing in this paragraph may be construed to provide that any loan made under a governmental plan under section 414(d), or a contract or account under section 403(b), of the Internal Revenue Code of 1986 constitutes a claim or a debt under this title.

Complementary to the new exception from discharge, chapter 13 plans, under new § 1322(f), may not alter the terms of a defined retirement account loan:

A plan may not materially alter the terms of a loan described in section 362(b)(19) and any amounts required to repay such loan shall not constitute 'disposable income' under section 1325.

Section 522 is further amended to add a $1 million dollar cap on the new exemptions of assets in individual retirement accounts, by adding a new section (n):

(n) For assets in individual retirement accounts described in section 408 or 408A of the Internal Revenue Code of 1986, other than a simplified employee pension under section 408(k) of such Code or a simple retirement account under section 408(p) of such Code, the aggregate value of such assets exempted under this section, without regard to amounts attributable to rollover contributions under section 402(c), 402(e)(6), 403(a)(4), 403(a)(5), and 403(b)(8) of the Internal Revenue Code of 1986, and earnings thereon, shall not exceed $1,000,000 in a case filed by a debtor who is an individual, except that such amount may be increased if the interests of justice so require.

This monetary cap is subject to the same periodic adjustment as are other exemption amounts.

The fact that the amended Code now permits exemption of funds held in IRAs whether the debtor claims exemptions under § 522(d) or under state law gives a short effective life to the Supreme Court's recent decision in *Rousey v. Jacoway*, 125 S. Ct. 1561, 34 Employee Benefits Cas. (BNA) 1929, 2005-1 U.S. Tax Cas. (CCH) P 50258, 95 A.F.T.R.2d 2005-1716 (U.S. 2005), on which certiorari had been granted from the Eighth Circuit. The Court reversed the Circuit Court opinion, holding that the chapter 7 debtors could exempt their IRAs from the bankruptcy estate under § 522(d)(10)(E). The opinion states that IRAs fulfill the requirements of that Code exemption because they confer a right to receive payment in the future on account of age, and they are similar plans or contracts to those enumerated in the Code section. The Court rejected the chapter 7 trustee's argument that the funds should not be exempt since the debtors could access the IRAs prior to reaching 59 1/2 years, with the Court's rationale being that the 10% penalty for early withdrawal was a substantial one and that it prevented the debtors from accessing all of the funds. This decision was a resolution to the dispute in the circuits on this issue under former Bankruptcy Code exemptions, but Congress has intervened to end any future dispute over treatment of IRAs in bankruptcy. Without the current amendments, the effect of *Rousey* could have been to permit an unlimited amount of IRA exemptions, so long as the debtor could satisfy § 522(d)(10(E)'s "reasonably necessary" test. The amended § 522(n) limits the IRA exemptions to $ 1 million, "except that such amount may be increased if the interests of justice so require." Whether this amendment results in the potential exemption of IRAs being more than would have been allowed under *Rousey's* interpretation of § 522(d)(10(E) remains to be seen, but clearly debtors who may use the § 522(d) exemptions now have a choice between § 522(d)(10(E) and the new § 522(d)(12). It is doubtful that debtors may use both of these sections to double up on IRA exemptions, especially in view of the $1 million cap. Debtors claiming exemptions under state law may nevertheless claim an exemption in IRAs, up to the $1 million cap, under amended § 522(b)(3)(C).

D. OTHER ASSET PROTECTION ISSUES UNDER THE 2005 CODE

1. SECTION 548(E)

Transfers to self-settled trusts may be subject to avoidance attack under new § 548(e), which provides that the trustee "may avoid any transfer of an interest of the debtor in property that was made on or within 10 years before the filing of the petition, if":

- the transfer was made to a self-settled trust or similar device
- the transfer was made by the debtor
- the debtor is the beneficiary of the trust
- the transfer was made with fraudulent intent as to an entity to which the debtor was indebted

The final factor is expressed in a way that seems to indicate that the trustee must prove that the debtor made the transfer to the self-settled trust with the intent to hinder, delay, or defraud a specific creditor or creditors to whom the debtor was indebted at the time of the transfer or to whom the debtor became indebted after the transfer. The specific language is that "the debtor made such transfer with actual intent to hinder, delay, or defraud any entity to which the debtor was or became, on or after the date that such transfer was made, indebted." In other words, the trustee would need to show the existence of actual creditors and relate the debtor's intent to those creditors, rather than merely showing that the debtor created or transferred to an asset-protection device. Code § 548(e) will, however, require those engaged in asset-protection planning to analyze the potential of an avoidance and to balance that with the effects of leaving assets in such devices as

IRA or other tax-sheltered funds that now enjoy exclusion or exemption from the bankruptcy estate.

2. NEW EXEMPTION TIMING ISSUES

To illustrate the approach to the new rules for exemption choices, we have created two hypothetical illustrations from which we may draw some conclusions. The potential fact variations are virtually endless. We conclude this discussion of the "consumer" provisions of the Bankruptcy Code in the hope that this will illustrate a road map to these difficult new exemption provisions.

Example 1: A Tennessee businessman left his business partnership after a conflict with his former partners. This conflict resulted in extensive litigation and the risk of a judgment in the amount of $5 million. The businessman liquidated his real estate and other liquid assets in Tennessee where his homestead exemption would be $5,000 (or $7,500 in a joint filing). The assets were liquidated after first transferring them to his wife's name. They moved on January 1, 2005, to the state of Florida where they acquired a home with $500,000 equity.

Discussion: Assuming that the former business partners succeed in obtaining an overwhelming judgment, the debtor has several difficult choices:

- If he files within two years (730 days) after moving his domicile to Florida, his homestead exemption will be capped at the amount of the Tennessee limit, ($5,000/$7,500), or, if Tennessee prohibits nonresidents from using its rules, he may elect the federal exemption scheme (with its $18,450 homestead). 11 U.S.C.A. § 522(b).
- If he files more than two years but less than three years and four months (1,215 days) after acquiring the Florida home, the (otherwise unlimited) Florida exemption will be capped at $125,000. 11 U.S.C.A. § 522(p).
- If he files more than 1,215 days after acquiring the house but within 10 years and if the value in the house can be found to be attributable to the disposition of property with intent to hinder, delay, or defraud a creditor, all or such attributable part of the homestead exemption may be set aside. 11 U.S.C.A. § 522(o).

Example 2: An attorney retired from a successful legal career and went into the business of selling proprietary legal software. In his practice, he had accumulated some assets of substance, including a $2 million tax-qualified Individual Retirement Account and a house with $250,000 worth of equity, all of which was covered by his state's homestead exemption. In his new career, however, he incurred substantial contingent liabilities as a guarantor the debts of his new company, which was not well capitalized.

Discussion: If this debtor is forced into bankruptcy, the IRA will be capped at $1 million, and the balance may be subject to administration in the bankruptcy estate. 11 U.S.C.A. § 522(n). Whether this debtor's creditors could reach the IRA if the debtor could avoid bankruptcy depends in part upon the protections built in to an IRA by its creating statute and upon whether the debtor's domiciliary state law grants any exemption to such funds. If the latter should be true, the Supreme Court's *Rousey* decision could have some influence on how the particular state courts would interpret the reach of that state's nonbankruptcy exemption.

For an excellent article reviewing the issues that were and were not decided by Rousey, see Anthony Michael Sabino, A Final Battle at the Last Line of Defense—The Struggle to Keep ERISA-Qualified Pension Funds Outside the Reach of Creditors in Bankruptcy Cases, 12 ABI Law Review 501 (2004).

The remainder of this work deals with the BAPCPA "business" rules, which are surprisingly numerous in what many think of as a "consumer" statute. We start with three types of commercial cases that have received some broader focus in the 2005 amendments: small business cases, health care cases, and cross-border cases. We then turn to a group of general administrative issues, starting with several rules of general application that were actually enacted as a part of the "small business" provisions in BAPCPA. Finally, we conclude with a series of areas in which Congress has responded in some detail to the interest of various constituencies in commercial cases: secured creditors, parties to executory contracts and unexpired leases, unsecured creditors and committees, employees, attorneys, and other officers and professionals.

A. SMALL BUSINESS CASES

1. INTRODUCTION

The Bankruptcy Abuse Prevention and Consumer Protection Act of 2005 builds on the 1994 attempt to provide a statutory framework for easier reorganization of smaller businesses in chapter 11. While this goal has been attempted from place to place in various local jurisdictions, a real, comprehensive statutory framework for such a procedure has been lacking. It is doubtful that 2005 sees the perfection of such a procedure. Many of the amendments impose new deadlines and reporting requirements that may be viewed as burdensome by debtors. These rules do, however, contain some provisions that will facilitate smaller companies' obtaining the benefits of chapter 11 reorganization. Thus some of these provisions seem designed to facilitate a more economical and efficient reorganization of a smaller debtor in a nonconsumer case while others seem to be a product of skepticism about these debtors' prospects for reorganization. The latter sense arises from the heavy burden of reporting, with strict deadlines imposed by these rules under the threat of dismissal or conversion.

2. "SMALL BUSINESS" DEFINED

BAPCPA § 432 provides a definition of a "small business" in Code § 101. A small business is a person engaged in commercial or business activities other than owning or operating real estate. It may not have more than $2 million in debt (excluding debt to insiders or affiliates). This definition may be problematic at times, however. For the debtor to be a "small business debtor," the U.S. trustee may not have appointed a creditors' committee. Further, if a committee has been appointed, it is necessary that the committee not be "sufficiently active and representative to provide effective oversight of the debtor." It is conceivable, therefore, that a case might be filed with the debtor otherwise meeting the definition of a small business debtor but losing that status if and when a committee is appointed. Might it reacquire the status of a small business debtor if and when the committee becomes insufficiently active and representative? It is hard to imagine how to apply the strict small business rules applicable under such circumstances. We will turn to those rules now.

3. REPORTING REQUIREMENTS

New Code § 308 is added by BAPCPA § 434, imposing new reporting requirements on small business debtors. These obligations do not become effective, however, until 60 days after rules are promulgated to establish the forms for use in reporting the data. BAPCPA § 435 requires the Judicial Conference to prescribe the forms. When effective, the requirements are significant. Periodic reports must be filed by these debtors describing their "profitability," defined as "the amount of money that the debtor has earned or lost during current and recent fiscal periods." The report must also provide reasonable approximations of projected cash receipts and disbursements and comparisons of actual receipts and disbursements to earlier projections and it must confirm compliance with the Rules of Bankruptcy, tax, other governmental filing obligations, and payment of taxes.

The draconian nature of these reporting requirements is underscored by the fact that the unexcused failure to meet them is grounds for conversion or dismissal of the case. 11 U.S.C.A. § 1112 (b)(4)(F). It appears that if a debtor misses a reporting deadline and cannot prove a "reasonable justification" for such error, 11 U.S.C.A. § 1112 (b)(2)(B)(i), BAPCPA would mandate dismissal or conversion upon motion of any party in interest, even if confirmation of a plan could be obtained within a reasonable time. Apart from the possibility that the court might consider the interests of other creditors or constituencies that would be harmed by conversion or dismissal as a part of its assessing the "reasonableness" of a justification for missing the deadline, there is no provision in the amended Code for considering those interests or balancing the gravity of the error and the consequences. Moreover, these deadlines are established by the Code rather than by the Rules of Bankruptcy Procedure. Therefore, it is debatable whether any such deadlines can be extended by application of Rule 9006. While missed deadlines under Rule 9006 can sometimes be excused by its "excusable neglect" provision (see *Pioneer Inv. Services Co. v. Brunswick Associates Ltd. Partnership*, 507 U.S. 380, 113 S. Ct. 1489, 123 L. Ed. 2d 74, 24 Bankr. Ct. Dec. (CRR) 63, 28 Collier Bankr. Cas. 2d (MB) 267, Bankr. L. Rep. (CCH) P 75157A, 25 Fed. R. Serv. 3d 401 (1993)), a statutory deadline is much more problematic. See *In re Butcher*, 829 F.2d 596, 16 Bankr. Ct. Dec. (CRR) 821, 17 Collier Bankr. Cas. 2d (MB) 1204, Bankr. L. Rep. (CCH) P 71989, 9 Fed. R. Serv. 3d 68 (6th Cir. 1987) (abrogated by, *Bartlik v. U.S. Dept. of Labor*, 62 F.3d 163, 10 I.E.R. Cas. (BNA) 1571, 130 Lab. Cas. (CCH) P 11407, 32 Fed. R. Serv. 3d 1032, 1995 FED App. 0247P (6th Cir. 1995)) (holding preference deadline "jurisdictional" and therefore not subject to Rule 9006).

4. INITIAL INTERVIEW

BAPCPA § 439 adds Code § 586(a)(7), under which the U.S. trustee has a new obligation to conduct initial interviews with small business debtors prior to the meeting of creditors under 11 U.S.C.A. § 341. The interview is to evaluate the debtor's financial viability and business plan and to reach an agreement on scheduling. The U.S. trustee is also given an opportunity at this meeting to advise the debtor of its reporting and filing obligations, which, as described above, are significant. The U.S. trustee must also move promptly for conversion or dismissal whenever he or she discovers that there are grounds for such a motion.

5. NEW DUTIES IN SMALL BUSINESS CASES

A new 11 U.S.C.A. § 1116 is added to the Code by BAPCPA § 436. That section sets out a list of duties for the trustee or debtor in possession in small business cases:

(1) Append to the voluntary petition or, in an involuntary case, filed not later than seven days after the date of the order for relief—

    (A) its most recent balance sheet, statement of operations, cash-flow statement, and Federal income tax return; or

    (B) a statement made under penalty of perjury that no balance sheet, statement of operations, or cash-flow statement has been prepared and no Federal tax return has been filed;

(2) attend, through its senior management personnel and counsel, meetings scheduled by the Court or the United States trustee, including initial debtor interviews, scheduling conferences, and meetings of creditors convened under § 341 unless the court, after notice and a hearing, waives that requirement upon a finding of extraordinary and compelling circumstances;

(3) timely file all schedules and statements of financial affairs, unless the court, after notice and a hearing, grants an extension, which shall not extend such time period to a date later than thirty days after the date of the order for relief, absent extraordinary and compelling circumstances;

(4) file all postpetition financial and other reports required by the Federal Rules of Bankruptcy Procedure or by local rule of the district court;

(5) subject to § 363(c)(2), maintain insurance customary and appropriate to the industry;

(6)(A) timely file tax returns and other required government filings; and (B) subject to § 363(c)(2), timely pay all taxes entitled to administrative expense priority except those being contested by appropriate proceedings being diligently prosecuted; and

(7) allow the United States trustee, or a designated representative of the United States trustee, to inspect the debtor's business premises, books, and records at reasonable times, after reasonable prior written notice, unless notice is waived by the debtor.

Remember, it may be difficult at a given moment in some cases to determine whether the debtor is a small business debtor. See the discussion, above, of the new definition of a "small business" debtor added to Code § 101 by BAPCPA § 432. So the existence of these duties may vary from time to time. After appointment of an actual trustee, it is unlikely that a committee will remain very active, however.

6. EXCLUSIVITY, DISCLOSURE, AND CONFIRMATION

11 U.S.C.A. § 1125 is altered by BAPCPA § 431 and establishes the basis for a more flexible confirmation process in small business cases. The court may now determine that the plan contains sufficient information, and, in that event, no disclosure statement is required. Disclosure statements can also be submitted on standard forms. Conditional approval is allowed with final approval to be given at the confirmation hearing. It is also possible now to combine the hearing on approval of the disclosure statement and the confirmation hearing itself. These may prove to be real improvements that may allow the case confirmation process to operate at reduced cost to all participants.

The tradeoff for those improvements, however, is a set of new deadlines for plan exclusivity and the filing and confirmation of a plan in a small business case, which are added by BAPCPA §§ 437 and 438.

The exclusive period in 11 U.S.C.A. § 1121 within which the debtor may file a plan is cut off by BAPCPA § 437 at 180 days after the order for relief. A plan and disclosure statement (if any), by whomever filed, must be filed no later than 300 days after the order for relief. Both of these deadlines may be extended but only by an order entered before the existing deadline expires and setting a new date, and only upon the debtor's showing "by a preponderance of the evidence that it is more likely than not that the court will confirm a plan within a reasonable period of time." 11 U.S.C.A. § 1121(e)(3)(A). A motion for an extension must therefore be made in time to allow the court to hear and determine whether an extension is warranted.

Under new 11 U.S.C.A. § 1129(e), as amended by BAPCPA § 438, the bankruptcy court is to confirm a plan in a small business case not later than 45 days after the plan is filed if it complies with the applicable provisions of the Bankruptcy Code. Like the deadlines for the exclusivity period and the time for filing plans, this time for confirmation of a filed plan can only be extended upon a showing by the debtor that confirmation of a plan will result at the end of the time. 11 U.S.C.A. § 1121(e)(3). Remember that an order extending this deadline must be signed before the existing deadline has expired. 11 U.S.C.A. § 1121(e)(3). The consequence of missing the deadline would seem to be that the debtor would not have a confirmable plan, providing a basis for conversion or dismissal of the case. 11 U.S.C.A. § 1112(b)(4)(J). Again, the consequence of this may be harsh. The confirmation deadline can be extended only if the *debtor* demonstrates that it is more likely than not that confirmation of a plan would occur within a reasonable time (as well as again showing "reasonable justification" for the missed deadline), a new deadline is imposed when the extension is granted, and the extension order is entered before the existing deadline has expired.

B. HEALTH CARE CASES

The Bankruptcy Code as amended in 2005 contains several provisions designed to address concerns that are particularly applicable to bankruptcies involving health care providers. "Health care business," "patient," and "patient records" are all new definitions added to Code § 101 and are clearly designed to cover a broad range of health care institutions. See 11 U.S.C.A. § 101(27A) (defining "health care business" to include a variety of hospitals, treatment facilities, hospices, home health agencies, and "similar" institutions as well as long-term care facilities).

1. PATIENT RECORDS

We will see elsewhere that the "dot com" collapse of the early 21st Century prompted concern in the 2005 amendments to Code § 362 over the handling of "personally identifiable information" collected in Internet businesses. Similarly, the occurrence of a financial crisis in the health care industry during the drafting that produced the 2005 legislation also led to a new Code § 351, in which the amended statute addresses preservation of patient records. Anticipating that some health care businesses may not have resources available to pay for proper handling of patient records under applicable law, the trustee is obligated to publish a notice that provides patients and insurance providers a year within which to assert a claim to such information, after which the trustee may destroy the records. 11 U.S.C.A. § 351(1)(A). Thereafter, the trustee still must ask any appropriate federal agency for permission to deposit the patient records with that agency, although no duty is imposed on any such agency. 11 U.S.C.A. § 351(2). During the first 180 days of the one-year period notice, the trustee is also "promptly" to attempt to make direct contact with patients and insurance companies. 11 U.S.C.A. § 351(1)(B).

2. PATIENT TRANSFER

The concern for patients in failing health care institutions goes beyond their records. New patient care duties are imposed on the debtor or trustee by amendment of Code § 704(a). The trustee is to "use all reasonable and best efforts to transfer patients from a health care business that is in the process of being closed to an appropriate health care business," according to 11 U.S.C.A. § 704(a)(12), which also specifies that the transferee institution should be in the vicinity of the closing facility, should provide the patient with substantially similar services, and should maintain a reasonable quality of care.

3. NEW ADMINISTRATIVE EXPENSE CLAIM

Recognizing that the obligations described in the preceding paragraphs may create a burden on the estate and the government, BAPCPA amends Code § 503(b) to allow an administrative expense claim for "actual necessary costs and expenses of closing a health care business incurred by a trustee or by a Federal agency," including those costs of disposing of records as well as the transfer of patients.

4. PATIENT CARE OMBUDSMAN

In another similarity to the rules related to personally identifiable information, we have after 2005 a new third party professional, the patient care "ombudsman." The debtor, trustee, and ombudsman all have special duties under these new provisions of chapter 11. An entirely new Code § 333 was added by the 2005 amendments to establish the role of ombudsman in health care business bankruptcies in chapter 7, 9, or 11 cases. BAPCPA § 1104. This new ombudsman is a "professional person" covered by Code § 330(a)(1). The ombudsman is to be appointed within 30 days after the commencement of the case and is to "monitor the quality of patient care and to represent the interests of the patients of the health care business unless the court finds that the appointment of such ombudsman is not necessary for the protection of patients under the specific facts of the case." 11 U.S.C.A. § 333(a)(1).

The ombudsman is required to report to the court regarding the quality of patient care within 60 days after appointment and every 60 days thereafter. 11 U.S.C.A. § 333(b)(2). The ombudsman is also required to file a special, immediate report upon determining "that the quality of patient care provided to patients of the debtor is declining significantly or is otherwise being materially compromised." 11 U.S.C.A. § 333(b)(3).

5. RESTRICTION ON TRANSFER OF ASSETS BY NON-PROFIT ENTITIES

The amended Bankruptcy Code also restricts the use, sale, or lease of property by other than moneyed, business, or commercial entities, discussed below. These new rules will be of particular concern in nonprofit health care cases.

6. RELIEF FROM STAY FOR DEPARTMENT OF HEALTH AND HUMAN SERVICES

As a final expression of the focus of Congress on these cases, BAPCPA § 1106 adds a new exception to the automatic stay. 11 U.S.C.A. § 362(b)(28). Under this provision, the Secretary of Heath and Human Services is allowed to exclude the debtor from participation in Medicare or any other federal health care program, as defined in and pursuant to the Social Security Act.

C. CROSS-BORDER CASES

1. INTRODUCTION

The Bankruptcy Abuse Prevention and Consumer Protection Act of 2005 adds a new chapter 15 to the Bankruptcy Code, which is almost identical to a model law proposed by the United Nations Commission on International Trade Law (UNCITRAL). The legislation is based on UNCITRAL's extensive work in numerous areas of international commercial law, which have resulted in several international conventions and model laws that have been widely adopted around the world and, most recently, the Model Law on Cross-Border Insolvency, which is the basis for chapter 15 of the revised Bankruptcy Code. Chapter 15 replaces former Code § 304 and provides much more breadth and detail than that earlier attempt to address these issues.

Chapter 15 is somewhat beyond the scope of this publication. Its primary goals, however, are to increase international cooperation in cross-border cases, largely by enabling bankruptcy courts in the United States to recognize foreign insolvency proceedings. Such insolvency proceedings are divided into two categories, as defined in 11 U.S.C.A. § 1502(4) and (5). An insolvency proceeding that is pending in a country in which the debtor has "the center of its main interests" is defined as a "foreign main proceeding," while other insolvency proceedings in countries in which the debtor is carrying on "nontransitory economic activity" are defined as "foreign nonmain proceedings."

2. COMMENCEMENT OF CHAPTER 15 CASE

A chapter 15 case is commenced by the filing of a petition for "recognition" of a foreign proceeding (either main or nonmain) under § 1515. Upon recognition of a foreign proceeding, §§ 361, 362, 365, 349, and 352 automatically apply with respect to the debtor, the property of the debtor, and transfers of interests of the debtor in property within the territorial jurisdiction of the United States, and a foreign representative may operate the debtor's business and exercise the rights and powers of a trustee under Code §§ 363 and 552. 11 U.S.C.A. § 1520. The court may also grant additional stays against individual actions and proceedings to protect the debtor's assets, obligations, and liabilities in the United States beyond the scope of those basic provisions of the Bankruptcy Code. 11 U.S.C.A. § 1521. Such protection may even be granted on an expedited basis upon the filing of the petition under proper circumstances. 11 U.S.C.A. § 1519.

3. ADMINISTRATIVE ISSUES

Additional actions may be undertaken by the foreign representative under §§ 522, 544, 545, 547, 548, 550, 553, and 724 (a). 11 U.S.C.A. § 1523. However, those powers to commence such actions (to avoid acts detrimental to creditors) are limited where the foreign proceeding is "nonmain" in nature. 11 U.S.C.A. § 1523.

Chapter 15 contains several provisions to facilitate cooperation and communication between the United States bankruptcy courts and trustees with the foreign courts and representatives. 11 U.S.C.A. §§ 1525-30. For example, the courts may communicate directly with each other, under Code § 1525(b), "by any means considered appropriate by the court." 11 U.S.C.A. § 1527(2).

D. OTHER CASE ADMINISTRATION ISSUES

1. INTRODUCTION

The Bankruptcy Abuse Prevention and Consumer Protection Act of 2005, which purports to deal with small businesses, also has a number of provisions that seem to be more generally applicable in chapter 11. Those and other rules of general interest in nonconsumer cases are addressed next.

2. STATUS CONFERENCES

11 U.S.C.A. § 105(d), as amended BAPCPA § 440, now affirmatively requires the bankruptcy court to hold "such status conferences as are necessary to further the expeditious and economical resolution of the case." This is an expansion of the effort begun in 1994 to reintroduce the bankruptcy judge into the general administration of a bankruptcy case.

3. AUTOMATIC STAY

a. IN REM PERMANENT RELIEF AFTER SMALL BUSINESS FILING

The stay imposed by 11 U.S.C.A. § 362 is significantly limited by new subsection (n) when the small business debtor has filed a previous bankruptcy case. Under the amendment, the automatic stay would not apply in a small business case if the debtor has another case pending simultaneously (although perhaps the stay in that case might still be in effect), and the stay would not operate if the debtor was in a small business case that was dismissed within two years of the order for relief in the second case or if the debtor had a plan confirmed in a small business case within two years of the new case.

Here is the broader application: This limitation of the stay is also triggered in the case of an entity that acquired all or substantially all of the assets of a small business under the circumstances described above. 11 U.S.C.A. § 362(n)(1)(D). This successor debtor can overcome the denial of stay protection if it can show by a preponderance of the evidence that the subsequent bankruptcy filing resulted from circumstances beyond the debtor's control and that it is more likely than not that the court will confirm a plan, other than a liquidating plan, in a reasonable time. 11 U.S.C.A. § 362(n)(1)(D).

b. SINGLE-ASSET REAL ESTATE CASES

Section 362 is further amended by BAPCPA § 444 to deal with the oft-criticized "single-asset real estate case." The scope of such cases has been significantly increased by amendment of the definition of that phrase in 11 U.S.C.A. § 101(51B), which eliminates the debt limitation. Thus larger real estate developments may now be subject to these provisions. However, the definition now excludes a family farmer.

The section now imposes a requirement in such a case that the debtor must have either (1) filed a confirmable plan or (2) commenced monthly payments to the secured creditor in order to keep the automatic stay in effect. Under the former Code, this was an obligation that arose 90 days after the entry of the order for relief. Former Code § 362(d)(3). However, because there was sometimes difficulty determining whether a particular case was a single-asset real estate case, the amended Code § 362(d)(3) provides that the date on which the requirement commences is the end of the 90-day period or 30 days after the court determines that the debtor has "single-asset real estate," whichever occurs later. Presumably, if there is some doubt, some interested party will wish to raise the issue before the running of the 90-day period. The law also now allows the debtor to make such payments from the rents or other income generated by the property.

Code § 362 also changes the amount of the payment necessary to continue the stay in effect. Under the former Code, the debtor was required to pay an amount "equal to interest at a current fair market rate on the value of the creditor's interest in the real estate." Now, in cases governed by BAPCPA § 444, the payment must be in the amount of the "nondefault contract rate of interest on the value of the creditor's interest in the real estate." Of course, prescribing rates in legislation is risky business. In a rising interest rate environment, this provision may actually benefit single-asset real estate debtors.

The monthly payments required under 11 U.S.C.A. § 362(d)(3) may be made notwithstanding the failure of the debtor to obtain consent for use of a lender's cash collateral under 11 U.S.C.A. § 363(c)(2). Thus the payments "may, in the debtor's sole discretion, notwithstanding section 363(c)(2), be made from rents or other income generated before, on, or after the date of the commencement of the case by or from the property to each creditor whose claim is secured by such real estate." 11 U.S.C.A. § 362(d)(3)(B)(i). This language is not perfectly clear, but it appears to require a correspondence between the collateral and the creditor to be paid. In other words, creditor A may be paid from its rents or other income generated by its collateral. Creditor B may not be paid from the collateral of creditor A.

4. NETTING AGREEMENTS

The amended Bankruptcy Code contains a series of complex rules championed by the federal securities and banking regulators and designed to reduce the risk of a systemic financial and economic failure in the United States. These provisions relate to securities contracts, commodity contracts, forward contracts, repurchase agreements, swap agreements, and master netting agreements.

A detailed discussion of these provisions is beyond the scope of this publication. Let us simply say for these purposes that the former rules that had addressed this concern have been expanded to include a wide range of "financial participants," defined in 11 U.S.C.A. § 101 (22A). Their netting actions are removed from the coverage of the automatic stay. 11 U.S.C.A. § 362(b)(27). Their interests are not subject to avoidance as statutory liens or otherwise under sections 544, 545, 547, or 548. 11 U.S.C.A. § 546(e)-(h) & (j). Thus, for example, under Code § 546(j), a trustee may not avoid a transfer made by or to a master netting agreement participant in connection with any master netting agreement or any individual contract under such a master agreement prior to the commencement of the case unless it was actually a fraudulent conveyance and could have otherwise been avoided under an individual contract.

5. USE, SALE, AND LEASE OF PROPERTY

a. TRANSFERS MADE BY NON-PROFITS

As suggested above in our discussion of health care cases, Congress has shifted the balance of power substantially in cases involving non-profit hospitals and other corporations or trusts that are not moneyed, business, or commercial in nature. Prior to enactment of BAPCPA, sales of such debtors' assets could be made to moneyed, commercial entities unless the sale was met with an objection that was upheld by the court. Now, Bankruptcy Code §§ 363, 541, and 1129 have been amended to reverse the order of such proceedings. Note that these changes were effective as of the date of enactment and applied to cases pending on that date, except that the court is not to confirm a plan under chapter 11 without consideration of the possibility that the changes would substantially affect the rights of a party in interest who first acquired rights with respect to the debtor after the commencement of such a pre-enactment case. BAPCPA § 1221 (d). Note that this and several other rules on this subject are found in extended rules of construction that apparently will not be codified.

Code § 363(d) has been amended to add a new proviso that the trustee may use, sell, or lease such property only "in accordance with applicable nonbankruptcy law that governs the transfer of property by a corporation or trust that is not a moneyed, business, or commercial corporation or trust." 11 U.S.C.A. § 363(d)(1). Thus Congress has deferred to nonbankruptcy law governing such debtors.

Similarly, a new clause has been added to Code § 1129(a), providing a new confirmation requirement that the court find that all transfers of property under the plan were made in accordance with applicable provisions in nonbankruptcy law that govern the transfer of property by a corporation or trust that is not a moneyed, business, or commercial corporation or trust. 11 U.S.C.A. § 1129(a)(16). Again, this is a significant deference to nonbankruptcy law.

Finally, BAPCPA adds a new subsection (f) to Code § 541 (as an apparent limitation on property of the estate) as follows:

> (f) Notwithstanding any other provision of this title, property that is held by a debtor that is a corporation described in § 501(c)(3) of the Internal Revenue Code of 1986 and exempt from tax under § 501(a) of such Code may be transferred to an entity that is not such a corporation, but only after the same conditions as would apply if the debtor had not filed a case under this title.

11 U.S.C.A. § 541(f).

With these substantive changes, BAPCPA makes two additional procedural changes. The attorney general of the state in which the debtor is incorporated, was formed, or does business is given standing to appear in a proceeding with respect to these issues. Again, the attorney general no longer must object to a sale in violation of one of the substantive provisions; however, nothing in these amendments is to be construed to require the bankruptcy court to remand or refer any proceeding or controversy to any other court or to require the approval of any other court for the transfer of property. BAPCPA § 1221 (e) (establishing a Rule of Construction).

b. TRANSFER OF PERSONALLY IDENTIFIABLE INFORMATION

Code § 363 is amended in several ways to deal with narrow but significant issues of public interest. The first of these was prompted by the notoriety of a few "dot com" cases in which the courts were asked to authorize the liquidation of contact information on customers and other visitors to commercial websites. Under the amendment, if a debtor was in the business of offering products or services to individuals and had a policy of prohibiting the transfer of "personally identifiable information" about those individuals, then the trustee may not transfer such information unless (1) the proposed sale or lease is consistent with the policy or (2) the court approves the transaction after giving it due consideration and finding that no showing has been made that the transaction would violate applicable nonbankruptcy law. 11 U.S.C.A. § 362(b)(1)(B).

Before the second route described above (i.e., a sale or lease in violation of a privacy policy but not violating nonbankruptcy law) may be taken, the court must order the U.S. trustee to appoint a "consumer privacy ombudsman" not later than five days before the commencement of the hearing. This ombudsman is a creature of new Code § 332, which suggests several issues for consideration at the hearing and prohibits the ombudsman from disclosing any personally identifiable information that he or she may obtain in the process.

6. APPOINTMENT OF A TRUSTEE OR EXAMINER IN A CHAPTER 11 CASE

Related to the increased emphasis on potential conversion or dismissal of a chapter 11 case, the grounds for appointment of a trustee are expanded under the amended Bankruptcy Code. New 11 U.S.C.A. § 1104(a)(3), added by BAPCPA § 442, allows the court to appoint a trustee or examiner as an option instead of converting or dismissing the case. The court may appoint a trustee or examiner if grounds exist to convert or dismiss and if the court determines that such appointment is in the best interest of creditors and the estate. 11 U.S.C.A. § 1104(a)(3). At the same time, the United States trustee must move for appointment of a trustee in more circumstances, reflecting an increasing and more specific concern about corporate governance:

> (e) The United States trustee shall move for the appointment of a trustee under subsection (a) if there are reasonable grounds to suspect that current members of the governing body of the debtor, the debtor's chief executive or chief financial officer, or members of the governing body who selected the debtor's chief executive or chief financial officer, participated in actual fraud, dishonesty, or criminal conduct in the management of the debtor or the debtor's public financial reporting.

11 U.S.C.A. § 1104(e).

If the "cause" for dismissal or conversion, however, is "substantial or continuing loss or diminution of the estate and an absence of a reasonable likelihood of rehabilitation," the court may not deny dismissal or conversion. This is true even if the debtor attempts to show a reasonable likelihood of timely confirmation of a plan. Otherwise, as mentioned above and discussed next, the court may deny a motion for conversion or dismissal if it can be established that there is a reasonable likelihood of plan confirmation and that, as to the grounds for granting the motion, there is a reasonable justification for the act or omission, and such failings will be cured within a reasonable time. 11 U.S.C.A. § 1112(b)(2).

7. CONVERSION AND DISMISSAL

The amendment of the Bankruptcy Code in 2005 has expanded the grounds for conversion or dismissal of a chapter 11 case. Simultaneously, it makes it more difficult to defeat such a request and accelerates the procedures applicable to a conversion/dismissal motion. 11 U.S.C.A. § 1112 has been amended by BAPCPA § 442 to list examples of cause for conversion or dismissal of chapter 11 cases. Note that section 442 is among the amendments categorized for "small business," but it actually applies to all cases.

First, the "cause" for dismissal or conversion under 11 U.S.C.A. § 1112(b)(4) has been expanded to include 16 items:

(A) Substantial or continuing loss to or diminution of the estate and the absence of a reasonable likelihood of rehabilitation;

(B) gross mismanagement of the estate;

(C) failure to maintain appropriate insurance that poses a risk to the estate or to the public;

(D) unauthorized use of cash collateral substantially harmful to one or more creditors;

(E) failure to comply with an order of the court;

(F) unexcused failure to satisfy timely any filing or reporting requirement established by this title or by any rule applicable to a case under this chapter;

(G) failure to attend the meeting of creditors convened under § 341(a) or an examination ordered under Rule 2004 of the Federal Rules of Bankruptcy Procedure without good cause shown by the debtor;

(H) failure timely to provide information or attend meetings reasonably requested by the United States trustee (or the bankruptcy administrator, if any);

(I) failure timely to pay taxes owed after the date of the order for relief or to file tax returns due after the date of the order for relief;

(J) failure to file a disclosure statement, or to file or confirm a plan, within the time fixed by this title or by order of the court;

(K) failure to pay any fees or charges required under chapter 123 of Title 28;

(L) revocation of an order of confirmation under § 1144;

(M) inability to effectuate substantial consummation of a confirmed plan,

(N) material default by the debtor with respect to a confirmed plan;

(O) termination of confirmed plan by reason of the occurrence of a condition specified in the plan; and

(P) failure of the debtor to pay any domestic support obligation that first becomes payable after the date of the filing of the petition.

Thus former Code § 1112(b) has been embellished to add examples of grounds for dismissal or conversion. In a semantic difference from former Code § 1112(b)(1), however, the parties eligible to move for conversion or dismissal seem to have been reduced from "a party in interest or the United States trustee or bankruptcy administrator" in the former law to only "a party in interest." The U.S. trustee and bankruptcy administrator have been deleted as parties who may raise this issue. The Supreme Court has recently construed such a deletion (in the 1994 amendments) strictly. *Lamie v. U.S. Trustee*, 540 U.S. 526, 124 S. Ct. 1023, 157 L. Ed. 2d 1024, 42 Bankr. Ct. Dec. (CRR) 122, 50 Collier Bankr. Cas. 2d (MB) 1299, Bankr. L. Rep. (CCH) P 80038 (2004) (holding that removal of debtor's attorney from list of persons entitled to payment from estate prevented payment of fees to debtor's attorney). The deletion of the U.S. trustee and the bankruptcy administrator from existing § 1112(b), however, may be less likely to be construed as a Congressional determination that those parties cannot raise the issue of conversion or dismissal of chapter 11 cases, because 11 U.S.C.A. § 307 separately gives the U.S. trustee standing to appear and be heard on any issue. If this at least creates an ambiguity so that the courts may look behind the narrow language of

Code § 1112(b)(1), it is fair for the U.S. trustee to argue that Congress could not have intended to exclude this standing from the panoply of other powers so that the U.S. trustee could not move to dismiss or convert in appropriate circumstances. The omission of the bankruptcy administrators may be more difficult to get around in Alabama and North Carolina cases.

Like a motion for relief from the stay, filing a motion for conversion or dismissal is now given accelerated docketing by the statute. Under 11 U.S.C.A. § 1112(b)(3), the court must commence the hearing not later than 30 days after the filing of the motion and must decide the motion no later than 15 days after commencement of the hearing unless the movant agrees to a delay or unless there are "compelling circumstances" that "prevent the court from meeting the time limits established."

In the context of considering the motion, the court is required to grant conversion or dismissal, whichever is in the best interest of the creditors and the estate, if the movant establishes one of the many grounds for conversion or dismissal, unless the court specifically identifies unusual circumstances such that the relief is not in the best interest of the creditors and the estate. In particular, the debtor or other party in interest objecting to the motion must establish:

> (A) there is a reasonable likelihood that a plan will be confirmed within the time frames established in §§ 1121(e) and 1129(e) of this title, or if such sections did not apply, within a reasonable period of time; and
>
> (B) the grounds for granting such relief includes an act or omission of the debtor other than under paragraph (4)(A)—
>
> > (i) for which there exists a reasonable justification for the act or omission; and
> >
> > (ii) that will be cured within a reasonable period of time fixed by the court.

11 U.S.C.A. § 1112(b)(2)(A) and (B).

8. "PREPACKAGED" CHAPTER 11 PLANS

a. SOLICITATION

The amendments deal with "prepackaged" plans by slightly altering the language in 11 U.S.C.A. § 1125. If a creditor received a solicitation prior to bankruptcy to vote in favor of a plan in a prepackaged chapter 11, other lawful solicitations can now be made during the pendency of the case. Section 1125, as amended by BAPCPA § 408, now authorizes the solicitation of acceptances or rejections of a plan if the entity "was solicited before the commencement of the case in a manner complying with applicable nonbankruptcy law." Under prior law, solicitation could not continue after the commencement of the case until the disclosure statement had been approved by the court. Now, provided that a prepetition solicitation was commenced in compliance with applicable law, it may continue after filing.

b. FIRST MEETING OF CREDITORS

The amendments also facilitate the approval of a prepackaged plan even before conducting the meeting of creditors under section 341. This is accomplished by a new 11 U.S.C.A. § 341(e), which allows the court to cancel ("order that the United States trustee not convene") the meeting of creditors in the event that a plan has been filed with prepetition acceptance. This overrides some pre-amendment suggestion that a prepackaged plan could not be confirmed prior to the "first meeting." Thus if the debtor has filed a plan and solicited acceptances of the plan prior to the commencement of the case, new Code § 341(e) now allows the court, after notice and a hearing, to waive the requirement of a meeting of creditors.

9. CONFIRMATION AND RELATED ISSUES

a. EXCLUSIVITY

The expeditious filing and confirmation of the plan in chapter 11 has been a frequent theme of creditor concern and Congressional action in the past. The amendments of 2005 are no exception. Again Congress has responded to the comments of a variety of creditors who wish to expedite the administration of chapter 11 cases by focusing on the debtors' exclusive right to file a plan under 11 U.S.C.A. § 1121, and the Bankruptcy Code now substantially limits a debtor's ability to obtain extensions of its time to file and confirm its plan.

Under BAPCPA § 411, the long-standing 120-day exclusivity period may not be extended beyond 18 months from the date of the order for relief. The former Code allowed the court to extend or reduce the 120-day period for "cause," and the only limit on the extent to which the court could reduce or extend the period was a mandatory interlocutory appeal imposed by the 1994 legislation and later embodied in Rule 8001(a) of the Federal Rules of Bankruptcy Procedure. Now there is also an unconditional limit on the exclusivity period at 18 months from the date of the order for relief. 11 U.S.C.A. § 1121(d)(2)(A). Good cause is still required for an extension of the period, but no extension can be granted beyond the 18-month period. 11 U.S.C.A. § 1121(d)(2)(B).

b. POSTPETITION DISCLOSURE STATEMENTS

(1) Tax Issues

The Bankruptcy Code now imposes additional requirements upon the disclosure statement as a part of the plan confirmation process. First, 11 U.S.C.A. § 1125(a) now requires the debtor to include (in the disclosure statement) a discussion of the "potential material Federal tax consequences of the plan to the debtor, any successor to the debtor, and a hypothetical investor typical of the holders of claims or interests in the case," thus confirming by statute what has been the practice in many cases.

(2) Consideration of Complexity/Benefit

The Code's disclosure requirements, however, are modified by language (also in 11 U.S.C.A. § 1125(a)) allowing the court to consider the complexity of the case, the benefit of additional information to creditors and other parties in interest, and the cost of providing such additional information in determining whether a disclosure statement provides adequate information. In an extremely complex case, this may be a greater burden on the debtor, but this would seem to allow the court to consider the disclosure statement more leniently in a smaller and less complex case.

c. MODIFICATION OF CHAPTER 11 PLAN

In addition to the new requirements for modification of an individual's chapter 11 plan, discussed elsewhere, a new Code § 1127(f) makes it clear that all of the confirmation requirements of sections 1121 through 1129 apply to any modification. The court is to direct the level of disclosure for such a modification and is to approve it after notice and a hearing. The definition of "notice and a hearing" has not changed. 11 U.S.C.A. § 102(1).

10. GENERAL TAX ISSUES

In § 701 et seq., BAPCPA deals at length with a number of issues regarding tax-related obligations of the bankruptcy estate and tax claims in bankruptcy cases. While many of these changes are beyond the scope of this publication, a few will be of interest to bankruptcy practitioners more generally.

a. NOTICE TO TAXING AUTHORITIES

Under Code § 575(b), the clerk is required to maintain a list of addresses designated by taxing authorities for requesting determination of a tax. In the absence of such a designation, the estate's request may be made to the address for filing a return or a protest.

b. INTEREST ON TAX CLAIMS

The applicable interest rate on a tax claim, including the rate to be used in determining the present value of a tax claim, is the rate that would be applicable under nonbankruptcy law. 11 U.S.C.A. § 511. The rate is to be determined in the context of confirmation as of the month of confirmation. 11 U.S.C.A. § 511.

c. PRIORITY CLAIMS

Code § 507(a) has been amended to clarify the date and extent of priority tax claims. The priority now extends to taxes assessed during the 240-day period prior to the commencement of the case, plus any time that a stay was in effect, plus 90 days. 11 U.S.C.A. § 507(a)(8). The time is also extended by a pending request for a hearing or appeal. 11 U.S.C.A. § 507(a)(8). The one-year time for computing property taxes is to be determined as of the date the debt was incurred rather than the date on which it was assessed. 11 U.S.C.A. § 507(a)(8)(B).

d. CONFIRMATION STANDARDS

Confirmation standards for treatment of tax payments have been changed significantly in chapter 11. Tax payments were formerly to be paid in an indeterminate fashion over a period of six years measured from the date of assessment. Former Code § 1129(a)(9). Paragraph (9) has now been amended to require "regular installment payments in cash" that equal the allowed amount of the claim and may not extend beyond five years from the date of the order for relief. 11 U.S.C.A. § 1129(a)(9). In addition, they must be paid in a fashion that is at least as favorable as the most favorable treatment of non-priority unsecured claims under the plan. 11 U.S.C.A. § 1129(a)(9)(C). The same rules apply to secured claims that otherwise qualify as priority tax claims. 11 U.S.C.A. § 1129(a)(9)(D).

e. TAX RETURNS

The 2005 amendments also give some special attention to issues related to tax returns. A tax return includes a return that satisfies the requirements of applicable bankruptcy law. 11 U.S.C.A. § 523(a)(1). It also includes a return prepared by taxing authorities or a written stipulation to a judgment or final order outside bankruptcy. BAPCPA § 714. It does not include, however, a return made pursuant to Internal Revenue Code § 6020(b) (by the Internal Revenue Service in case of the taxpayer's failure to make a return or submission of a false or fraudulent return) or similar state or local law. Code § 521 has been amended to allow a taxing authority to seek conversion or dismissal of the case based on a debtor's failure either to file a tax return that is due after commencement or to properly request an extension. Upon such a request by the taxing authority, the debtor has 90 days within which to file the return or request, after which the case is required to be converted or dismissed, whichever is in the best interest of creditors and the estate. 11 U.S.C.A. § 521(j)(2).

11. UTILITY SERVICE

The amendments improve the protection given to utilities in bankruptcy. 11 U.S.C.A. § 366 now includes a detailed definition of "assurance of payment" for the purpose of maintaining utility service. The rights of the utility in cases in which the debtor fails to furnish adequate assurance under 11 U.S.C.A. § 366, however, are somewhat troubling under the new amendments. Code § 366(a) allows a utility to alter, refuse, or discontinue service if such assurance is not furnished within 20 days after the order for relief. Subsection (c)(2), however, allows the utility to alter, refuse, or discontinue if assurance is not received, satisfactory to the utility, within 30 days beginning on the date of the filing of the petition.

There are several express options now for assuring payment, including prepayment or surety bonds. 11 U.S.C.A. § 366(C)(1)(A). Note that the amendment specifically precludes the timely payment of utility charges in the past as evidence of assurance of payment in the future. Similarly, it is not enough to rely on the availability of an administrative expense priority as "assurance." Ultimately, however, the adequate assurance of payment must be "satisfactory to the utility." 11 U.S.C.A. § 366(c)(2).

A new provision in Code § 366(c)(3) specifically allows the court to order modification of the amount of assurance of payment upon the request of a party in interest and after notice and a hearing.

New Code § 366(c)(4) explicitly allows a utility to recover or offset against a prepetition security deposit with neither notice nor any order of the court.

Taken together, these changes represent a significant shift in the balance of power toward utilities and may make it much more difficult in many cases for a debtor to satisfy utilities' adequate protection demands, and these factors will need to be considered in budgeting for operations in chapter 11.

12. PREFERENTIAL AND FRAUDULENT TRANSFERS

a. INTRODUCTION

Congress has given special attention to two groups of creditors who, as practitioners may attest, are uniquely aggrieved by the bankruptcy process. Perhaps no bankruptcy-related client is more deeply offended by the process than a vendor who is sued for a preference. They perceive that they have delivered value to the debtor, they have been paid something to which they are entitled, they often have a claim on which they expect little or no distribution, and, adding insult to injury, they are being asked to pay back something that they lawfully received. In 2005,

Congress responded to these complaints about preferences in several positive ways but also added to the trustee's power to recover fraudulent transfers.

b. THE "ORDINARY COURSE" DEFENSE

First, BAPCPA § 409 amended § 547(c)(2). This provision of section 547 is one of the affirmative defenses to a preference action, the "ordinary course defense." There has been some confusion over the meaning of paragraphs (B) and (C) of section 547(c)(2). Especially confusing is the meaning of the language of paragraph (C), which appeared to some courts to require that the preference defendant must qualify a transfer two ways: (1) as being in the ordinary course of the business of financial affairs of the parties and (2) also as conforming to some broader industry standard. Congress now has attempted to eliminate this problem by restructuring and tweaking the language to change its meaning dramatically. Former phrase (A) has been moved up into the preamble of section 547(c)(2). The remaining phrases, previously found in (B) and (C), have now been re-lettered as (A) and (B). The smallest but most significant change, however, is that the "and," between former subparagraphs (B) and (C), becomes an "or" in the new section. The effect of this is to wipe out the difficulty formerly created by the conjunctively linked elements under § 547(c)(2). Now, as long as the defendant can show either that the transfer was "made in the ordinary course of business or financial affairs of the debtor and the transferee" or that the transfer was "made according to ordinary business terms," then the defendant has a valid affirmative defense to an otherwise voidable preference action.

The amendment should reduce the cost of defending a preference action because the defendant will no longer be required to produce expert testimony regarding industry standards. Moreover, the debate over whether expert testimony is even required to prove industry standards will no longer materialize so long as the defendant can show that the transfer was made in the ordinary course of business or financial affairs of the debtor and the transferee.

c. PREFERENCE CAPS IN NONCONSUMER CASES

In addition to the other "affirmative defenses" to avoidance of preferences in Code § 547(c), a new item has been added as (c)(9). In nonconsumer cases, the recovery of preferences is precluded unless the aggregate property at issue is equal to or greater than $5,000. Although subsection (c)(8) has heretofore capped recoveries at $600, this is the first time that nonconsumer preferences have been so limited.

d. VENUE FOR NONCONSUMER ACTIONS TO COLLECT MONEY OR PROPERTY

The next change favoring defendants in these avoidance actions is found in BAPCPA § 410. This is an amendment to 28 U.S.C.A. § 1409(b), the venue provision governing actions to collect money or property. By this amendment to title 28, BAPCPA restricts actions on nonconsumer debts against noninsiders. Such actions seeking less than $10,000 must be filed in the district court in the district in which the defendant resides, even if the bankruptcy is pending in another district. 28 U.S.C.A. § 1409(b). Under the amendment, these actions must be brought in the defendant's home district for any action to collect a consumer debt of less than $15,000 or any other debt less than $10,000. Note that these limits on such actions are not limited to preference actions, although that seems likely to be the area of greatest impact of this change. Also note that the $10,000 debt limit does not protect a defendant that is an insider, in which case the $1,000 venue limit continues.

In the wake of the mass prosecution of preference actions in large commercial cases across the country, these new caps will provide relief to at least some defendants who otherwise could not justify the expense of defending the preference action, particularly where the lawsuit filed would have been in a foreign state.

e. ANOTHER ATTEMPT TO FIX THE *DEPRIZIO* PROBLEM

In *Levit v. Ingersoll Rand Financial Corp.*, 874 F.2d 1186, 19 Bankr. Ct. Dec. (CRR) 574, 22 Collier Bankr. Cas. 2d (MB) 36, 11 Employee Benefits Cas. (BNA) 1323, Bankr. L. Rep. (CCH) P 72910 (7th Cir. 1989) (disapproved of by, In re Arundel Housing Components, Inc., 126 B.R. 216, 21 Bankr. Ct. Dec. (CRR) 959, Bankr. L. Rep. (CCH) P 73922 (Bankr. D. Md. 1991)), the Seventh Circuit shocked the lending community by deciding that a noninsider creditor was subject to the one-year preference period when the transfer simply benefited an insider-guarantor. Thus a bank with no insider relationship with its borrower might be exposed to preference actions for up to a year after a payment to the bank simply because it had a guaranty from an insider who was indirectly benefited by the payment.

In 1994, Congress attempted to address this problem by an amendment to Code § 550(b), which precludes *recovery* from a noninsider outside the basic 90-day preference period. Now, in an amendment to Code § 547, a new subparagraph (i) has been added to make it clear that not only may such transfers not be recovered, they may not be *avoided* if such a transfer was made more than 90 days prior to bankruptcy except with respect to an insider creditor. This is one of the changes that becomes effective immediately upon enactment of BAPCPA.

f. FRAUDULENT TRANSFER LOOK-BACK PERIOD

11 U.S.C.A. § 548(a)(1) has been changed to double the size of the window through which the trustee may look back to recover or avoid fraudulent transfers. The transfers subject to scrutiny are expanded from those made within one year to those made within two years. 11 U.S.C.A. § 548(a)(1). This is a provision that applies, however, only to cases commenced one year after enactment of BAPCPA.

g. KEY EMPLOYEE RETENTION PLANS AS FRAUDULENT TRANSFERS

The scrutiny of key employee retention plans is discussed at length below, in the context of labor relations in chapter 11 more generally. It includes an amendment to the fraudulent transfer rules in the Bankruptcy Code. A benefit paid to an insider under a KERP may be avoided as a fraudulent transfer unless it was made in the ordinary course of business. 11 U.S.C.A. § 548(a)(1)(B)(ii)(IV). Although subsection (a)(1)(B) requires a showing that less than reasonably equivalent value was received in exchange for such transfer or obligation, note that the new KERP provision does not require a showing of insolvency.

13. INVESTOR PROTECTION

11 U.S.C.A. § 362 is amended by BAPCPA to provide governmental protection for investors. This is accomplished by excepting "securities self-regulatory orga-

nizations" from the automatic stay. Such an organization is defined as a securities association registered with the Securities and Exchange Commission. 11 U.S.C.A. § 101(48A). Protected activity includes commencement or continuation of such organizations' investigations and actions, including enforcement and such other action as delisting, that are related to the regulatory power of such an organization or the failure to meet applicable regulatory requirements. 11 U.S.C.A. § 362(b)(25).

14. COLLECTION OF DATA ON OTHER ENTITIES

BAPCPA § 419 continues the effort to measure progress in the reorganization process by ordering the Judicial Conference of the United States to promulgate forms by which chapter 11 debtors are to disclose the "value, operations, and profitability" of entities in which the debtor holds a controlling or substantial interest. This is a curious provision, as practitioners will quickly realize, because the subject of the report is an entity that is not in bankruptcy and may not be controlled by the debtor but may simply be one in which the debtor's interest is "substantial." This entity is not a debtor, and the debtor may not be in a position either to obtain the information or to force the entity to complete the form. Nevertheless, failure to make such a report may be cause for conversion or dismissal, 11 U.S.C.A. § 1112(b)(4)(F), triggering the harsh procedures for dismissal previously discussed.

15. POSTCONFIRMATION DISCHARGE

The amended Code imposes two new kinds of limitations on discharges in chapter 11. In addition to the new limitation in individual cases contained in 11 U.S.C.A. § 1142(d)(5) and discussed above, corporations are now precluded from obtaining a discharge by confirmation from two new categories of debt: (1) debts arising from obtaining money, credit, etc., by false pretenses, false representations, actual fraud or a false financial statement (as described in Code § 523(a)(2)(A)(B)) if those debts are owed to a domestic governmental unit or owed as a result of an action filed on a claim against the United States government (under subchapter III of chapter 37 of title 31) or under any similar State statute; and (2) debts for a tax or customs duty with respect to which the debtor made a fraudulent return or "willfully attempted in any manner to evade or defeat such tax or such customs duty." 11 U.S.C.A. § 1141(d)(6)(B)(ii).

E. SECURED CREDITORS

1. PERFECTION AND THE PREFERENCE RULES

BAPCPA § 403 amends 11 U.S.C.A. § 547(e)(2) to provide additional protection for secured creditors in the context of the preference rules. Subsection (e)(2) generally provides a grace period to a transferee within which to file its documents and "perfect" the transfer. Under the new law, that grace period has been extended from 10 days to 30 days. Thus, for example, a secured party taking a security interest in the equipment of a debtor should have 30 days within which to file its financing statement under Article 9. If the filing occurs within this time, the transfer is deemed to have taken effect at the time of the granting of a security interest.

2. PERFECTION OF THE PURCHASE-MONEY SECURITY INTEREST

More problematic is a similar attempt to expand the grace period allowed by Code § 547(c)(3). This is the provision that protects purchase money security interests (enabling loans). Until the amendment of the Bankruptcy Code in 2005, both the Bankruptcy Code and Article 9 (section 9-324(a)) allowed 20 days within which to perfect after the debtor received possession of goods other than inventory or livestock. Now, the Bankruptcy Code has been amended to increase the grace period to 30 days. Commercial practitioners should not be misled by this, however, and should remember that purchase-money priority, being governed by nonbankruptcy law, is dependent on filing within the 20 days allowed by the Uniform Commercial Code.

3. WAREHOUSEMAN'S LIEN

Congress has also addressed the interests of warehousemen who may have statutory liens for storage, transportation, and other charges. BAPCPA § 406 adds protections for such liens by protecting them from avoidance actions under Code § 545, although they are otherwise statutory liens subject to attack under that section. Now, under Code § 546(i), the trustee may not avoid such liens. The provision is to "be applied in a manner consistent with any State statute applicable to such lien that is similar to section 7-209 of the Uniform Commercial Code." 11 U.S.C.A. § 546(i)(2).

F. PARTIES TO EXECUTORY CONTRACTS AND UNEXPIRED LEASES

1. NEW (AND IMPROVED?) DEADLINE TO ASSUME OR REJECT NONRESIDENTIAL REAL ESTATE LEASES

Practitioners who represent real estate developers and others who own commercial space may confirm anecdotal evidence that their clients have been frustrated by their experiences as landlords in chapter 11. A reorganization in bankruptcy is, by its nature, designed to give a business some time to reorganize. Thus, for example, retail businesses often wish to wait through a business cycle before assuming all of their obligations to their landlords. The Bankruptcy Code already required that leases be assumed or rejected within 60 days after the filing of a petition. Former Code § 365(d) (applying the 60-day standard with varying degrees of severity in cases under all of the chapters of the Code). The courts were allowed to extend this deadline, however, and the reality has been that the deadline was often extended. These extensions often lasted for many months and, especially in large cases, might delay the landlords' ability to exercise their rights for years. The 2005 amendment of the Bankruptcy Code tilts the playing field considerably. Landlords may feel that the effect of this is simply to level the field. Other creditors may be less happy with the outcome.

BAPCPA § 404 amends former Code § 365(d)(4) to provide that unexpired leases of nonresidential real estate in which the debtor is the lessee are deemed rejected and must be immediately surrendered to the lessor by the earlier of 120 days after the commencement of the case or the date of the confirmation of a plan. The court, for cause, may extend the 120-day period for an additional 90 days, but any extension subsequent to the additional 90 days is available only with the consent of the lessor.

Thus the new law provides for *automatic* rejection of a nonresidential real estate lease if the reorganizing tenant does not assume the lease, and it imposes a strict timeline on this process. 11 U.S.C.A. § 365(d)(4). At the end of those scheduled events, the landlord is given a veto over the tenant's ability to extend the deadline further. This new timeline is designed to focus the judge's attention on the interests of landlords and, over the course of the bankruptcy process, to increase the pressure on the tenant.

It works this way: The timeline starts, in a voluntary chapter 11 filed after October 17, 2005, with the filing of the petition itself. 11 U.S.C.A. § 365(d)(4) (measuring the deadline is from the order for relief). Measuring from that starting date, the tenant has 120 days within which to make a decision about the wisdom of assuming the lease. If, in the meantime, the tenant proposes a plan, then the 120 days is cut short at the date of confirmation. In other words, there is automatic rejection if the lease is not assumed by the earlier of (1) 120 days after the commencement of the voluntary case or (2) the entry of a confirmation order. After that initial four-month grace period, the court may only extend the deadline (1) for cause and (2) for time not to exceed 90 days.

C. AMENDMENTS EFECTIVE IMMEDIATELY UPON ENACTMENT

Code Section	General Topic
§104(b)	New sections added to adjustment of dollar amounts
§303(b)(1)	Involuntary bankruptcy; retroactive effect
§363, 541 & 1129	Rules for nonprofit property sales, subject to court considering effect in a confirmation
§507(a)(4) & (5)	Priority of employee claims
§547(i)	Insider avoidance; retroactive to proceeding pending
§548(a) & (e)	Insider transfers
§522(o)	Reduces homestead
§522(p)	$125,000 cap on homestead
§522(q)	$125,000 cap on homestead
§727(a)(12)	Delays discharge for § 522(q) determination
§1104(e)	Chapter 11 trustee appointment
§1114(l)	Modification of retiree insurance benefits
§1141(d)	Delays discharge for § 522(q) determination
§1222(a)(2) & 1231(b)	Governmental claims, effective but specifically not retroactive
§1228(f)	Delays discharge for § 522(q) determination
§1328(h)	Delays discharge for § 522(q) determination
28 U.S.C.A. §152	New bankruptcy judgeships
28 U.S.C.A. §1334	Jurisdiction over 11 U.S.C.A. §327
28 U.S.C.A. §1930	Changes in filing fees and U.S. trustee system fund

So, the tenant reorganizing in bankruptcy has a maximum possible seven-month grace period within which to assume the lease. After four of those months (more precisely, 120 days), it must show "cause" for the extension, perhaps because it must wait to see whether its business turns up. At the end of another three months (90 days), however, the lease may only be assumed with "the prior written consent of the lessor" who may thus stop the process. It may be that granting additional time makes sense, but at that point it is the landlord's prerogative to make that decision.

2. POSTASSUMPTION, POSTREJECTION LEASE CLAIMS

These rules may have some unpleasant (and perhaps unintended) consequences. Trade creditors (and even other landlords whose leases are *not* assumed) may find themselves distressed by this development because the landlords who are able to force the tenant to assume their leases will put themselves in a priority position that may eviscerate the value of the estate in an ultimate liquidation. These side effects of the new law should not be ignored as trade creditors and landlords consider the dynamics of dealing with a tenant under the new chapter 11 regime.

The amendments attempt to deal with this reality that the debtor may be forced into a premature assumption of a lease that is ultimately defaulted. Apparently to ameliorate the effect on unsecured creditors that would be caused by such a premature assumption followed by later rejection, the amended Code limits the administrative claim resulting from that circumstance. The landlord may have a priority claim of up to two years' rent and other monetary damages after the ultimate rejection or turnover of the leased property, whichever occurs later. This amount is to be reduced by "sums actually received or to be received" from third parties (guarantors, etc.). The statute expresses this as follows:

> (b) after notice and a hearing, there shall be allowed administrative expenses, other than claims allowed under § 502 (f) of this title, including—
> ****

>> (7) with respect to a nonresidential real property lease previously assumed under § 365, and subsequently rejected, a settlement equal to all monetary obligations due, excluding those arising from or relating to a failure to operate or a penalty provision, for the period of two years following the later of the rejection date or the date of actual turnover of the premises, without reduction or setoff for any reason whatsoever except for sums actually received or to be received from an entity other than the debtor, and the claim for remaining sums due for the balance of the term of the lease shall be a claim under § 502(b)(6);

11 U.S.C.A. § 503(b)(7). The balance of the landlord's claim would be relegated to unsecured status, subject to the cap imposed by 11 U.S.C.A. § 502(b)(6).

3. CURE OF NONMONETARY DEFAULTS

One of the recent and more contentious battles between landlords, tenants, and other parties to executory contracts has been fought over the need to cure defaults in the assumption process. Before 2005, paragraph (1) of former Code § 365(b) required an assuming trustee/DIP to cure or provide for cure of defaults before assumption but subsection (b) went on to provide:

> (2) paragraph (1) of this subsection does not apply to a default that is a breach of a provision relating to—
> ****

>> (D) the satisfaction of any penalty rate or provision relating to a default arising from any failure by the debtor to perform non-monetary obligations under the executory contract or unexpired lease.

Former Code § 365(b)(2)(D). This language produced a split in its interpretation by the circuits, which Congress has now attempted to resolve.

The circuit split is found in *In re Claremont Acquisition Corp., Inc.*, 113 F.3d 1029, 30 Bankr. Ct. Dec. (CRR) 1045, Bankr. L. Rep. (CCH) P 77469 (9th Cir. 1997) and In re BankVest Capital Corp., 360 F.3d 291, 42 Bankr. Ct. Dec. (CRR) 210, Bankr. L. Rep. (CCH) P 80062 (1st Cir. 2004), cert. denied, 124 S. Ct. 2874, 159 L. Ed. 2d 776 (U.S. 2004). In *BankVest* and *Claremont*, the two circuits analyzed former Code § 365(b)(2)(D) and came to different conclusions as to whether that language required that debtors cure nonmonetary defaults prior to assuming executory contracts and unexpired leases.

The *Claremont* decision arose from the attempted assumption of a franchise agreement for a car dealership. Prior to the debtor's bankruptcy, the debtor had ceased operations for a period of 14 days. The franchise agreement required that the operations at the dealership be continuous, and thus the shutdown breached the franchise agreement. When the debtor attempted to assume the franchise agreement, the franchisor objected and argued that the debtor's failure to abide by the continuous operation requirement constituted an "historical" default that the debtor could not cure. See *Claremont*, 113 F.3d 1029, 1033. The debtor argued that the continuous operation requirement is a nonmonetary obligation, and, under former Code § 365(b)(2)(D), the debtor is not required to cure nonmonetary defaults. *Claremont*, 113 F.3d 1029, 1033.

Siding with the franchisor, the court determined that former Code § 365(b)(2)(D) *only* exempted from the debtor's cure requirements the *payment of monetary penalties* resulting from the failure to perform nonmonetary obligations. *Claremont*, 113 F.3d 1029, 1034. Thus the Ninth Circuit read the word "penalty" (meaning penalty payment) in former paragraph (2)(D) to modify both nouns following that modifier, "rate" and "provision," determining this to be the only proper grammatical reading of the former language. So, if either a penalty rate or other penalty payment was tied to a nonmonetary obligation, it need not be cured, but other nonmonetary defaults had to be cured, regardless of whether it was possible to do so. The court's decision was based in part on its review of the limited legislative history of the former Code section which suggested that debtors will be able to assume a lease by curing any default at the nondefault interest rate. The *Claremont* court took this to mean that Congress only intended to protect debtors from being required to pay monetary penalties resulting from nonmonetary defaults. The Ninth Circuit reasoned that the debtor's proposed reading of former Code § 365(b)(2)(D) would render the other three subsections useless or superfluous in that they would be covered by subsection (D). *Claremont*, 113 F.3d 1029. Thus all nonmonetary defaults were to be cured unless such default requires a payment by the debtor of a monetary penalty.

In *BankVest*, the First Circuit took the opposite approach. The court observed that the *Claremont* ruling produced a harsh result for debtors by creating situations in which the debtor's ability to cure a default under an expired lease or executory contract is impossible. See *BankVest*, 360 F.3d 291, 299. The *BankVest* court found the result reached in *Claremont* to be at odds with the underlying principles of the Bankruptcy Code, namely the rehabilitation of debtors. *BankVest*, 360 F.3d 291, 300. The First Circuit concluded that debtors may assume executory contracts and unexpired leases without first curing *any* nonmonetary defaults.

In BAPCPA, Congress has addressed this split in the circuits by taking pages from both the *Claremont* and *BankVest* opinions. First, in construing the language of former Code § 365(b)(2)(D), Congress sided with the *Claremont* Court. Subsection (b)(2)(D) now reads as follows:

> (2) Paragraph (1) of this subsection does not apply to a default that is a breach of a provision relating to—
> ****
>> (D) The satisfaction of any penalty rate or *penalty* provision relating to a default arising from any failure by the debtor to perform non-monetary obligations under the executory contract or unexpired lease.

11 U.S.C.A. § 365(b)(2)(D) (new text in italics). This change results in the same phrasing inferred by the *Claremont* court with the word "penalty" modifying both nouns, "rate" and "provision." Congress therefore has agreed with the view that Code § 365(b)(2)(D) should only except from debtors' cure obligations the payment of penalty rates or penalty provisions but that the escape clause (b)(2)(D) does not provide a catch-all exception for nonmonetary defaults. Unless the nonmonetary default requires some type of penalty payment, the debtor must cure the nonmonetary default prior to assumption.

However, in order to reduce somewhat the harsh effects illuminated in *BankVest*, Congress added the following language to Code § 365(b)(1)(A):

> (b)(1) if there has been a default in an executory contract or unexpired lease of the debtor, the trustee may not assume such contract or lease unless, at the time of assumption of such contract or lease, the trustee—
>> (A) cures, or provides adequate assurance that the trustee will promptly cure, such default other than a default that is a breach of a provision relating to the satisfaction of any provision (other than a penalty rate or penalty provision) relating to a default arising from any failure to perform non-monetary obligations under any unexpired lease of real property, if it is impossible for the trustee to cure such default by performing non-monetary acts at and after the time of assumption, except that if such default arises from a failure to operate in accordance with a non-residential real property lease, then such default shall be cured by performance at and after the time of assumption in accordance with such lease, and pecuniary losses resulting from such default shall be compensated in accordance with the provisions of this paragraph;

11 U.S.C.A. § 365(b)(1)(A) (new text in italics).

The analysis of this complex language might start with the observation that it repeats the phrase "penalty rate or penalty provision." Do these phrases conflict, or does the appearance in paragraph (b)(2)(D) simply clarify that the debtor never needs to make such penalty payments?

Beyond that, the additional language of the BAPCPA specifically exempts certain nonmonetary cure obligations of the debtor. These exceptions, however, only apply to unexpired leases of real property. Thus the result reached in *Claremont* would be the same today under the 2005 Code § 365(b)(1) and (2) because *Claremont* dealt with a franchise agreement and not a real property lease.

Note that 2005 changes do not except from the debtor's cure requirements every nonmonetary obligation under leases of real property. This is true in two respects. First, the 2005 Code only excepts those nonmonetary acts which are "impossible" for the debtor to cure at or after the time of assumption. A new debate will certainly arise over what cure obligations are impossible.

Further, the language under new paragraph 365(b)(1)(A) specifically requires that, at and after the time of assumption, the debtor perform any breach related to the failure to operate in accordance with a nonresidential real property lease. Debtors are therefore compelled to comply prospectively with all operational terms in nonresidential real property leases. The distinction between "operating" and nonoperating obligations may also be a source of debate.

Congress' modifications to former Code § 365 should add some clarity to the proper interpretation of 11 U.S.C.A. § 365(b)(2)(D). In the case of real property leases, the new language will prevent the harsh result enunciated in *BankVest*. However, in all other situations including franchise agreements, leases of personal property, and any other executory contracts or unexpired leases that are not leases of real property, the existence of a nonmonetary default that triggers a nonmonetary obligation of the debtor seems to provide the nondebtor party a means to block the assumption of otherwise valuable contracts. In many situations, these counterparties will thus continue to hold a trump card that may affect the debtor's ability to successfully reorganize. This is true because the *Claremont* rule continues to apply for all executory contracts and unexpired leases except "impossible" cure obligations in residential real estate leases and impossible cure of nonoperational obligations in nonresidential real estate leases.

The outcome of the particular facts in *Claremont* apparently would be the same under the 2005 Code, while the *BankVest* decision would be reversed as illustrated by the following matrix of facts and results.

Analysis of Possible Circumstances and Outcomes Under New Code § 365

	Default and Penalty Circumstances		
	Monetary Default	Non-Monetary Default	
		Penalty Payment	No Penalty Payment
Personal Property Lease	Cure required	Cure not required	Cure required (Note: These are the *Bankvest* facts and cure would be required.)
Executory Contract (e.g, Franchise Agreement)	Cure required	Cure not required	Cure required (Note: These are the *Claremont* facts and cure would still be required.)
Non-Residential Real Estate Lease	Cure required	Cure not required	Cure not required if "impossible" *except* cure for failure to operate in accordance with the lease *prospectively*
Residential Real Estate Lease	Cure required	Cure not required	Cure not required if "impossible"
Note: It continues to be necessary to provide compensation to the lessor or counterparty for pecuniary losses resulting from any such default.			

4. PERSONAL PROPERTY LEASES

A chapter 7 debtor would be specifically permitted to assume an unexpired lease of personalty. In chapter 11 or 13 cases, however, if an individual debtor does not assume the lease in a plan, the lease would be rejected and not subject to the automatic stay.

5. AIRCRAFT GATES

11 U.S.C.A. § 365 as amended also deletes extensive language dealing with leases of aircraft gates and similar issues of interest in airline bankruptcies. These appear simply to be [long overdue] housekeeping changes. The provisions expired in 1993 but, like many other issues, were trapped in the Congressional deadlock on bankruptcy issues in the interim and had not been removed from the Code even though they are no longer applicable.

G. UNSECURED CREDITORS AND COMMITTEES

1. COMMITTEE COMPOSITION

The 2005 amendments specifically address some of the concerns of smaller and trade creditors. The first of these changes involves the desire of trade creditors sometimes to serve on creditors' committees and the likelihood that they are excluded in favor of those listed as the debtor's largest creditors. This concern is addressed by confirmation of the authority of a bankruptcy court to order adjustment (by the U.S. trustee) of the number and makeup of committee members under 11 U.S.C.A. § 1102.

The provision also adds specific authority to order the U.S. trustee to include "small" businesses, as defined in Section 3(a)(1) of the Small Business Act, on a creditors' committee, if the claim held by the small business concern is disproportionately large in comparison with its annual gross revenue. Thus a small business with a disproportionately large claim may be given a role in the case by allowing it to serve on a committee (with expenses paid by the estate). The power of the court to order a change in the membership of a committee is a change from prior law, under which the power to change membership rested with the U.S. trustee.

2. COMMITTEE DISCLOSURE REQUIREMENTS

11 U.S.C.A. § 1102 is further amended in subsection (b) to require that a committee provide its constituency with access to information and solicit and obtain comments from such creditors who are not appointed to the committee. The court may also compel additional reporting or disclosure.

These rules do not clearly state the kinds of information that the committee is to disclose. Presumably, a hearing on a request for such an order would provide some opportunity to raise questions of confidentiality and competitive interests because creditors who are not members of a committee may not have the same fiduciary or contractual duty to maintain the confidentiality of such information. However, again, the amendment does not clearly address the consequences of refusal to release such information. There is likely to be debate over whether the committee's constituency is entitled to its private analysis and strategic information or whether this simply requires the disclosure of information generally available from the records in the case.

3. COMMITTEE MEMBERS' PROFESSIONAL FEES

The amendments drew the line at one point, however. 11 U.S.C.A. § 503(b)(4) has been amended to reverse the result in the *First Merchants* case (*First Merchants Acceptance Corp. v. J.C. Bradford & Co.*, 198 F.3d 394, 35 Bankr. Ct. Dec.

(CRR) 96, 43 Collier Bankr. Cas. 2d (MB) 442, Bankr. L. Rep. (CCH) P 78072 (3d Cir. 1999)). In that case, the Third Circuit concluded that the language of the 1994 amendments, strictly construed, allowed individual committee members to apply for reimbursement of their attorney's fees. By excluding persons listed in subsection (b)(3)(F) from those who are entitled to ask for reimbursement of attorney's fees under 11 U.S.C.A. § 503(b)(4), Congress has limited the professional fees related to creditors' committees to only those professionals who are retained by the committee under 11 U.S.C.A. § 1103.

4. PRO SE REPRESENTATION

The interests of creditors and equity security holders in participating in the process without excessive cost have been further enhanced by an amendment to Code § 341(c), allowing appearances and participation at the "first meeting" without an attorney. The new rule is, by its terms, applicable only to creditors holding consumer debts, but Congress expressly provided that this should not be "construed to require any creditor to be represented by an attorney at any meeting of creditors." 11 U.S.C.A. § 341(c). Whether this will be effective to override state law outside the consumer setting remains to be seen.

5. RECLAMATION CLAIMS

On the other hand, Congress was more considerate of trade creditors with reclamation claims. The amended Bankruptcy Code contains a complex series of changes designed to enhance the reclamation rights of trade creditors who deliver goods on the eve of bankruptcy. First, that "eve" of bankruptcy is now extended from 10 days to 45 days before the date of commencement of the case. The trustee's avoidance rights are subject to the right of an ordinary course seller who delivered goods to the debtor within 45 days prior to the filing of the petition and while the debtor is insolvent. 11 U.S.C.A. § 546(c)(1). The seller's right to reclaim, however, is contingent on making a demand in writing either (1) within 45 after the debtor's receipt of the goods or (2) if the 45 days expires after the commencement of the case, the demand must be made not later than 20 days after the date of commencement. 11 U.S.C.A. § 546(c)(1).

Reclaiming sellers should be sensitive to a dangerous interpretation of this rule. Congress may have intended to allow reclamation within 20 days or the remainder of a 45-day reclamation window, whichever deadline occurs last. The language does not clearly say "whichever occurs later," however, and therefore some courts may conclude that the smaller window applies. For example, suppose the seller delivers to debtor 10 days prior to the filing of debtor's petition. The 45-day window would not run until 35 days after the petition. Because "the 45-day period expires after the commencement of the case," however, the notice might have to be given in writing "not later than 20 days after the date of commencement." 11 U.S.C.A. § 546(c)(1)(B).

Thus the time to reclaim is either (1) not later than 45 days after receipt or (2) not later than 20 days after the date of commencement of the case. The second deadline seems to apply by its terms only if the 45-day window expires postpetition. It is unclear which deadline would apply. Moral: Make a demand within 20 days after the date of bankruptcy.

On the other hand, Code § 546 now also confirms the proposition that a security interest in goods subject to reclamation is prior to the rights of the reclaiming creditor. 11 U.S.C.A. § 546(c)(1). Reclamation claims are fragile rights. The debtor may simply consume the goods on hand. The debtor may have already sold the goods or may simply ignore the notice. These circumstances can be the source of considerable frustration to the reclaiming creditor. Congress attempted to ease this frustration by further amendments to Code § 503 that provide administrative expense treatment to a creditor with reclamation rights even if the seller fails to make a demand. 11 U.S.C.A. § 503(b)(9). This claim is limited, however, to the value of goods received by the debtor in the ordinary course of business within 20 days prior to the commencement of the case. 11 U.S.C.A. § 503(b)(9).

H. LABOR RELATIONS

1. KEY EMPLOYEE RETENTION PLANS

A recurring complaint, both from organized labor and from media and regulatory observers, is the payment of what may be perceived as excessive amounts to management of troubled companies under the category of "key employee retention plans" (KERPs) or other devices such as those referred to in the pejorative as "golden parachutes." See *In re Georgetown Steel Co., LLC*, 306 B.R. 549, 42 Bankr. Ct. Dec. (CRR) 217 (Bankr. D. S.C. 2004) (approving implementation of key employee retention program over objections of union employees). An amendment of 11 U.S.C.A. § 503 late in the legislative process reflects Congress's desire to respond to these concerns. BAPCPA § 331.

Code § 503 now sets forth limitations on the payment or allowance of claims for retention bonuses or severance pay to the debtor's insiders, "key" or otherwise. It disallows payments to induce persons who are insiders to remain in the debtor's employ unless the payment is essential to retain a person who has "a bona fide job offer from another business at the same or a greater rate of compensation," with the reference rate being the amount to be paid under the KERP. 11 U.S.C.A. § 503(c)(1).

In addition, the amount of the payment may not exceed 10 times the amount of a similar transfer to a nonmanagement employee during the calendar year of the proposed transfer. 11 U.S.C.A. § 503(c)(1)(C)(i). If no such transfer has been made to nonmanagement personnel during the calendar year, then it may not exceed 25 times the amount of any similar transfer to an insider in the calendar year prior to commencement of the case. 11 U.S.C.A. § 503(c)(1)(C)(ii).

2. SEVERANCE COMPENSATION

In the same theme, severance pay is now limited to an amount not to exceed 10 times the amount of the mean severance pay given to nonmanagement employees unless the severance pay is a part of a program generally applicable to all employees. 11 U.S.C.A. § 503(c)(2). Notice that the maximum amounts are linked to payments made to other employees during the calendar year of the case, which seems to include both pre and postbankruptcy payments.

3. LIMITATION OF PRIORITY EXPENSES

The amendment also more generally proscribes the payment or allowance of any other obligations outside of the ordinary course of business as priority administrative expenses unless they are "justified by the facts and circumstances of the case." 11 U.S.C.A. § 503(c)(3).

4. RETIREE HEALTH PLANS

Another change reflecting concern over labor relations in chapter 11 is found in an amendment to Code § 1114 that restricts even prepetition modification of retiree health plans by debtors. Under the amendment, the court is to issue an order of reinstatement of retiree benefits as of the date that the modification was made if (1) the debtor modified the benefits during the 180 days preceding the commencement of the case and (2) the debtor was insolvent at the time the benefits were modified. 11 U.S.C.A. § 1114(*l*). This requirement is qualified by allowing the court to find "that the balance of the equities clearly favors such modification." 11 U.S.C.A. § 1114(*l*)(2).

I. ATTORNEYS AND OTHER OFFICERS AND PROFESSIONALS

1. DISINTERESTEDNESS

The "disinterestedness" definition in 11 U.S.C.A. § 101(14) has been made more permissive in a narrow but important situation by deleting language that automatically rendered investment bankers for a security of the debtor (without regard to the timing of the issuance of the securities) and their attorneys not disinterested. Section 101(14) was amended as follows (deleted material in strikethrough; new material in italics):

(14) ~~"disinterested person" means person that~~

~~(A) is not a creditor, an equity security holder, or an insider;~~

~~(B) is not and was not an investment banker for any outstanding security of the debtor;~~

~~(C) has not been, within three years before the date of the filing of the petition, an investment banker for a security of the debtor, or an attorney for such an investment banker in connection with the offer, sale, or issuance of a security of the debtor;~~ The term 'disinterested person' means a person that—

(A) is not a creditor, an equity security holder, or an insider;

(B) is not and was not, within 2 years before the date of the filing of the petition, a director, officer, or employee of the debtor; and

(C) does not have an interest materially adverse to the interest of the estate or of any class of creditors or equity security holders, by reason of any direct or indirect relationship to, connection with, or interest in, the debtor, or for any other reason;

~~(D) is not and was not, within two years before the date of the filing of the petition, a director, officer, or employee of the debtor or of an investment banker specified in subparagraph (B) or (C) of this paragraph; and~~

~~(E) does not have an interest materially adverse to the interest of the estate or of any class of creditors or equity security holders, by reason of any direct or indirect relationship to, connection with, or interest in, the debtor or an investment banker specified in subparagraph (B) or (C) of this paragraph, or for any other reason;.~~

Now, the only circumstance that would render investment banks not disinterested is found in the general provision that they may not have an interest materially adverse to the estate or any class of creditors or equity security holders.

This loosening of the disinterestedness standard prevailed in an arcane legislative and lobbying debate. The Securities and Exchange Commission resisted the change. In the course of debate, however, it was noted that a tiny group of banking houses would benefit from retention of the former restriction. In the end, more investment bankers were allowed into the coveted business of representing debtors in possession, although at the expense of customary disinterestedness.

2. CERTIFICATION AND OTHER ENHANCEMENT OF COMPENSATION

Section 415 of the bill adds a new subparagraph (E) to § 330(a)(3) of the Code, directing the court to consider whether a professional person is board certified or has otherwise demonstrated skill and experience in the bankruptcy field. The amendment makes board certification a specific factor in the award of compensation to professionals.

HIGHLIGHTED TEXT OF TITLES 11, 18, AND 28

CHAPTER 1—GENERAL PROVISIONS

CHAPTER 3—CASE ADMINISTRATION

CHAPTER 5—CREDITORS, THE DEBTOR, AND THE ESTATE

CHAPTER 7—LIQUIDATION

CHAPTER 9—ADJUSTMENT OF DEBTS OF A MUNICIPALITY

CHAPTER 11—REORGANIZATION

CHAPTER 12—ADJUSTMENT OF DEBTS OF A FAMILY FARMER OR FISHERMAN WITH REGULAR ANNUAL INCOME

CHAPTER 13—ADJUSTMENT OF DEBTS OF AN INDIVIDUAL WITH REGULAR INCOME

CHAPTER 15

CHAPTER 1—GENERAL PROVISIONS

§ 101. Definitions

~~In this title~~—*In this title thefollowing definitions shall apply:*

(1) *The term* "accountant" means accountant authorized under applicable law to practice public accounting, and includes professional accounting association, corporation, or partnership, if so authorized.~~;~~

(2) *The term* "affiliate" means—

(A) entity that directly or indirectly owns, controls, or holds with power to vote, 20 percent or more of the outstanding voting securities of the debtor, other than an entity that holds such securities—

(i) in a fiduciary or agency capacity without sole discretionary power to vote such securities; or

(ii) solely to secure a debt, if such entity has not in fact exercised such power to vote;

(B) corporation 20 percent or more of whose outstanding voting securities are directly or indirectly owned, controlled, or held with power to vote, by the debtor, or by an entity that directly or indirectly owns, controls, or holds with power to vote, 20 percent or more of the outstanding voting securities of the debtor, other than an entity that holds such securities—

(i) in a fiduciary or agency capacity without sole discretionary power to vote such securities; or

(ii) solely to secure a debt, if such entity has not in fact exercised such power to vote;

(C) person whose business is operated under a lease or operating agreement by a debtor, or person substantially all of whose property is operated under an operating agreement with the debtor; or

(D) entity that operates the business or substantially all of the property of the debtor under a lease or operating agreement.~~;~~

(3) The term 'assisted person' means any person whose debts consist primarily of consumer debts and the value of whose nonexempt property is less than $150,000.

[(3) Redesignated (21B)]

(4) *The term* "attorney" means attorney, professional law association, corporation, or partnership, authorized under applicable law to practice law.~~;~~

(4A) The term 'bankruptcy assistance' means any goods or services sold or otherwise provided to an assisted person with the express or implied purpose of providing information, advice, counsel, document preparation, or filing, or attendance at a creditors' meeting or appearing in a case or proceeding on behalf of another or providing legal representation with respect to a case or proceeding under this title.

(5) *The term* "claim" means—

(A) right to payment, whether or not such right is reduced to judgment, liquidated, unliquidated, fixed, contingent, matured, unmatured, disputed, undisputed, legal, equitable, secured, or unsecured; or

(B) right to an equitable remedy for breach of performance if such breach gives rise to a right to payment, whether or not such right to an equitable remedy is reduced to judgment, fixed, contingent, matured, unmatured, disputed, undisputed, secured, or unsecured;.

(6) *The term* "commodity broker" means futures commission merchant, foreign futures commission merchant, clearing organization, leverage transaction merchant, or commodity options dealer, as defined in section 761 of this title, with respect to which there is a customer, as defined in section 761 of this title;.

(7) *The term* "community claim" means claim that arose before the commencement of the case concerning the debtor for which property of the kind specified in section 541(a)(2) of this title is liable, whether or not there is any such property at the time of the commencement of the case;.

(7A) The term 'commercial fishing operation' means—

> *(A) the catching or harvesting of fish, shrimp, lobsters, urchins, seaweed, shellfish, or other aquatic species or products of such species; or*

> *(B) for purposes of section 109 and chapter 12, aquaculture activities consisting of raising for market any species or product described in subparagraph (A).*

(7B) The term 'commercial fishing vessel' means a vessel used by a family fisherman to carry out a commercial fishing operation.;

(8) *The term* "consumer debt" means debt incurred by an individual primarily for a personal, family, or household purpose;.

(9) *The term* "corporation"—

> (A) includes—

>> (i) association having a power or privilege that a private corporation, but not an individual or a partnership, possesses;

>> (ii) partnership association organized under a law that makes only the capital subscribed responsible for the debts of such association;

>> (iii) joint-stock company;

>> (iv) unincorporated company or association; or

>> (v) business trust; but

> (B) does not include limited partnership;.

(10) *The term* "creditor" means—

> (A) entity that has a claim against the debtor that arose at the time of or before the order for relief concerning the debtor;

> (B) entity that has a claim against the estate of a kind specified in section 348(d), 502(f), 502(g), 502(h) or 502(i) of this title; or

> (C) entity that has a community claim;.

(10A) The term 'current monthly income'—

> *(A) means the average monthly income from all sources that the debtor receives (or in a joint case the debtor and the debtor's spouse receive) without regard to whether such income is taxable income, derived during the 6-month period ending on—*

(i) the last day of the calendar month immediately preceding the date of the commencement of the case if the debtor files the schedule of current income required by section 521(a)(1)(B)(ii); or

(ii) the date on which current income is determined by the court for purposes of this title if the debtor does not file the schedule of current income required by section 521(a)(1)(B)(ii); and

(B) includes any amount paid by any entity other than the debtor (or in a joint case the debtor and the debtor's spouse), on a regular basis for the household expenses of the debtor or the debtor's dependents (and in a joint case the debtor's spouse if not otherwise a dependent), but excludes benefits received under the Social Security Act, payments to victims of war crimes or crimes against humanity on account of their status as victims of such crimes, and payments to victims of international terrorism (as defined in section 2331 of title 18) or domestic terrorism (as defined in section 2331 of title 18) on account of their status as victims of such terrorism.

(11) *The term* "custodian" *means*—

(A) receiver or trustee of any of the property of the debtor, appointed in a case or proceeding not under this title;

(B) assignee under a general assignment for the benefit of the debtor's creditors; or

(C) trustee, receiver, or agent under applicable law, or under a contract, that is appointed or authorized to take charge of property of the debtor for the purpose of enforcing a lien against such property, or for the purpose of general administration of such property for the benefit of the debtor's creditors.~;~

(12) *The term* "debt" *means liability on a claim.~;~*

(12A) The term 'debt relief agency' means any person who provides any bankruptcy assistance to an assisted person in return for the payment of money or other valuable consideration, or who is a bankruptcy petition preparer under section 110, but does not include—

(A) any person who is an officer, director, employee, or agent of a person who provides such assistance or of the bankruptcy petition preparer;

(B) a nonprofit organization that is exempt from taxation under section 501(c)(3) of the Internal Revenue Code of 1986;

(C) a creditor of such assisted person, to the extent that the creditor is assisting such assisted person to restructure any debt owed by such assisted person to the creditor;

(D) a depository institution (as defined in section 3 of the Federal Deposit Insurance Act) or any Federal credit union or State credit union (as those terms are defined in section 101 of the Federal Credit Union Act), or any affiliate or subsidiary of such depository institution or credit union; or

(E) an author, publisher, distributor, or seller of works subject to copyright protection under title 17, when acting in such capacity.

~(12A) "debt for child support" means a debt of a kind specified in section 523(a)(5) of this title for maintenance or support of a child of the debtor;~

(13) *The term* "debtor" *means person or municipality concerning which a case under this title has been commenced~;~.*

(13A) The term 'debtor's principal residence'—

(A) means a residential structure, including incidental property, without regard to whether that structure is attached to real property; and

(B) includes an individual condominium or cooperative unit, a mobile or manufactured home, or trailer.

(14) ~~"disinterested person" means person that—~~

~~(A) is not a creditor, an equity security holder, or an insider;~~

~~(B) is not and was not an investment banker for any outstanding security of the debtor;~~

~~(C) has not been, within three years before the date of the filing of the petition, an investment banker for a security of the debtor, or an attorney for such an investment banker in connection with the offer, sale, or issuance of a security of the debtor;~~ The term 'disinterested person' means a person that—

(A) is not a creditor, an equity security holder, or an insider;

(B) is not and was not, within 2 years before the date of the filing of the petition, a director, officer, or employee of the debtor; and

(C) does not have an interest materially adverse to the interest of the estate or of any class of creditors or equity security holders, by reason of any direct or indirect relationship to, connection with, or interest in, the debtor, or for any other reason;

~~(D) is not and was not, within two years before the date of the filing of the petition, a director, officer, or employee of the debtor or of an investment banker specified in subparagraph (B) or (C) of this paragraph; and~~

~~(E) does not have an interest materially adverse to the interest of the estate or of any class of creditors or equity security holders, by reason of any direct or indirect relationship to, connection with, or interest in, the debtor or an investment banker specified in subparagraph (B) or (C) of this paragraph, or for any other reason;.~~

(14A) The term 'domestic support obligation' means a debt that accrues before, on, or after the date of the order for relief in a case under this title, including interest that accrues on that debt as provided under applicable nonbankruptcy law notwithstanding any other provision of this title, that is—

(A) owed to or recoverable by—

(i) a spouse, former spouse, or child of the debtor or such child's parent, legal guardian, or responsible relative; or

(ii) a governmental unit;

(B) in the nature of alimony, maintenance, or support (including assistance provided by a governmental unit) of such spouse, former spouse, or child of the debtor or such child's parent, without regard to whether such debt is expressly so designated;

(C) established or subject to establishment before, on, or after the date of the order for relief in a case under this title, by reason of applicable provisions of—

(i) a separation agreement, divorce decree, or property settlement agreement;

(ii) an order of a court of record; or

(iii) a determination made in accordance with applicable nonbankruptcy law by a governmental unit; and

(D) not assigned to a nongovernmental entity, unless that obligation is assigned voluntarily by the spouse, former spouse, child of the debtor, or such child's parent, legal guardian, or responsible relative for the purpose of collecting the debt.

(15) *The term* "entity" includes person, estate, trust, governmental unit, and United States trustee.~~;~~

(16) *The term* "equity security" means—

(A) share in a corporation, whether or not transferable or denominated "stock", or similar security;

(B) interest of a limited partner in a limited partnership; or

(C) warrant or right, other than a right to convert, to purchase, sell, or subscribe to a share, security, or interest of a kind specified in subparagraph (A) or (B) of this paragraph~~.~~;

(17) *The term* "equity security holder" means holder of an equity security of the debtor.~~;~~

(18) *The term* "family farmer" means—

(A) individual or individual and spouse engaged in a farming operation whose aggregate debts do not exceed $~~1,500,000~~*3,237,000* and not less than ~~80~~*50* percent of whose aggregate noncontingent, liquidated debts (excluding a debt for the principal residence of such individual or such individual and spouse unless such debt arises out of a farming operation), on the date the case is filed, arise out of a farming operation owned or operated by such individual or such individual and spouse, and such individual or such individual and spouse receive from such farming operation more than 50 percent of such individual's or such individual and spouse's gross income ~~for the taxable year preceding the taxable year~~ *for—*

(i) the taxable year preceding; or

(ii) each of the 2d and 3d taxable years preceding; the taxable year in which the case concerning such individual or such individual and spouse was filed; or

(B) corporation or partnership in which more than 50 percent of the outstanding stock or equity is held by one family, or by one family and the relatives of the members of such family, and such family or such relatives conduct the farming operation, and

(i) more than 80 percent of the value of its assets consists of assets related to the farming operation;

(ii) its aggregate debts do not exceed $~~1,500,000~~*3,237,000* and not less than ~~80~~*50* percent of its aggregate noncontingent, liquidated debts (excluding a debt for one dwelling which is owned by such corporation or partnership and which a shareholder or partner maintains as a principal residence, unless such debt arises out of a farming operation), on the date the case is filed, arise out of the farming operation owned or operated by such corporation or such partnership; and

(iii) if such corporation issues stock, such stock is not publicly traded.~~;~~

(19) *The term* "family farmer with regular annual income" means family farmer whose annual income is sufficiently stable and regular to enable such family farmer to make payments under a plan under chapter 12 of this title;.

(19A) The term 'family fisherman' means

(A) an individual or individual and spouse engaged in a commercial fishing operation—

(i) whose aggregate debts do not exceed $1,500,000 and not less than 80 percent of whose aggregate noncontingent, liquidated debts (excluding a debt for the principal residence of such individual or such individual and spouse, unless such debt arises out of a commercial fishing operation), on the date the case is filed, arise out of a commercial fishing operation owned or operated by such individual or such individual and spouse; and

(ii) who receive from such commercial fishing operation more than 50 percent of such individual's or such individual's and spouse's gross income for the taxable year preceding the taxable year in which the case concerning such individual or such individual and spouse was filed; or

(B) a corporation or partnership—

(i) in which more than 50 percent of the outstanding stock or equity is held by—

(I) 1 family that conducts the commercial fishing operation; or

(II) 1 family and the relatives of the members of such family, and such family or such relatives conduct the commercial fishing operation; and

(ii)(I) more than 80 percent of the value of its assets consists of assets related to the commercial fishing operation;

(II) its aggregate debts do not exceed $1,500,000 and not less than 80 percent of its aggregate noncontingent, liquidated debts (excluding a debt for 1 dwelling which is owned by such corporation or partnership and which a shareholder or partner maintains as a principal residence, unless such debt arises out of a commercial fishing operation), on the date the case is filed, arise out of a commercial fishing operation owned or operated by such corporation or such partnership; and

(III) if such corporation issues stock, such stock is not publicly traded.

(19B) The term 'family fisherman with regular annual income' means a family fisherman whose annual income is sufficiently stable and regular to enable such family fisherman to make payments under a plan under chapter 12 of this title.

(20) *The term* "farmer" means (except when such term appears in the term "family farmer") person that received more than 80 percent of such person's gross income during the taxable year of such person immediately preceding the taxable year of such person during which the case under this title concerning such person was commenced from a farming operation owned or operated by such person;.

(21) *The term* "farming operation" includes farming, tillage of the soil, dairy farming, ranching, production or raising of crops, poultry, or livestock, and production of poultry or livestock products in an unmanufactured state;.

(21A) *The term* "farmout agreement" means a written agreement in which—

(A) the owner of a right to drill, produce, or operate liquid or gaseous hydrocarbons on property agrees or has agreed to transfer or assign all or a part of such right to another entity; and

(B) such other entity (either directly or through its agents or its assigns), as consideration, agrees to perform drilling, reworking, recompleting, testing, or similar or related operations, to develop or produce liquid or gaseous hydrocarbons on the property;.

(21B) *The term* "Federal depository institutions regulatory agency" means—

(A) with respect to an insured depository institution (as defined in section 3(c)(2) of the Federal Deposit Insurance Act) for which no conservator or receiver has been appointed, the appropriate Federal banking agency (as defined in section 3(q) of such Act);

(B) with respect to an insured credit union (including an insured credit union for which the National Credit Union Administration has been appointed conservator or liquidating agent), the National Credit Union Administration;

(C) with respect to any insured depository institution for which the Resolution Trust Corporation has been appointed conservator or receiver, the Resolution Trust Corporation; and

(D) with respect to any insured depository institution for which the Federal Deposit Insurance Corporation has been appointed conservator or receiver, the Federal Deposit Insurance Corporation.;

(22) the term "financial institution"—

(A) means—

(i) a Federal reserve bank or an entity (domestic or foreign) that is a commercial or savings bank, industrial savings bank, savings and loan association, trust company, or receiver or conservator for such entity and, when any such Federal reserve bank, receiver, conservator, or entity is acting as agent or custodian for a customer in connection with a securities contract, as defined in section 741 of this title, the customer; or

(ii) in connection with a securities contract, as defined in section 741 of this title, an investment company registered under the Investment Company Act of 1940; and

(B) includes any person described in subparagraph (A) which operates, or operates as, a multilateral clearing organization pursuant to section 409 of the Federal Deposit Insurance Corporation Improvement Act of 1991; *(22) The term 'financial institution' means—*

(A) a Federal reserve bank, or an entity (domestic or foreign) that is a commercial or savings bank, industrial savings bank, savings and loan association, trust company, federally-insured credit union, or receiver, liquidating agent, or conservator for such entity and, when any such Federal reserve bank, receiver, liquidating agent, conservator or entity is acting as agent or custodian for a customer in connection with a securities contract (as defined in section 741) such customer; or

(B) in connection with a securities contract (as defined in section 741) an investment company registered under the Investment Company Act of 1940.

(22A) The term 'financial participant' means—

(A) an entity that, at the time it enters into a securities contract, commodity contract, swap agreement, repurchase agreement, or forward contract, or at the time of the date of the filing of the petition, has one or more agreements or transactions described in paragraph (1), (2), (3), (4), (5), or (6) of section 561(a) with the debtor or any other entity (other than an affiliate) of a total gross dollar value of not less than $1,000,000,000 in notional or actual principal amount outstanding on any day during the previous 15-month period, or has gross mark-to-market positions of not less than $100,000,000 (aggregated across counterparties) in one or more such agreements or transactions with the debtor or any other entity (other than an affiliate) on any day during the previous 15-month period; or

(B) a clearing organization (as defined in section 402 of the Federal Deposit Insurance Corporation Improvement Act of 1991).

~~(23) "foreign proceeding" means proceeding, whether judicial or administrative and whether or not under bankruptcy law, in a foreign country in which the debtor's domicile, residence, principal place of business, or principal assets were located at the commencement of such proceeding, for the purpose of liquidating an estate, adjusting debts by composition, extension, or discharge, or effecting a reorganization;~~

(23) The term 'foreign proceeding' means a collective judicial or administrative proceeding in a foreign country, including an interim proceeding, under a law relating to insolvency or adjustment of debt in which proceeding the assets and affairs of the debtor are subject to control or supervision by a foreign court, for the purpose of reorganization or liquidation.

~~(24) "foreign representative" means duly selected trustee, administrator, or other representative of an estate in a foreign proceeding;~~

(24) The term 'foreign representative' means a person or body, including a person or body appointed on an interim basis, authorized in a foreign proceeding to administer the reorganization or the liquidation of the debtor's assets or affairs or to act as a representative of such foreign proceeding.

(25) *The term* "forward contract" ~~means a contract~~ *means—*

(A) a contract (other than a commodity contract) for the purchase, sale, or transfer of a commodity, as defined in section 761(8) of this title, or any similar good, article, service, right, or interest which is presently or in the future becomes the subject of dealing in the forward contract trade, or product or byproduct thereof, with a maturity date more than two days after the date the contract is entered into, including, but not limited to, a repurchase transaction, reverse repurchase transaction, consignment, lease, swap, hedge transaction, deposit, loan, option, allocated transaction, unallocated transaction, *or any other similar agreement;*

(B) any combination of agreements or transactions referred to in subparagraphs (A) and (C);

(C) any option to enter into an agreement or transaction referred to in subparagraph (A) or (B);

(D) a master agreement that provides for an agreement or transaction referred to in subparagraph (A), (B), or (C), together with all supplements to any such master agreement, without regard to whether such master agreement provides for an agreement or transaction that is not a forward contract under this paragraph, except that such master agreement shall be consid-

ered to be a forward contract under this paragraph only with respect to each agreement or transaction under such master agreement that is referred to in subparagraph (A), (B), or (C); or

(E) any security agreement or arrangement, or other credit enhancement related to any agreement or transaction referred to in subparagraph (A), (B), (C), or (D), including any guarantee or reimbursement obligation by or to a forward contract merchant or financial participant in connection with any agreement or transaction referred to in any such subparagraph, but not to exceed the damages in connection with any such agreement or transaction, measured in accordance with section 562.

~~(26) "forward contract merchant" means a person whose business consists in whole or in part of entering into forward contracts as or with merchants in a commodity, as defined in section 761(8) of this title, or any similar good, article, service, right, or interest which is presently or in the future becomes the subject of dealing in the forward contract trade;~~ *(26) The term 'forward contract merchant' means a Federal reserve bank, or an entity the business of which consists in whole or in part of entering into forward contracts as or with merchants in a commodity (as defined in section 761) or any similar good, article, service, right, or interest which is presently or in the future becomes the subject of dealing in the forward contract trade.*

(27) *The term* "governmental unit" means United States; State; Commonwealth; District; Territory; municipality; foreign state; department, agency, or instrumentality of the United States (but not a United States trustee while serving as a trustee in a case under this title), a State, a Commonwealth, a District, a Territory, a municipality, or a foreign state; or other foreign or domestic government.~~;~~

(27A) The term 'health care business'—

(A) means any public or private entity (without regard to whether that entity is organized for profit or not for profit) that is primarily engaged in offering to the general public facilities and services for—

(i) the diagnosis or treatment of injury, deformity, or disease; and

(ii) surgical, drug treatment, psychiatric, or obstetric care; and

(B) includes—

(i) any—

(I) general or specialized hospital;

(II) ancillary ambulatory, emergency, or surgical treatment facility;

(III) hospice;

(IV) home health agency; and

(V) other health care institution that is similar to an entity referred to in subclause (I), (II), (III), or (IV); and

(ii) any long-term care facility, including any—

(I) skilled nursing facility;

(II) intermediate care facility;

(III) assisted living facility;

(IV) home for the aged;

(V) domiciliary care facility; and

(VI) health care institution that is related to a facility referred to in subclause (I), (II), (III), (IV), or (V), if that institution is primarily engaged in offering room, board, laundry, or personal assistance with activities of daily living and incidentals to activities of daily living.

(27B) The term 'incidental property' means, with respect to a debtor's principal residence—

(A) property commonly conveyed with a principal residence in the area where the real property is located;

(B) all easements, rights, appurtenances, fixtures, rents, royalties, mineral rights, oil or gas rights or profits, water rights, escrow funds, or insurance proceeds; and

(C) all replacements or additions.

(28) *The term* "indenture" means mortgage, deed of trust, or indenture, under which there is outstanding a security, other than a voting-trust certificate, constituting a claim against the debtor, a claim secured by a lien on any of the debtor's property, or an equity security of the debtor.÷

(29) *The term* "indenture trustee" means trustee under an indenture.÷

(30) *The term* "individual with regular income" means individual whose income is sufficiently stable and regular to enable such individual to make payments under a plan under chapter 13 of this title, other than a stockbroker or a commodity broker÷.

(31) *The term* "insider" includes—

(A) if the debtor is an individual—

(i) relative of the debtor or of a general partner of the debtor;

(ii) partnership in which the debtor is a general partner;

(iii) general partner of the debtor; or

(iv) corporation of which the debtor is a director, officer, or person in control;

(B) if the debtor is a corporation—

(i) director of the debtor;

(ii) officer of the debtor;

(iii) person in control of the debtor;

(iv) partnership in which the debtor is a general partner;

(v) general partner of the debtor; or

(vi) relative of a general partner, director, officer, or person in control of the debtor;

(C) if the debtor is a partnership—

(i) general partner in the debtor;

(ii) relative of a general partner in, general partner of, or person in control of the debtor;

(iii) partnership in which the debtor is a general partner;

(iv) general partner of the debtor; or

(v) person in control of the debtor;

(D) if the debtor is a municipality, elected official of the debtor or relative of an elected official of the debtor;

(E) affiliate, or insider of an affiliate as if such affiliate were the debtor; and

(F) managing agent of the debtor.;

(32) *The term* "insolvent" means—

(A) with reference to an entity other than a partnership and a municipality, financial condition such that the sum of such entity's debts is greater than all of such entity's property, at a fair valuation, exclusive of—

(i) property transferred, concealed, or removed with intent to hinder, delay, or defraud such entity's creditors; and

(ii) property that may be exempted from property of the estate under section 522 of this title;

(B) with reference to a partnership, financial condition such that the sum of such partnership's debts is greater than the aggregate of, at a fair valuation—

(i) all of such partnership's property, exclusive of property of the kind specified in subparagraph (A)(i) of this paragraph; and

(ii) the sum of the excess of the value of each general partner's nonpartnership property, exclusive of property of the kind specified in subparagraph (A) of this paragraph, over such partner's nonpartnership debts; and

(C) with reference to a municipality, financial condition such that the municipality is—

(i) generally not paying its debts as they become due unless such debts are the subject of a bona fide dispute; or

(ii) unable to pay its debts as they become due.;

(33) *The term* "institution-affiliated party"—

(A) with respect to an insured depository institution (as defined in section 3(c)(2) of the Federal Deposit Insurance Act), has the meaning given it in section 3(u) of the Federal Deposit Insurance Act; and

(B) with respect to an insured credit union, has the meaning given it in section 206(r) of the Federal Credit Union Act.;

(34) *The term* "insured credit union" has the meaning given it in section 101(7) of the Federal Credit Union Act.;

(35) *The term* "insured depository institution"—

(A) has the meaning given it in section 3(c)(2) of the Federal Deposit Insurance Act; and

(B) includes an insured credit union (except in the case of paragraphs (21B) and (33)(A) *(23) and (35)* of this subsection).;

(35A) *The term* "intellectual property" means—

(A) trade secret;

(B) invention, process, design, or plant protected under title 35;

(C) patent application;

(D) plant variety;

(E) work of authorship protected under title 17; or

(F) mask work protected under chapter 9 of title 17;

to the extent protected by applicable nonbankruptcy law.; and

(36) *The term* "judicial lien" means lien obtained by judgment, levy, sequestration, or other legal or equitable process or proceeding.;

(37) "lien" means charge against or interest in property to secure payment of a debt or performance of an obligation.;

(38) *The term* "margin payment" means, for purposes of the forward contract provisions of this title, payment or deposit of cash, a security or other property, that is commonly known in the forward contract trade as original margin, initial margin, maintenance margin, or variation margin, including mark-to-market payments, or variation payments.; and

(38A) The term 'master netting agreement'—

(A) means an agreement providing for the exercise of rights, including rights of netting, setoff, liquidation, termination, acceleration, or close out, under or in connection with one or more contracts that are described in any one or more of paragraphs (1) through (5) of section 561(a), or any security agreement or arrangement or other credit enhancement related to one or more of the foregoing, including any guarantee or reimbursement obligation related to 1 or more of the foregoing; and

(B) if the agreement contains provisions relating to agreements or transactions that are not contracts described in paragraphs (1) through (5) of section 561(a), shall be deemed to be a master netting agreement only with respect to those agreements or transactions that are described in any one or more of paragraphs (1) through (5) of section 561(a).

(38B) The term 'master netting agreement participant' means an entity that, at any time before the date of the filing of the petition, is a party to an outstanding master netting agreement with the debtor.

(39) *The term* "mask work" has the meaning given it in section 901(a)(2) of title 17.

(39A) The term 'median family income' means for any year—

(A) the median family income both calculated and reported by the Bureau of the Census in the then most recent year; and

(B) if not so calculated and reported in the then current year, adjusted annually after such most recent year until the next year in which median family income is both calculated and reported by the Bureau of the Census, to reflect the percentage change in the Consumer Price Index for All Urban Consumers during the period of years occurring after such most recent year and before such current year.

(40) *The term* "municipality" means political subdivision or public agency or instrumentality of a State.;

(40A) The term 'patient' means any individual who obtains or receives services from a health care business.

(40B) The term 'patient records' means any written document relating to a patient or a record recorded in a magnetic, optical, or other form of electronic medium.

(41) *The term* "person" includes individual, partnership, and corporation, but does not include governmental unit, except that a governmental unit that—

(A) acquires an asset from a person—

(i) as a result of the operation of a loan guarantee agreement; or

(ii) as receiver or liquidating agent of a person;

(B) is a guarantor of a pension benefit payable by or on behalf of the debtor or an affiliate of the debtor; or

(C) is the legal or beneficial owner of an asset of—

(i) an employee pension benefit plan that is a governmental plan, as defined in section 414(d) of the Internal Revenue Code of 1986; or

(ii) an eligible deferred compensation plan, as defined in section 457(b) of the Internal Revenue Code of 1986;

shall be considered, for purposes of section 1102 of this title, to be a person with respect to such asset or such benefit.;

(41A) The term 'personally identifiable information' means—

(A) if provided by an individual to the debtor in connection with obtaining a product or a service from the debtor primarily for personal, family, or household purposes—

(i) the first name (or initial) and last name of such individual, whether given at birth or time of adoption, or resulting from a lawful change of name;

(ii) the geographical address of a physical place of residence of such individual;

(iii) an electronic address (including an e-mail address) of such individual;

(iv) a telephone number dedicated to contacting such individual at such physical place of residence;

(v) a social security account number issued to such individual; or

(vi) the account number of a credit card issued to such individual; or

(B) if identified in connection with 1 or more of the items of information specified in subparagraph (A)—

(i) a birth date, the number of a certificate of birth or adoption, or a place of birth; or

(ii) any other information concerning an identified individual that, if disclosed, will result in contacting or identifying such individual physically or electronically.

(42) *The term* "petition" means petition filed under section 301, 302, 303, or 304 of this title, as the case may be, commencing a case under this title.;

(42A) *The term* "production payment" means a term overriding royalty satisfiable in cash or in kind—

(A) contingent on the production of a liquid or gaseous hydrocarbon from particular real property; and

(B) from a specified volume, or a specified value, from the liquid or gaseous hydrocarbon produced from such property, and determined without regard to production costs.;

(43) *The term* "purchaser" means transferee of a voluntary transfer, and includes immediate or mediate transferee of such a transferee.;

(44) *The term* "railroad" means common carrier by railroad engaged in the transportation of individuals or property or owner of trackage facilities leased by such a common carrier.;

(45) *The term* "relative" means individual related by affinity or consanguinity within the third degree as determined by the common law, or individual in a step or adoptive relationship within such third degree.;

(46) *The term* "repo participant" means an entity that, on any day during the period beginning 90 days before the date of *at any time before* the filing of the petition, has an outstanding repurchase agreement with the debtor.;

(47) *The term* "repurchase agreement" ~~(which definition also applies to a reverse repurchase agreement) means an agreement, including related terms, which provides for the transfer of certificates of deposit, eligible bankers' acceptances, or securities that are direct obligations of, or that are fully guaranteed as to principal and interest by, the United States or any agency of the United States against the transfer of funds by the transferee of such certificates of deposit, eligible bankers' acceptances, or securities with a simultaneous agreement by such transferee to transfer to the transferor thereof certificates of deposit, eligible bankers' acceptances, or securities as described above, at a date certain not later than one year after such transfers or on demand, against the transfer of funds;~~ *(which definition also applies to a reverse repurchase agreement)—*

(A) means—

(i) an agreement, including related terms, which provides for the transfer of one or more certificates of deposit, mortgage related securities (as defined in section 3 of the Securities Exchange Act of 1934), mortgage loans, interests in mortgage related securities or mortgage loans, eligible bankers' acceptances, qualified foreign government securities (defined as a security that is a direct obligation of, or that is fully guaranteed by, the central government of a member of the Organization for Economic Cooperation and Development), or securities that are direct obligations of, or that are fully guaranteed by, the United States or any agency of the United States against the transfer of funds by the transferee of such certificates of deposit, eligible bankers' acceptances, securities, mortgage loans, or interests, with a simultaneous agreement by such transferee to transfer to the transferor thereof certificates of deposit, eligible bankers' acceptance, securities, mortgage loans, or interests of the kind described in this clause, at a date certain not later than 1 year after such transfer or on demand, against the transfer of funds;

(ii) any combination of agreements or transactions referred to in clauses (i) and (iii);

(iii) an option to enter into an agreement or transaction referred to in clause (i) or (ii);

(iv) a master agreement that provides for an agreement or transaction referred to in clause (i), (ii), or (iii), together with all supplements to any such master agreement, without regard to whether such master agreement provides for an agreement or transaction that is not a repurchase agreement under this paragraph, except that such master agreement shall be considered to be a repurchase agreement under this paragraph only with

respect to each agreement or transaction under the master agreement that is referred to in clause (i), (ii), or (iii); or

(v) any security agreement or arrangement or other credit enhancement related to any agreement or transaction referred to in clause (i), (ii), (iii), or (iv), including any guarantee or reimbursement obligation by or to a repo participant or financial participant in connection with any agreement or transaction referred to in any such clause, but not to exceed the damages in connection with any such agreement or transaction, measured in accordance with section 562 of this title; and

(B) does not include a repurchase obligation under a participation in a commercial mortgage loan.

(48) *The term* "securities clearing agency" means person that is registered as a clearing agency under section 17A of the Securities Exchange Act of 1934, *or exempt from such registration under such section pursuant to an order of the Securities and Exchange Commission,* or whose business is confined to the performance of functions of a clearing agency with respect to exempted securities, as defined in section 3(a)(12) of such Act for the purposes of such section 17A.;

(48A) The term 'securities self regulatory organization' means either a securities association registered with the Securities and Exchange Commission under section 15A of the Securities Exchange Act of 1934 or a national securities exchange registered with the Securities and Exchange Commission under section 6 of the Securities Exchange Act of 1934.

(49) *The term* "security"—

  (A) includes—

    (i) note;

    (ii) stock;

    (iii) treasury stock;

    (iv) bond;

    (v) debenture;

    (vi) collateral trust certificate;

    (vii) pre-organization certificate or subscription;

    (viii) transferable share;

    (ix) voting-trust certificate;

    (x) certificate of deposit;

    (xi) certificate of deposit for security;

    (xii) investment contract or certificate of interest or participation in a profit-sharing agreement or in an oil, gas, or mineral royalty or lease, if such contract or interest is required to be the subject of a registration statement filed with the Securities and Exchange Commission under the provisions of the Securities Act of 1933, or is exempt under section 3(b) of such Act from the requirement to file such a statement;

    (xiii) interest of a limited partner in a limited partnership;

    (xiv) other claim or interest commonly known as "security"; and

    (xv) certificate of interest or participation in, temporary or interim certificate for, receipt for, or warrant or right to subscribe to or purchase or sell, a security; but

(B) does not include—

(i) currency, check, draft, bill of exchange, or bank letter of credit;

(ii) leverage transaction, as defined in section 761 of this title;

(iii) commodity futures contract or forward contract;

(iv) option, warrant, or right to subscribe to or purchase or sell a commodity futures contract;

(v) option to purchase or sell a commodity;

(vi) contract or certificate of a kind specified in subparagraph (A)(xii) of this paragraph that is not required to be the subject of a registration statement filed with the Securities and Exchange Commission and is not exempt under section 3(b) of the Securities Act of 1933 from the requirement to file such a statement; or

(vii) debt or evidence of indebtedness for goods sold and delivered or services rendered.;

(50) *The term* "security agreement" means agreement that creates or provides for a security interest.;

(51) *The term* "security interest" means lien created by an agreement.;

(51A) *The term* "settlement payment" means, for purposes of the forward contract provisions of this title, a preliminary settlement payment, a partial settlement payment, an interim settlement payment, a settlement payment on account, a final settlement payment, a net settlement payment, or any other similar payment commonly used in the forward contract trade.;

(51B) *The term* "single asset real estate" means real property constituting a single property or project, other than residential real property with fewer than 4 residential units, which generates substantially all of the gross income of a debtor *who is not a family farmer* and on which no substantial business is being conducted by a debtor other than the business of operating the real property and activities incidental ~~thereto having aggregate noncontingent, liquidated secured debts in an amount no more than $4,000,000.~~;

~~(51C) "small business" means a person engaged in commercial or business activities (but does not include a person whose primary activity is the business of owning or operating real property and activities incidental thereto) whose aggregate noncontingent liquidated secured and unsecured debts as of the date of the petition do not exceed $2,000,000;~~

(51C) The term 'small business case' means a case filed under chapter 11 of this title in which the debtor is a small business debtor.

(51D) The term 'small business debtor'—

(A) subject to subparagraph (B), means a person engaged in commercial or business activities (including any affiliate of such person that is also a debtor under this title and excluding a person whose primary activity is the business of owning or operating real property or activities incidental thereto) that has aggregate noncontingent liquidated secured and unsecured debts as of the date of the petition or the date of the order for relief in an amount not more than $2,000,000 (excluding debts owed to 1 or more affiliates or insiders) for a case in which the United States trustee has not appointed under section 1102(a)(1) a committee of unsecured creditors or where the court has determined that the committee of unsecured creditors is

not sufficiently active and representative to provide effective oversight of the debtor; and

(B) does not include any member of a group of affiliated debtors that has aggregate noncontingent liquidated secured and unsecured debts in an amount greater than $2,000,000 (excluding debt owed to 1 or more affiliates or insiders).

(52) *The term* "State" includes the District of Columbia and Puerto Rico, except for the purpose of defining who may be a debtor under chapter 9 of this title.;

(53) *The term* "statutory lien" means lien arising solely by force of a statute on specified circumstances or conditions, or lien of distress for rent, whether or not statutory, but does not include security interest or judicial lien, whether or not such interest or lien is provided by or is dependent on a statute and whether or not such interest or lien is made fully effective by statute.;

(53A) *The term* "stockbroker" means person—

(A) with respect to which there is a customer, as defined in section 741 of this title; and

(B) that is engaged in the business of effecting transactions in securities—

(i) for the account of others; or

(ii) with members of the general public, from or for such person's own account.;

(53B) ~~"swap agreement" means—~~

~~(A) an agreement (including terms and conditions incorporated by reference therein) which is a rate swap agreement, basis swap, forward rate agreement, commodity swap, interest rate option, forward foreign exchange agreement, spot foreign exchange agreement, rate cap agreement, rate floor agreement, rate collar agreement, currency swap agreement, cross-currency rate swap agreement, currency option, any other similar agreement (including any option to enter into any of the foregoing);~~

~~(B) any combination of the foregoing; or~~

~~(C) a master agreement for any of the foregoing together with all supplements;~~ *The term 'swap agreement'—*

(A) means—

(i) any agreement, including the terms and conditions incorporated by reference in such agreement, which is—

(I) an interest rate swap, option, future, or forward agreement, including a rate floor, rate cap, rate collar, cross-currency rate swap, and basis swap;

(II) a spot, same day-tomorrow, tomorrow-next, forward, or other foreign exchange or precious metals agreement;

(III) a currency swap, option, future, or forward agreement;

(IV) an equity index or equity swap, option, future, or forward agreement;

(V) a debt index or debt swap, option, future, or forward agreement;

(VI) a total return, credit spread or credit swap, option, future, or forward agreement;

(VII) a commodity index or a commodity swap, option, future, or forward agreement; or

(VIII) a weather swap, weather derivative, or weather option;

(ii) any agreement or transaction that is similar to any other agreement or transaction referred to in this paragraph and that—

(I) is of a type that has been, is presently, or in the future becomes, the subject of recurrent dealings in the swap markets (including terms and conditions incorporated by reference therein); and

(II) is a forward, swap, future, or option on one or more rates, currencies, commodities, equity securities, or other equity instruments, debt securities or other debt instruments, quantitative measures associated with an occurrence, extent of an occurrence, or contingency associated with a financial, commercial, or economic consequence, or economic or financial indices or measures of economic or financial risk or value;

(iii) any combination of agreements or transactions referred to in this subparagraph;

(iv) any option to enter into an agreement or transaction referred to in this subparagraph;

(v) a master agreement that provides for an agreement or transaction referred to in clause (i), (ii), (iii), or (iv), together with all supplements to any such master agreement, and without regard to whether the master agreement contains an agreement or transaction that is not a swap agreement under this paragraph, except that the master agreement shall be considered to be a swap agreement under this paragraph only with respect to each agreement or transaction under the master agreement that is referred to in clause (i), (ii), (iii), or (iv); or

(vi) any security agreement or arrangement or other credit enhancement related to any agreements or transactions referred to in clause (i) through (v), including any guarantee or reimbursement obligation by or to a swap participant or financial participant in connection with any agreement or transaction referred to in any such clause, but not to exceed the damages in connection with any such agreement or transaction, measured in accordance with section 562; and

(B) is applicable for purposes of this title only, and shall not be construed or applied so as to challenge or affect the characterization, definition, or treatment of any swap agreement under any other statute, regulation, or rule, including the Securities Act of 1933, the Securities Exchange Act of 1934, the Public Utility Holding Company Act of 1935, the Trust Indenture Act of 1939, the Investment Company Act of 1940, the Investment Advisers Act of 1940, the Securities Investor Protection Act of 1970, the Commodity Exchange Act, the Gramm-Leach-Bliley Act, and the Legal Certainty for Bank Products Act of 2000.

(53C) *The term* "swap participant" means an entity that, at any time before the filing of the petition, has an outstanding swap agreement with the debtor.;

(56A) "term overriding royalty" means an interest in liquid or gaseous hydrocarbons in place or to be produced from particular real property that entitles the owner thereof to a share of production, or the value thereof, for a term limited by time, quantity, or value realized;

(53D) *The term* "timeshare plan" means and shall include that interest purchased in any arrangement, plan, scheme, or similar device, but not including exchange programs, whether by membership, agreement, tenancy in common, sale, lease, deed, rental agreement, license, right to use agreement, or by any other means, whereby a purchaser, in exchange for consideration, receives a right to use accommodations, facilities, or recreational sites, whether improved or unimproved, for a specific period of time less than a full year during any given year, but not necessarily for consecutive years, and which extends for a period of more than three years. A "timeshare interest" is that interest purchased in a timeshare plan which grants the purchaser the right to use and occupy accommodations, facilities, or recreational sites, whether improved or unimproved, pursuant to a timeshare plan.~;~

~(54) "transfer" means every mode, direct or indirect, absolute or conditional, voluntary or involuntary, of disposing of or parting with property or with an interest in property, including retention of title as a security interest and foreclosure of the debtor's equity of redemption;~ *(54) The term 'transfer' means—*

   (A) the creation of a lien;

   (B) the retention of title as a security interest;

   (C) the foreclosure of a debtor's equity of redemption; or

   (D) each mode, direct or indirect, absolute or conditional, voluntary or involuntary, of disposing of or parting with—

     (i) property; or

     (ii) an interest in property.

(54A) *T*~t~he term "uninsured State member bank" means a State member bank (as defined in section 3 of the Federal Deposit Insurance Act) the deposits of which are not insured by the Federal Deposit Insurance Corporation. ~; and~

(55) *The term* "United States", when used in a geographical sense, includes all locations where the judicial jurisdiction of the United States extends, including territories and possessions of the United States~;~.

§ 102. Rules of construction

In this title—

   (1) "after notice and a hearing", or a similar phrase—

     (A) means after such notice as is appropriate in the particular circumstances, and such opportunity for a hearing as is appropriate in the particular circumstances; but

     (B) authorizes an act without an actual hearing if such notice is given properly and if—

       (i) such a hearing is not requested timely by a party in interest; or

       (ii) there is insufficient time for a hearing to be commenced before such act must be done, and the court authorizes such act;

   (2) "claim against the debtor" includes claim against property of the debtor;

   (3) "includes" and "including" are not limiting;

   (4) "may not" is prohibitive, and not permissive;

   (5) "or" is not exclusive;

(6) "order for relief" means entry of an order for relief;

(7) the singular includes the plural;

(8) a definition, contained in a section of this title that refers to another section of this title, does not, for the purpose of such reference, affect the meaning of a term used in such other section; and

(9) "United States trustee" includes a designee of the United States trustee.

§ 103. Applicability of chapters

(a) Except as provided in section 1161 of this title, chapters 1, 3, and 5 of this title apply in a case under chapter 7, 11, 12, or 13 of this title, *and this chapter, sections 307, 362(n), 555 through 557, and 559 through 562 apply in a case under chapter 15.*

(b) Subchapters I and II of chapter 7 of this title apply only in a case under such chapter.

(c) Subchapter III of chapter 7 of this title applies only in a case under such chapter concerning a stockbroker.

(d) Subchapter IV of chapter 7 of this title applies only in a case under such chapter concerning a commodity broker.

(e) Scope of application.—Subchapter V of chapter 7 of this title shall apply only in a case under such chapter concerning the liquidation of an uninsured State member bank, or a corporation organized under section 25A of the Federal Reserve Act, which operates, or operates as, a multilateral clearing organization pursuant to section 409 of the Federal Deposit Insurance Corporation Improvement Act of 1991.

(f) Except as provided in section 901 of this title, only chapters 1 and 9 of this title apply in a case under such chapter 9.

(g) Except as provided in section 901 of this title, subchapters I, II, and III of chapter 11 of this title apply only in a case under such chapter.

(h) Subchapter IV of chapter 11 of this title applies only in a case under such chapter concerning a railroad.

(i) Chapter 13 of this title applies only in a case under such chapter.

(j) Chapter 12 of this title applies only in a case under such chapter.

(k) Chapter 15 applies only in a case under such chapter, except that—

(1) sections 1505, 1513, and 1514 apply in all cases under this title; and

(2) section 1509 applies whether or not a case under this title is pending.

§ 104. Adjustment of dollar amounts

(a) The Judicial Conference of the United States shall transmit to the Congress and to the President before May 1, 1985, and before May 1 of every sixth year after May 1, 1985, a recommendation for the uniform percentage adjustment of each dollar amount in this title and in section 1930 of title 28.

(b)(1) On April 1, 1998, and at each 3-year interval ending on April 1 thereafter, each dollar amount in effect under sections *101(3),101(18), 101(19A), 101(51D),* 109(e), 303(b), 507(a), 522(d), *522(f)(3) and 522(f)(4), 522(n),522(p), 522(q),* and 523(a)(2)(C), *541(b), 547(c)(9), 707(b), 1322(d),*

1325(b)(3) and 1326(b)(3) of this title and section 1409(b) of title 28 immediately before such April 1 shall be adjusted—

(A) to reflect the change in the Consumer Price Index for All Urban Consumers, published by the Department of Labor, for the most recent 3-year period ending immediately before January 1 preceding such April 1, and

(B) to round to the nearest $25 the dollar amount that represents such change.

(2) Not later than March 1, 1998, and at each 3-year interval ending on March 1 thereafter, the Judicial Conference of the United States shall publish in the Federal Register the dollar amounts that will become effective on such April 1 under sections *101(3), 101(18), 101(19A), 101(51D),* 109(e), 303(b), 507(a), 522(d), *522(f)(3) and 522(f)(4), 522(n)* and 523(a)(2)(C), *541(b), 547(c)(9), 707(b), and 1322(d), 1325(b), and 1326(b)(3) of this title and section 1409(b) of title 28* of this title.

(3) Adjustments made in accordance with paragraph (1) shall not apply with respect to cases commenced before the date of such adjustments.

§ 105. Power of court

(a) The court may issue any order, process, or judgment that is necessary or appropriate to carry out the provisions of this title. No provision of this title providing for the raising of an issue by a party in interest shall be construed to preclude the court from, sua sponte, taking any action or making any determination necessary or appropriate to enforce or implement court orders or rules, or to prevent an abuse of process.

(b) Notwithstanding subsection (a) of this section, a court may not appoint a receiver in a case under this title.

(c) The ability of any district judge or other officer or employee of a district court to exercise any of the authority or responsibilities conferred upon the court under this title shall be determined by reference to the provisions relating to such judge, officer, or employee set forth in title 28. This subsection shall not be interpreted to exclude bankruptcy judges and other officers or employees appointed pursuant to chapter 6 of title 28 from its operation.

(d) The court, on its own motion or on the request of a party in interest, may—

(1) hold a status conference regarding any case or proceeding under this title after notice to the parties in interest; and *shall hold such status conferences as are necessary to further the expeditious and economical resolution of the case; and*

(2) unless inconsistent with another provision of this title or with applicable Federal Rules of Bankruptcy Procedure, issue an order at any such conference prescribing such limitations and conditions as the court deems appropriate to ensure that the case is handled expeditiously and economically, including an order that—

(A) sets the date by which the trustee must assume or reject an executory contract or unexpired lease; or

(B) in a case under chapter 11 of this title—

(i) sets a date by which the debtor, or trustee if one has been appointed, shall file a disclosure statement and plan;

    (ii) sets a date by which the debtor, or trustee if one has been appointed, shall solicit acceptances of a plan;

    (iii) sets the date by which a party in interest other than a debtor may file a plan;

    (iv) sets a date by which a proponent of a plan, other than the debtor, shall solicit acceptances of such plan;

    (v) fixes the scope and format of the notice to be provided regarding the hearing on approval of the disclosure statement; or

    (vi) provides that the hearing on approval of the disclosure statement may be combined with the hearing on confirmation of the plan.

§ 106. Waiver of sovereign immunity

 (a) Notwithstanding an assertion of sovereign immunity, sovereign immunity is abrogated as to a governmental unit to the extent set forth in this section with respect to the following:

    (1) Sections 105, 106, 107, 108, 303, 346, 362, 363, 364, 365, 366, 502, 503, 505, 506, 510, 522, 523, 524, 525, 542, 543, 544, 545, 546, 547, 548, 549, 550, 551, 552, 553, 722, 724, 726, 728, 744, 749, 764, 901, 922, 926, 928, 929, 944, 1107, 1141, 1142, 1143, 1146, 1201, 1203, 1205, 1206, 1227, 1231, 1301, 1303, 1305, and 1327 of this title.

    (2) The court may hear and determine any issue arising with respect to the application of such sections to governmental units.

    (3) The court may issue against a governmental unit an order, process, or judgment under such sections or the Federal Rules of Bankruptcy Procedure, including an order or judgment awarding a money recovery, but not including an award of punitive damages. Such order or judgment for costs or fees under this title or the Federal Rules of Bankruptcy Procedure against any governmental unit shall be consistent with the provisions and limitations of section 2412(d)(2)(A) of title 28.

    (4) The enforcement of any such order, process, or judgment against any governmental unit shall be consistent with appropriate nonbankruptcy law applicable to such governmental unit and, in the case of a money judgment against the United States, shall be paid as if it is a judgment rendered by a district court of the United States.

    (5) Nothing in this section shall create any substantive claim for relief or cause of action not otherwise existing under this title, the Federal Rules of Bankruptcy Procedure, or nonbankruptcy law.

 (b) A governmental unit that has filed a proof of claim in the case is deemed to have waived sovereign immunity with respect to a claim against such governmental unit that is property of the estate and that arose out of the same transaction or occurrence out of which the claim of such governmental unit arose.

 (c) Notwithstanding any assertion of sovereign immunity by a governmental unit, there shall be offset against a claim or interest of a governmental unit any claim against such governmental unit that is property of the estate.

§ 107. Public access to papers

(a) Except as provided in ~~subsection (b)~~ *subsections (b) and (c)* of this section *and subject to section 112*, a paper filed in a case under this title and the dockets of a bankruptcy court are public records and open to examination by an entity at reasonable times without charge.

(b) On request of a party in interest, the bankruptcy court shall, and on the bankruptcy court's own motion, the bankruptcy court may—

(1) protect an entity with respect to a trade secret or confidential research, development, or commercial information; or

(2) protect a person with respect to scandalous or defamatory matter contained in a paper filed in a case under this title.

(c)(1) The bankruptcy court, for cause, may protect an individual, with respect to the following types of information to the extent the court finds that disclosure of such information would create undue risk of identity theft or other unlawful injury to the individual or the individual's property:

(A) Any means of identification (as defined in section 1028(d) of title 18) contained in a paper filed, or to be filed, in a case under this title.

(B) Other information contained in a paper described in subparagraph (A).

(2) Upon ex parte application demonstrating cause, the court shall provide access to information protected pursuant to paragraph (1) to an entity acting pursuant to the police or regulatory power of a domestic governmental unit.

(3) The United States trustee, bankruptcy administrator, trustee, and any auditor serving under section 586(f) of title 28—

(A) shall have full access to all information contained in any paper filed or submitted in a case under this title; and

(B) shall not disclose information specifically protected by the court under this title.

§ 108. Extension of time

(a) If applicable nonbankruptcy law, an order entered in a nonbankruptcy proceeding, or an agreement fixes a period within which the debtor may commence an action, and such period has not expired before the date of the filing of the petition, the trustee may commence such action only before the later of—

(1) the end of such period, including any suspension of such period occurring on or after the commencement of the case; or

(2) two years after the order for relief.

(b) Except as provided in subsection (a) of this section, if applicable nonbankruptcy law, an order entered in a nonbankruptcy proceeding, or an agreement fixes a period within which the debtor or an individual protected under section 1201 or 1301 of this title may file any pleading, demand, notice, or proof of claim or loss, cure a default, or perform any other similar act, and such period has not expired before the date of the filing of the petition, the trustee may only file, cure, or perform, as the case may be, before the later of—

(1) the end of such period, including any suspension of such period occurring on or after the commencement of the case; or

(2) 60 days after the order for relief.

(c) Except as provided in section 524 of this title, if applicable nonbankruptcy law, an order entered in a nonbankruptcy proceeding, or an agreement fixes a period for commencing or continuing a civil action in a court other than a bankruptcy court on a claim against the debtor, or against an individual with respect to which such individual is protected under section 1201 or 1301 of this title, and such period has not expired before the date of the filing of the petition, then such period does not expire until the later of—

(1) the end of such period, including any suspension of such period occurring on or after the commencement of the case; or

(2) 30 days after notice of the termination or expiration of the stay under section 362, 922, 1201, or 1301 of this title, as the case may be, with respect to such claim.

§ 109. Who may be a debtor

(a) Notwithstanding any other provision of this section, only a person that resides or has a domicile, a place of business, or property in the United States, or a municipality, may be a debtor under this title.

(b) A person may be a debtor under chapter 7 of this title only if such person is not—

(1) a railroad;

(2) a domestic insurance company, bank, savings bank, cooperative bank, savings and loan association, building and loan association, homestead association, a New Markets Venture Capital company as defined in section 351 of the Small Business Investment Act of 1958, a small business investment company licensed by the Small Business Administration under ~~subsection (c) or (d) of~~ section 301 of the Small Business Investment Act of 1958, credit union, or industrial bank or similar institution which is an insured bank as defined in section 3(h) of the Federal Deposit Insurance Act, except that an uninsured State member bank, or a corporation organized under section 25A of the Federal Reserve Act, which operates, or operates as, a multilateral clearing organization pursuant to section 409 of the Federal Deposit Insurance Corporation Improvement Act of 1991 may be a debtor if a petition is filed at the direction of the Board of Governors of the Federal Reserve System; or

~~(3) a foreign insurance company, bank, savings bank, cooperative bank, savings and loan association, building and loan association, homestead association, or credit union, engaged in such business in the United States.~~

(3)(A) a foreign insurance company, engaged in such business in the United States; or

(B) a foreign bank, savings bank, cooperative bank, savings and loan association, building and loan association, or credit union, that has a branch or agency (as defined in section 1(b) of the International Banking Act of 1978 in the United States.

(c) An entity may be a debtor under chapter 9 of this title if and only if such entity—

(1) is a municipality;

(2) is specifically authorized, in its capacity as a municipality or by name, to be a debtor under such chapter by State law, or by a governmental officer or orga-

nization empowered by State law to authorize such entity to be a debtor under such chapter;

(3) is insolvent;

(4) desires to effect a plan to adjust such debts; and

(5)(A) has obtained the agreement of creditors holding at least a majority in amount of the claims of each class that such entity intends to impair under a plan in a case under such chapter;

(B) has negotiated in good faith with creditors and has failed to obtain the agreement of creditors holding at least a majority in amount of the claims of each class that such entity intends to impair under a plan in a case under such chapter;

(C) is unable to negotiate with creditors because such negotiation is impracticable; or

(D) reasonably believes that a creditor may attempt to obtain a transfer that is avoidable under section 547 of this title.

(d) Only a railroad, a person that may be a debtor under chapter 7 of this title (except a stockbroker or a commodity broker), and an uninsured State member bank, or a corporation organized under section 25A of the Federal Reserve Act, which operates, or operates as, a multilateral clearing organization pursuant to section 409 of the Federal Deposit Insurance Corporation Improvement Act of 1991 may be a debtor under chapter 11 of this title.

(c) Only an individual with regular income that owes, on the date of the filing of the petition, noncontingent, liquidated, unsecured debts of less than $307,675 and noncontingent, liquidated, secured debts of less than $922,975, or an individual with regular income and such individual's spouse, except a stockbroker or a commodity broker, that owe, on the date of the filing of the petition, noncontingent, liquidated, unsecured debts that aggregate less than $307,675 and noncontingent, liquidated, secured debts of less than $922,975 may be a debtor under chapter 13 of this title.

(f) Only a family farmer *or family fisherman* with regular annual income may be a debtor under chapter 12 of this title.

(g) Notwithstanding any other provision of this section, no individual or family farmer may be a debtor under this title who has been a debtor in a case pending under this title at any time in the preceding 180 days if—

(1) the case was dismissed by the court for willful failure of the debtor to abide by orders of the court, or to appear before the court in proper prosecution of the case; or

(2) the debtor requested and obtained the voluntary dismissal of the case following the filing of a request for relief from the automatic stay provided by section 362 of this title.

(h)(1) Subject to paragraphs (2) and (3), and notwithstanding any other provision of this section, an individual may not be a debtor under this title unless such individual has, during the 180-day period preceding the date of filing of the petition by such individual, received from an approved nonprofit budget and credit counseling agency described in section 111(a) an individual or group briefing (including a briefing conducted by telephone or on the Internet) that outlined the opportunities for available credit counseling and assisted such individual in performing a related budget analysis.

*****

(2)(A) *Paragraph (1) shall not apply with respect to a debtor who resides in a district for which the United States trustee (or the bankruptcy administrator, if any) determines that the approved nonprofit budget and credit counseling agencies for such district are not reasonably able to provide adequate services to the additional individuals who would otherwise seek credit counseling from such agencies by reason of the requirements of paragraph (1).*

(B) *The United States trustee (or the bankruptcy administrator, if any) who makes a determination described in subparagraph (A) shall review such determination not later than 1 year after the date of such determination, and not less frequently than annually thereafter. Notwithstanding the preceding sentence, a nonprofit budget and credit counseling agency may be disapproved by the United States trustee (or the bankruptcy administrator, if any) at any time.*

(3)(A) *Subject to subparagraph (B), the requirements of paragraph (1) shall not apply with respect to a debtor who submits to the court a certification that—*

(i) *describes exigent circumstances that merit a waiver of the requirements of paragraph (1);*

(ii) *states that the debtor requested credit counseling services from an approved nonprofit budget and credit counseling agency, but was unable to obtain the services referred to in paragraph (1) during the 5-day period beginning on the date on which the debtor made that request; and*

(iii) *is satisfactory to the court.*

(B) *With respect to a debtor, an exemption under subparagraph (A) shall cease to apply to that debtor on the date on which the debtor meets the requirements of paragraph (1), but in no case may the exemption apply to that debtor after the date that is 30 days after the debtor files a petition, except that the court, for cause, may order an additional 15 days.*

(4) *The requirements of paragraph (1) shall not apply with respect to a debtor whom the court determines, after notice and hearing, is unable to complete those requirements because of incapacity, disability, or active military duty in a military combat zone. For the purposes of this paragraph, incapacity means that the debtor is impaired by reason of mental illness or mental deficiency so that he is incapable of realizing and making rational decisions with respect to his financial responsibilities; and 'disability' means that the debtor is so physically impaired as to be unable, after reasonable effort, to participate in an in person, telephone, or Internet briefing required under paragraph (1).*

§ 110. Penalty for persons who negligently or fraudulently prepare bankruptcy petitions

(a) In this section—

(1) "bankruptcy petition preparer" means a person, other than an attorney ~~or an employee of an attorney~~ *for the debtor or an employee of such attorney under the direct supervision of such attorney*, who prepares for compensation a document for filing; and

(2) "document for filing" means a petition or any other document prepared for filing by a debtor in a United States bankruptcy court or a United States district court in connection with a case under this title.

(b)(1) A bankruptcy petition preparer who prepares a document for filing shall sign the document and print on the document the preparer's name and address. *If a bankruptcy petition preparer is not an individual, then an officer, principal, responsible person, or partner of the bankruptcy petition preparer shall be required to—*

(A) sign the document for filing; and

(B) print on the document the name and address of that officer, principal, responsible person, or partner.

~~(2) A bankruptcy petition preparer who fails to comply with paragraph (1) may be fined not more than $500 for each such failure unless the failure is due to reasonable cause.~~

(2)(A) Before preparing any document for filing or accepting any fees from a debtor, the bankruptcy petition preparer shall provide to the debtor a written notice which shall be on an official form prescribed by the Judicial Conference of the United States in accordance with rule 9009 of the Federal Rules of Bankruptcy Procedure.

(B) The notice under subparagraph (A)—

(i) shall inform the debtor in simple language that a bankruptcy petition preparer is not an attorney and may not practice law or give legal advice;

(ii) may contain a description of examples of legal advice that a bankruptcy petition preparer is not authorized to give, in addition to any advice that the preparer may not give by reason of subsection (e)(2); and

(iii) shall—

(I) be signed by the debtor and, under penalty of perjury, by the bankruptcy petition preparer; and

(II) be filed with any document for filing.

(c)(1) A bankruptcy petition preparer who prepares a document for filing shall place on the document, after the preparer's signature, an identifying number that identifies individuals who prepared the document.

(2)*(A) Subject to Subparagraph (B), for* ~~For~~ purposes of this section, the identifying number of a bankruptcy petition preparer shall be the Social Security account number of each individual who prepared the document or assisted in its preparation.

(B) If a bankruptcy petition preparer is not an individual, the identifying number of the bankruptcy petition preparer shall be the Social Security account number of the officer, principal, responsible person, or partner of the bankruptcy petition preparer.

~~(3) A bankruptcy petition preparer who fails to comply with paragraph (1) may be fined not more than $500 for each such failure unless the failure is due to reasonable cause.~~

(d)(1) A bankruptcy petition preparer shall, not later than the time at which a document for filing is presented for the debtor's signature, furnish to the debtor a copy of the document.

143

~~(2) A bankruptcy petition preparer who fails to comply with paragraph (1) may be fined not more than $500 for each such failure unless the failure is due to reasonable cause.~~

(e)(1) A bankruptcy petition preparer shall not execute any document on behalf of a debtor.

~~(2) A bankruptcy petition preparer may be fined not more than $500 for each document executed in violation of paragraph (1).~~

(2)(A) A bankruptcy petition preparer may not offer a potential bankruptcy debtor any legal advice, including any legal advice described in subparagraph (B).

(B) The legal advice referred to in subparagraph (A) includes advising the debtor—

(i) whether—

(I) to file a petition under this title; or

(II) commencing a case under chapter 7, 11, 12, or 13 is appropriate;

(ii) whether the debtor's debts will be discharged in a case under this title;

(iii) whether the debtor will be able to retain the debtor's home, car, or other property after commencing a case under this title;

(iv) concerning—

(I) the tax consequences of a case brought under this title; or

(II) the dischargeability of tax claims;

(v) whether the debtor may or should promise to repay debts to a creditor or enter into a reaffirmation agreement with a creditor to reaffirm a debt;

(vi) concerning how to characterize the nature of the debtor's interests in property or the debtor's debts; or

(vii) concerning bankruptcy procedures and rights.

(f)(1) A bankruptcy petition preparer shall not use the word "legal" or any similar term in any advertisements, or advertise under any category that includes the word "legal" or any similar term.

~~(2) A bankruptcy petition preparer shall be fined not more than $500 for each violation of paragraph (1).~~

(g)(1) A bankruptcy petition preparer shall not collect or receive any payment from the debtor or on behalf of the debtor for the court fees in connection with filing the petition.

~~(2) A bankruptcy petition preparer shall be fined not more than $500 for each violation of paragraph (1).~~

(h)*(1) The Supreme Court may promulgate rules under section 2075 of title 28, or the Judicial Conference of the United States may prescribe guidelines, for setting a maximum allowable fee chargeable by a bankruptcy petition preparer. A bankruptcy petition preparer shall notify the debtor of any such maximum amount before preparing any document for filing for a debtor or accepting any fee from the debtor.*

(1*2*) ~~Within 10 days after the date of the filing of a petition, a bankruptcy petition preparer shall file a~~ *A* declaration under penalty of perjury *by the bankruptcy petition preparer shall be filed together with the petition* disclosing any fee received from or on behalf of the debtor within 12 months immediately prior to the filing of the case, and any unpaid fee charged to the debtor. *If rules or guidelines setting a maximum fee for services have been promulgated or prescribed under paragraph (1), the declaration under this paragraph shall include a certification that the bankruptcy petition preparer complied with the notification requirement under paragraph (1).*

~~(2) The court shall disallow and order the immediate turnover to the bankruptcy trustee of any fee referred to in paragraph (1) found to be in excess of the value of services rendered for the documents prepared. An individual debtor may exempt any funds so recovered under section 522(b).~~

(3)*(A) The court shall disallow and order the immediate turnover to the bankruptcy trustee any fee referred to in paragraph (2) found to be in excess of the value of any services—*

(i) rendered by the bankruptcy petition preparer during the 12-month period immediately preceding the date of the filing of the petition; or

(ii) found to be in violation of any rule or guideline promulgated or prescribed under paragraph (1).

(B) All fees charged by a bankruptcy petition preparer may be forfeited in any case in which the bankruptcy petition preparer fails to comply with this subsection or subsection (b), (c), (d), (e), (f), or (g).

(C) An individual may exempt any funds recovered under this paragraph under section 522(b).

(~~3~~4) The debtor, the trustee, a creditor, ~~or~~ the United States trustee *(or the bankruptcy administrator, if any) or the court, on the initiative of the court,* may file a motion for an order under paragraph (2).

(~~4~~5) A bankruptcy petition preparer shall be fined not more than $500 for each failure to comply with a court order to turn over funds within 30 days of service of such order.

~~(i)(1) If a bankruptcy case or related proceeding is dismissed because of the failure to file bankruptcy papers, including papers specified in section 521(1) of this title, the negligence or intentional disregard of this title or the Federal Rules of Bankruptcy Procedure by a bankruptcy petition preparer, or if a bankruptcy petition preparer violates this section or commits any fraudulent, unfair, or deceptive act, the bankruptcy court shall certify that fact to the district court, and the district court, on motion of the debtor, the trustee, or a creditor and after a hearing, shall order the bankruptcy petition preparer to pay to the debtor——~~

(i)(1) If a bankruptcy petition preparer violates this section or commits any act that the court finds to be fraudulent, unfair, or deceptive, on the motion of the debtor, trustee, United States trustee (or the bankruptcy administrator, if any), and after notice and a hearing, the court shall order the bankruptcy petition preparer to pay to the debtor—

(A) the debtor's actual damages;

(B) the greater of—

(i) $2,000; or

(ii) twice the amount paid by the debtor to the bankruptcy petition preparer for the preparer's services; and

(C) reasonable attorneys' fees and costs in moving for damages under this subsection.

(2) If the trustee or creditor moves for damages on behalf of the debtor under this subsection, the bankruptcy petition preparer shall be ordered to pay the movant the additional amount of $1,000 plus reasonable attorneys' fees and costs incurred.

(j)(1) A debtor for whom a bankruptcy petition preparer has prepared a document for filing, the trustee, a creditor, or the United States trustee in the district in which the bankruptcy petition preparer resides, has conducted business, or the United States trustee in any other district in which the debtor resides may bring a civil action to enjoin a bankruptcy petition preparer from engaging in any conduct in violation of this section or from further acting as a bankruptcy petition preparer.

(2)(A) In an action under paragraph (1), if the court finds that—

(i) a bankruptcy petition preparer has—

(I) engaged in conduct in violation of this section or of any provision of this title a violation of which subjects a person to criminal penalty;

(II) misrepresented the preparer's experience or education as a bankruptcy petition preparer; or

(III) engaged in any other fraudulent, unfair, or deceptive conduct; and

(ii) injunctive relief is appropriate to prevent the recurrence of such conduct,

the court may enjoin the bankruptcy petition preparer from engaging in such conduct.

(B) If the court finds that a bankruptcy petition preparer has continually engaged in conduct described in subclause (I), (II), or (III) of clause (i) and that an injunction prohibiting such conduct would not be sufficient to prevent such person's interference with the proper administration of this title, or has not paid a penalty *has not paid a penalty* imposed under this section *or failed to disgorge all fees ordered by the court*, the court may enjoin the person from acting as a bankruptcy petition preparer.

(3) The court, as part of its contempt power, may enjoin a bankruptcy petition preparer that has failed to comply with a previous order issued under this section. The injunction under this paragraph may be issued on the motion of the court, the trustee, or the United States trustee (or the bankruptcy administrator, if any).

(34) The court shall award to a debtor, trustee, or creditor that brings a successful action under this subsection reasonable attorneys's fees and costs of the action, to be paid by the bankruptcy petition preparer.

(k) Nothing in this section shall be construed to permit activities that are otherwise prohibited by law, including rules and laws that prohibit the unauthorized practice of law.

(l)(1) A bankruptcy petition preparer who fails to comply with any provision of subsection (b), (c), (d), (e), (f), (g), or (h) may be fined not more than $500 for each such failure.

****

(2) The court shall triple the amount of a fine assessed under paragraph (1) in any case in which the court finds that a bankruptcy petition preparer—

(A) advised the debtor to exclude assets or income that should have been included on applicable schedules;

(B) advised the debtor to use a false Social Security account number;

(C) failed to inform the debtor that the debtor was filing for relief under this title; or

(D) prepared a document for filing in a manner that failed to disclose the identity of the bankruptcy petition preparer.

(3) A debtor, trustee, creditor, or United States trustee (or the bankruptcy administrator, if any) may file a motion for an order imposing a fine on the bankruptcy petition preparer for any violation of this section.

(4)(A) Fines imposed under this subsection in judicial districts served by United States trustees shall be paid to the United States trustee, who shall deposit an amount equal to such fines in a special account of the United States Trustee System Fund referred to in section 586(e)(2) of title 28. Amounts deposited under this subparagraph shall be available to fund the enforcement of this section on a national basis.

(B) Fines imposed under this subsection in judicial districts served by bankruptcy administrators shall be deposited as offsetting receipts to the fund established under section 1931 of title 28, and shall remain available until expended to reimburse any appropriation for the amount paid out of such appropriation for expenses of the operation and maintenance of the courts of the United States.

§ 111. Nonprofit budget and credit counseling agencies; financial management instructional courses

(a) The clerk shall maintain a publicly available list of—

(1) nonprofit budget and credit counseling agencies that provide 1 or more services described in section 109(h) currently approved by the United States trustee (or the bankruptcy administrator, if any); and

(2) instructional courses concerning personal financial management currently approved by the United States trustee (or the bankruptcy administrator, if any), as applicable.

(b) The United States trustee (or bankruptcy administrator, if any) shall only approve a nonprofit budget and credit counseling agency or an instructional course concerning personal financial management as follows:

(1) The United States trustee (or bankruptcy administrator, if any) shall have thoroughly reviewed the qualifications of the nonprofit budget and credit counseling agency or of the provider of the instructional course under the standards set forth in this section, and the services or instructional courses that will be offered by such agency or such provider, and may require such agency or such provider that has sought approval to provide information with respect to such review.

(2) The United States trustee (or bankruptcy administrator, if any) shall have determined that such agency or such instructional course fully satisfies the applicable standards set forth in this section.

(3) If a nonprofit budget and credit counseling agency or instructional course did not appear on the approved list for the district under subsection (a) imme-

diately before approval under this section, approval under this subsection of such agency or such instructional course shall be for a probationary period not to exceed 6 months.

(4) At the conclusion of the applicable probationary period under paragraph (3), the United States trustee (or bankruptcy administrator, if any) may only approve for an additional 1-year period, and for successive 1- year periods thereafter, an agency or instructional course that has demonstrated during the probationary or applicable subsequent period of approval that such agency or instructional course—

(A) has met the standards set forth under this section during such period; and

(B) can satisfy such standards in the future.

(5) Not later than 30 days after any final decision under paragraph (4), an interested person may seek judicial review of such decision in the appropriate district court of the United States.

(c)(1) The United States trustee (or the bankruptcy administrator, if any) shall only approve a nonprofit budget and credit counseling agency that demonstrates that it will provide qualified counselors, maintain adequate provision for safekeeping and payment of client funds, provide adequate counseling with respect to client credit problems, and deal responsibly and effectively with other matters relating to the quality, effectiveness, and financial security of the services it provides.

(2) To be approved by the United States trustee (or the bankruptcy administrator, if any), a nonprofit budget and credit counseling agency shall, at a minimum—

(A) have a board of directors the majority of which—

(i) are not employed by such agency; and

(ii) will not directly or indirectly benefit financially from the outcome of the counseling services provided by such agency;

(B) if a fee is charged for counseling services, charge a reasonable fee, and provide services without regard to ability to pay the fee;

(C) provide for safekeeping and payment of client funds, including an annual audit of the trust accounts and appropriate employee bonding;

(D) provide full disclosures to a client, including funding sources, counselor qualifications, possible impact on credit reports, and any costs of such program that will be paid by such client and how such costs will be paid;

(E) provide adequate counseling with respect to a client's credit problems that includes an analysis of such client's current financial condition, factors that caused such financial condition, and how such client can develop a plan to respond to the problems without incurring negative amortization of debt;

(F) provide trained counselors who receive no commissions or bonuses based on the outcome of the counseling services provided by such agency, and who have adequate experience, and have been adequately trained to provide counseling services to individuals in financial difficulty, including the matters described in subparagraph (E);

(G) demonstrate adequate experience and background in providing credit counseling; and

(H) have adequate financial resources to provide continuing support services for budgeting plans over the life of any repayment plan.

(d) The United States trustee (or the bankruptcy administrator, if any) shall only approve an instructional course concerning personal financial management—

(1) for an initial probationary period under subsection (b)(3) if the course will provide at a minimum—

(A) trained personnel with adequate experience and training in providing effective instruction and services;

(B) learning materials and teaching methodologies designed to assist debtors in understanding personal financial management and that are consistent with stated objectives directly related to the goals of such instructional course;

(C) adequate facilities situated in reasonably convenient locations at which such instructional course is offered, except that such facilities may include the provision of such instructional course by telephone or through the Internet, if such instructional course is effective;

(D) the preparation and retention of reasonable records (which shall include the debtor's bankruptcy case number) to permit evaluation of the effectiveness of such instructional course, including any evaluation of satisfaction of instructional course requirements for each debtor attending such instructional course, which shall be available for inspection and evaluation by the Executive Office for United States Trustees, the United States trustee (or the bankruptcy administrator, if any), or the chief bankruptcy judge for the district in which such instructional course is offered; and

(E) if a fee is charged for the instructional course, charge a reasonable fee, and provide services without regard to ability to pay the fee.

(2) for any 1-year period if the provider thereof has demonstrated that the course meets the standards of paragraph (1) and, in addition—

(A) has been effective in assisting a substantial number of debtors to understand personal financial management; and

(B) is otherwise likely to increase substantially the debtor's understanding of personal financial management.

(e) The district court may, at any time, investigate the qualifications of a nonprofit budget and credit counseling agency referred to in subsection (a), and request production of documents to ensure the integrity and effectiveness of such agency. The district court may, at any time, remove from the approved list under subsection (a) a nonprofit budget and credit counseling agency upon finding such agency does not meet the qualifications of subsection (b).

(f) The United States trustee (or the bankruptcy administrator, if any) shall notify the clerk that a nonprofit budget and credit counseling agency or an instructional course is no longer approved, in which case the clerk shall remove it from the list maintained under subsection (a).

(g)(1) No nonprofit budget and credit counseling agency may provide to a credit reporting agency information concerning whether a debtor has received or sought instruction concerning personal financial management from such agency.

(2) *A nonprofit budget and credit counseling agency that willfully or negligently fails to comply with any requirement under this title with respect to a debtor shall be liable for damages in an amount equal to the sum of—*

   (A) any actual damages sustained by the debtor as a result of the violation; and

   (B) any court costs or reasonable attorneys' fees (as determined by the court) incurred in an action to recover those damages.

§ 112. Prohibition on disclosure of name of minor children

The debtor may be required to provide information regarding a minor child involved in matters under this title but may not be required to disclose in the public records in the case the name of such minor child. The debtor may be required to disclose the name of such minor child in a nonpublic record that is maintained by the court and made available by the court for examination by the United States trustee, the trustee, and the auditor (if any) serving under section 586(f) of title 28, in the case. The court, the United States trustee, the trustee, and such auditor shall not disclose the name of such minor child maintained in such nonpublic record.

CHAPTER 3—CASE ADMINISTRATION

SUBCHAPTER I—COMMENCEMENT OF A CASE

§ 301. Voluntary cases

(a) A voluntary case under a chapter of this title is commenced by the filing with the bankruptcy court of a petition under such chapter by an entity that may be a debtor under such chapter. ~~The commencement of a voluntary case under a chapter of this title constitutes an order for relief under such chapter.~~

(b) *The commencement of a voluntary case under a chapter of this title constitutes an order for relief under such chapter.*

§ 302. Joint cases

(a) A joint case under a chapter of this title is commenced by the filing with the bankruptcy court of a single petition under such chapter by an individual that may be a debtor under such chapter and such individual's spouse. The commencement of a joint case under a chapter of this title constitutes an order for relief under such chapter.

(b) After the commencement of a joint case, the court shall determine the extent, if any, to which the debtors' estates shall be consolidated.

§ 303. Involuntary cases

(a) An involuntary case may be commenced only under chapter 7 or 11 of this title, and only against a person, except a farmer, family farmer, or a corporation that is not a moneyed, business, or commercial corporation, that may be a debtor under the chapter under which such case is commenced.

(c) An order under subsection (a) of this section dismissing a case or suspending all proceedings in a case, or a decision not so to dismiss or suspend, is not reviewable by appeal or otherwise by the court of appeals under section 158(d), 1291, or 1292 of title 28 or by the Supreme Court of the United States under section 1254 of title 28.

§ 306. Limited appearance

An appearance in a bankruptcy court by a foreign representative in connection with a petition or request under section 303, ~~304,~~ or 305 of this title does not submit such foreign representative to the jurisdiction of any court in the United States for any other purpose, but the bankruptcy court may condition any order under section 303, ~~304,~~ or 305 of this title on compliance by such foreign representative with the orders of such bankruptcy court.

§ 307. United States trustee

The United States trustee may raise and may appear and be heard on any issue in any case or proceeding under this title but may not file a plan pursuant to section 1121(c) of this title.

§ 308. *Debtor Reporting Requirements*

(a) For purposes of this section, the term "profitability" means, with respect to a debtor, the amount of money that the debtor has earned or lost during current and recent fiscal periods.

(b) A small business debtor shall file periodic financial and other reports containing information including—

(1) the debtor's profitability;

(2) reasonable approximations of the debtor's projected cash receipts and cash disbursements over a reasonable period;

(3) comparisons of actual cash receipts and disbursements with projections in prior reports;

(4)(A) whether the debtor is—

(i) in compliance in all material respects with postpetition requirements imposed by this title and the Federal Rules of Bankruptcy Procedure; and

(ii) timely filing tax returns and other required government filings and paying taxes and other administrative expenses when due;

(B) if the debtor is not in compliance with the requirements referred to in subparagraph (A)(i) or filing tax returns and other required government filings and making the payments referred to in subparagraph (A)(ii), what the failures are and how, at what cost, and when the debtor intends to remedy such failures; and

(C) such other matters as are in the best interests of the debtor and creditors, and in the public interest in fair and efficient procedures under chapter 11 of this title.

(b) An involuntary case against a person is commenced by the filing with the bankruptcy court of a petition under chapter 7 or 11 of this title—

(1) by three or more entities, each of which is either a holder of a claim against such person that is not contingent as to liability or the subject of a bona fide dispute *as to liability or amount,* or an indenture trustee representing such a holder, ~~if such claims~~ *if such noncontingent, undisputed claims* aggregate at least $12,300 more than the value of any lien on property of the debtor securing such claims held by the holders of such claims;

(2) if there are fewer than 12 such holders, excluding any employee or insider of such person and any transferee of a transfer that is voidable under section 544, 545, 547, 548, 549, or 724(a) of this title, by one or more of such holders that hold in the aggregate at least $12,300 of such claims;

(3) if such person is a partnership—

(A) by fewer than all of the general partners in such partnership; or

(B) if relief has been ordered under this title with respect to all of the general partners in such partnership, by a general partner in such partnership, the trustee of such a general partner, or a holder of a claim against such partnership; or

(4) by a foreign representative of the estate in a foreign proceeding concerning such person.

(c) After the filing of a petition under this section but before the case is dismissed or relief is ordered, a creditor holding an unsecured claim that is not contingent, other than a creditor filing under subsection (b) of this section, may join in the petition with the same effect as if such joining creditor were a petitioning creditor under subsection (b) of this section.

(d) The debtor, or a general partner in a partnership debtor that did not join in the petition, may file an answer to a petition under this section.

(e) After notice and a hearing, and for cause, the court may require the petitioners under this section to file a bond to indemnify the debtor for such amounts as the court may later allow under subsection (i) of this section.

(f) Notwithstanding section 363 of this title, except to the extent that the court orders otherwise, and until an order for relief in the case, any business of the debtor may continue to operate, and the debtor may continue to use, acquire, or dispose of property as if an involuntary case concerning the debtor had not been commenced.

(g) At any time after the commencement of an involuntary case under chapter 7 of this title but before an order for relief in the case, the court, on request of a party in interest, after notice to the debtor and a hearing, and if necessary to preserve the property of the estate or to prevent loss to the estate, may order the United States trustee to appoint an interim trustee under section 701 of this title to take possession of the property of the estate and to operate any business of the debtor. Before an order for relief, the debtor may regain possession of property in the possession of a trustee ordered appointed under this subsection if the debtor files such bond as the court requires, conditioned on the debtor's accounting for and delivering to the trustee, if there is an order for relief in the case, such property, or the value, as of the date the debtor regains possession, of such property.

(h) If the petition is not timely controverted, the court shall order relief against the debtor in an involuntary case under the chapter under which the petition was filed. Otherwise, after trial, the court shall order relief against the debtor in an involuntary case under the chapter under which the petition was filed, only if—

    (1) the debtor is generally not paying such debtor's debts as such debts become due unless such debts are the subject of a bona fide dispute *as to liability or amount;* or

    (2) within 120 days before the date of the filing of the petition, a custodian, other than a trustee, receiver, or agent appointed or authorized to take charge of less than substantially all of the property of the debtor for the purpose of enforcing a lien against such property, was appointed or took possession.

(i) If the court dismisses a petition under this section other than on consent of all petitioners and the debtor, and if the debtor does not waive the right to judgment under this subsection, the court may grant judgment—

    (1) against the petitioners and in favor of the debtor for—

      (A) costs; or

      (B) a reasonable attorney's fee; or

    (2) against any petitioner that filed the petition in bad faith, for—

      (A) any damages proximately caused by such filing; or

      (B) punitive damages.

(j) Only after notice to all creditors and a hearing may the court dismiss a petition filed under this section—

    (1) on the motion of a petitioner;

    (2) on consent of all petitioners and the debtor; or

    (3) for want of prosecution.

(k) Notwithstanding subsection (a) of this section, an involuntary case may be commenced against a foreign bank that is not engaged in such business in the United States only under chapter 7 of this title and only if a foreign proceeding concerning such bank is pending.

(l)(1) If—

    (A) the petition under this section is false or contains any materially false, fictitious, or fraudulent statement;

    (B) the debtor is an individual; and

    (C) the court dismisses such petition,

the court, upon the motion of the debtor, shall seal all the records of the court relating to such petition, and all references to such petition.

    (2) If the debtor is an individual and the court dismisses a petition under this section, the court may enter an order prohibiting all consumer reporting agencies (as defined in section 603(f) of the Fair Credit Reporting Act (15 U.S.C. 1681a(f))) from making any consumer report (as defined in section 603(d) of that Act) that contains any information relating to such petition or to the case commenced by the filing of such petition.

    (3) Upon the expiration of the statute of limitations described in section 3282 of title 18, for a violation of section 152 or 157 of such title, the court, upon the motion of the debtor and for good cause, may expunge any records relating to a petition filed under this section.

§ 304. Cases ancillary to foreign proceedings

(a) A case ancillary to a foreign proceeding is commenced by the filing with the bankruptcy court of a petition under this section by a foreign representative.

(b) Subject to the provisions of subsection (c) of this section, if a party in interest does not timely controvert the petition, or after trial, the court may—

    (1) enjoin the commencement or continuation of—

      (A) any action against—

        (i) a debtor with respect to property involved in such foreign proceeding; or

        (ii) such property; or

      (B) the enforcement of any judgment against the debtor with respect to such property, or any act or the commencement or continuation of any judicial proceeding to create or enforce a lien against the property of such estate;

    (2) order turnover of the property of such estate, or the proceeds of such property, to such foreign representative; or

    (3) order other appropriate relief.

(c) In determining whether to grant relief under subsection (b) of this section, the court shall be guided by what will best assure an economical and expeditious administration of such estate, consistent with—

    (1) just treatment of all holders of claims against or interests in such estate;

    (2) protection of claim holders in the United States against prejudice and inconvenience in the processing of claims in such foreign proceeding;

    (3) prevention of preferential or fraudulent dispositions of property of such estate;

    (4) distribution of proceeds of such estate substantially in accordance with the order prescribed by this title;

    (5) comity; and

    (6) if appropriate, the provision of an opportunity for a fresh start for the individual that such foreign proceeding concerns.

§ 305. Abstention

(a) The court, after notice and a hearing, may dismiss a case under this title, or may suspend all proceedings in a case under this title, at any time if—

    (1) the interests of creditors and the debtor would be better served by such dismissal or suspension; or

    (2)(A) there is pending a foreign proceeding; and

      (B) the factors specified in section 304(c) of this title warrant such dismissal or suspension. *(2)(A) a petition under section 1515 for recognition of a foreign proceeding has been granted; and*

      (B) the purposes of chapter 15 of this title would be best served by such dismissal or suspension.

(b) A foreign representative may seek dismissal or suspension under subsection (a)(2) of this section.

§ 321. Eligibility to serve as trustee

(a) A person may serve as trustee in a case under this title only if such person is—

(1) an individual that is competent to perform the duties of trustee and, in a case under chapter 7, 12, or 13 of this title, resides or has an office in the judicial district within which the case is pending, or in any judicial district adjacent to such district; or

(2) a corporation authorized by such corporation's charter or bylaws to act as trustee, and, in a case under chapter 7, 12, or 13 of this title, having an office in at least one of such districts.

(b) A person that has served as an examiner in the case may not serve as trustee in the case.

(c) The United States trustee for the judicial district in which the case is pending is eligible to serve as trustee in the case if necessary.

§ 322. Qualification of trustee

(a) Except as provided in subsection (b)(1), a person selected under section 701, 702, 703, 1104, 1163, 1202, or 1302 of this title to serve as trustee in a case under this title qualifies if before five days after such selection, and before beginning official duties, such person has filed with the court a bond in favor of the United States conditioned on the faithful performance of such official duties.

(b)(1) The United States trustee qualifies wherever such trustee serves as trustee in a case under this title.

(2) The United States trustee shall determine—

(A) the amount of a bond required to be filed under subsection (a) of this section; and

(B) the sufficiency of the surety on such bond.

(c) A trustee is not liable personally or on such trustee's bond in favor of the United States for any penalty or forfeiture incurred by the debtor.

(d) A proceeding on a trustee's bond may not be commenced after two years after the date on which such trustee was discharged.

§ 323. Role and capacity of trustee

(a) The trustee in a case under this title is the representative of the estate.

(b) The trustee in a case under this title has capacity to sue and be sued.

§ 324. Removal of trustee or examiner

(a) The court, after notice and a hearing, may remove a trustee, other than the United States trustee, or an examiner, for cause.

(b) Whenever the court removes a trustee or examiner under subsection (a) in a case under this title, such trustee or examiner shall thereby be removed in all other cases under this title in which such trustee or examiner is then serving unless the court orders otherwise.

§ 325. Effect of vacancy

A vacancy in the office of trustee during a case does not abate any pending action or proceeding, and the successor trustee shall be substituted as a party in such action or proceeding.

§ 326. Limitation on compensation of trustee

(a) In a case under chapter 7 or 11, the court may allow reasonable compensation under section 330 of this title of the trustee for the trustee's services, payable after the trustee renders such services, not to exceed 25 percent on the first $5,000 or less, 10 percent on any amount in excess of $5,000 but not in excess of $50,000, 5 percent on any amount in excess of $50,000 but not in excess of $1,000,000, and reasonable compensation not to exceed 3 percent of such moneys in excess of $1,000,000, upon all moneys disbursed or turned over in the case by the trustee to parties in interest, excluding the debtor, but including holders of secured claims.

(b) In a case under chapter 12 or 13 of this title, the court may not allow compensation for services or reimbursement of expenses of the United States trustee or of a standing trustee appointed under section 586(b) of title 28, but may allow reasonable compensation under section 330 of this title of a trustee appointed under section 1202(a) or 1302(a) of this title for the trustee's services, payable after the trustee renders such services, not to exceed five percent upon all payments under the plan.

(c) If more than one person serves as trustee in the case, the aggregate compensation of such persons for such service may not exceed the maximum compensation prescribed for a single trustee by subsection (a) or (b) of this section, as the case may be.

(d) The court may deny allowance of compensation for services or reimbursement of expenses of the trustee if the trustee failed to make diligent inquiry into facts that would permit denial of allowance under section 328(c) of this title or, with knowledge of such facts, employed a professional person under section 327 of this title.

§ 327. Employment of professional persons

(a) Except as otherwise provided in this section, the trustee, with the court's approval, may employ one or more attorneys, accountants, appraisers, auctioneers, or other professional persons, that do not hold or represent an interest adverse to the estate, and that are disinterested persons, to represent or assist the trustee in carrying out the trustee's duties under this title.

(b) If the trustee is authorized to operate the business of the debtor under section 721, 1202, or 1108 of this title, and if the debtor has regularly employed attorneys, accountants, or other professional persons on salary, the trustee may retain or replace such professional persons if necessary in the operation of such business.

(c) In a case under chapter 7, 12, or 11 of this title, a person is not disqualified for employment under this section solely because of such person's employment by or representation of a creditor, unless there is objection by another creditor or the United States trustee, in which case the court shall disapprove such employment if there is an actual conflict of interest.

(d) The court may authorize the trustee to act as attorney or accountant for the estate if such authorization is in the best interest of the estate.

(e) The trustee, with the court's approval, may employ, for a specified special purpose, other than to represent the trustee in conducting the case, an attorney that has represented the debtor, if in the best interest of the estate, and if such attorney does not represent or hold any interest adverse to the debtor or to the estate with respect to the matter on which such attorney is to be employed.

(f) The trustee may not employ a person that has served as an examiner in the case.

§ 328. Limitation on compensation of professional persons

(a) The trustee, or a committee appointed under section 1102 of this title, with the court's approval, may employ or authorize the employment of a professional person under section 327 or 1103 of this title, as the case may be, on any reasonable terms and conditions of employment, including on a retainer, on an hourly basis *on a fixed or percentage fee basis,* or on a contingent fee basis. Notwithstanding such terms and conditions, the court may allow compensation different from the compensation provided under such terms and conditions after the conclusion of such employment, if such terms and conditions prove to have been improvident in light of developments not capable of being anticipated at the time of the fixing of such terms and conditions.

(b) If the court has authorized a trustee to serve as an attorney or accountant for the estate under section 327(d) of this title, the court may allow compensation for the trustee's services as such attorney or accountant only to the extent that the trustee performed services as attorney or accountant for the estate and not for performance of any of the trustee's duties that are generally performed by a trustee without the assistance of an attorney or accountant for the estate.

(c) Except as provided in section 327(c), 327(e), or 1107(b) of this title, the court may deny allowance of compensation for services and reimbursement of expenses of a professional person employed under section 327 or 1103 of this title if, at any time during such professional person's employment under section 327 or 1103 of this title, such professional person is not a disinterested person, or represents or holds an interest adverse to the interest of the estate with respect to the matter on which such professional person is employed.

§ 329. Debtor's transactions with attorneys

(a) Any attorney representing a debtor in a case under this title, or in connection with such a case, whether or not such attorney applies for compensation under this title, shall file with the court a statement of the compensation paid or agreed to be paid, if such payment or agreement was made after one year before the date of the filing of the petition, for services rendered or to be rendered in contemplation of or in connection with the case by such attorney, and the source of such compensation.

(b) If such compensation exceeds the reasonable value of any such services, the court may cancel any such agreement, or order the return of any such payment, to the extent excessive, to—

(1) the estate, if the property transferred—

(A) would have been property of the estate; or

(B) was to be paid by or on behalf of the debtor under a plan under chapter 11, 12, or 13 of this title; or

(2) the entity that made such payment.

§ 330. Compensation of officers

(a)(1) After notice to the parties in interest and the United States Trustee and a hearing, and subject to sections 326, 328, and 329, the court may award to a trustee, *a consumer privacy ombudsman appointed under section 332,* an examiner, *an ombudsman appointed under section 333,* or a professional person employed under section 327 or 1103—

(A) reasonable compensation for actual, necessary services rendered by the trustee, examiner, ombudsman, professional person, or attorney and by any paraprofessional person employed by any such person; and

(B) reimbursement for actual, necessary expenses.

(2) The court may, on its own motion or on the motion of the United States Trustee, the United States Trustee for the District or Region, the trustee for the estate, or any other party in interest, award compensation that is less than the amount of compensation that is requested.

(3)(A) In determining the amount of reasonable compensation to be awarded *to an examiner, trustee under chapter 11, or professional person,* the court shall consider the nature, the extent, and the value of such services, taking into account all relevant factors, including—

(A) the time spent on such services;

(B) the rates charged for such services;

(C) whether the services were necessary to the administration of, or beneficial at the time at which the service was rendered toward the completion of, a case under this title;

(D) whether the services were performed within a reasonable amount of time commensurate with the complexity, importance, and nature of the problem, issue, or task addressed; and

(E) with respect to a professional person, whether the person is board certified or otherwise has demonstrated skill and experience in the bankruptcy field; and

(EF) whether the compensation is reasonable based on the customary compensation charged by comparably skilled practitioners in cases other than cases under this title.

(4)(A) Except as provided in subparagraph (B), the court shall not allow compensation for—

(i) unnecessary duplication of services; or

(ii) services that were not—

(I) reasonably likely to benefit the debtor's estate; or

(II) necessary to the administration of the case.

(B) In a chapter 12 or chapter 13 case in which the debtor is an individual, the court may allow reasonable compensation to the debtor's attorney for representing the interests of the debtor in connection with the bankruptcy case based on a consideration of the benefit and necessity of such services to the debtor and the other factors set forth in this section.

(5) The court shall reduce the amount of compensation awarded under this section by the amount of any interim compensation awarded under section 331, and, if the amount of such interim compensation exceeds the amount of compensation awarded under this section, may order the return of the excess to the estate.

(6) Any compensation awarded for the preparation of a fee application shall be based on the level and skill reasonably required to prepare the application.

(7) In determining the amount of reasonable compensation to be awarded to a trustee, the court shall treat such compensation as a commission, based on section 326.

(b)(1) There shall be paid from the filing fee in a case under chapter 7 of this title $45 to the trustee serving in such case, after such trustee's services are rendered.

(2) The Judicial Conference of the United States—

(A) shall prescribe additional fees of the same kind as prescribed under section 1914(b) of title 28; and

(B) may prescribe notice of appearance fees and fees charged against distributions in cases under this title;

to pay $15 to trustees serving in cases after such trustees' services are rendered. Beginning 1 year after the date of the enactment of the Bankruptcy Reform Act of 1994, such $15 shall be paid in addition to the amount paid under paragraph (1).

(c) Unless the court orders otherwise, in a case under chapter 12 or 13 of this title the compensation paid to the trustee serving in the case shall not be less than $5 per month from any distribution under the plan during the administration of the plan.

(d) In a case in which the United States trustee serves as trustee, the compensation of the trustee under this section shall be paid to the clerk of the bankruptcy court and deposited by the clerk into the United States Trustee System Fund established by section 589a of title 28.

§ 331. Interim compensation

A trustee, an examiner, a debtor's attorney, or any professional person employed under section 327 or 1103 of this title may apply to the court not more than once every 120 days after an order for relief in a case under this title, or more often if the court permits, for such compensation for services rendered before the date of such an application or reimbursement for expenses incurred before such date as is provided under section 330 of this title. After notice and a hearing, the court may allow and disburse to such applicant such compensation or reimbursement.

§ 332. Consumer privacy ombudsman

(a) If a hearing is required under section 363(b)(1)(B), the court shall order the United States trustee to appoint, not later than 5 days before the commencement of the hearing, 1 disinterested person (other than the United States trustee) to serve as the consumer privacy ombudsman in the case and shall require that notice of such hearing be timely given to such ombudsman.

(b) The consumer privacy ombudsman may appear and be heard at such hearing and shall provide to the court information to assist the court in its consideration of the facts, circumstances, and conditions of the proposed sale or lease of personally identifiable information under section 363(b)(1)(B). Such information may include presentation of—

(1) the debtor's privacy policy;

(2) the potential losses or gains of privacy to consumers if such sale or such lease is approved by the court;

(3) the potential costs or benefits to consumers if such sale or such lease is approved by the court; and

(4) the potential alternatives that would mitigate potential privacy losses or potential costs to consumers.

(c) A consumer privacy ombudsman shall not disclose any personally identifiable information obtained by the ombudsman under this title.

§ 333. *Appointment of patient care ombudsman*

(a)(1) If the debtor in a case under chapter 7, 9, or 11 is a health care business, the court shall order, not later than 30 days after the commencement of the case, the appointment of an ombudsman to monitor the quality of patient care and to represent the interests of the patients of the health care business unless the court finds that the appointment of such ombudsman is not necessary for the protection of patients under the specific facts of the case.

(2)(A) If the court orders the appointment of an ombudsman under paragraph (1), the United States trustee shall appoint 1 disinterested person (other than the United States trustee) to serve as such ombudsman.

(B) If the debtor is a health care business that provides long-term care, then the United States trustee may appoint the State Long-Term Care Ombudsman appointed under the Older Americans Act of 1965 for the State in which the case is pending to serve as the ombudsman required by paragraph (1).

(C) If the United States trustee does not appoint a State Long-Term Care Ombudsman under subparagraph (B), the court shall notify the State Long-Term Care Ombudsman appointed under the Older Americans Act of 1965 for the State in which the case is pending, of the name and address of the person who is appointed under subparagraph (A).

(b) An ombudsman appointed under subsection (a) shall—

(1) monitor the quality of patient care provided to patients of the debtor, to the extent necessary under the circumstances, including interviewing patients and physicians;

(2) not later than 60 days after the date of appointment, and not less frequently than at 60-day intervals thereafter, report to the court after notice to the parties in interest, at a hearing or in writing, regarding the quality of patient care provided to patients of the debtor; and

(3) if such ombudsman determines that the quality of patient care provided to patients of the debtor is declining significantly or is otherwise being materially compromised, file with the court a motion or a written report, with notice to the parties in interest immediately upon making such determination.

(c)(1) An ombudsman appointed under subsection (a) shall maintain any information obtained by such ombudsman under this section that relates to patients (including information relating to patient records) as confidential information. Such ombudsman may not review confidential patient records unless the court approves such review in advance and imposes restrictions on such ombudsman to protect the confidentiality of such records.

(2) An ombudsman appointed under subsection (a)(2)(B) shall have access to patient records consistent with authority of such ombudsman under the Older Americans Act of 1965 and under non-Federal laws governing the State Long-Term Care Ombudsman program.

§ 341. Meetings of creditors and equity security holders

(a) Within a reasonable time after the order for relief in a case under this title, the United States trustee shall convene and preside at a meeting of creditors.

(b) The United States trustee may convene a meeting of any equity security holders.

(c) The court may not preside at, and may not attend, any meeting under this section including any final meeting of creditors. *Notwithstanding any local court rule, provision of a State constitution, any otherwise applicable nonbankruptcy law, or any other requirement that representation at the meeting of creditors under subsection (a) be by an attorney, a creditor holding a consumer debt or any representative of the creditor (which may include an entity or an employee of an entity and may be a representative for more than 1 creditor) shall be permitted to appear at and participate in the meeting of creditors in a case under chapter 7 or 13, either alone or in conjunction with an attorney for the creditor. Nothing in this subsection shall be construed to require any creditor to be represented by an attorney at any meeting of creditors.*

(d) Prior to the conclusion of the meeting of creditors or equity security holders, the trustee shall orally examine the debtor to ensure that the debtor in a case under chapter 7 of this title is aware of—

(1) the potential consequences of seeking a discharge in bankruptcy, including the effects on credit history;

(2) the debtor's ability to file a petition under a different chapter of this title;

(3) the effect of receiving a discharge of debts under this title; and

(4) the effect of reaffirming a debt, including the debtor's knowledge of the provisions of section 524(d) of this title.

(e) Notwithstanding subsections (a) and (b), the court, on the request of a party in interest and after notice and a hearing, for cause may order that the United States trustee not convene a meeting of creditors or equity security holders if the debtor has filed a plan as to which the debtor solicited acceptances prior to the commencement of the case.

§ 342. Notice

(a) There shall be given such notice as is appropriate, including notice to any holder of a community claim, of an order for relief in a case under this title.

(b) Prior to the commencement of a case under this title by an individual whose debts are primarily consumer debts, the clerk shall give written notice to such

~~individual that indicates each chapter of this title under which such individual may proceed.~~

(b) Before the commencement of a case under this title by an individual whose debts are primarily consumer debts, the clerk shall give to such individual written notice containing—

(1) a brief description of—

(A) chapters 7, 11, 12, and 13 and the general purpose, benefits, and costs of proceeding under each of those chapters; and

(B) the types of services available from credit counseling agencies; and

(2) statements specifying that—

(A) a person who knowingly and fraudulently conceals assets or makes a false oath or statement under penalty of perjury in connection with a case under this title shall be subject to fine, imprisonment, or both; and

(B) all information supplied by a debtor in connection with a case under this title is subject to examination by the Attorney General.

(c)*(1)* If notice is required to be given by the debtor to a creditor under this title, any rule, any applicable law, or any order of the court, such notice shall contain the name, address, and last four digits of the taxpayer identification number of the debtor~~, but the failure of such notice to contain such information shall not invalidate the legal effect of such notice~~. *If the notice concerns an amendment that adds a creditor to the schedules of assets and liabilities, the debtor shall include the full taxpayer identification number in the notice sent to that creditor, but the debtor shall include only the last 4 digits of the taxpayer identification number in the copy of the notice filed with the court.*

(2)(A) If, within the 90 days before the commencement of a voluntary case, a creditor supplies the debtor in at least 2 communications sent to the debtor with the current account number of the debtor and the address at which such creditor requests to receive correspondence, then any notice required by this title to be sent by the debtor to such creditor shall be sent to such address and shall include such account number.

(B) If a creditor would be in violation of applicable nonbankruptcy law by sending any such communication within such 90-day period and if such creditor supplies the debtor in the last 2 communications with the current account number of the debtor and the address at which such creditor requests to receive correspondence, then any notice required by this title to be sent by the debtor to such creditor shall be sent to such address and shall include such account number.

(d) In a case under chapter 7 of this title in which the debtor is an individual and in which the presumption of abuse arises under section 707(b), the clerk shall give written notice to all creditors not later than 10 days after the date of the filing of the petition that the presumption of abuse has arisen.

(e)(1) In a case under chapter 7 or 13 of this title of a debtor who is an individual, a creditor at any time may both file with the court and serve on the debtor a notice of address to be used to provide notice in such case to such creditor.

(2) Any notice in such case required to be provided to such creditor by the debtor or the court later than 5 days after the court and the debtor receive such creditor's notice of address, shall be provided to such address.

(f)(1) An entity may file with any bankruptcy court a notice of address to be used by all the bankruptcy courts or by particular bankruptcy courts, as so specified by such entity at the time such notice is filed, to provide notice to such entity in all cases under chapters 7 and 13 pending in the courts with respect to which such notice is filed, in which such entity is a creditor.

(2) In any case filed under chapter 7 or 13, any notice required to be provided by a court with respect to which a notice is filed under paragraph (1), to such entity later than 30 days after the filing of such notice under paragraph (1) shall be provided to such address unless with respect to a particular case a different address is specified in a notice filed and served in accordance with subsection (e).

(3) A notice filed under paragraph (1) may be withdrawn by such entity.

(g)(1) Notice provided to a creditor by the debtor or the court other than in accordance with this section (excluding this subsection) shall not be effective notice until such notice is brought to the attention of such creditor. If such creditor designates a person or an organizational subdivision of such creditor to be responsible for receiving notices under this title and establishes reasonable procedures so that such notices receivable by such creditor are to be delivered to such person or such subdivision, then a notice provided to such creditor other than in accordance with this section (excluding this subsection) shall not be considered to have been brought to the attention of such creditor until such notice is received by such person or such subdivision.

(2) A monetary penalty may not be imposed on a creditor for a violation of a stay in effect under section 362(a) (including a monetary penalty imposed under section 362(k)) or for failure to comply with section 542 or 543 unless the conduct that is the basis of such violation or of such failure occurs after such creditor receives notice effective under this section of the order for relief.

§ 343. Examination of the debtor

The debtor shall appear and submit to examination under oath at the meeting of creditors under section 341(a) of this title. Creditors, any indenture trustee, any trustee or examiner in the case, or the United States trustee may examine the debtor. The United States trustee may administer the oath required under this section.

§ 344. Self-incrimination; immunity

Immunity for persons required to submit to examination, to testify, or to provide information in a case under this title may be granted under part V of title 18.

§ 345. Money of estates

(a) A trustee in a case under this title may make such deposit or investment of the money of the estate for which such trustee serves as will yield the maximum reasonable net return on such money, taking into account the safety of such deposit or investment.

(b) Except with respect to a deposit or investment that is insured or guaranteed by the United States or by a department, agency, or instrumentality of the United States or backed by the full faith and credit of the United States, the trustee shall require from an entity with which such money is deposited or invested—

(1) a bond—

 (A) in favor of the United States;

 (B) secured by the undertaking of a corporate surety approved by the United States trustee for the district in which the case is pending; and

 (C) conditioned on—

   (i) a proper accounting for all money so deposited or invested and for any return on such money;

   (ii) prompt repayment of such money and return; and

   (iii) faithful performance of duties as a depository; or

 (2) the deposit of securities of the kind specified in section 9303 of title 31;

unless the court for cause orders otherwise.

 (c) An entity with which such moneys are deposited or invested is authorized to deposit or invest such moneys as may be required under this section.

§ 346. Special tax provisions

(a) Except to the extent otherwise provided in this section, subsections (b), (c), (d), (e), (g), (h), (i), and (j) of this section apply notwithstanding any State or local law imposing a tax, but subject to the Internal Revenue Code of 1986.

(b)(1) In a case under chapter 7, 12, or 11 of this title concerning an individual, any income of the estate may be taxed under a State or local law imposing a tax on or measured by income only to the estate, and may not be taxed to such individual. Except as provided in section 728 of this title, if such individual is a partner in a partnership, any gain or loss resulting from a distribution of property from such partnership, or any distributive share of income, gain, loss, deduction, or credit of such individual that is distributed, or considered distributed, from such partnership, after the commencement of the case is gain, loss, income, deduction, or credit, as the case may be, of the estate.

(2) Except as otherwise provided in this section and in section 728 of this title, any income of the estate in such a case, and any State or local tax on or measured by such income, shall be computed in the same manner as the income and the tax of an estate.

(3) The estate in such a case shall use the same accounting method as the debtor used immediately before the commencement of the case.

(c)(1) The commencement of a case under this title concerning a corporation or a partnership does not effect a change in the status of such corporation or partnership for the purposes of any State or local law imposing a tax on or measured by income. Except as otherwise provided in this section and in section 728 of this title, any income of the estate in such case may be taxed only as though such case had not been commenced.

(2) In such a case, except as provided in section 728 of this title, the trustee shall make any tax return otherwise required by State or local law to be filed by or on behalf of such corporation or partnership in the same manner and form as such corporation or partnership, as the case may be, is required to make such return.

~~(d) In a case under chapter 13 of this title, any income of the estate or the debtor may be taxed under a State or local law imposing a tax on or measured by income only to the debtor, and may not be taxed to the estate.~~

~~(e) A claim allowed under section 502(f) or 503 of this title, other than a claim for a tax that is not otherwise deductible or a capital expenditure that is not otherwise deductible, is deductible by the entity to which income of the estate is taxed unless such claim was deducted by another entity, and a deduction for such a claim is deemed to be a deduction attributable to a business.~~

~~(f) The trustee shall withhold from any payment of claims for wages, salaries, commissions, dividends, interest, or other payments, or collect, any amount required to be withheld or collected under applicable State or local tax law, and shall pay such withheld or collected amount to the appropriate governmental unit at the time and in the manner required by such tax law, and with the same priority as the claim from which such amount was withheld was paid.~~

~~(g)(1) Neither gain nor loss shall be recognized on a transfer—~~

~~(A) by operation of law, of property to the estate;~~

~~(B) other than a sale, of property from the estate to the debtor; or~~

~~(C) in a case under chapter 11 or 12 of this title concerning a corporation, of property from the estate to a corporation that is an affiliate participating in a joint plan with the debtor, or that is a successor to the debtor under the plan, except that gain or loss may be recognized to the same extent that such transfer results in the recognition of gain or loss under section 371 of the Internal Revenue Code of 1986.~~

~~(2) The transferee of a transfer of a kind specified in this subsection shall take the property transferred with the same character, and with the transferor's basis, as adjusted under subsection (j)(5) of this section, and holding period.~~

~~(h) Notwithstanding sections 728(a) and 1146(a) of this title, for the purpose of determining the number of taxable periods during which the debtor or the estate may use a loss carryover or a loss carryback, the taxable period of the debtor during which the case is commenced is deemed not to have been terminated by such commencement.~~

~~(i)(1) In a case under chapter 7, 12, or 11 of this title concerning an individual, the estate shall succeed to the debtor's tax attributes, including—~~

~~(A) any investment credit carryover;~~

~~(B) any recovery exclusion;~~

~~(C) any loss carryover;~~

~~(D) any foreign tax credit carryover;~~

~~(E) any capital loss carryover; and~~

~~(F) any claim of right.~~

~~(2) After such a case is closed or dismissed, the debtor shall succeed to any tax attribute to which the estate succeeded under paragraph (1) of this subsection but that was not utilized by the estate. The debtor may utilize such tax attributes as though any applicable time limitations on such utilization by the debtor were suspended during the time during which the case was pending.~~

~~(3) In such a case, the estate may carry back any loss of the estate to a taxable period of the debtor that ended before the order for relief under such chapter the same as the debtor could have carried back such loss had the debtor~~

incurred such loss and the case under this title had not been commenced, but the debtor may not carry back any loss of the debtor from a taxable period that ends after such order to any taxable period of the debtor that ended before such order until after the case is closed.

(j)(1) Except as otherwise provided in this subsection, income is not realized by the estate, the debtor, or a successor to the debtor by reason of forgiveness or discharge of indebtedness in a case under this title.

(2) For the purposes of any State or local law imposing a tax on or measured by income, a deduction with respect to a liability may not be allowed for any taxable period during or after which such liability is forgiven or discharged under this title. In this paragraph, "a deduction with respect to a liability" includes a capital loss incurred on the disposition of a capital asset with respect to a liability that was incurred in connection with the acquisition of such asset.

(3) Except as provided in paragraph (4) of this subsection, for the purpose of any State or local law imposing a tax on or measured by income, any net operating loss of an individual or corporate debtor, including a net operating loss carryover to such debtor, shall be reduced by the amount of indebtedness forgiven or discharged in a case under this title, except to the extent that such forgiveness or discharge resulted in a disallowance under paragraph (2) of this subsection.

(4) A reduction of a net operating loss or a net operating loss carryover under paragraph (3) of this subsection or of basis under paragraph (5) of this subsection is not required to the extent that the indebtedness of an individual or corporate debtor forgiven or discharged—

(A) consisted of items of a deductible nature that were not deducted by such debtor; or

(B) resulted in an expired net operating loss carryover or other deduction that—

(i) did not offset income for any taxable period; and

(ii) did not contribute to a net operating loss in or a net operating loss carryover to the taxable period during or after which such indebtedness was discharged.

(5) For the purposes of a State or local law imposing a tax on or measured by income, the basis of the debtor's property or of property transferred to an entity required to use the debtor's basis in whole or in part shall be reduced by the lesser of—

(A)(i) the amount by which the indebtedness of the debtor has been forgiven or discharged in a case under this title; minus

(ii) the total amount of adjustments made under paragraphs (2) and (3) of this subsection; and

(B) the amount by which the total basis of the debtor's assets that were property of the estate before such forgiveness or discharge exceeds the debtor's total liabilities that were liabilities both before and after such forgiveness or discharge.

(6) Notwithstanding paragraph (5) of this subsection, basis is not required to be reduced to the extent that the debtor elects to treat as taxable income, of the taxable period in which indebtedness is forgiven or discharged, the amount of

~~indebtedness forgiven or discharged that otherwise would be applied in reduction of basis under paragraph (5) of this subsection.~~

~~(7) For the purposes of this subsection, indebtedness with respect to which an equity security, other than an interest of a limited partner in a limited partnership, is issued to the creditor to whom such indebtedness was owed, or that is forgiven as a contribution to capital by an equity security holder other than a limited partner in the debtor, is not forgiven or discharged in a case under this title—~~

~~(A) to any extent that such indebtedness did not consist of items of a deductible nature; or~~

~~(B) if the issuance of such equity security has the same consequences under a law imposing a tax on or measured by income to such creditor as a payment in cash to such creditor in an amount equal to the fair market value of such equity security, then to the lesser of—~~

~~(i) the extent that such issuance has the same such consequences; and~~

~~(ii) the extent of such fair market value.~~

§ 346. Special provisions related to the treatment of State and local taxes

(a) Whenever the Internal Revenue Code of 1986 provides that a separate taxable estate or entity is created in a case concerning a debtor under this title, and the income, gain, loss, deductions, and credits of such estate shall be taxed to or claimed by the estate, a separate taxable estate is also created for purposes of any State and local law imposing a tax on or measured by income and such income, gain, loss, deductions, and credits shall be taxed to or claimed by the estate and may not be taxed to or claimed by the debtor. The preceding sentence shall not apply if the case is dismissed. The trustee shall make tax returns of income required under any such State or local law.

(b) Whenever the Internal Revenue Code of 1986 provides that no separate taxable estate shall be created in a case concerning a debtor under this title, and the income, gain, loss, deductions, and credits of an estate shall be taxed to or claimed by the debtor, such income, gain, loss, deductions, and credits shall be taxed to or claimed by the debtor under a State or local law imposing a tax on or measured by income and may not be taxed to or claimed by the estate. The trustee shall make such tax returns of income of corporations and of partnerships as are required under any State or local law, but with respect to partnerships, shall make such returns only to the extent such returns are also required to be made under such Code. The estate shall be liable for any tax imposed on such corporation or partnership, but not for any tax imposed on partners or members.

(c) With respect to a partnership or any entity treated as a partnership under a State or local law imposing a tax on or measured by income that is a debtor in a case under this title, any gain or loss resulting from a distribution of property from such partnership, or any distributive share of any income, gain, loss, deduction, or credit of a partner or member that is distributed, or considered distributed, from such partnership, after the commencement of the case, is gain, loss, income, deduction, or credit, as the case may be, of the partner or member, and if such partner or member is a debtor in a case under this title, shall be subject to tax in accordance with subsection (a) or (b).

(d) For purposes of any State or local law imposing a tax on or measured by income, the taxable period of a debtor in a case under this title shall terminate only if and to the extent that the taxable period of such debtor terminates under the Internal Revenue Code of 1986.

(e) The estate in any case described in subsection (a) shall use the same accounting method as the debtor used immediately before the commencement of the case, if such method of accounting complies with applicable nonbankruptcy tax law.

(f) For purposes of any State or local law imposing a tax on or measured by income, a transfer of property from the debtor to the estate or from the estate to the debtor shall not be treated as a disposition for purposes of any provision assigning tax consequences to a disposition, except to the extent that such transfer is treated as a disposition under the Internal Revenue Code of 1986.

(g) Whenever a tax is imposed pursuant to a State or local law imposing a tax on or measured by income pursuant to subsection (a) or (b), such tax shall be imposed at rates generally applicable to the same types of entities under such State or local law.

(h) The trustee shall withhold from any payment of claims for wages, salaries, commissions, dividends, interest, or other payments, or collect, any amount required to be withheld or collected under applicable State or local tax law, and shall pay such withheld or collected amount to the appropriate governmental unit at the time and in the manner required by such tax law, and with the same priority as the claim from which such amount was withheld or collected was paid.

(i)(1) To the extent that any State or local law imposing a tax on or measured by income provides for the carryover of any tax attribute from one taxable period to a subsequent taxable period, the estate shall succeed to such tax attribute in any case in which such estate is subject to tax under subsection (a).

(2) After such a case is closed or dismissed, the debtor shall succeed to any tax attribute to which the estate succeeded under paragraph (1) to the extent consistent with the Internal Revenue Code of 1986.

(3) The estate may carry back any loss or tax attribute to a taxable period of the debtor that ended before the date of the order for relief under this title to the extent that—

(A) applicable State or local tax law provides for a carryback in the case of the debtor; and

(B) the same or a similar tax attribute may be carried back by the estate to such a taxable period of the debtor under the Internal Revenue Code of 1986.

(j)(1) For purposes of any State or local law imposing a tax on or measured by income, income is not realized by the estate, the debtor, or a successor to the debtor by reason of discharge of indebtedness in a case under this title, except to the extent, if any, that such income is subject to tax under the Internal Revenue Code of 1986.

(2) Whenever the Internal Revenue Code of 1986 provides that the amount excluded from gross income in respect of the discharge of indebtedness in a case under this title shall be applied to reduce the tax attributes of the debtor or the estate, a similar reduction shall be made under any State or local law imposing a tax on or measured by income to the extent such State or local law recognizes such attributes. Such State or local law may also provide for the

reduction of other attributes to the extent that the full amount of income from the discharge of indebtedness has not been applied.

(k)(1) Except as provided in this section and section 505, the time and manner of filing tax returns and the items of income, gain, loss, deduction, and credit of any taxpayer shall be determined under applicable nonbankruptcy law.

(2) For Federal tax purposes, the provisions of this section are subject to the Internal Revenue Code of 1986 and other applicable Federal nonbankruptcy law.

§ 347. Unclaimed property

(a) Ninety days after the final distribution under section 726, 1226, or 1326 of this title in a case under chapter 7, 12, or 13 of this title, as the case may be, the trustee shall stop payment on any check remaining unpaid, and any remaining property of the estate shall be paid into the court and disposed of under chapter 129 of title 28.

(b) Any security, money, or other property remaining unclaimed at the expiration of the time allowed in a case under chapter 9, 11, or 12 of this title for the presentation of a security or the performance of any other act as a condition to participation in the distribution under any plan confirmed under section 943(b), 1129, 1173, or 1225 of this title, as the case may be, becomes the property of the debtor or of the entity acquiring the assets of the debtor under the plan, as the case may be.

§ 348. Effect of conversion

(a) Conversion of a case from a case under one chapter of this title to a case under another chapter of this title constitutes an order for relief under the chapter to which the case is converted, but, except as provided in subsections (b) and (c) of this section, does not effect a change in the date of the filing of the petition, the commencement of the case, or the order for relief.

(b) Unless the court for cause orders otherwise, in sections 701(a), 727(a)(10), 727(b), 728(a), 728(b), 1102(a), 1110(a)(1), 1121(b), 1121(c), 1141(d)(4), 1146(a), 1146(b), 1201(a), 1221, 1228(a), 1301(a), and 1305(a) of this title, "the order for relief under this chapter" in a chapter to which a case has been converted under section 706, 1112, 1208, or 1307 of this title means the conversion of such case to such chapter.

(c) Sections 342 and 365(d) of this title apply in a case that has been converted under section 706, 1112, 1208, or 1307 of this title, as if the conversion order were the order for relief.

(d) A claim against the estate or the debtor that arises after the order for relief but before conversion in a case that is converted under section 1112, 1208, or 1307 of this title, other than a claim specified in section 503(b) of this title, shall be treated for all purposes as if such claim had arisen immediately before the date of the filing of the petition.

(e) Conversion of a case under section 706, 1112, 1208, or 1307 of this title terminates the service of any trustee or examiner that is serving in the case before such conversion.

(f)(1) Except as provided in paragraph (2), when a case under chapter 13 of this title is converted to a case under another chapter under this title—

(A) property of the estate in the converted case shall consist of property of the estate, as of the date of filing of the petition, that remains in the possession of or is under the control of the debtor on the date of conversion; ~~and~~

(B) valuations of property and of allowed secured claims in the chapter 13 case shall apply ~~in the converted case, with allowed secured claims~~ *only in a case converted to a case under chapter 11 or 12, but not in a case converted to a case under chapter 7, with allowed secured claims in cases under chapters 11 and 12* reduced to the extent that they have been paid in accordance with the chapter 13 plan~~.~~*; and*

(C) with respect to cases converted from chapter 13—

(i) the claim of any creditor holding security as of the date of the petition shall continue to be secured by that security unless the full amount of such claim determined under applicable nonbankruptcy law has been paid in full as of the date of conversion, notwithstanding any valuation or determination of the amount of an allowed secured claim made for the purposes of the case under chapter 13; and

(ii) unless a prebankruptcy default has been fully cured under the plan at the time of conversion, in any proceeding under this title or otherwise, the default shall have the effect given under applicable nonbankruptcy law.

(2) If the debtor converts a case under chapter 13 of this title to a case under another chapter under this title in bad faith, the property *of the estate* in the converted case shall consist of the property of the estate as of the date of conversion.

§ 349. Effect of dismissal

(a) Unless the court, for cause, orders otherwise, the dismissal of a case under this title does not bar the discharge, in a later case under this title, of debts that were dischargeable in the case dismissed; nor does the dismissal of a case under this title prejudice the debtor with regard to the filing of a subsequent petition under this title, except as provided in section 109(g) of this title.

(b) Unless the court, for cause, orders otherwise, a dismissal of a case other than under section 742 of this title—

(1) reinstates—

(A) any proceeding or custodianship superseded under section 543 of this title;

(B) any transfer avoided under section 522, 544, 545, 547, 548, 549, or 724(a) of this title, or preserved under section 510(c)(2), 522(i)(2), or 551 of this title; and

(C) any lien voided under section 506(d) of this title;

(2) vacates any order, judgment, or transfer ordered, under section 522(i)(1), 542, 550, or 553 of this title; and

(3) revests the property of the estate in the entity in which such property was vested immediately before the commencement of the case under this title.

§ 350. Closing and reopening cases

(a) After an estate is fully administered and the court has discharged the trustee, the court shall close the case.

(b) A case may be reopened in the court in which such case was closed to administer assets, to accord relief to the debtor, or for other cause.

§ 351. Disposal of patient records

If a health care business commences a case under chapter 7, 9, or 11, and the trustee does not have a sufficient amount of funds to pay for the storage of patient records in the manner required under applicable Federal or State law, the following requirements shall apply:

(1) The trustee shall—

(A) promptly publish notice, in 1 or more appropriate newspapers, that if patient records are not claimed by the patient or an insurance provider (if applicable law permits the insurance provider to make that claim) by the date that is 365 days after the date of that notification, the trustee will destroy the patient records; and

(B) during the first 180 days of the 365-day period described in subparagraph (A), promptly attempt to notify directly each patient that is the subject of the patient records and appropriate insurance carrier concerning the patient records by mailing to the most recent known address of that patient, or a family member or contact person for that patient, and to the appropriate insurance carrier an appropriate notice regarding the claiming or disposing of patient records.

(2) If, after providing the notification under paragraph (1), patient records are not claimed during the 365-day period described under that paragraph, the trustee shall mail, by certified mail, at the end of such 365- day period a written request to each appropriate Federal agency to request permission from that agency to deposit the patient records with that agency, except that no Federal agency is required to accept patient records under this paragraph.

(3) If, following the 365-day period described in paragraph (2) and after providing the notification under paragraph (1), patient records are not claimed by a patient or insurance provider, or request is not granted by a Federal agency to deposit such records with that agency, the trustee shall destroy those records by—

(A) if the records are written, shredding or burning the records; or

(B) if the records are magnetic, optical, or other electronic records, by otherwise destroying those records so that those records cannot be retrieved.

§ 361. Adequate protection

When adequate protection is required under section 362, 363, or 364 of this title of an interest of an entity in property, such adequate protection may be provided by—

(1) requiring the trustee to make a cash payment or periodic cash payments to such entity, to the extent that the stay under section 362 of this title, use, sale, or lease under section 363 of this title, or any grant of a lien under section 364 of

this title results in a decrease in the value of such entity's interest in such property;

(2) providing to such entity an additional or replacement lien to the extent that such stay, use, sale, lease, or grant results in a decrease in the value of such entity's interest in such property; or

(3) granting such other relief, other than entitling such entity to compensation allowable under section 503(b)(1) of this title as an administrative expense, as will result in the realization by such entity of the indubitable equivalent of such entity's interest in such property.

§ 362. Automatic stay

(a) Except as provided in subsection (b) of this section, a petition filed under section 301, 302, or 303 of this title, or an application filed under section 5(a)(3) of the Securities Investor Protection Act of 1970, operates as a stay, applicable to all entities, of—

(1) the commencement or continuation, including the issuance or employment of process, of a judicial, administrative, or other action or proceeding against the debtor that was or could have been commenced before the commencement of the case under this title, or to recover a claim against the debtor that arose before the commencement of the case under this title;

(2) the enforcement, against the debtor or against property of the estate, of a judgment obtained before the commencement of the case under this title;

(3) any act to obtain possession of property of the estate or of property from the estate or to exercise control over property of the estate;

(4) any act to create, perfect, or enforce any lien against property of the estate;

(5) any act to create, perfect, or enforce against property of the debtor any lien to the extent that such lien secures a claim that arose before the commencement of the case under this title;

(6) any act to collect, assess, or recover a claim against the debtor that arose before the commencement of the case under this title;

(7) the setoff of any debt owing to the debtor that arose before the commencement of the case under this title against any claim against the debtor; and

(8) the commencement or continuation of a proceeding before the United States Tax Court concerning the debtor *a corporate debtor's tax liability for a taxable period the bankruptcy court may determine or concerning the tax liability of a debtor who is an individual for a taxable period ending before the date of the order for relief under this title.*

(b) The filing of a petition under section 301, 302, or 303 of this title, or of an application under section 5(a)(3) of the Securities Investor Protection Act of 1970, does not operate as a stay—

(1) under subsection (a) of this section, of the commencement or continuation of a criminal action or proceeding against the debtor;

(2) under subsection (a) of this section—

(A) of the commencement or continuation of an action or proceeding for—

(i) the establishment of paternity; or

~~(ii) the establishment or modification of an order for alimony, maintenance, or support; or~~

~~(B) of the collection of alimony, maintenance, or support from property that is not property of the estate;~~

(2) under subsection (a)—

(A) of the commencement or continuation of a civil action or proceeding—

(i) for the establishment of paternity;

(ii) for the establishment or modification of an order for domestic support obligations;

(iii) concerning child custody or visitation;

(iv) for the dissolution of a marriage, except to the extent that such proceeding seeks to determine the division of property that is property of the estate; or

(v) regarding domestic violence;

(B) of the collection of a domestic support obligation from property that is not property of the estate;

(C) with respect to the withholding of income that is property of the estate or property of the debtor for payment of a domestic support obligation under a judicial or administrative order or a statute;

(D) of the withholding, suspension, or restriction of a driver's license, a professional or occupational license, or a recreational license, under State law, as specified in section 466(a)(16) of the Social Security Act;

(E) of the reporting of overdue support owed by a parent to any consumer reporting agency as specified in section 466(a)(7) of the Social Security Act;

(F) of the interception of a tax refund, as specified in sections 464 and 466(a)(3) of the Social Security Act or under an analogous State law; or

(G) of the enforcement of a medical obligation, as specified under title IV of the Social Security Act;

(3) under subsection (a) of this section, of any act to perfect, or to maintain or continue the perfection of, an interest in property to the extent that the trustee's rights and powers are subject to such perfection under section 546(b) of this title or to the extent that such act is accomplished within the period provided under section 547(e)(2)(A) of this title;

(4) under paragraph (1), (2), (3), or (6) of subsection (a) of this section, of the commencement or continuation of an action or proceeding by a governmental unit or any organization exercising authority under the Convention on the Prohibition of the Development, Production, Stockpiling and Use of Chemical Weapons and on Their Destruction, opened for signature on January 13, 1993, to enforce such governmental unit's or organization's police and regulatory power, including the enforcement of a judgment other than a money judgment, obtained in an action or proceeding by the governmental unit to enforce such governmental unit's or organization's police or regulatory power;

[(5) Repealed. Pub.L. 105-277, Div. I, Title VI, § 603(1), Oct. 21, 1998, 112 Stat. 2681-886]

(6) under subsection (a) of this section, of the setoff by a commodity broker, forward contract merchant, stockbroker, financial institutions, *financial partici-*

pant, or securities clearing agency of any mutual debt and claim under or in connection with commodity contracts, as defined in section 761 of this title, forward contracts, or securities contracts, as defined in section 741 of this title, that constitutes the setoff of a claim against the debtor for a margin payment, as defined in section 101, 741, or 761 of this title, or settlement payment, as defined in section 101 or 741 of this title, arising out of commodity contracts, forward contracts, or securities contracts against cash, securities, or other property held by, *pledged to, under the control of,* or due from such commodity broker, forward contract merchant, stockbroker, financial institutions, *financial participant,* or securities clearing agency to margin, guarantee, secure, or settle commodity contracts, forward contracts, or securities contracts;

(7) under subsection (a) of this section, of the setoff by a repo participant *or financial participant,* of any mutual debt and claim under or in connection with repurchase agreements that constitutes the setoff of a claim against the debtor for a margin payment, as defined in section 741 or 761 of this title, or settlement payment, as defined in section 741 of this title, arising out of repurchase agreements against cash, securities, or other property held by, *pledged to, under the control of,* or due from such repo participant *or financial participant* to margin, guarantee, secure or settle repurchase agreements;

(8) under subsection (a) of this section, of the commencement of any action by the Secretary of Housing and Urban Development to foreclose a mortgage or deed of trust in any case in which the mortgage or deed of trust held by the Secretary is insured or was formerly insured under the National Housing Act and covers property, or combinations of property, consisting of five or more living units;

(9) under subsection (a), of—

(A) an audit by a governmental unit to determine tax liability;

(B) the issuance to the debtor by a governmental unit of a notice of tax deficiency;

(C) a demand for tax returns; or

(D) the making of an assessment for any tax and issuance of a notice and demand for payment of such an assessment (but any tax lien that would otherwise attach to property of the estate by reason of such an assessment shall not take effect unless such tax is a debt of the debtor that will not be discharged in the case and such property or its proceeds are transferred out of the estate to, or otherwise revested in, the debtor).

(10) under subsection (a) of this section, of any act by a lessor to the debtor under a lease of nonresidential real property that has terminated by the expiration of the stated term of the lease before the commencement of or during a case under this title to obtain possession of such property;

(11) under subsection (a) of this section, of the presentment of a negotiable instrument and the giving of notice of and protesting dishonor of such an instrument;

(12) under subsection (a) of this section, after the date which is 90 days after the filing of such petition, of the commencement or continuation, and conclusion to the entry of final judgment, of an action which involves a debtor subject to reorganization pursuant to chapter 11 of this title and which was brought by the Secretary of Transportation under section 31325 of title 46 (including distribution of any proceeds of sale) to foreclose a preferred ship or fleet mort-

gage, or a security interest in or relating to a vessel or vessel under construction, held by the Secretary of Transportation under section 207 or title XI of the Merchant Marine Act, 1936, or under applicable State law;

(13) under subsection (a) of this section, after the date which is 90 days after the filing of such petition, of the commencement or continuation, and conclusion to the entry of final judgment, of an action which involves a debtor subject to reorganization pursuant to chapter 11 of this title and which was brought by the Secretary of Commerce under section 31325 of title 46 (including distribution of any proceeds of sale) to foreclose a preferred ship or fleet mortgage in a vessel or a mortgage, deed of trust, or other security interest in a fishing facility held by the Secretary of Commerce under section 207 or title XI of the Merchant Marine Act, 1936;

(14) under subsection (a) of this section, of any action by an accrediting agency regarding the accreditation status of the debtor as an educational institution;

(15) under subsection (a) of this section, of any action by a State licensing body regarding the licensure of the debtor as an educational institution;

(16) under subsection (a) of this section, of any action by a guaranty agency, as defined in section 435(j) of the Higher Education Act of 1965 or the Secretary of Education regarding the eligibility of the debtor to participate in programs authorized under such Act;

~~(17) under subsection (a) of this section, of the setoff by a swap participant, of any mutual debt and claim under or in connection with any swap agreement that constitutes the setoff of a claim against the debtor for any payment due from the debtor under or in connection with any swap agreement against any payment due to the debtor from the swap participant under or in connection with any swap agreement or against cash, securities, or other property of the debtor held by or due from such swap participant to guarantee, secure or settle any swap agreement; or~~ *(17) under subsection (a), of the setoff by a swap participant or financial participant of a mutual debt and claim under or in connection with one or more swap agreements that constitutes the setoff of a claim against the debtor for any payment or other transfer of property due from the debtor under or in connection with any swap agreement against any payment due to the debtor from the swap participant or financial participant under or in connection with any swap agreement or against cash, securities, or other property held by, pledged to, under the control of, or due from such swap participant or financial participant to margin, guarantee, secure, or settle any swap agreement;*

(18) ~~under subsection (a) of the creation or perfection of a statutory lien for an ad valorem property tax imposed by the District of Columbia, or a political subdivision of a State, if such tax comes due after the filing of the petition.~~ *under subsection (a) of the creation or perfection of a statutory lien for an ad valorem property tax, or a special tax or special assessment on real property whether or not ad valorem, imposed by a governmental unit, if such tax or assessment comes due after the date of the filing of the petition;*

(19) under subsection (a), of withholding of income from a debtor's wages and collection of amounts withheld, under the debtor's agreement authorizing that withholding and collection for the benefit of a pension, profit-sharing, stock bonus, or other plan established under section 401, 403, 408, 408A, 414, 457,

or 501(c) of the Internal Revenue Code of 1986, that is sponsored by the employer of the debtor, or an affiliate, successor, or predecessor of such employer—

(A) to the extent that the amounts withheld and collected are used solely for payments relating to a loan from a plan under section 408(b)(1) of the Employee Retirement Income Security Act of 1974 or is subject to section 72(p) of the Internal Revenue Code of 1986; or

(B) a loan from a thrift savings plan permitted under subchapter III of chapter 84 of title 5, that satisfies the requirements of section 8433(g) of such title;

but nothing in this paragraph may be construed to provide that any loan made under a governmental plan under section 414(d), or a contract or account under section 403(b), of the Internal Revenue Code of 1986 constitutes a claim or a debt under this title;

(20) under subsection (a), of any act to enforce any lien against or security interest in real property following entry of the order under subsection (d)(4) as to such real property in any prior case under this title, for a period of 2 years after the date of the entry of such an order, except that the debtor, in a subsequent case under this title, may move for relief from such order based upon changed circumstances or for other good cause shown, after notice and a hearing;

(21) under subsection (a), of any act to enforce any lien against or security interest in real property—

(A) if the debtor is ineligible under section 109(g) to be a debtor in a case under this title; or

(B) if the case under this title was filed in violation of a bankruptcy court order in a prior case under this title prohibiting the debtor from being a debtor in another case under this title;

(22) subject to subsection (l), under subsection (a)(3), of the continuation of any eviction, unlawful detainer action, or similar proceeding by a lessor against a debtor involving residential property in which the debtor resides as a tenant under a lease or rental agreement and with respect to which the lessor has obtained before the date of the filing of the bankruptcy petition, a judgment for possession of such property against the debtor;

(23) subject to subsection (m), under subsection (a)(3), of an eviction action that seeks possession of the residential property in which the debtor resides as a tenant under a lease or rental agreement based on endangerment of such property or the illegal use of controlled substances on such property, but only if the lessor files with the court, and serves upon the debtor, a certification under penalty of perjury that such an eviction action has been filed, or that the debtor, during the 30-day period preceding the date of the filing of the certification, has endangered property or illegally used or allowed to be used a controlled substance on the property;

(24) under subsection (a), of any transfer that is not avoidable under section 544 and that is not avoidable under section 549;

(25) under subsection (a), of—

(A) the commencement or continuation of an investigation or action by a securities self regulatory organization to enforce such organization's regulatory power;

(B) the enforcement of an order or decision, other than for monetary sanctions, obtained in an action by such securities self regulatory organization to enforce such organization's regulatory power; or

(C) any act taken by such securities self regulatory organization to delist, delete, or refuse to permit quotation of any stock that does not meet applicable regulatory requirements;

(26) under subsection (a), of the setoff under applicable nonbankruptcy law of an income tax refund, by a governmental unit, with respect to a taxable period that ended before the date of the order for relief against an income tax liability for a taxable period that also ended before the date of the order for relief, except that in any case in which the setoff of an income tax refund is not permitted under applicable nonbankruptcy law because of a pending action to determine the amount or legality of a tax liability, the governmental unit may hold the refund pending the resolution of the action, unless the court, on the motion of the trustee and after notice and a hearing, grants the taxing authority adequate protection (within the meaning of section 361) for the secured claim of such authority in the setoff under section 506(a);

(27) under subsection (a), of the setoff by a master netting agreement participant of a mutual debt and claim under or in connection with one or more master netting agreements or any contract or agreement subject to such agreements that constitutes the setoff of a claim against the debtor for any payment or other transfer of property due from the debtor under or in connection with such agreements or any contract or agreement subject to such agreements against any payment due to the debtor from such master netting agreement participant under or in connection with such agreements or any contract or agreement subject to such agreements or against cash, securities, or other property held by, pledged to, under the control of, or due from such master netting agreement participant to margin, guarantee, secure, or settle such agreements or any contract or agreement subject to such agreements, to the extent that such participant is eligible to exercise such offset rights under paragraph (6), (7), or (17) for each individual contract covered by the master netting agreement in issue; and

(28) under subsection (a), of the exclusion by the Secretary of Health and Human Services of the debtor from participation in the medicare program or any other Federal health care program (as defined in section 1128B(f) of the Social Security Act pursuant to title XI or XVIII of such Act).

The provisions of paragraphs (12) and (13) of this subsection shall apply with respect to any such petition filed on or before December 31, 1989.

(c) Except as provided in subsections (d), (e), ~~and~~ (f), *and (h)* of this section—

(1) the stay of an act against property of the estate under subsection (a) of this section continues until such property is no longer property of the estate; ~~and~~

(2) the stay of any other act under subsection (a) of this section continues until the earliest of—

(A) the time the case is closed;

(B) the time the case is dismissed; or

(C) if the case is a case under chapter 7 of this title concerning an individual or a case under chapter 9, 11, 12, or 13 of this title, the time a discharge is granted or denied.

(3) if a single or joint case is filed by or against debtor who is an individual in a case under chapter 7, 11, or 13, and if a single or joint case of the debtor was pending within the preceding 1-year period but was dismissed, other than a case refiled under a chapter other than chapter 7 after dismissal under section 707(b)—

(A) the stay under subsection (a) with respect to any action taken with respect to a debt or property securing such debt or with respect to any lease shall terminate with respect to the debtor on the 30th day after the filing of the later case;

(B) on the motion of a party in interest for continuation of the automatic stay and upon notice and a hearing, the court may extend the stay in particular cases as to any or all creditors (subject to such conditions or limitations as the court may then impose) after notice and a hearing completed before the expiration of the 30-day period only if the party in interest demonstrates that the filing of the later case is in good faith as to the creditors to be stayed; and

(C) for purposes of subparagraph (B), a case is presumptively filed not in good faith (but such presumption may be rebutted by clear and convincing evidence to the contrary)—

(i) as to all creditors, if—

(I) more than 1 previous case under any of chapters 7, 11, and 13 in which the individual was a debtor was pending within the preceding 1-year period;

(II) a previous case under any of chapters 7, 11, and 13 in which the individual was a debtor was dismissed within such 1-year period, after the debtor failed to—

(aa) file or amend the petition or other documents as required by this title or the court without substantial excuse (but mere inadvertence or negligence shall not be a substantial excuse unless the dismissal was caused by the negligence of the debtor's attorney);

(bb) provide adequate protection as ordered by the court; or

(cc) perform the terms of a plan confirmed by the court; or

(III) there has not been a substantial change in the financial or personal affairs of the debtor since the dismissal of the next most previous case under chapter 7, 11, or 13 or any other reason to conclude that the later case will be concluded—

(aa) if a case under chapter 7, with a discharge; or

(bb) if a case under chapter 11 or 13, with a confirmed plan that will be fully performed; and

(ii) as to any creditor that commenced an action under subsection (d) in a previous case in which the individual was a debtor if, as of the date of dismissal of such case, that action was still pending or had been resolved by terminating, conditioning, or limiting the stay as to actions of such creditor; and

(4)(A)(i) if a single or joint case is filed by or against a debtor who is an individual under this title, and if 2 or more single or joint cases of the debtor were pending within the previous year but were dismissed, other than a case refiled under section 707(b), the stay under subsection (a) shall not go into effect upon the filing of the later case; and

(ii) on request of a party in interest, the court shall promptly enter an order confirming that no stay is in effect;

(B) if, within 30 days after the filing of the later case, a party in interest requests the court may order the stay to take effect in the case as to any or all creditors (subject to such conditions or limitations as the court may impose), after notice and a hearing, only if the party in interest demonstrates that the filing of the later case is in good faith as to the creditors to be stayed;

(C) a stay imposed under subparagraph (B) shall be effective on the date of the entry of the order allowing the stay to go into effect; and

(D) for purposes of subparagraph (B), a case is presumptively filed not in good faith (but such presumption may be rebutted by clear and convincing evidence to the contrary)—

(i) as to all creditors if—

(I) 2 or more previous cases under this title in which the individual was a debtor were pending within the 1-year period;

(II) a previous case under this title in which the individual was a debtor was dismissed within the time period stated in this paragraph after the debtor failed to file or amend the petition or other documents as required by this title or the court without substantial excuse (but mere inadvertence or negligence shall not be substantial excuse unless the dismissal was caused by the negligence of the debtor's attorney), failed to provide adequate protection as ordered by the court, or failed to perform the terms of a plan confirmed by the court; or

(III) there has not been a substantial change in the financial or personal affairs of the debtor since the dismissal of the next most previous case under this title, or any other reason to conclude that the later case will not be concluded, if a case under chapter 7, with a discharge, and if a case under chapter 11 or 13, with a confirmed plan that will be fully performed; or

(ii) as to any creditor that commenced an action under subsection (d) in a previous case in which the individual was a debtor if, as of the date of dismissal of such case, such action was still pending or had been resolved by terminating, conditioning, or limiting the stay as to such action of such creditor.

(d) On request of a party in interest and after notice and a hearing, the court shall grant relief from the stay provided under subsection (a) of this section, such as by terminating, annulling, modifying, or conditioning such stay—

(1) for cause, including the lack of adequate protection of an interest in property of such party in interest;

(2) with respect to a stay of an act against property under subsection (a) of this section, if—

(A) the debtor does not have an equity in such property; and

(B) such property is not necessary to an effective reorganization; ~~or~~

(3) with respect to a stay of an act against single asset real estate under subsection (a), by a creditor whose claim is secured by an interest in such real estate, unless, not later than the date that is 90 days after the entry of the order for relief (or such later date as the court may determine for cause by order entered within that 90-day period) *or 30 days after the court determines that the debtor is subject to this paragraph, whichever is later—*

(A) the debtor has filed a plan of reorganization that has a reasonable possibility of being confirmed within a reasonable time; or

~~(B) the debtor has commenced monthly payments to each creditor whose claim is secured by such real estate (other than a claim secured by a judgment lien or by an unmatured statutory lien), which payments are in an amount equal to interest at a current fair market rate on the value of the creditor's interest in the real estate.~~

(B) the debtor has commenced monthly payments that—

(i) may, in the debtor's sole discretion, notwithstanding section 363(c)(2), be made from rents or other income generated before, on, or after the date of the commencement of the case by or from the property to each creditor whose claim is secured by such real estate (other than a claim secured by a judgment lien or by an unmatured statutory lien); and

(ii) are in an amount equal to interest at the then applicable nondefault contract rate of interest on the value of the creditor's interest in the real estate; or

(4) with respect to a stay of an act against real property under subsection (a), by a creditor whose claim is secured by an interest in such real property, if the court finds that the filing of the petition was part of a scheme to delay, hinder, and defraud creditors that involved either—

(A) transfer of all or part ownership of, or other interest in, such real property without the consent of the secured creditor or court approval; or

(B) multiple bankruptcy filings affecting such real property.

If recorded in compliance with applicable State laws governing notices of interests or liens in real property, an order entered under paragraph (4) shall be binding in any other case under this title purporting to affect such real property filed not later than 2 years after the date of the entry of such order by the court, except that a debtor in a subsequent case under this title may move for relief from such order based upon changed circumstances or for good cause shown, after notice and a hearing. Any Federal, State, or local governmental unit that accepts notices of interests or liens in real property shall accept any certified copy of an order described in this subsection for indexing and recording.

(e)*(1)* Thirty days after a request under subsection (d) of this section for relief from the stay of any act against property of the estate under subsection (a) of this section, such stay is terminated with respect to the party in interest making such request, unless the court, after notice and a hearing, orders such stay continued in effect pending the conclusion of, or as a result of, a final hearing and determination under subsection (d) of this section. A hearing under this subsection may be a preliminary hearing, or may be consolidated with the final hearing under subsection (d) of this section. The court shall order such stay continued in effect pending the conclusion of the final hearing under subsection

(d) of this section if there is a reasonable likelihood that the party opposing relief from such stay will prevail at the conclusion of such final hearing. If the hearing under this subsection is a preliminary hearing, then such final hearing shall be concluded not later than thirty days after the conclusion of such preliminary hearing, unless the 30-day period is extended with the consent of the parties in interest or for a specific time which the court finds is required by compelling circumstances.

(2) Notwithstanding paragraph (1), in a case under chapter 7, 11, or 13 in which the debtor is an individual, the stay under subsection (a) shall terminate on the date that is 60 days after a request is made by a party in interest under subsection (d), unless

(A) a final decision is rendered by the court during the 60-day period beginning on the date of the request; or

(B) such 60-day period is extended—

(i) by agreement of all parties in interest; or

(ii) by the court for such specific period of time as the court finds is required for good cause, as described in findings made by the court.

(f) Upon request of a party in interest, the court, with or without a hearing, shall grant such relief from the stay provided under subsection (a) of this section as is necessary to prevent irreparable damage to the interest of an entity in property, if such interest will suffer such damage before there is an opportunity for notice and a hearing under subsection (d) or (e) of this section.

(g) In any hearing under subsection (d) or (e) of this section concerning relief from the stay of any act under subsection (a) of this section—

(1) the party requesting such relief has the burden of proof on the issue of the debtor's equity in property; and

(2) the party opposing such relief has the burden of proof on all other issues.

(h)(1) In a case in which the debtor is an individual, the stay provided by subsection (a) is terminated with respect to personal property of the estate or of the debtor securing in whole or in part a claim, or subject to an unexpired lease, and such personal property shall no longer be property of the estate if the debtor fails within the applicable time set by section 521(a)(2)—

(A) to file timely any statement of intention required under section 521(a)(2) with respect to such personal property or to indicate in such statement that the debtor will either surrender such personal property or retain it and, if retaining such personal property, either redeem such personal property pursuant to section 722, enter into an agreement of the kind specified in section 524(c) applicable to the debt secured by such personal property, or assume such unexpired lease pursuant to section 365(p) if the trustee does not do so, as applicable; and

(B) to take timely the action specified in such statement, as it may be amended before expiration of the period for taking action, unless such statement specifies the debtor's intention to reaffirm such debt on the original contract terms and the creditor refuses to agree to the reaffirmation on such terms.

(2) Paragraph (1) does not apply if the court determines, on the motion of the trustee filed before the expiration of the applicable time set by section 521(a)(2), after notice and a hearing, that such personal property is of conse-

quential value or benefit to the estate, and orders appropriate adequate protection of the creditor's interest, and orders the debtor to deliver any collateral in the debtor's possession to the trustee. If the court does not so determine, the stay provided by subsection (a) shall terminate upon the conclusion of the hearing on the motion.

(h) An individual injured by any willful violation of a stay provided by this section shall recover actual damages, including costs and attorneys' fees, and, in appropriate circumstances, may recover punitive damages.

(i) If a case commenced under chapter 7, 11, or 13 is dismissed due to the creation of a debt repayment plan, for purposes of subsection (c)(3), any subsequent case commenced by the debtor under any such chapter shall not be presumed to be filed not in good faith.

(j) On request of a party in interest, the court shall issue an order under subsection (c) confirming that the automatic stay has been terminated.

(k)(1) Except as provided in paragraph (2), an individual injured by any willful violation of a stay provided by this section shall recover actual damages, including costs and attorneys' fees, and, in appropriate circumstances, may recover punitive damages.

(2) If such violation is based on an action taken by an entity in the good faith belief that subsection (h) applies to the debtor, the recovery under paragraph (1) of this subsection against such entity shall be limited to actual damages.

(l)(1) Except as otherwise provided in this subsection, subsection (b)(22) shall apply on the date that is 30 days after the date on which the bankruptcy petition is filed, if the debtor files with the petition and serves upon the lessor a certification under penalty of perjury that—

(A) under nonbankruptcy law applicable in the jurisdiction, there are circumstances under which the debtor would be permitted to cure the entire monetary default that gave rise to the judgment for possession, after that judgment for possession was entered; and

(B) the debtor (or an adult dependent of the debtor) has deposited with the clerk of the court, any rent that would become due during the 30-day period after the filing of the bankruptcy petition.

(2) If, within the 30-day period after the filing of the bankruptcy petition, the debtor (or an adult dependent of the debtor) complies with paragraph (1) and files with the court and serves upon the lessor a further certification under penalty of perjury that the debtor (or an adult dependent of the debtor) has cured, under nonbankrupcty law applicable in the jurisdiction, the entire monetary default that gave rise to the judgment under which possession is sought by the lessor, subsection (b)(22) shall not apply, unless ordered to apply by the court under paragraph (3).

(3)(A) If the lessor files an objection to any certification filed by the debtor under paragraph (1) or (2), and serves such objection upon the debtor, the court shall hold a hearing within 10 days after the filing and service of such objection to determine if the certification filed by the debtor under paragraph (1) or (2) is true.

(B) If the court upholds the objection of the lessor filed under subparagraph (A)—

     (i) subsection (b)(22) shall apply immediately and relief from the stay provided under subsection (a)(3) shall not be required to enable the lessor to complete the process to recover full possession of the property; and

     (ii) the clerk of the court shall immediately serve upon the lessor and the debtor a certified copy of the court's order upholding the lessor's objection.

(4) If a debtor, in accordance with paragraph (5), indicates on the petition that there was a judgment for possession of the residential rental property in which the debtor resides and does not file a certification under paragraph (1) or (2)—

     (A) subsection (b)(22) shall apply immediately upon failure to file such certification, and relief from the stay provided under subsection (a)(3) shall not be required to enable the lessor to complete the process to recover full possession of the property; and

     (B) the clerk of the court shall immediately serve upon the lessor and the debtor a certified copy of the docket indicating the absence of a filed certification and the applicability of the exception to the stay under subsection (b)(22).

(5)(A) Where a judgment for possession of residential property in which the debtor resides as a tenant under a lease or rental agreement has been obtained by the lessor, the debtor shall so indicate on the bankruptcy petition and shall provide the name and address of the lessor that obtained that pre-petition judgment on the petition and on any certification filed under this subsection.

     (B) The form of certification filed with the petition, as specified in this subsection, shall provide for the debtor to certify, and the debtor shall certify—

          (i) whether a judgment for possession of residential rental housing in which the debtor resides has been obtained against the debtor before the date of the filing of the petition; and

          (ii) whether the debtor is claiming under paragraph (1) that under nonbankruptcy law applicable in the jurisdiction, there are circumstances under which the debtor would be permitted to cure the entire monetary default that gave rise to the judgment for possession, after that judgment of possession was entered, and has made the appropriate deposit with the court.

     (C) The standard forms (electronic and otherwise) used in a bankruptcy proceeding shall be amended to reflect the requirements of this subsection.

     (D) The clerk of the court shall arrange for the prompt transmittal of the rent deposited in accordance with paragraph (1)(B) to the lessor.

(m)(1) Except as otherwise provided in this subsection, subsection (b)(23) shall apply on the date that is 15 days after the date on which the lessor files and serves a certification described in subsection (b)(23).

     (2)(A) If the debtor files with the court an objection to the truth or legal sufficiency of the certification described in subsection (b)(23) and serves such objection upon the lessor, subsection (b)(23) shall not apply, unless ordered to apply by the court under this subsection.

     (B) If the debtor files and serves the objection under subparagraph (A), the court shall hold a hearing within 10 days after the filing and service of such

objection to determine if the situation giving rise to the lessor's certification under paragraph (1) existed or has been remedied.

(C) If the debtor can demonstrate to the satisfaction of the court that the situation giving rise to the lessor's certification under paragraph (1) did not exist or has been remedied, the stay provided under subsection (a)(3) shall remain in effect until the termination of the stay under this section.

(D) If the debtor cannot demonstrate to the satisfaction of the court that the situation giving rise to the lessor's certification under paragraph (1) did not exist or has been remedied—

(i) relief from the stay provided under subsection (a)(3) shall not be required to enable the lessor to proceed with the eviction; and

(ii) the clerk of the court shall immediately serve upon the lessor and the debtor a certified copy of the court's order upholding the lessor's certification.

(3) If the debtor fails to file, within 15 days, an objection under paragraph (2)(A)—

(A) subsection (b)(23) shall apply immediately upon such failure and relief from the stay provided under subsection (a)(3) shall not be required to enable the lessor to complete the process to recover full possession of the property; and

(B) the clerk of the court shall immediately serve upon the lessor and the debtor a certified copy of the docket indicating such failure.

(n)(1) Except as provided in paragraph (2), subsection (a) does not apply in a case in which the debtor—

(A) is a debtor in a small business case pending at the time the petition is filed;

(B) was a debtor in a small business case that was dismissed for any reason by an order that became final in the 2-year period ending on the date of the order for relief entered with respect to the petition;

(C) was a debtor in a small business case in which a plan was confirmed in the 2-year period ending on the date of the order for relief entered with respect to the petition; or

(D) is an entity that has acquired substantially all of the assets or business of a small business debtor described in subparagraph (A), (B), or (C), unless such entity establishes by a preponderance of the evidence that such entity acquired substantially all of the assets or business of such small business debtor in good faith and not for the purpose of evading this paragraph.

(2) Paragraph (1) does not apply—

(A) to an involuntary case involving no collusion by the debtor with creditors; or

(B) to the filing of a petition if—

(i) the debtor proves by a preponderance of the evidence that the filing of the petition resulted from circumstances beyond the control of the debtor not foreseeable at the time the case then pending was filed; and

(ii) it is more likely than not that the court will confirm a feasible plan, but not a liquidating plan, within a reasonable period of time.

(o) The exercise of rights not subject to the stay arising under subsection (a) pursuant to paragraph (6), (7), (17), or (27) of subsection (b) shall not be stayed by any order of a court or administrative agency in any proceeding under this title.

§ 363. Use, sale, or lease of property

(a) In this section, "cash collateral" means cash, negotiable instruments, documents of title, securities, deposit accounts, or other cash equivalents whenever acquired in which the estate and an entity other than the estate have an interest and includes the proceeds, products, offspring, rents, or profits of property and the fees, charges, accounts or other payments for the use or occupancy of rooms and other public facilities in hotels, motels, or other lodging properties subject to a security interest as provided in section 552(b) of this title, whether existing before or after the commencement of a case under this title.

(b)(1) The trustee, after notice and a hearing, may use, sell, or lease, other than in the ordinary course of business, property of the estate-, *except that if the debtor in connection with offering a product or a service discloses to an individual a policy prohibiting the transfer of personally identifiable information about individuals to persons that are not affiliated with the debtor and if such policy is in effect on the date of the commencement of the case, then the trustee may not sell or lease personally identifiable information to any person unless—*

(A) such sale or such lease is consistent with such policy; or

(B) after appointment of a consumer privacy ombudsman in accordance with section 332, and after notice and a hearing, the court approves such sale or such lease—

(i) giving due consideration to the facts, circumstances, and conditions of such sale or such lease; and

(ii) finding that no showing was made that such sale or such lease would violate applicable nonbankruptcy law.

(2) If notification is required under subsection (a) of section 7A of the Clayton Act in the case of a transaction under this subsection, then—

(A) notwithstanding subsection (a) of such section, the notification required by such subsection to be given by the debtor shall be given by the trustee; and

(B) notwithstanding subsection (b) of such section, the required waiting period shall end on the 15th day after the date of the receipt, by the Federal Trade Commission and the Assistant Attorney General in charge of the Antitrust Division of the Department of Justice, of the notification required under such subsection (a), unless such waiting period is extended—

(i) pursuant to subsection (e)(2) of such section, in the same manner as such subsection (e)(2) applies to a cash tender offer;

(ii) pursuant to subsection (g)(2) of such section; or

(iii) by the court after notice and a hearing.

(c)(1) If the business of the debtor is authorized to be operated under section 721, 1108, 1203, 1204, or 1304 of this title and unless the court orders otherwise, the trustee may enter into transactions, including the sale or lease of property of the estate, in the ordinary course of business, without notice or a hearing, and may use property of the estate in the ordinary course of business without notice or a hearing.

(2) The trustee may not use, sell, or lease cash collateral under paragraph (1) of this subsection unless—

(A) each entity that has an interest in such cash collateral consents; or

(B) the court, after notice and a hearing, authorizes such use, sale, or lease in accordance with the provisions of this section.

(3) Any hearing under paragraph (2)(B) of this subsection may be a preliminary hearing or may be consolidated with a hearing under subsection (e) of this section, but shall be scheduled in accordance with the needs of the debtor. If the hearing under paragraph (2)(B) of this subsection is a preliminary hearing, the court may authorize such use, sale, or lease only if there is a reasonable likelihood that the trustee will prevail at the final hearing under subsection (e) of this section. The court shall act promptly on any request for authorization under paragraph (2)(B) of this subsection.

(4) Except as provided in paragraph (2) of this subsection, the trustee shall segregate and account for any cash collateral in the trustee's possession, custody, or control.

(d) The trustee may use, sell, or lease property under subsection (b) or (c) of this section only —— to the extent not inconsistent with any relief granted under section 362(c), 362(d), 362(e), or 362(f) of this title.

(1) in accordance with applicable nonbankruptcy law that governs the transfer of property by a corporation or trust that is not a moneyed, business, or commercial corporation or trust; and

(2) to the extent not inconsistent with any relief granted under subsection (c), (d), (e), or (f) of section 362.

(e) Notwithstanding any other provision of this section, at any time, on request of an entity that has an interest in property used, sold, or leased, or proposed to be used, sold, or leased, by the trustee, the court, with or without a hearing, shall prohibit or condition such use, sale, or lease as is necessary to provide adequate protection of such interest. This subsection also applies to property that is subject to any unexpired lease of personal property (to the exclusion of such property being subject to an order to grant relief from the stay under section 362).

(f) The trustee may sell property under subsection (b) or (c) of this section free and clear of any interest in such property of an entity other than the estate, only if—

(1) applicable nonbankruptcy law permits sale of such property free and clear of such interest;

(2) such entity consents;

(3) such interest is a lien and the price at which such property is to be sold is greater than the aggregate value of all liens on such property;

(4) such interest is in bona fide dispute; or

(5) such entity could be compelled, in a legal or equitable proceeding, to accept a money satisfaction of such interest.

(g) Notwithstanding subsection (f) of this section, the trustee may sell property under subsection (b) or (c) of this section free and clear of any vested or contingent right in the nature of dower or curtesy.

(h) Notwithstanding subsection (f) of this section, the trustee may sell both the estate's interest, under subsection (b) or (c) of this section, and the interest of any co-owner in property in which the debtor had, at the time of the commencement of the case, an undivided interest as a tenant in common, joint tenant, or tenant by the entirety, only if—

(1) partition in kind of such property among the estate and such co-owners is impracticable;

(2) sale of the estate's undivided interest in such property would realize significantly less for the estate than sale of such property free of the interests of such co-owners;

(3) the benefit to the estate of a sale of such property free of the interests of co owners outweighs the detriment, if any, to such co-owners; and

(4) such property is not used in the production, transmission, or distribution, for sale, of electric energy or of natural or synthetic gas for heat, light, or power.

(i) Before the consummation of a sale of property to which subsection (g) or (h) of this section applies, or of property of the estate that was community property of the debtor and the debtor's spouse immediately before the commencement of the case, the debtor's spouse, or a co-owner of such property, as the case may be, may purchase such property at the price at which such sale is to be consummated.

(j) After a sale of property to which subsection (g) or (h) of this section applies, the trustee shall distribute to the debtor's spouse or the co-owners of such property, as the case may be, and to the estate, the proceeds of such sale, less the costs and expenses, not including any compensation of the trustee, of such sale, according to the interests of such spouse or co-owners, and of the estate.

(k) At a sale under subsection (b) of this section of property that is subject to a lien that secures an allowed claim, unless the court for cause orders otherwise the holder of such claim may bid at such sale, and, if the holder of such claim purchases such property, such holder may offset such claim against the purchase price of such property.

(l) Subject to the provisions of section 365, the trustee may use, sell, or lease property under subsection (b) or (c) of this section, or a plan under chapter 11, 12, or 13 of this title may provide for the use, sale, or lease of property, notwithstanding any provision in a contract, a lease, or applicable law that is conditioned on the insolvency or financial condition of the debtor, on the commencement of a case under this title concerning the debtor, or on the appointment of or the taking possession by a trustee in a case under this title or a custodian, and that effects, or gives an option to effect, a forfeiture, modification, or termination of the debtor's interest in such property.

(m) The reversal or modification on appeal of an authorization under subsection (b) or (c) of this section of a sale or lease of property does not affect the validity of a sale or lease under such authorization to an entity that purchased or leased such property in good faith, whether or not such entity knew of the pendency of the appeal, unless such authorization and such sale or lease were stayed pending appeal.

(n) The trustee may avoid a sale under this section if the sale price was controlled by an agreement among potential bidders at such sale, or may recover from a party to such agreement any amount by which the value of the property sold exceeds the price at which such sale was consummated, and may recover any costs, attorneys' fees, or expenses incurred in avoiding such sale or recovering such amount. In addition to any recovery under the preceding sentence, the court may grant judgment for punitive damages in favor of the estate and against any such party that entered into such an agreement in willful disregard of this subsection.

(o) Notwithstanding subsection (f), if a person purchases any interest in a consumer credit transaction that is subject to the Truth in Lending Act or any interest in a consumer credit contract (as defined in section 433.1 of title 16 of the Code of Federal Regulations (January 1, 2004), as amended from time to time), and if such interest is purchased through a sale under this section, then such person shall remain subject to all claims and defenses that are related to such consumer credit transaction or such consumer credit contract, to the same extent as such person would be subject to such claims and defenses of the consumer had such interest been purchased at a sale not under this section.

(~~o~~*p*) In any hearing under this section—

(1) the trustee has the burden of proof on the issue of adequate protection; and

(2) the entity asserting an interest in property has the burden of proof on the issue of the validity, priority, or extent of such interest.

§ 364. Obtaining credit

(a) If the trustee is authorized to operate the business of the debtor under section 721, 1108, 1203, 1204, or 1304 of this title, unless the court orders otherwise, the trustee may obtain unsecured credit and incur unsecured debt in the ordinary course of business allowable under section 503(b)(1) of this title as an administrative expense.

(b) The court, after notice and a hearing, may authorize the trustee to obtain unsecured credit or to incur unsecured debt other than under subsection (a) of this section, allowable under section 503(b)(1) of this title as an administrative expense.

(c) If the trustee is unable to obtain unsecured credit allowable under section 503(b)(1) of this title as an administrative expense, the court, after notice and a hearing, may authorize the obtaining of credit or the incurring of debt—

(1) with priority over any or all administrative expenses of the kind specified in section 503(b) or 507(b) of this title;

(2) secured by a lien on property of the estate that is not otherwise subject to a lien; or

(3) secured by a junior lien on property of the estate that is subject to a lien.

(d)(1) The court, after notice and a hearing, may authorize the obtaining of credit or the incurring of debt secured by a senior or equal lien on property of the estate that is subject to a lien only if—

(A) the trustee is unable to obtain such credit otherwise; and

(B) there is adequate protection of the interest of the holder of the lien on the property of the estate on which such senior or equal lien is proposed to be granted.

(2) In any hearing under this subsection, the trustee has the burden of proof on the issue of adequate protection.

(e) The reversal or modification on appeal of an authorization under this section to obtain credit or incur debt, or of a grant under this section of a priority or a lien, does not affect the validity of any debt so incurred, or any priority or lien so granted, to an entity that extended such credit in good faith, whether or not such entity knew of the pendency of the appeal, unless such authorization and the incurring of such debt, or the granting of such priority or lien, were stayed pending appeal.

(f) Except with respect to an entity that is an underwriter as defined in section 1145(b) of this title, section 5 of the Securities Act of 1933, the Trust Indenture Act of 1939, and any State or local law requiring registration for offer or sale of a security or registration or licensing of an issuer of, underwriter of, or broker or dealer in, a security does not apply to the offer or sale under this section of a security that is not an equity security.

§ 365. Executory contracts and unexpired leases

(a) Except as provided in sections 765 and 766 of this title and in subsections (b), (c), and (d) of this section, the trustee, subject to the court's approval, may assume or reject any executory contract or unexpired lease of the debtor.

(b)(1) If there has been a default in an executory contract or unexpired lease of the debtor, the trustee may not assume such contract or lease unless, at the time of assumption of such contract or lease, the trustee—

(A) cures, or provides adequate assurance that the trustee will promptly cure, such default; *other than a default that is a breach of a provision relating to the satisfaction of any provision (other than a penalty rate or penalty provision) relating to a default arising from any failure to perform nonmonetary obligations under an unexpired lease of real property, if it is impossible for the trustee to cure such default by performing nonmonetary acts at and after the time of assumption, except that if such default arises from a failure to operate in accordance with a nonresidential real property lease, then such default shall be cured by performance at and after the time of assumption in accordance with such lease, and pecuniary losses resulting from such default shall be compensated in accordance with the provisions of this paragraph;*

(B) compensates, or provides adequate assurance that the trustee will promptly compensate, a party other than the debtor to such contract or lease, for any actual pecuniary loss to such party resulting from such default; and

(C) provides adequate assurance of future performance under such contract or lease.

(2) Paragraph (1) of this subsection does not apply to a default that is a breach of a provision relating to—

(A) the insolvency or financial condition of the debtor at any time before the closing of the case;

(B) the commencement of a case under this title;

(C) the appointment of or taking possession by a trustee in a case under this title or a custodian before such commencement; or

(D) the satisfaction of any ~~penalty rate or provision~~ *penalty rate or penalty provision* relating to a default arising from any failure by the debtor to perform nonmonetary obligations under the executory contract or unexpired lease.

(3) For the purposes of paragraph (1) of this subsection and paragraph (2)(B) of subsection (f), adequate assurance of future performance of a lease of real property in a shopping center includes adequate assurance—

(A) of the source of rent and other consideration due under such lease, and in the case of an assignment, that the financial condition and operating performance of the proposed assignee and its guarantors, if any, shall be similar to the financial condition and operating performance of the debtor and its guarantors, if any, as of the time the debtor became the lessee under the lease;

(B) that any percentage rent due under such lease will not decline substantially;

(C) that assumption or assignment of such lease is subject to all the provisions thereof, including (but not limited to) provisions such as a radius, location, use, or exclusivity provision, and will not breach any such provision contained in any other lease, financing agreement, or master agreement relating to such shopping center; and

(D) that assumption or assignment of such lease will not disrupt any tenant mix or balance in such shopping center.

(4) Notwithstanding any other provision of this section, if there has been a default in an unexpired lease of the debtor, other than a default of a kind specified in paragraph (2) of this subsection, the trustee may not require a lessor to provide services or supplies incidental to such lease before assumption of such lease unless the lessor is compensated under the terms of such lease for any services and supplies provided under such lease before assumption of such lease.

(c) The trustee may not assume or assign any executory contract or unexpired lease of the debtor, whether or not such contract or lease prohibits or restricts assignment of rights or delegation of duties, if—

(1)(A) applicable law excuses a party, other than the debtor, to such contract or lease from accepting performance from or rendering performance to an entity other than the debtor or the debtor in possession, whether or not such contract or lease prohibits or restricts assignment of rights or delegation of duties; and

(B) such party does not consent to such assumption or assignment; or

(2) such contract is a contract to make a loan, or extend other debt financing or financial accommodations, to or for the benefit of the debtor, or to issue a security of the debtor; or

(3) such lease is of nonresidential real property and has been terminated under applicable nonbankruptcy law prior to the order for relief; or

(4) such lease is of nonresidential real property under which the debtor is the lessee of an aircraft terminal or aircraft gate at an airport at which the debtor is the lessee under one or more additional nonresidential leases of an aircraft terminal or aircraft gate and the trustee, in connection with such assumption or assignment, does not assume all such leases or does not assume and assign all of such leases to the same person, except that the trustee may assume or assign less than all of such leases with the airport operator's written consent.

(d)(1) In a case under chapter 7 of this title, if the trustee does not assume or reject an executory contract or unexpired lease of residential real property or of personal property of the debtor within 60 days after the order for relief, or within such additional time as the court, for cause, within such 60- day period, fixes, then such contract or lease is deemed rejected.

(2) In a case under chapter 9, 11, 12, or 13 of this title, the trustee may assume or reject an executory contract or unexpired lease of residential real property or of personal property of the debtor at any time before the confirmation of a plan but the court, on the request of any party to such contract or lease, may order the trustee to determine within a specified period of time whether to assume or reject such contract or lease.

(3) The trustee shall timely perform all the obligations of the debtor, except those specified in section 365(b)(2), arising from and after the order for relief under any unexpired lease of nonresidential real property, until such lease is assumed or rejected, notwithstanding section 503(b)(1) of this title. The court may extend, for cause, the time for performance of any such obligation that arises within 60 days after the date of the order for relief, but the time for performance shall not be extended beyond such 60-day period. This subsection shall not be deemed to affect the trustee's obligations under the provisions of subsection (b) or (f) of this section. Acceptance of any such performance does not constitute waiver or relinquishment of the lessor's rights under such lease or under this title.

(4) ~~Notwithstanding paragraphs (1) and (2), in a case under any chapter of this title, if the trustee does not assume or reject an unexpired lease of nonresidential real property under which the debtor is the lessee within 60 days after the date of the order for relief, or within such additional time as the court, for cause, within such 60-day period, fixes, then such lease is deemed rejected, and the trustee shall immediately surrender such nonresidential real property to the lessor.~~ *(A) Subject to subparagraph (B), an unexpired lease of nonresidential real property under which the debtor is the lessee shall be deemed rejected, and the trustee shall immediately surrender that nonresidential real property to the lessor, if the trustee does not assume or reject the unexpired lease by the earlier of—*

(i) the date that is 120 days after the date of the order for relief; or

(ii) the date of the entry of an order confirming a plan.

(B)(i) The court may extend the period determined under subparagraph (A), prior to the expiration of the 120-day period, for 90 days on the motion of the trustee or lessor for cause.

(ii) If the court grants an extension under clause (i), the court may grant a subsequent extension only upon prior written consent of the lessor in each instance.

~~(5) Notwithstanding paragraphs (1) and (4) of this subsection, in a case under any chapter of this title, if the trustee does not assume or reject an unexpired lease of nonresidential real property under which the debtor is an affected air carrier that is the lessee of an aircraft terminal or aircraft gate before the occurrence of a termination event, then (unless the court orders the trustee to assume such unexpired leases within 5 days after the termination event), at the option of the airport operator, such lease is deemed rejected 5 days after the occurrence of a termination event and the trustee shall immediately surrender possession of the premises to the airport operator; except that the lease shall not be deemed to be rejected unless the airport operator first waives the right to damages related to the rejection. In the event that the lease is deemed to be rejected under this paragraph, the airport operator shall provide the affected air carrier~~

~~adequate opportunity after the surrender of the premises to remove the fixtures and equipment installed by the affected air carrier.~~

~~(6) For the purpose of paragraph (5) of this subsection and paragraph (f)(1) of this section, the occurrence of a termination event means, with respect to a debtor which is an affected air carrier that is the lessee of an aircraft terminal or aircraft gate—~~

~~(A) the entry under section 301 or 302 of this title of an order for relief under chapter 7 of this title;~~

~~(B) the conversion of a case under any chapter of this title to a case under chapter 7 of this title; or~~

~~(C) the granting of relief from the stay provided under section 362(a) of this title with respect to aircraft, aircraft engines, propellers, appliances, or spare parts, as defined in section 40102(a) of title 49, except for property of the debtor found by the court not to be necessary to an effective reorganization.~~

~~(7) Any order entered by the court pursuant to paragraph (4) extending the period within which the trustee of an affected air carrier must assume or reject an unexpired lease of nonresidential real property shall be without prejudice to—~~

~~(A) the right of the trustee to seek further extensions within such additional time period granted by the court pursuant to paragraph (4); and~~

~~(B) the right of any lessor or any other party in interest to request, at any time, a shortening or termination of the period within which the trustee must assume or reject an unexpired lease of nonresidential real property.~~

~~(8) The burden of proof for establishing cause for an extension by an affected air carrier under paragraph (4) or the maintenance of a previously granted extension under paragraph (7)(A) and (B) shall at all times remain with the trustee.~~

~~(9) For purposes of determining cause under paragraph (7) with respect to an unexpired lease of nonresidential real property between the debtor that is an affected air carrier and an airport operator under which such debtor is the lessee of an airport terminal or an airport gate, the court shall consider, among other relevant factors, whether substantial harm will result to the airport operator or airline passengers as a result of the extension or the maintenance of a previously granted extension. In making the determination of substantial harm, the court shall consider, among other relevant factors, the level of actual use of the terminals or gates which are the subject of the lease, the public interest in actual use of such terminals or gates, the existence of competing demands for the use of such terminals or gates, the effect of the court's extension or termination of the period of time to assume or reject the lease on such debtor's ability to successfully reorganize under chapter 11 of this title, and whether the trustee of the affected air carrier is capable of continuing to comply with its obligations under section 365(d)(3) of this title.~~

(~~10~~5) The trustee shall timely perform all of the obligations of the debtor, except those specified in section 365(b)(2), first arising from or after 60 days after the order for relief in a case under chapter 11 of this title under an unexpired lease of personal property (other than personal property leased to an individual primarily for personal, family, or household purposes), until such lease is assumed or rejected notwithstanding section 503(b)(1) of this title, unless the court, after notice and a hearing and based on the equities of the case, orders otherwise with respect to the obligations or timely performance thereof. This subsection shall not be deemed to affect the trustee's obligations under the provisions of subsection (b) or (f). Acceptance of any such performance does not constitute waiver or relinquishment of the lessor's rights under such lease or under this title.

(e)(1) Notwithstanding a provision in an executory contract or unexpired lease, or in applicable law, an executory contract or unexpired lease of the debtor may not be terminated or modified, and any right or obligation under such contract or lease may not be terminated or modified, at any time after the commencement of the case solely because of a provision in such contract or lease that is conditioned on—

   (A) the insolvency or financial condition of the debtor at any time before the closing of the case;

   (B) the commencement of a case under this title; or

   (C) the appointment of or taking possession by a trustee in a case under this title or a custodian before such commencement.

 (2) Paragraph (1) of this subsection does not apply to an executory contract or unexpired lease of the debtor, whether or not such contract or lease prohibits or restricts assignment of rights or delegation of duties, if—

   (A)(i) applicable law excuses a party, other than the debtor, to such contract or lease from accepting performance from or rendering performance to the trustee or to an assignee of such contract or lease, whether or not such contract or lease prohibits or restricts assignment of rights or delegation of duties; and

      (ii) such party does not consent to such assumption or assignment; or

   (B) such contract is a contract to make a loan, or extend other debt financing or financial accommodations, to or for the benefit of the debtor, or to issue a security of the debtor.

(f)(1) Except as provided in subsections *(b) and (c)* of this section, notwithstanding a provision in an executory contract or unexpired lease of the debtor, or in applicable law, that prohibits, restricts, or conditions the assignment of such contract or lease, the trustee may assign such contract or lease under paragraph (2) of this subsection; except that the trustee may not assign an unexpired lease of nonresidential real property under which the debtor is an affected air carrier that is the lessee of an aircraft terminal or aircraft gate if there has occurred a termination event.

 (2) The trustee may assign an executory contract or unexpired lease of the debtor only if—

   (A) the trustee assumes such contract or lease in accordance with the provisions of this section; and

   (B) adequate assurance of future performance by the assignee of such contract or lease is provided, whether or not there has been a default in such contract or lease.

 (3) Notwithstanding a provision in an executory contract or unexpired lease of the debtor, or in applicable law that terminates or modifies, or permits a party other than the debtor to terminate or modify, such contract or lease or a right or obligation under such contract or lease on account of an assignment of such contract or lease, such contract, lease, right, or obligation may not be termi-

nated or modified under such provision because of the assumption or assignment of such contract or lease by the trustee.

(g) Except as provided in subsections (h)(2) and (i)(2) of this section, the rejection of an executory contract or unexpired lease of the debtor constitutes a breach of such contract or lease—

   (1) if such contract or lease has not been assumed under this section or under a plan confirmed under chapter 9, 11, 12, or 13 of this title, immediately before the date of the filing of the petition; or

   (2) if such contract or lease has been assumed under this section or under a plan confirmed under chapter 9, 11, 12, or 13 of this title—

      (A) if before such rejection the case has not been converted under section 1112, 1208, or 1307 of this title, at the time of such rejection; or

      (B) if before such rejection the case has been converted under section 1112, 1208, or 1307 of this title—

         (i) immediately before the date of such conversion, if such contract or lease was assumed before such conversion; or

         (ii) at the time of such rejection, if such contract or lease was assumed after such conversion.

(h)(1)(A) If the trustee rejects an unexpired lease of real property under which the debtor is the lessor and—

      (i) if the rejection by the trustee amounts to such a breach as would entitle the lessee to treat such lease as terminated by virtue of its terms, applicable nonbankruptcy law, or any agreement made by the lessee, then the lessee under such lease may treat such lease as terminated by the rejection; or

      (ii) if the term of such lease has commenced, the lessee may retain its rights under such lease (including rights such as those relating to the amount and timing of payment of rent and other amounts payable by the lessee and any right of use, possession, quiet enjoyment, subletting, assignment, or hypothecation) that are in or appurtenant to the real property for the balance of the term of such lease and for any renewal or extension of such rights to the extent that such rights are enforceable under applicable nonbankruptcy law.

   (B) If the lessee retains its rights under subparagraph (A)(ii), the lessee may offset against the rent reserved under such lease for the balance of the term after the date of the rejection of such lease and for the term of any renewal or extension of such lease, the value of any damage caused by the nonperformance after the date of such rejection, of any obligation of the debtor under such lease, but the lessee shall not have any other right against the estate or the debtor on account of any damage occurring after such date caused by such nonperformance.

   (C) The rejection of a lease of real property in a shopping center with respect to which the lessee elects to retain its rights under subparagraph (A)(ii) does not affect the enforceability under applicable nonbankruptcy law of any provision in the lease pertaining to radius, location, use, exclusivity, or tenant mix or balance.

   (D) In this paragraph, "lessee" includes any successor, assign, or mortgagee permitted under the terms of such lease.

(2)(A) If the trustee rejects a timeshare interest under a timeshare plan under which the debtor is the timeshare interest seller and—

(i) if the rejection amounts to such a breach as would entitle the timeshare interest purchaser to treat the timeshare plan as terminated under its terms, applicable nonbankruptcy law, or any agreement made by timeshare interest purchaser, the timeshare interest purchaser under the timeshare plan may treat the timeshare plan as terminated by such rejection; or

(ii) if the term of such timeshare interest has commenced, then the timeshare interest purchaser may retain its rights in such timeshare interest for the balance of such term and for any term of renewal or extension of such timeshare interest to the extent that such rights are enforceable under applicable nonbankruptcy law.

(B) If the timeshare interest purchaser retains its rights under subparagraph (A), such timeshare interest purchaser may offset against the moneys due for such timeshare interest for the balance of the term after the date of the rejection of such timeshare interest, and the term of any renewal or extension of such timeshare interest, the value of any damage caused by the nonperformance after the date of such rejection, of any obligation of the debtor under such timeshare plan, but the timeshare interest purchaser shall not have any right against the estate or the debtor on account of any damage occurring after such date caused by such nonperformance.

(i)(1) If the trustee rejects an executory contract of the debtor for the sale of real property or for the sale of a timeshare interest under a timeshare plan, under which the purchaser is in possession, such purchaser may treat such contract as terminated, or, in the alternative, may remain in possession of such real property or timeshare interest.

(2) If such purchaser remains in possession—

(A) such purchaser shall continue to make all payments due under such contract, but may offset against such payments any damages occurring after the date of the rejection of such contract caused by the nonperformance of any obligation of the debtor after such date, but such purchaser does not have any rights against the estate on account of any damages arising after such date from such rejection, other than such offset; and

(B) the trustee shall deliver title to such purchaser in accordance with the provisions of such contract, but is relieved of all other obligations to perform under such contract.

(j) A purchaser that treats an executory contract as terminated under subsection (i) of this section, or a party whose executory contract to purchase real property from the debtor is rejected and under which such party is not in possession, has a lien on the interest of the debtor in such property for the recovery of any portion of the purchase price that such purchaser or party has paid.

(k) Assignment by the trustee to an entity of a contract or lease assumed under this section relieves the trustee and the estate from any liability for any breach of such contract or lease occurring after such assignment.

(l) If an unexpired lease under which the debtor is the lessee is assigned pursuant to this section, the lessor of the property may require a deposit or other security for the performance of the debtor's obligations under the lease substantially the same as would have been required by the landlord upon the initial leasing to a similar tenant.

(m) For purposes of this section 365 and sections 541(b)(2) and 362(b)(10), leases of real property shall include any rental agreement to use real property.

(n)(1) If the trustee rejects an executory contract under which the debtor is a licensor of a right to intellectual property, the licensee under such contract may elect—

(A) to treat such contract as terminated by such rejection if such rejection by the trustee amounts to such a breach as would entitle the licensee to treat such contract as terminated by virtue of its own terms, applicable nonbankruptcy law, or an agreement made by the licensee with another entity; or

(B) to retain its rights (including a right to enforce any exclusivity provision of such contract, but excluding any other right under applicable nonbankruptcy law to specific performance of such contract) under such contract and under any agreement supplementary to such contract, to such intellectual property (including any embodiment of such intellectual property to the extent protected by applicable nonbankruptcy law), as such rights existed immediately before the case commenced, for—

(i) the duration of such contract; and

(ii) any period for which such contract may be extended by the licensee as of right under applicable nonbankruptcy law.

(2) If the licensee elects to retain its rights, as described in paragraph (1)(B) of this subsection, under such contract—

(A) the trustee shall allow the licensee to exercise such rights;

(B) the licensee shall make all royalty payments due under such contract for the duration of such contract and for any period described in paragraph (1)(B) of this subsection for which the licensee extends such contract; and

(C) the licensee shall be deemed to waive—

(i) any right of setoff it may have with respect to such contract under this title or applicable nonbankruptcy law; and

(ii) any claim allowable under section 503(b) of this title arising from the performance of such contract.

(3) If the licensee elects to retain its rights, as described in paragraph (1)(B) of this subsection, then on the written request of the licensee the trustee shall—

(A) to the extent provided in such contract, or any agreement supplementary to such contract, provide to the licensee any intellectual property (including such embodiment) held by the trustee; and

(B) not interfere with the rights of the licensee as provided in such contract, or any agreement supplementary to such contract, to such intellectual property (including such embodiment) including any right to obtain such intellectual property (or such embodiment) from another entity.

(4) Unless and until the trustee rejects such contract, on the written request of the licensee the trustee shall—

(A) to the extent provided in such contract or any agreement supplementary to such contract—

(i) perform such contract; or

(ii) provide to the licensee such intellectual property (including any embodiment of such intellectual property to the extent protected by applicable nonbankruptcy law) held by the trustee; and

(B) not interfere with the rights of the licensee as provided in such contract, or any agreement supplementary to such contract, to such intellectual property (including such embodiment), including any right to obtain such intellectual property (or such embodiment) from another entity.

(o) In a case under chapter 11 of this title, the trustee shall be deemed to have assumed (consistent with the debtor's other obligations under section 507), and shall immediately cure any deficit under, any commitment by the debtor to a Federal depository institutions regulatory agency (or predecessor to such agency) to maintain the capital of an insured depository institution, and any claim for a subsequent breach of the obligations thereunder shall be entitled to priority under section 507. This subsection shall not extend any commitment that would otherwise be terminated by any act of such an agency.

(p)(1) If a lease of personal property is rejected or not timely assumed by the trustee under subsection (d), the leased property is no longer property of the estate and the stay under section 362(a) is automatically terminated.

(2)(A) If the debtor in a case under chapter 7 is an individual, the debtor may notify the creditor in writing that the debtor desires to assume the lease. Upon being so notified, the creditor may, at its option, notify the debtor that it is willing to have the lease assumed by the debtor and may condition such assumption on cure of any outstanding default on terms set by the contract.

(B) If, not later than 30 days after notice is provided under subparagraph (A), the debtor notifies the lessor in writing that the lease is assumed, the liability under the lease will be assumed by the debtor and not by the estate.

(C) The stay under section 362 and the injunction under section 524(a)(2) shall not be violated by notification of the debtor and negotiation of cure under this subsection.

(3) In a case under chapter 11 in which the debtor is an individual and in a case under chapter 13, if the debtor is the lessee with respect to personal property and the lease is not assumed in the plan confirmed by the court, the lease is deemed rejected as of the conclusion of the hearing on confirmation. If the lease is rejected, the stay under section 362 and any stay under section 1301 is automatically terminated with respect to the property subject to the lease.

§ 366. Utility service

(a) Except as provided in subsections (b) and (c) of this section, a utility may not alter, refuse, or discontinue service to, or discriminate against, the trustee or the debtor solely on the basis of the commencement of a case under this title or that a debt owed by the debtor to such utility for service rendered before the order for relief was not paid when due.

(b) Such utility may alter, refuse, or discontinue service if neither the trustee nor the debtor, within 20 days after the date of the order for relief, furnishes adequate assurance of payment, in the form of a deposit or other security, for service after such date. On request of a party in interest and after notice and a hearing, the court may order reasonable modification of the amount of the deposit or other security necessary to provide adequate assurance of payment.

(c)(1)(A) For purposes of this subsection, the term 'assurance of payment' means—

(i) a cash deposit;

(ii) a letter of credit;

(iii) a certificate of deposit;

(iv) a surety bond;

(v) a prepayment of utility consumption; or

(vi) another form of security that is mutually agreed on between the utility and the debtor or the trustee.

(B) For purposes of this subsection an administrative expense priority shall not constitute an assurance of payment.

(2) Subject to paragraphs (3) and (4), with respect to a case filed under chapter 11, a utility referred to in subsection (a) may alter, refuse, or discontinue utility service, if during the 30-day period beginning on the date of the filing of the petition, the utility does not receive from the debtor or the trustee adequate assurance of payment for utility service that is satisfactory to the utility.

(3)(A) On request of a party in interest and after notice and a hearing, the court may order modification of the amount of an assurance of payment under paragraph (2).

(B) In making a determination under this paragraph whether an assurance of payment is adequate, the court may not consider—

(i) the absence of security before the date of the filing of the petition;

(ii) the payment by the debtor of charges for utility service in a timely manner before the date of the filing of the petition; or

(iii) the availability of an administrative expense priority.

(4) Notwithstanding any other provision of law, with respect to a case subject to this subsection, a utility may recover or set off against a security deposit provided to the utility by the debtor before the date of the filing of the petition without notice or order of the court.

CHAPTER 5—CREDITORS, THE DEBTOR, AND THE ESTATE

SUBCHAPTER I—CREDITORS AND CLAIMS

§ 501. Filing of proofs of claims or interests

(a) A creditor or an indenture trustee may file a proof of claim. An equity security holder may file a proof of interest.

(b) If a creditor does not timely file a proof of such creditor's claim, an entity that is liable to such creditor with the debtor, or that has secured such creditor, may file a proof of such claim.

(c) If a creditor does not timely file a proof of such creditor's claim, the debtor or the trustee may file a proof of such claim.

(d) A claim of a kind specified in section 502(e)(2), 502(f), 502(g), 502(h) or 502(i) of this title may be filed under subsection (a), (b), or (c) of this section the same as if such claim were a claim against the debtor and had arisen before the date of the filing of the petition.

(e) A claim arising from the liability of a debtor for fuel use tax assessed consistent with the requirements of section 31705 of title 49 may be filed by the base jurisdiction designated pursuant to the International Fuel Tax Agreement (as defined in section 31701 of title 49) and, if so filed, shall be allowed as a single claim.

§ 502. Allowance of claims or interests

(a) A claim or interest, proof of which is filed under section 501 of this title, is deemed allowed, unless a party in interest, including a creditor of a general partner in a partnership that is a debtor in a case under chapter 7 of this title, objects.

(b) Except as provided in subsections (e)(2), (f), (g), (h) and (i) of this section, if such objection to a claim is made, the court, after notice and a hearing, shall determine the amount of such claim in lawful currency of the United States as of the date of the filing of the petition, and shall allow such claim in such amount, except to the extent that—

(1) such claim is unenforceable against the debtor and property of the debtor, under any agreement or applicable law for a reason other than because such claim is contingent or unmatured;

(2) such claim is for unmatured interest;

(3) if such claim is for a tax assessed against property of the estate, such claim exceeds the value of the interest of the estate in such property;

(4) if such claim is for services of an insider or attorney of the debtor, such claim exceeds the reasonable value of such services;

(5) such claim is for a debt that is unmatured on the date of the filing of the petition and that is excepted from discharge under section 523(a)(5) of this title;

(6) if such claim is the claim of a lessor for damages resulting from the termination of a lease of real property, such claim exceeds—

(A) the rent reserved by such lease, without acceleration, for the greater of one year, or 15 percent, not to exceed three years, of the remaining term of such lease, following the earlier of—

(i) the date of the filing of the petition; and

(ii) the date on which such lessor repossessed, or the lessee surrendered, the leased property; plus

(B) any unpaid rent due under such lease, without acceleration, on the earlier of such dates;

(7) if such claim is the claim of an employee for damages resulting from the termination of an employment contract, such claim exceeds—

(A) the compensation provided by such contract, without acceleration, for one year following the earlier of—

(i) the date of the filing of the petition; or

(ii) the date on which the employer directed the employee to terminate, or such employee terminated, performance under such contract; plus

(B) any unpaid compensation due under such contract, without acceleration, on the earlier of such dates;

(8) such claim results from a reduction, due to late payment, in the amount of an otherwise applicable credit available to the debtor in connection with an employment tax on wages, salaries, or commissions earned from the debtor; or

(9) proof of such claim is not timely filed, except to the extent tardily filed as permitted under paragraph (1), (2), or (3) of section 726(a) of this title or under the Federal Rules of Bankruptcy Procedure, except that a claim of a governmental unit shall be timely filed if it is filed before 180 days after the date of the order for relief or such later time as the Federal Rules of Bankruptcy Procedure may provide, *and except that in a case under chapter 13, a claim of a governmental unit for a tax with respect to a return filed under section 1308 shall be timely if the claim is filed on or before the date that is 60 days after the date on which such return was filed as required.*

(c) There shall be estimated for purpose of allowance under this section—

(1) any contingent or unliquidated claim, the fixing or liquidation of which, as the case may be, would unduly delay the administration of the case; or

(2) any right to payment arising from a right to an equitable remedy for breach of performance.

(d) Notwithstanding subsections (a) and (b) of this section, the court shall disallow any claim of any entity from which property is recoverable under section 542, 543, 550, or 553 of this title or that is a transferee of a transfer avoidable under section 522(f), 522(h), 544, 545, 547, 548, 549, or 724(a) of this title, unless such entity or transferee has paid the amount, or turned over any such property, for which such entity or transferee is liable under section 522(i), 542, 543, 550, or 553 of this title.

(e)(1) Notwithstanding subsections (a), (b), and (c) of this section and paragraph (2) of this subsection, the court shall disallow any claim for reimbursement or contribution of an entity that is liable with the debtor on or has secured the claim of a creditor, to the extent that—

(A) such creditor's claim against the estate is disallowed;

(B) such claim for reimbursement or contribution is contingent as of the time of allowance or disallowance of such claim for reimbursement or contribution; or

(C) such entity asserts a right of subrogation to the rights of such creditor under section 509 of this title.

(2) A claim for reimbursement or contribution of such an entity that becomes fixed after the commencement of the case shall be determined, and shall be allowed under subsection (a), (b), or (c) of this section, or disallowed under subsection (d) of this section, the same as if such claim had become fixed before the date of the filing of the petition.

(f) In an involuntary case, a claim arising in the ordinary course of the debtor's business or financial affairs after the commencement of the case but before the earlier of the appointment of a trustee and the order for relief shall be determined as of the date such claim arises, and shall be allowed under subsection (a), (b), or

(c) of this section or disallowed under subsection (d) or (e) of this section, the same as if such claim had arisen before the date of the filing of the petition.

(g)*(1)* A claim arising from the rejection, under section 365 of this title or under a plan under chapter 9, 11, 12, or 13 of this title, of an executory contract or unexpired lease of the debtor that has not been assumed shall be determined, and shall be allowed under subsection (a), (b), or (c) of this section or disallowed under subsection (d) or (e) of this section, the same as if such claim had arisen before the date of the filing of the petition.

(2) A claim for damages calculated in accordance with section 562 shall be allowed under subsection (a), (b), or (c), or disallowed under subsection (d) or (e), as if such claim had arisen before the date of the filing of the petition.

(h) A claim arising from the recovery of property under section 522, 550, or 553 of this title shall be determined, and shall be allowed under subsection (a), (b), or (c) of this section, or disallowed under subsection (d) or (e) of this section, the same as if such claim had arisen before the date of the filing of the petition.

(i) A claim that does not arise until after the commencement of the case for a tax entitled to priority under section 507(a)(8) of this title shall be determined, and shall be allowed under subsection (a), (b), or (c) of this section, or disallowed under subsection (d) or (e) of this section, the same as if such claim had arisen before the date of the filing of the petition.

(j) A claim that has been allowed or disallowed may be reconsidered for cause. A reconsidered claim may be allowed or disallowed according to the equities of the case. Reconsideration of a claim under this subsection does not affect the validity of any payment or transfer from the estate made to a holder of an allowed claim on account of such allowed claim that is not reconsidered, but if a reconsidered claim is allowed and is of the same class as such holder's claim, such holder may not receive any additional payment or transfer from the estate on account of such holder's allowed claim until the holder of such reconsidered and allowed claim receives payment on account of such claim proportionate in value to that already received by such other holder. This subsection does not alter or modify the trustee's right to recover from a creditor any excess payment or transfer made to such creditor.

(k)*(1) The court, on the motion of the debtor and after a hearing, may reduce a claim filed under this section based in whole on an unsecured consumer debt by not more than 20 percent of the claim, if—*

(A) the claim was filed by a creditor who unreasonably refused to negotiate a reasonable alternative repayment schedule proposed on behalf of the debtor by an approved nonprofit budget and credit counseling agency described in section 111;

(B) the offer of the debtor under subparagraph (A)—

(i) was made at least 60 days before the date of the filing of the petition; and

(ii) provided for payment of at least 60 percent of the amount of the debt over a period not to exceed the repayment period of the loan, or a reasonable extension thereof; and

(C) no part of the debt under the alternative repayment schedule is nondischargeable.

(2) The debtor shall have the burden of proving, by clear and convincing evidence, that—

(A) the creditor unreasonably refused to consider the debtor's proposal; and

(B) the proposed alternative repayment schedule was made prior to expiration of the 60-day period specified in paragraph (1)(B)(i).

§ 503. Allowance of administrative expenses

(a) An entity may timely file a request for payment of an administrative expense, or may tardily file such request if permitted by the court for cause.

(b) After notice and a hearing, there shall be allowed administrative expenses, other than claims allowed under section 502(f) of this title, including—

(1)(A) ~~the actual, necessary costs and expenses of preserving the estate, including wages, salaries, or commissions for services rendered after the commencement of the case;~~ *the actual, necessary costs and expenses of preserving the estate including—*

(i) wages, salaries, and commissions for services rendered after the commencement of the case; and

(ii) wages and benefits awarded pursuant to a judicial proceeding or a proceeding of the National Labor Relations Board as back pay attributable to any period of time occurring after commencement of the case under this title, as a result of a violation of Federal or State law by the debtor, without regard to the time of the occurrence of unlawful conduct on which such award is based or to whether any services were rendered, if the court determines that payment of wages and benefits by reason of the operation of this clause will not substantially increase the probability of layoff or termination of current employees, or of nonpayment of domestic support obligations, during the case under this title;

(B) any tax—

(i) incurred by the estate, *whether secured or unsecured, including property taxes for which liability is in rem, in personam, or both,* except a tax of a kind specified in section 507(a)(8) of this title; or

(ii) attributable to an excessive allowance of a tentative carryback adjustment that the estate received, whether the taxable year to which such adjustment relates ended before or after the commencement of the case; ~~and~~

(C) any fine, penalty, or reduction in credit relating to a tax of a kind specified in subparagraph (B) of this paragraph*; and*

(D) notwithstanding the requirements of subsection (a), a governmental unit shall not be required to file a request for the payment of an expense described in subparagraph (B) or (C), as a condition of its being an allowed administrative expense;

(2) compensation and reimbursement awarded under section 330(a) of this title;

(3) the actual, necessary expenses, other than compensation and reimbursement specified in paragraph (4) of this subsection, incurred by—

(A) a creditor that files a petition under section 303 of this title;

(B) a creditor that recovers, after the court's approval, for the benefit of the estate any property transferred or concealed by the debtor;

(C) a creditor in connection with the prosecution of a criminal offense relating to the case or to the business or property of the debtor;

(D) a creditor, an indenture trustee, an equity security holder, or a committee representing creditors or equity security holders other than a committee appointed under section 1102 of this title, in making a substantial contribution in a case under chapter 9 or 11 of this title;

(E) a custodian superseded under section 543 of this title, and compensation for the services of such custodian; or

(F) a member of a committee appointed under section 1102 of this title, if such expenses are incurred in the performance of the duties of such committee;

(4) reasonable compensation for professional services rendered by an attorney or an accountant of an entity whose expense is allowable under subparagraph (A), (B), (C), (D), or (E) of paragraph (3) of this subsection, based on the time, the nature, the extent, and the value of such services, and the cost of comparable services other than in a case under this title, and reimbursement for actual, necessary expenses incurred by such attorney or accountant;

(5) reasonable compensation for services rendered by an indenture trustee in making a substantial contribution in a case under chapter 9 or 11 of this title, based on the time, the nature, the extent, and the value of such services, and the cost of comparable services other than in a case under this title; ~~and~~

(6) the fees and mileage payable under chapter 119 of title 28;~~.~~

(7) with respect to a nonresidential real property lease previously assumed under section 365, and subsequently rejected, a sum equal to all monetary obligations due, excluding those arising from or relating to a failure to operate or a penalty provision, for the period of 2 years following the later of the rejection date or the date of actual turnover of the premises, without reduction or setoff for any reason whatsoever except for sums actually received or to be received from an entity other than the debtor, and the claim for remaining sums due for the balance of the term of the lease shall be a claim under section 502(b)(6);

(8) the actual, necessary costs and expenses of closing a health care business incurred by a trustee or by a Federal agency (as defined in section 551(1) of title 5) or a department or agency of a State or political subdivision thereof, including any cost or expense incurred—

(A) in disposing of patient records in accordance with section 351; or

(B) in connection with transferring patients from the health care business that is in the process of being closed to another health care business; and

(9) the value of any goods received by the debtor within 20 days before the date of commencement of a case under this title in which the goods have been sold to the debtor in the ordinary course of such debtor's business.

(c) Notwithstanding subsection (b), there shall neither be allowed, nor paid—

(1) a transfer made to, or an obligation incurred for the benefit of, an insider of the debtor for the purpose of inducing such person to remain with the debtor's business, absent a finding by the court based on evidence in the record that—

(A) the transfer or obligation is essential to retention of the person because the individual has a bona fide job offer from another business at the same or greater rate of compensation;

(B) the services provided by the person are essential to the survival of the business; and

(C) either—

(i) the amount of the transfer made to, or obligation incurred for the benefit of, the person is not greater than an amount equal to 10 times the amount of the mean transfer or obligation of a similar kind given to non-management employees for any purpose during the calendar year in which the transfer is made or the obligation is incurred; or

(ii) if no such similar transfers were made to, or obligations were incurred for the benefit of, such nonmanagement employees during such calendar year, the amount of the transfer or obligation is not greater than an amount equal to 25 percent of the amount of any similar transfer or obligation made to or incurred for the benefit of such insider for any purpose during the calendar year before the year in which such transfer is made or obligation is incurred;

(2) a severance payment to an insider of the debtor, unless—

(A) the payment is part of a program that is generally applicable to all full-time employees; and

(B) the amount of the payment is not greater than 10 times the amount of the mean severance pay given to nonmanagement employees during the calendar year in which the payment is made; or

(3) other transfers or obligations that are outside the ordinary course of business and not justified by the facts and circumstances of the case, including transfers made to, or obligations incurred for the benefit of, officers, managers, or consultants hired after the date of the filing of the petition.

§ 504. Sharing of compensation

(a) Except as provided in subsection (b) of this section, a person receiving compensation or reimbursement under section 503(b)(2) or 503(b)(4) of this title may not share or agree to share—

(1) any such compensation or reimbursement with another person; or

(2) any compensation or reimbursement received by another person under such sections.

(b)(1) A member, partner, or regular associate in a professional association, corporation, or partnership may share compensation or reimbursement received under section 503(b)(2) or 503(b)(4) of this title with another member, partner, or regular associate in such association, corporation, or partnership, and may share in any compensation or reimbursement received under such sections by another member, partner, or regular associate in such association, corporation, or partnership.

(2) An attorney for a creditor that files a petition under section 303 of this title may share compensation and reimbursement received under section 503(b)(4) of this title with any other attorney contributing to the services rendered or expenses incurred by such creditor's attorney.

(c) This section shall not apply with respect to sharing, or agreeing to share, compensation with a bona fide public service attorney referral program that operates in accordance with non-Federal law regulating attorney referral services and with rules of professional responsibility applicable to attorney acceptance of referrals.

§ 505. Determination of tax liability

(a)(1) Except as provided in paragraph (2) of this subsection, the court may determine the amount or legality of any tax, any fine or penalty relating to a tax, or any addition to tax, whether or not previously assessed, whether or not paid, and whether or not contested before and adjudicated by a judicial or administrative tribunal of competent jurisdiction.

(2) The court may not so determine—

(A) the amount or legality of a tax, fine, penalty, or addition to tax if such amount or legality was contested before and adjudicated by a judicial or administrative tribunal of competent jurisdiction before the commencement of the case under this title; ~~or~~

(B) any right of the estate to a tax refund, before the earlier of—

(i) 120 days after the trustee properly requests such refund from the governmental unit from which such refund is claimed; or

(ii) a determination by such governmental unit of such request~~;~~*; or*

(C) the amount or legality of any amount arising in connection with an ad valorem tax on real or personal property of the estate, if the applicable period for contesting or redetermining that amount under any law (other than a bankruptcy law) has expired.

(b)(1)(A) *The clerk shall maintain a list under which a Federal, State, or local governmental unit responsible for the collection of taxes within the district may—*

(i) designate an address for service of requests under this subsection; and

(ii) describe where further information concerning additional requirements for filing such requests may be found.

(B) If such governmental unit does not designate an address and provide such address to the clerk under subparagraph (A), any request made under this subsection may be served at the address for the filing of a tax return or protest with the appropriate taxing authority of such governmental unit.

(~~b~~2) A trustee may request a determination of any unpaid liability of the estate for any tax incurred during the administration of the case by submitting a tax return for such tax and a request for such a determination to the governmental unit charged with responsibility for collection or determination of such tax *at the address and in the manner designated in paragraph (1)*. Unless such return is fraudulent, or contains a material misrepresentation, *the estate,* the trustee, the debtor, and any successor to the debtor are discharged from any liability for such tax—

(~~1~~*A*) upon payment of the tax shown on such return, if—

(~~A~~*i*) such governmental unit does not notify the trustee, within 60 days after such request, that such return has been selected for examination; or

    (~~B~~*ii*) such governmental unit does not complete such an examination and notify the trustee of any tax due, within 180 days after such request or within such additional time as the court, for cause, permits;

    (~~2~~*B*) upon payment of the tax determined by the court, after notice and a hearing, after completion by such governmental unit of such examination; or

    (~~3~~*C*) upon payment of the tax determined by such governmental unit to be due.

(c) Notwithstanding section 362 of this title, after determination by the court of a tax under this section, the governmental unit charged with responsibility for collection of such tax may assess such tax against the estate, the debtor, or a successor to the debtor, as the case may be, subject to any otherwise applicable law.

§ 506. Determination of secured status

(a)*(1)* An allowed claim of a creditor secured by a lien on property in which the estate has an interest, or that is subject to setoff under section 553 of this title, is a secured claim to the extent of the value of such creditor's interest in the estate's interest in such property, or to the extent of the amount subject to setoff, as the case may be, and is an unsecured claim to the extent that the value of such creditor's interest or the amount so subject to setoff is less than the amount of such allowed claim. Such value shall be determined in light of the purpose of the valuation and of the proposed disposition or use of such property, and in conjunction with any hearing on such disposition or use or on a plan affecting such creditor's interest.

    (2) If the debtor is an individual in a case under chapter 7 or 13, such value with respect to personal property securing an allowed claim shall be determined based on the replacement value of such property as of the date of the filing of the petition without deduction for costs of sale or marketing. With respect to property acquired for personal, family, or household purposes, replacement value shall mean the price a retail merchant would charge for property of that kind considering the age and condition of the property at the time value is determined.

(b) To the extent that an allowed secured claim is secured by property the value of which, after any recovery under subsection (c) of this section, is greater than the amount of such claim, there shall be allowed to the holder of such claim, interest on such claim, and any reasonable fees, costs, or charges provided for under the agreement or State statute under which such claim arose.

(c) The trustee may recover from property securing an allowed secured claim the reasonable, necessary costs and expenses of preserving, or disposing of, such property to the extent of any benefit to the holder of such claim, *including the payment of all ad valorem property taxes with respect to the property.*

(d) To the extent that a lien secures a claim against the debtor that is not an allowed secured claim, such lien is void, unless—

    (1) such claim was disallowed only under section 502(b)(5) or 502(e) of this title; or

    (2) such claim is not an allowed secured claim due only to the failure of any entity to file a proof of such claim under section 501 of this title.

§ 507. Priorities

(a) The following expenses and claims have priority in the following order:

(1) First:

(A) Allowed unsecured claims for domestic support obligations that, as of the date of the filing of the petition in a case under this title, are owed to or recoverable by a spouse, former spouse, or child of the debtor, or such child's parent, legal guardian, or responsible relative, without regard to whether the claim is filed by such person or is filed by a governmental unit on behalf of such person, on the condition that funds received under this paragraph by a governmental unit under this title after the date of the filing of the petition shall be applied and distributed in accordance with applicable nonbankruptcy law.

(B) Subject to claims under subparagraph (A), allowed unsecured claims for domestic support obligations that, as of the date of the filing of the petition, are assigned by a spouse, former spouse, child of the debtor, or such child's parent, legal guardian, or responsible relative to a governmental unit (unless such obligation is assigned voluntarily by the spouse, former spouse, child, parent, legal guardian, or responsible relative of the child for the purpose of collecting the debt) or are owed directly to or recoverable by a governmental unit under applicable nonbankruptcy law, on the condition that funds received under this paragraph by a governmental unit under this title after the date of the filing of the petition be applied and distributed in accordance with applicable nonbankruptcy law.

(C) If a trustee is appointed or elected under section 701, 702, 703, 1104, 1202, or 1302, the administrative expenses of the trustee allowed under paragraphs (1)(A), (2), and (6) of section 503(b) shall be paid before payment of claims under subparagraphs (A) and (B), to the extent that the trustee administers assets that are otherwise available for the payment of such claims.

(~~+2~~) ~~First~~ *Second*, administrative expenses allowed under section 503(b) of this title, and any fees and charges assessed against the estate under chapter 123 of title 28.

(~~23~~) ~~Second~~ *Third*, unsecured claims allowed under section 502(f) of this title.

(~~34~~) ~~Third~~ *Fourth*, allowed unsecured claims, but only to the extent of $~~4,925~~ [$~~4,000~~] *$10,000* for each individual or corporation, as the case may be, earned within *180* ~~90~~ days before the date of the filing of the petition or the date of the cessation of the debtor's business, whichever occurs first, for—

(A) wages, salaries, or commissions, including vacation, severance, and sick leave pay earned by an individual; or

(B) sales commissions earned by an individual or by a corporation with only 1 employee, acting as an independent contractor in the sale of goods or services for the debtor in the ordinary course of the debtor's business if, and only if, during the 12 months preceding that date, at least 75 percent of the amount that the individual or corporation earned by acting as an independent contractor in the sale of goods or services was earned from the debtor;.

(~~45~~) ~~Fourth~~ *Fifth*, allowed unsecured claims for contributions to an employee benefit plan—

(A) arising from services rendered within 180 days before the date of the filing of the petition or the date of the cessation of the debtor's business, whichever occurs first; but only

(B) for each such plan, to the extent of—

(i) the number of employees covered by each such plan multiplied by $4,925[$4,000] *$10,000*; less

(ii) the aggregate amount paid to such employees under paragraph (*43*) of this subsection, plus the aggregate amount paid by the estate on behalf of such employees to any other employee benefit plan.

(*56*) Fifth *Sixth*, allowed unsecured claims of persons—

(A) engaged in the production or raising of grain, as defined in section 557(b) of this title, against a debtor who owns or operates a grain storage facility, as defined in section 557(b) of this title, for grain or the proceeds of grain, or

(B) engaged as a United States fisherman against a debtor who has acquired fish or fish produce from a fisherman through a sale or conversion, and who is engaged in operating a fish produce storage or processing facility—

but only to the extent of $4,925[$4,000] *$10,000* for each such individual.

(*67*) Sixth *Seventh*, allowed unsecured claims of individuals, to the extent of $1,800 [$2,225] for each such individual, arising from the deposit, before the commencement of the case, of money in connection with the purchase, lease, or rental of property, or the purchase of services, for the personal, family, or household use of such individuals, that were not delivered or provided.

(7) Seventh, allowed claims for debts to a spouse, former spouse, or child of the debtor, for alimony to, maintenance for, or support of such spouse or child, in connection with a separation agreement, divorce decree or other order of a court of record, determination made in accordance with State or territorial law by a governmental unit, or property settlement agreement, but not to the extent that such debt—

(A) is assigned to another entity, voluntarily, by operation of law, or otherwise; or

(B) includes a liability designated as alimony, maintenance, or support, unless such liability is actually in the nature of alimony, maintenance or support.

(8) Eighth, allowed unsecured claims of governmental units, only to the extent that such claims are for—

(A) a tax on or measured by income or gross receipts *for a taxable year ending on or before the date of the filing of the petition* —

(i) for a taxable year ending on or before the date of the filing of the petition for which a return, if required, is last due, including extensions, after three years before the date of the filing of the petition;

(ii) assessed within 240 days, plus any time plus 30 days during which an offer in compromise with respect to such tax that was made within 240 days after such assessment was pending, before the date of the filing of the petition; or *(ii) assessed within 240 days before the date of the filing of the petition, exclusive of—*

(I) any time during which an offer in compromise with respect to that tax was pending or in effect during that 240-day period, plus 30 days; and

(II) any time during which a stay of proceedings against collections was in effect in a prior case under this title during that 240-day period, plus 90 days.

An otherwise applicable time period specified in this paragraph shall be suspended for any period during which a governmental unit is prohibited under applicable nonbankruptcy law from collecting a tax as a result of a request by the debtor for a hearing and an appeal of any collection action taken or proposed against the debtor, plus 90 days; plus any time during which the stay of proceedings was in effect in a prior case under this title or during which collection was precluded by the existence of 1 or more confirmed plans under this title, plus 90 days.

(iii) other than a tax of a kind specified in section 523(a)(1)(B) or 523(a)(1)(C) of this title, not assessed before, but assessable, under applicable law or by agreement, after, the commencement of the case;

(B) a property tax ~~assessed~~ *incurred* before the commencement of the case and last payable without penalty after one year before the date of the filing of the petition;

(C) a tax required to be collected or withheld and for which the debtor is liable in whatever capacity;

(D) an employment tax on a wage, salary, or commission of a kind specified in paragraph (34) of this subsection earned from the debtor before the date of the filing of the petition, whether or not actually paid before such date, for which a return is last due, under applicable law or under any extension, after three years before the date of the filing of the petition;

(E) an excise tax on

(i) a transaction occurring before the date of the filing of the petition for which a return, if required, is last due, under applicable law or under any extension, after three years before the date of the filing of the petition; or

(ii) if a return is not required, a transaction occurring during the three years immediately preceding the date of the filing of the petition;

(F) a customs duty arising out of the importation of merchandise—

(i) entered for consumption within one year before the date of the filing of the petition;

(ii) covered by an entry liquidated or reliquidated within one year before the date of the filing of the petition; or

(iii) entered for consumption within four years before the date of the filing of the petition but unliquidated on such date, if the Secretary of the Treasury certifies that failure to liquidate such entry was due to an investigation pending on such date into assessment of antidumping or countervailing duties or fraud, or if information needed for the proper appraisement or classification of such merchandise was not available to the appropriate customs officer before such date; or

(G) a penalty related to a claim of a kind specified in this paragraph and in compensation for actual pecuniary loss.

(9) Ninth, allowed unsecured claims based upon any commitment by the debtor to a Federal depository institutions regulatory agency (or predecessor to such agency) to maintain the capital of an insured depository institution.

(10) Tenth, allowed claims for death or personal injury resulting from the operation of a motor vehicle or vessel if such operation was unlawful because the debtor was intoxicated from using alcohol, a drug, or another substance.

(b) If the trustee, under section 362, 363, or 364 of this title, provides adequate protection of the interest of a holder of a claim secured by a lien on property of the debtor and if, notwithstanding such protection, such creditor has a claim allowable under subsection (a)(2~~1~~) of this section arising from the stay of action against such property under section 362 of this title, from the use, sale, or lease of such property under section 363 of this title, or from the granting of a lien under section 364(d) of this title, then such creditor's claim under such subsection shall have priority over every other claim allowable under such subsection.

(c) For the purpose of subsection (a) of this section, a claim of a governmental unit arising from an erroneous refund or credit of a tax has the same priority as a claim for the tax to which such refund or credit relates.

(d) An entity that is subrogated to the rights of a holder of a claim of a kind specified in subsection (a)(1~~3~~), (a)(4), (a)(5), (a)(6), (a)(7), (a)(8), or (a)(9) of this section is not subrogated to the right of the holder of such claim to priority under such subsection.

§ 508. Effect of distribution other than under this title

~~(a) If a creditor receives, in a foreign proceeding, payment of, or a transfer of property on account of, a claim that is allowed under this title, such creditor may not receive any payment under this title on account of such claim until each of the other holders of claims on account of which such holders are entitled to share equally with such creditor under this title has received payment under this title equal in value to the consideration received by such creditor in such foreign proceeding.~~

~~(b)~~ If a creditor of a partnership debtor receives, from a general partner that is not a debtor in a case under chapter 7 of this title, payment of, or a transfer of property on account of, a claim that is allowed under this title and that is not secured by a lien on property of such partner, such creditor may not receive any payment under this title on account of such claim until each of the other holders of claims on account of which such holders are entitled to share equally with such creditor under this title has received payment under this title equal in value to the consideration received by such creditor from such general partner.

§ 509. Claims of codebtors

(a) Except as provided in subsection (b) or (c) of this section, an entity that is liable with the debtor on, or that has secured, a claim of a creditor against the debtor, and that pays such claim, is subrogated to the rights of such creditor to the extent of such payment.

(b) Such entity is not subrogated to the rights of such creditor to the extent that—

(1) a claim of such entity for reimbursement or contribution on account of such payment of such creditor's claim is—

(A) allowed under section 502 of this title;

(B) disallowed other than under section 502(e) of this title; or

(C) subordinated under section 510 of this title; or

(2) as between the debtor and such entity, such entity received the consideration for the claim held by such creditor.

(c) The court shall subordinate to the claim of a creditor and for the benefit of such creditor an allowed claim, by way of subrogation under this section, or for reimbursement or contribution, of an entity that is liable with the debtor on, or that has secured, such creditor's claim, until such creditor's claim is paid in full, either through payments under this title or otherwise.

§ 510. Subordination

(a) A subordination agreement is enforceable in a case under this title to the same extent that such agreement is enforceable under applicable nonbankruptcy law.

(b) For the purpose of distribution under this title, a claim arising from rescission of a purchase or sale of a security of the debtor or of an affiliate of the debtor, for damages arising from the purchase or sale of such a security, or for reimbursement or contribution allowed under section 502 on account of such a claim, shall be subordinated to all claims or interests that are senior to or equal the claim or interest represented by such security, except that if such security is common stock, such claim has the same priority as common stock.

(c) Notwithstanding subsections (a) and (b) of this section, after notice and a hearing, the court may—

(1) under principles of equitable subordination, subordinate for purposes of distribution all or part of an allowed claim to all or part of another allowed claim or all or part of an allowed interest to all or part of another allowed interest; or

(2) order that any lien securing such a subordinated claim be transferred to the estate.

§ 511. Rate of interest on tax claims

(a) If any provision of this title requires the payment of interest on a tax claim or on an administrative expense tax, or the payment of interest to enable a creditor to receive the present value of the allowed amount of a tax claim, the rate of interest shall be the rate determined under applicable nonbankruptcy law.

(b) In the case of taxes paid under a confirmed plan under this title, the rate of interest shall be determined as of the calendar month in which the plan is confirmed.

SUBCHAPTER II—DEBTOR'S DUTIES AND BENEFITS

§ 521. Debtor's duties

(a) The debtor shall—

~~(1) file a list of creditors, and unless the court orders otherwise, a schedule of assets and liabilities, a schedule of current income and current expenditures, and a statement of the debtor's financial affairs;~~

(1) file—

    (A) a list of creditors; and

    (B) unless the court orders otherwise—

        (i) a schedule of assets and liabilities;

        (ii) a schedule of current income and current expenditures;

        (iii) a statement of the debtor's financial affairs and, if section 342(b) applies, a certificate—

            (I) of an attorney whose name is indicated on the petition as the attorney for the debtor, or a bankruptcy petition preparer signing the petition under section 110(b)(1), indicating that such attorney or the bankruptcy petition preparer delivered to the debtor the notice required by section 342(b); or

            (II) if no attorney is so indicated, and no bankruptcy petition preparer signed the petition, of the debtor that such notice was received and read by the debtor;

        (iv) copies of all payment advices or other evidence of payment received within 60 days before the date of the filing of the petition, by the debtor from any employer of the debtor;

        (v) a statement of the amount of monthly net income, itemized to show how the amount is calculated; and

        (vi) a statement disclosing any reasonably anticipated increase in income or expenditures over the 12-month period following the date of the filing of the petition;

(2) if an individual debtor's schedule of assets and liabilities includes ~~consumer~~ debts which are secured by property of the estate—

  (A) within thirty days after the date of the filing of a petition under chapter 7 of this title or on or before the date of the meeting of creditors, whichever is earlier, or within such additional time as the court, for cause, within such period fixes, the debtor shall file with the clerk a statement of his intention with respect to the retention or surrender of such property and, if applicable, specifying that such property is claimed as exempt, that the debtor intends to redeem such property, or that the debtor intends to reaffirm debts secured by such property;

  (B) within *30 days after the first date set for the meeting of creditors under section 341(a)*~~forty-five days after the filing of a notice of intent under this section~~, or within such additional time as the court, for cause, within such ~~forty-five~~ *30*-day period fixes, the debtor shall perform his intention with respect to such property, as specified by subparagraph (A) of this paragraph; and

  (C) nothing in subparagraphs (A) and (B) of this paragraph shall alter the debtor's or the trustee's rights with regard to such property under this title, *except as provided in section 362(h)*;

(3) if a trustee is serving in the case *or an auditor serving under section 586(f) of title 28,* cooperate with the trustee as necessary to enable the trustee to perform the trustee's duties under this title;

(4) if a trustee is serving in the case *or an auditor serving under section 586(f) of title 28,* surrender to the trustee all property of the estate and any recorded information, including books, documents, records, and papers, relating to property of the estate, whether or not immunity is granted under section 344 of this title; ~~and~~

(5) appear at the hearing required under section 524(d) of this title~~.~~*; and*

(6) in a case under chapter 7 of this title in which the debtor is an individual, not retain possession of personal property as to which a creditor has an allowed claim for the purchase price secured in whole or in part by an interest in such personal property unless the debtor, not later than 45 days after the first meeting of creditors under section 341(a), either—

(A) enters into an agreement with the creditor pursuant to section 524(c) with respect to the claim secured by such property; or

(B) redeems such property from the security interest pursuant to section 722.

If the debtor fails to so act within the 45-day period referred to in paragraph (6), the stay under section 362(a) is terminated with respect to the personal property of the estate or of the debtor which is affected, such property shall no longer be property of the estate, and the creditor may take whatever action as to such property as is permitted by applicable nonbankruptcy law, unless the court determines on the motion of the trustee filed before the expiration of such 45-day period, and after notice and a hearing, that such property is of consequential value or benefit to the estate, orders appropriate adequate protection of the creditor's interest, and orders the debtor to deliver any collateral in the debtor's possession to the trustee; and

(7) unless a trustee is serving in the case, continue to perform the obligations required of the administrator (as defined in section 3 of the Employee Retirement Income Security Act of 1974) of an employee benefit plan if at the time of the commencement of the case the debtor (or any entity designated by the debtor) served as such administrator.

(b) In addition to the requirements under subsection (a), a debtor who is an individual shall file with the court—

(1) a certificate from the approved nonprofit budget and credit counseling agency that provided the debtor services under section 109(h) describing the services provided to the debtor; and

(2) a copy of the debt repayment plan, if any, developed under section 109(h) through the approved nonprofit budget and credit counseling agency referred to in paragraph (1).

(c) In addition to meeting the requirements under subsection (a), a debtor shall file with the court a record of any interest that a debtor has in an education individual retirement account (as defined in section 530(b)(1) of the Internal Revenue Code of 1986) or under a qualified State tuition program (as defined in section 529(b)(1) of such Code).

(d) If the debtor fails timely to take the action specified in subsection (a)(6) of this section, or in paragraphs (1) and (2) of section 362(h), with respect to prop-

erty which a lessor or bailor owns and has leased, rented, or bailed to the debtor or as to which a creditor holds a security interest not otherwise voidable under section 522(f), 544, 545, 547, 548, or 549, nothing in this title shall prevent or limit the operation of a provision in the underlying lease or agreement that has the effect of placing the debtor in default under such lease or agreement by reason of the occurrence, pendency, or existence of a proceeding under this title or the insolvency of the debtor. Nothing in this subsection shall be deemed to justify limiting such a provision in any other circumstance.

(e)(1) If the debtor in a case under chapter 7 or 13 is an individual and if a creditor files with the court at any time a request to receive a copy of the petition, schedules, and statement of financial affairs filed by the debtor, then the court shall make such petition, such schedules, and such statement available to such creditor.

(2)(A) The debtor shall provide—

(i) not later than 7 days before the date first set for the first meeting of creditors, to the trustee a copy of the Federal income tax return required under applicable law (or at the election of the debtor, a transcript of such return) for the most recent tax year ending immediately before the commencement of the case and for which a Federal income tax return was filed; and

(ii) at the same time the debtor complies with clause (i), a copy of such return (or if elected under clause (i), such transcript) to any creditor that timely requests such copy.

(B) If the debtor fails to comply with clause (i) or (ii) of subparagraph (A), the court shall dismiss the case unless the debtor demonstrates that the failure to so comply is due to circumstances beyond the control of the debtor.

(C) If a creditor requests a copy of such tax return or such transcript and if the debtor fails to provide a copy of such tax return or such transcript to such creditor at the time the debtor provides such tax return or such transcript to the trustee, then the court shall dismiss the case unless the debtor demonstrates that the failure to provide a copy of such tax return or such transcript is due to circumstances beyond the control of the debtor.

(3) If a creditor in a case under chapter 13 files with the court at any time a request to receive a copy of the plan filed by the debtor, then the court shall make available to such creditor a copy of the plan—

(A) at a reasonable cost; and

(B) not later than 5 days after such request is filed.

(f) At the request of the court, the United States trustee, or any party in interest in a case under chapter 7, 11, or 13, a debtor who is an individual shall file with the court—

(1) at the same time filed with the taxing authority, a copy of each Federal income tax return required under applicable law (or at the election of the debtor, a transcript of such tax return) with respect to each tax year of the debtor ending while the case is pending under such chapter;

(2) at the same time filed with the taxing authority, each Federal income tax return required under applicable law (or at the election of the debtor, a transcript of such tax return) that had not been filed with such authority as of the date of the commencement of the case and that was subsequently filed for any

tax year of the debtor ending in the 3-year period ending on the date of the commencement of the case;

(3) a copy of each amendment to any Federal income tax return or transcript filed with the court under paragraph (1) or (2); and

(4) in a case under chapter 13—

(A) on the date that is either 90 days after the end of such tax year or 1 year after the date of the commencement of the case, whichever is later, if a plan is not confirmed before such later date; and

(B) annually after the plan is confirmed and until the case is closed, not later than the date that is 45 days before the anniversary of the confirmation of the plan;

a statement, under penalty of perjury, of the income and expenditures of the debtor during the tax year of the debtor most recently concluded before such statement is filed under this paragraph, and of the monthly income of the debtor, that shows how income, expenditures, and monthly income are calculated.

(g)(1) A statement referred to in subsection (f)(4) shall disclose—

(A) the amount and sources of the income of the debtor;

(B) the identity of any person responsible with the debtor for the support of any dependent of the debtor; and

(C) the identity of any person who contributed, and the amount contributed, to the household in which the debtor resides.

(2) The tax returns, amendments, and statement of income and expenditures described in subsections (e)(2)(A) and (f) shall be available to the United States trustee (or the bankruptcy administrator, if any), the trustee, and any party in interest for inspection and copying, subject to the requirements of section 315(c) of the Bankruptcy Abuse Prevention and Consumer Protection Act of 2005.

(h) If requested by the United States trustee or by the trustee, the debtor shall provide—

(1) a document that establishes the identity of the debtor, including a driver's license, passport, or other document that contains a photograph of the debtor; or

(2) such other personal identifying information relating to the debtor that establishes the identity of the debtor.

(i)(1) Subject to paragraphs (2) and (4) and notwithstanding section 707(a), if an individual debtor in a voluntary case under chapter 7 or 13 fails to file all of the information required under subsection (a)(1) within 45 days after the date of the filing of the petition, the case shall be automatically dismissed effective on the 46th day after the date of the filing of the petition.

(2) Subject to paragraph (4) and with respect to a case described in paragraph (1), any party in interest may request the court to enter an order dismissing the case. If requested, the court shall enter an order of dismissal not later than 5 days after such request.

(3) Subject to paragraph (4) and upon request of the debtor made within 45 days after the date of the filing of the petition described in paragraph (1), the court may allow the debtor an additional period of not to exceed 45 days to file

the information required under subsection (a)(1) if the court finds justification for extending the period for the filing.

(4) Notwithstanding any other provision of this subsection, on the motion of the trustee filed before the expiration of the applicable period of time specified in paragraph (1), (2), or (3), and after notice and a hearing, the court may decline to dismiss the case if the court finds that the debtor attempted in good faith to file all the information required by subsection (a)(1)(B)(iv) and that the best interests of creditors would be served by administration of the case.

(j)(1) Notwithstanding any other provision of this title, if the debtor fails to file a tax return that becomes due after the commencement of the case or to properly obtain an extension of the due date for filing such return, the taxing authority may request that the court enter an order converting or dismissing the case.

(2) If the debtor does not file the required return or obtain the extension referred to in paragraph (1) within 90 days after a request is filed by the taxing authority under that paragraph, the court shall convert or dismiss the case, whichever is in the best interests of creditors and the estate.

§ 522. Exemptions

(a) In this section—

(1) "dependent" includes spouse, whether or not actually dependent; and

(2) "value" means fair market value as of the date of the filing of the petition or, with respect to property that becomes property of the estate after such date, as of the date such property becomes property of the estate.

(b)*(1)* Notwithstanding section 541 of this title, an individual debtor may exempt from property of the estate the property listed in either ~~paragraph (1)~~*paragraph (2)* or, in the alternative, ~~paragraph (2)~~*paragraph (3)* of this subsection. In joint cases filed under section 302 of this title and individual cases filed under section 301 or 303 of this title by or against debtors who are husband and wife, and whose estates are ordered to be jointly administered under Rule 1015(b) of the Federal Rules of Bankruptcy Procedure, one debtor may not elect to exempt property listed in ~~paragraph (1)~~*paragraph (2)* and the other debtor elect to exempt property listed in ~~paragraph (2)~~*paragraph (3)* of this subsection. If the parties cannot agree on the alternative to be elected, they shall be deemed to elect ~~paragraph (1)~~*paragraph (2),* where such election is permitted under the law of the jurisdiction where the case is filed. ~~Such property is—~~

~~(1) property that is specified under subsection (d) of this section, unless the State law that is applicable to the debtor under paragraph (2)(A) of this subsection specifically does not so authorize; or, in the alternative,~~ *(2) Property listed in this paragraph is property that is specified under subsection (d), unless the State law that is applicable to the debtor under paragraph (3)(A) specifically does not so authorize.*

(3~~2~~) Property listed in this paragraph is

(A) *subject to subsections (o) and (p),* any property that is exempt under Federal law, other than subsection (d) of this section, or State or local law that is applicable on the date of the filing of the petition at the place in which the debtor's domicile has been located for the ~~180~~*730* days immediately preceding the date of the filing of the petition~~, or for a longer portion of such 180-day period than in any other place~~ *or if the debtor's domicile has not been located at a single State for such 730-day period, the place in which the debtor's domicile was located for 180 days immediately preceding the 730-day period or for a longer portion of such 180-day period than in any other place;* ~~and~~

(B) any interest in property in which the debtor had, immediately before the commencement of the case, an interest as a tenant by the entirety or joint tenant to the extent that such interest as a tenant by the entirety or joint tenant is exempt from process under applicable nonbankruptcy law~~;~~ *;and*

(C) retirement funds to the extent that those funds are in a fund or account that is exempt from taxation under section 401, 403, 408, 408A, 414, 457, or 501(a) of the Internal Revenue Code of 1986.

If the effect of the domiciliary requirement under subparagraph (A) is to render the debtor ineligible for any exemption, the debtor may elect to exempt property that is specified under subsection (d).

(4) For purposes of paragraph (3)(C) and subsection (d)(12), the following shall apply:

(A) If the retirement funds are in a retirement fund that has received a favorable determination under section 7805 of the Internal Revenue Code of 1986, and that determination is in effect as of the date of the filing of the petition in a case under this title, those funds shall be presumed to be exempt from the estate.

(B) If the retirement funds are in a retirement fund that has not received a favorable determination under such section 7805, those funds are exempt from the estate if the debtor demonstrates that—

(i) no prior determination to the contrary has been made by a court or the Internal Revenue Service; and

(ii)(I) the retirement fund is in substantial compliance with the applicable requirements of the Internal Revenue Code of 1986; or

(II) the retirement fund fails to be in substantial compliance with the applicable requirements of the Internal Revenue Code of 1986 and the debtor is not materially responsible for that failure.

(C) A direct transfer of retirement funds from 1 fund or account that is exempt from taxation under section 401, 403, 408, 408A, 414, 457, or 501(a) of the Internal Revenue Code of 1986, under section 401(a)(31) of the Internal Revenue Code of 1986, or otherwise, shall not cease to qualify for exemption under paragraph (3)(C) or subsection (d)(12) by reason of such direct transfer.

(D)(i) Any distribution that qualifies as an eligible rollover distribution within the meaning of section 402(c) of the Internal Revenue Code of 1986 or that is described in clause (ii) shall not cease to qualify for exemption under paragraph (3)(C) or subsection (d)(12) by reason of such distribution.

(ii) A distribution described in this clause is an amount that—

(I) has been distributed from a fund or account that is exempt from taxation under section 401, 403, 408, 408A, 414, 457, or 501(a) of the Internal Revenue Code of 1986; and

(II) to the extent allowed by law, is deposited in such a fund or account not later than 60 days after the distribution of such amount.

(c) Unless the case is dismissed, property exempted under this section is not liable during or after the case for any debt of the debtor that arose, or that is determined under section 502 of this title as if such debt had arisen, before the commencement of the case, except—

~~(1) a debt of a kind specified in section 523(a)(1) or 523(a)(5) of this title;~~

(1) a debt of a kind specified in paragraph (1) or (5) of section 523(a) (in which case, notwithstanding any provision of applicable nonbankruptcy law to the contrary, such property shall be liable for a debt of a kind specified in section 523(a)(5));

(2) a debt secured by a lien that is—

   (A)(i) not avoided under subsection (f) or (g) of this section or under section 544, 545, 547, 548, 549, or 724(a) of this title; and

   (ii) not void under section 506(d) of this title;

   (B) a tax lien, notice of which is properly filed; or

(3) a debt of a kind specified in section 523(a)(4) or 523(a)(6) of this title owed by an institution-affiliated party of an insured depository institution to a Federal depository institutions regulatory agency acting in its capacity as conservator, receiver, or liquidating agent for such institution; or

(4) a debt in connection with fraud in the obtaining or providing of any scholarship, grant, loan, tuition, discount, award, or other financial assistance for purposes of financing an education at an institution of higher education (as that term is defined in section 101 of the Higher Education Act of 1965 (20 U.S.C. 1001)).

(d) The following property may be exempted under ~~subsection (b)(1)~~ *subsection (b)(2)* of this section:

(1) The debtor's aggregate interest, not to exceed $18,450 in value, in real property or personal property that the debtor or a dependent of the debtor uses as a residence, in a cooperative that owns property that the debtor or a dependent of the debtor uses as a residence, or in a burial plot for the debtor or a dependent of the debtor.

(2) The debtor's interest, not to exceed $2,950 in value, in one motor vehicle.

(3) The debtor's interest, not to exceed $475 in value in any particular item or $9,850 in aggregate value, in household furnishings, household goods, wearing apparel, appliances, books, animals, crops, or musical instruments, that are held primarily for the personal, family, or household use of the debtor or a dependent of the debtor.

(4) The debtor's aggregate interest, not to exceed $1,225 in value, in jewelry held primarily for the personal, family, or household use of the debtor or a dependent of the debtor.

(5) The debtor's aggregate interest in any property, not to exceed in value $975 plus up to $9,250 of any unused amount of the exemption provided under paragraph (1) of this subsection.

(6) The debtor's aggregate interest, not to exceed $1,850 in value, in any implements, professional books, or tools, of the trade of the debtor or the trade of a dependent of the debtor.

(7) Any unmatured life insurance contract owned by the debtor, other than a credit life insurance contract.

(8) The debtor's aggregate interest, not to exceed in value $9,850 less any amount of property of the estate transferred in the manner specified in section 542(d) of this title, in any accrued dividend or interest under, or loan value of, any unmatured life insurance contract owned by the debtor under which the insured is the debtor or an individual of whom the debtor is a dependent.

(9) Professionally prescribed health aids for the debtor or a dependent of the debtor.

(10) The debtor's right to receive—

(A) a social security benefit, unemployment compensation, or a local public assistance benefit;

(B) a veterans' benefit;

(C) a disability, illness, or unemployment benefit;

(D) alimony, support, or separate maintenance, to the extent reasonably necessary for the support of the debtor and any dependent of the debtor;

(E) a payment under a stock bonus, pension, profitsharing, annuity, or similar plan or contract on account of illness, disability, death, age, or length of service, to the extent reasonably necessary for the support of the debtor and any dependent of the debtor, unless—

(i) such plan or contract was established by or under the auspices of an insider that employed the debtor at the time the debtor's rights under such plan or contract arose;

(ii) such payment is on account of age or length of service; and

(iii) such plan or contract does not qualify under section 401(a), 403(a), 403(b), or 408 of the Internal Revenue Code of 1986.

(11) The debtor's right to receive, or property that is traceable to—

(A) an award under a crime victim's reparation law;

(B) a payment on account of the wrongful death of an individual of whom the debtor was a dependent, to the extent reasonably necessary for the support of the debtor and any dependent of the debtor;

(C) a payment under a life insurance contract that insured the life of an individual of whom the debtor was a dependent on the date of such individual's death, to the extent reasonably necessary for the support of the debtor and any dependent of the debtor;

(D) a payment, not to exceed $18,450, on account of personal bodily injury, not including pain and suffering or compensation for actual pecuniary loss, of the debtor or an individual of whom the debtor is a dependent; or

(E) a payment in compensation of loss of future earnings of the debtor or an individual of whom the debtor is or was a dependent, to the extent reasonably necessary for the support of the debtor and any dependent of the debtor.

(12) Retirement funds to the extent that those funds are in a fund or account that is exempt from taxation under section 401, 403, 408, 408A, 414, 457, or 501(a) of the Internal Revenue Code of 1986.

(e) A waiver of an exemption executed in favor of a creditor that holds an unsecured claim against the debtor is unenforceable in a case under this title with respect to such claim against property that the debtor may exempt under subsection (b) of this section. A waiver by the debtor of a power under subsection (f) or

(h) of this section to avoid a transfer, under subsection (g) or (i) of this section to exempt property, or under subsection (i) of this section to recover property or to preserve a transfer, is unenforceable in a case under this title.

(f)(1) Notwithstanding any waiver of exemptions but subject to paragraph (3), the debtor may avoid the fixing of a lien on an interest of the debtor in property to the extent that such lien impairs an exemption to which the debtor would have been entitled under subsection (b) of this section, if such lien is—

(A) a judicial lien, other than a judicial lien that secures a debt *of a kind that is specified in section 523(a)(5); or*—

~~(i) to a spouse, former spouse, or child of the debtor, for alimony to, maintenance for, or support of such spouse or child, in connection with a separation agreement, divorce decree or other order of a court of record, determination made in accordance with State or territorial law by a governmental unit, or property settlement agreement; and~~

~~(ii) to the extent that such debt—~~

~~(I) is not assigned to another entity, voluntarily, by operation of law, or otherwise; and~~

~~(II) includes a liability designated as alimony, maintenance, or support, unless such liability is actually in the nature of alimony, maintenance or support.; or~~

(B) a nonpossessory, nonpurchase-money security interest in any—

(i) household furnishings, household goods, wearing apparel, appliances, books, animals, crops, musical instruments, or jewelry that are held primarily for the personal, family, or household use of the debtor or a dependent of the debtor;

(ii) implements, professional books, or tools, of the trade of the debtor or the trade of a dependent of the debtor; or

(iii) professionally prescribed health aids for the debtor or a dependent of the debtor.

(2)(A) For the purposes of this subsection, a lien shall be considered to impair an exemption to the extent that the sum of—

(i) the lien;

(ii) all other liens on the property; and

(iii) the amount of the exemption that the debtor could claim if there were no liens on the property;

exceeds the value that the debtor's interest in the property would have in the absence of any liens.

(B) In the case of a property subject to more than 1 lien, a lien that has been avoided shall not be considered in making the calculation under subparagraph (A) with respect to other liens.

(C) This paragraph shall not apply with respect to a judgment arising out of a mortgage foreclosure.

(3) In a case in which State law that is applicable to the debtor—

(A) permits a person to voluntarily waive a right to claim exemptions under subsection (d) or prohibits a debtor from claiming exemptions under subsection (d); and

(B) either permits the debtor to claim exemptions under State law without limitation in amount, except to the extent that the debtor has permitted the fixing of a consensual lien on any property or prohibits avoidance of a consensual lien on property otherwise eligible to be claimed as exempt property;

the debtor may not avoid the fixing of a lien on an interest of the debtor or a dependent of the debtor in property if the lien is a nonpossessory, nonpurchase-money security interest in implements, professional books, or tools of the trade of the debtor or a dependent of the debtor or farm animals or crops of the debtor or a dependent of the debtor to the extent the value of such implements, professional books, tools of the trade, animals, and crops exceeds $5,000.

(4)(A) Subject to subparagraph (B), for purposes of paragraph (1)(B), the term 'household goods' means—

(i) clothing;

(ii) furniture;

(iii) appliances;

(iv) 1 radio;

(v) 1 television;

(vi) 1 VCR;

(vii) linens;

(viii) china;

(ix) crockery;

(x) kitchenware;

(xi) educational materials and educational equipment primarily for the use of minor dependent children of the debtor;

(xii) medical equipment and supplies;

(xiii) furniture exclusively for the use of minor children, or elderly or disabled dependents of the debtor;

(xiv) personal effects (including the toys and hobby equipment of minor dependent children and wedding rings) of the debtor and the dependents of the debtor; and

(xv) 1 personal computer and related equipment.

(B) The term 'household goods' does not include—

(i) works of art (unless by or of the debtor, or any relative of the debtor);

(ii) electronic entertainment equipment with a fair market value of more than $500 in the aggregate (except 1 television, 1 radio, and 1 VCR);

(iii) items acquired as antiques with a fair market value of more than $500 in the aggregate;

(iv) jewelry with a fair market value of more than $500 in the aggregate (except wedding rings); and

(v) a computer (except as otherwise provided for in this section), motor vehicle (including a tractor or lawn tractor), boat, or a motorized recreational device, conveyance, vehicle, watercraft, or aircraft.

(g) Notwithstanding sections 550 and 551 of this title, the debtor may exempt under subsection (b) of this section property that the trustee recovers under section 510(c)(2), 542, 543, 550, 551, or 553 of this title, to the extent that the debtor could have exempted such property under subsection (b) of this section if such property had not been transferred, if—

(1)(A) such transfer was not a voluntary transfer of such property by the debtor; and

(B) the debtor did not conceal such property; or

(2) the debtor could have avoided such transfer under subsection (f)(2*1*)*(B)* of this section.

(h) The debtor may avoid a transfer of property of the debtor or recover a setoff to the extent that the debtor could have exempted such property under subsection (g)(1) of this section if the trustee had avoided such transfer, if—

(1) such transfer is avoidable by the trustee under section 544, 545, 547, 548, 549, or 724(a) of this title or recoverable by the trustee under section 553 of this title; and

(2) the trustee does not attempt to avoid such transfer.

(i)(1) If the debtor avoids a transfer or recovers a setoff under subsection (f) or (h) of this section, the debtor may recover in the manner prescribed by, and subject to the limitations of, section 550 of this title, the same as if the trustee had avoided such transfer, and may exempt any property so recovered under subsection (b) of this section.

(2) Notwithstanding section 551 of this title, a transfer avoided under section 544, 545, 547, 548, 549, or 724(a) of this title, under subsection (f) or (h) of this section, or property recovered under section 553 of this title, may be preserved for the benefit of the debtor to the extent that the debtor may exempt such property under subsection (g) of this section or paragraph (1) of this subsection.

(j) Notwithstanding subsections (g) and (i) of this section, the debtor may exempt a particular kind of property under subsections (g) and (i) of this section only to the extent that the debtor has exempted less property in value of such kind than that to which the debtor is entitled under subsection (b) of this section.

(k) Property that the debtor exempts under this section is not liable for payment of any administrative expense except—

(1) the aliquot share of the costs and expenses of avoiding a transfer of property that the debtor exempts under subsection (g) of this section, or of recovery of such property, that is attributable to the value of the portion of such property exempted in relation to the value of the property recovered; and

(2) any costs and expenses of avoiding a transfer under subsection (f) or (h) of this section, or of recovery of property under subsection (i)(1) of this section, that the debtor has not paid.

(l) The debtor shall file a list of property that the debtor claims as exempt under subsection (b) of this section. If the debtor does not file such a list, a dependent of the debtor may file such a list, or may claim property as exempt from property of the estate on behalf of the debtor. Unless a party in interest objects, the property claimed as exempt on such list is exempt.

(m) Subject to the limitation in subsection (b), this section shall apply separately with respect to each debtor in a joint case.

(n) For assets in individual retirement accounts described in section 408 or 408A of the Internal Revenue Code of 1986, other than a simplified employee pension

under section 408(k) of such Code or a simple retirement account under section 408(p) of such Code, the aggregate value of such assets exempted under this section, without regard to amounts attributable to rollover contributions under section 402(c), 402(e)(6), 403(a)(4), 403(a)(5), and 403(b)(8) of the Internal Revenue Code of 1986, and earnings thereon, shall not exceed $1,000,000 in a case filed by a debtor who is an individual, except that such amount may be increased if the interests of justice so require.

(o) For purposes of subsection (b)(3)(A), and notwithstanding subsection (a), the value of an interest in—

    (1) real or personal property that the debtor or a dependent of the debtor uses as a residence;

    (2) a cooperative that owns property that the debtor or a dependent of the debtor uses as a residence;

    (3) a burial plot for the debtor or a dependent of the debtor; or

    (4) real or personal property that the debtor or a dependent of the debtor claims as a homestead;

shall be reduced to the extent that such value is attributable to any portion of any property that the debtor disposed of in the 10-year period ending on the date of the filing of the petition with the intent to hinder, delay, or defraud a creditor and that the debtor could not exempt, or that portion that the debtor could not exempt, under subsection (b), if on such date the debtor had held the property so disposed of.

(p)(1) Except as provided in paragraph (2) of this subsection and sections 544 and 548, as a result of electing under subsection (b)(3)(A) to exempt property under State or local law, a debtor may not exempt any amount of interest that was acquired by the debtor during the 1215-day period preceding the date of the filing of the petition that exceeds in the aggregate $125,000 in value in—

    (A) real or personal property that the debtor or a dependent of the debtor uses as a residence;

    (B) a cooperative that owns property that the debtor or a dependent of the debtor uses as a residence;

    (C) a burial plot for the debtor or a dependent of the debtor; or

    (D) real or personal property that the debtor or dependent of the debtor claims as a homestead.

    (2)(A) The limitation under paragraph (1) shall not apply to an exemption claimed under subsection (b)(3)(A) by a family farmer for the principal residence of such farmer.

    (B) For purposes of paragraph (1), any amount of such interest does not include any interest transferred from a debtor's previous principal residence (which was acquired prior to the beginning of such 1215-day period) into the debtor's current principal residence, if the debtor's previous and current residences are located in the same State.

(q)(1) As a result of electing under subsection (b)(3)(A) to exempt property under State or local law, a debtor may not exempt any amount of an interest in property described in subparagraphs (A), (B), (C), and (D) of subsection (p)(1) which exceeds in the aggregate $125,000 if—

    (A) the court determines, after notice and a hearing, that the debtor has been convicted of a felony (as defined in section 3156 of title 18), which

under the circumstances, demonstrates that the filing of the case was an abuse of the provisions of this title; or

(B) the debtor owes a debt arising from—

(i) any violation of the Federal securities laws (as defined in section 3(a)(47) of the Securities Exchange Act of 1934), any State securities laws, or any regulation or order issued under Federal securities laws or State securities laws;

(ii) fraud, deceit, or manipulation in a fiduciary capacity or in connection with the purchase or sale of any security registered under section 12 or 15(d) of the Securities Exchange Act of 1934 or under section 6 of the Securities Act of 1933;

(iii) any civil remedy under section 1964 of title 18; or

(iv) any criminal act, intentional tort, or willful or reckless misconduct that caused serious physical injury or death to another individual in the preceding 5 years.

(2) Paragraph (1) shall not apply to the extent the amount of an interest in property described in subparagraphs (A), (B), (C), and (D) of subsection (p)(1) is reasonably necessary for the support of the debtor and any dependent of the debtor.

§ 523. Exceptions to discharge

(a) A discharge under section 727, 1141, 1228(a), 1228(b), or 1328(b) of this title does not discharge an individual debtor from any debt—

(1) for a tax or a customs duty—

(A) of the kind and for the periods specified in section 507(a)(2̶3) or 507(a)(8) of this title, whether or not a claim for such tax was filed or allowed;

(B) with respect to which a return, *or equivalent report or notice,* if required—

(i) was not filed or given; or

(ii) was filed *or given* after the date on which such return, *report, or notice* was last due, under applicable law or under any extension, and after two years before the date of the filing of the petition; or

(C) with respect to which the debtor made a fraudulent return or willfully attempted in any manner to evade or defeat such tax;

(2) for money, property, services, or an extension, renewal, or refinancing of credit, to the extent obtained by—

(A) false pretenses, a false representation, or actual fraud, other than a statement respecting the debtor's or an insider's financial condition;

(B) use of a statement in writing—

(i) that is materially false;

(ii) respecting the debtor's or an insider's financial condition;

(iii) on which the creditor to whom the debtor is liable for such money, property, services, or credit reasonably relied; and

(iv) that the debtor caused to be made or published with intent to deceive; or

(C) ~~for purposes of subparagraph (A) of this paragraph, consumer debts owed to a single creditor and aggregating more than $1,225 for "luxury goods or services" incurred by an individual debtor on or within 60 days before the order for relief under this title, or cash advances aggregating more than $1,225 that are extensions of consumer credit under an open end credit plan obtained by an individual debtor on or within 60 days before the order for relief under this title, are presumed to be nondischargeable; "luxury goods or services" do not include goods or services reasonably acquired for the support or maintenance of the debtor or a dependent of the debtor; an extension of consumer credit under an open end credit plan is to be defined for purposes of this subparagraph as it is defined in the Consumer Credit Protection Act;~~ *(i) for purposes of subparagraph (A)—*

(I) consumer debts owed to a single creditor and aggregating more than $500 for luxury goods or services incurred by an individual debtor on or within 90 days before the order for relief under this title are presumed to be nondischargeable; and

(II) cash advances aggregating more than $750 that are extensions of consumer credit under an open end credit plan obtained by an individual debtor on or within 70 days before the order for relief under this title, are presumed to be nondischargeable; and

(ii) for purposes of this subparagraph—

(I) the terms 'consumer', 'credit', and 'open end credit plan' have the same meanings as in section 103 of the Truth in Lending Act; and

(II) the term 'luxury goods or services' does not include goods or services reasonably necessary for the support or maintenance of the debtor or a dependent of the debtor.

(3) neither listed nor scheduled under section 521(1) of this title, with the name, if known to the debtor, of the creditor to whom such debt is owed, in time to permit—

(A) if such debt is not of a kind specified in paragraph (2), (4), or (6) of this subsection, timely filing of a proof of claim, unless such creditor had notice or actual knowledge of the case in time for such timely filing; or

(B) if such debt is of a kind specified in paragraph (2), (4), or (6) of this subsection, timely filing of a proof of claim and timely request for a determination of dischargeability of such debt under one of such paragraphs, unless such creditor had notice or actual knowledge of the case in time for such timely filing and request;

(4) for fraud or defalcation while acting in a fiduciary capacity, embezzlement, or larceny;

~~(5) to a spouse, former spouse, or child of the debtor, for alimony to, maintenance for, or support of such spouse or child, in connection with a separation agreement, divorce decree or other order of a court of record, determination made in accordance with State or territorial law by a governmental unit, or property settlement agreement, but not to the extent that——~~

(5) for a domestic support obligation;

~~(A) such debt is assigned to another entity, voluntarily, by operation of law, or otherwise (other than debts assigned pursuant to section 408(a)(3) of the Social Security Act, or any such debt which has been assigned to the Federal Government or to a State or any political subdivision of such State); or~~

~~(B) such debt includes a liability designated as alimony, maintenance, or support, unless such liability is actually in the nature of alimony, maintenance, or support;~~

(6) for willful and malicious injury by the debtor to another entity or to the property of another entity;

(7) to the extent such debt is for a fine, penalty, or forfeiture payable to and for the benefit of a governmental unit, and is not compensation for actual pecuniary loss, other than a tax penalty—

(A) relating to a tax of a kind not specified in paragraph (1) of this subsection; or

(B) imposed with respect to a transaction or event that occurred before three years before the date of the filing of the petition;

~~(8) for an educational benefit overpayment or loan made, insured or guaranteed by a governmental unit, or made under any program funded in whole or in part by a governmental unit or nonprofit institution, or for an obligation to repay funds received as an educational benefit, scholarship or stipend, unless excepting such debt from discharge under this paragraph will impose an undue hardship on the debtor and the debtor's dependents;~~

(8) unless excepting such debt from discharge under this paragraph would impose an undue hardship on the debtor and the debtor's dependents, for—

(A)(i) an educational benefit overpayment or loan made, insured, or guaranteed by a governmental unit, or made under any program funded in whole or in part by a governmental unit or nonprofit institution; or

(ii) an obligation to repay funds received as an educational benefit, scholarship, or stipend; or

(B) any other educational loan that is a qualified education loan, as defined in section 221(d)(1) of the Internal Revenue Code of 1986, incurred by a debtor who is an individual;

(9) for death or personal injury caused by the debtor's operation of a motor vehicle, *vessel, or aircraft* if such operation was unlawful because the debtor was intoxicated from using alcohol, a drug, or another substance;

(10) that was or could have been listed or scheduled by the debtor in a prior case concerning the debtor under this title or under the Bankruptcy Act in which the debtor waived discharge, or was denied a discharge under section 727(a)(2), (3), (4), (5), (6), or (7) of this title, or under section 14c(1), (2), (3), (4), (6), or (7) of such Act;

(11) provided in any final judgment, unreviewable order, or consent order or decree entered in any court of the United States or of any State, issued by a Federal depository institutions regulatory agency, or contained in any settlement agreement entered into by the debtor, arising from any act of fraud or defalcation while acting in a fiduciary capacity committed with respect to any depository institution or insured credit union;

(12) for malicious or reckless failure to fulfill any commitment by the debtor to a Federal depository institutions regulatory agency to maintain the capital of an

insured depository institution, except that this paragraph shall not extend any such commitment which would otherwise be terminated due to any act of such agency; or

(13) for any payment of an order of restitution issued under title 18, United States Code;

(14) incurred to pay a tax to the United States that would be nondischargeable pursuant to paragraph (1);

(14A) incurred to pay a tax to a governmental unit, other than the United States, that would be nondischargeable under paragraph (1);

(14B) incurred to pay fines or penalties imposed under Federal election law;

(15) *to a spouse, former spouse, or child of the debtor and* not of the kind described in paragraph (5) that is incurred by the debtor in the course of a divorce or separation or in connection with a separation agreement, divorce decree or other order of a court of record, or a determination made in accordance with State or territorial law by a governmental unit; unless—

(A) the debtor does not have the ability to pay such debt from income or property of the debtor not reasonably necessary to be expended for the maintenance or support of the debtor or a dependent of the debtor and, if the debtor is engaged in a business, for the payment of expenditures necessary for the continuation, preservation, and operation of such business; or

(B) discharging such debt would result in a benefit to the debtor that outweighs the detrimental consequences to a spouse, former spouse, or child of the debtor;

(16) for a fee or assessment that becomes due and payable after the order for relief to a membership association with respect to the debtor's interest in a dwelling-unit that has condominium ownership or *ownership,* in a share of a cooperative housing-corporation, but only if such fee or assessment is payable for a period during which—

(A) the debtor physically occupied a dwelling unit in the condominium or cooperative project; or

(B) the debtor rented the dwelling unit to a tenant and received payments from the tenant for such period *or a lot in a homeowners association, for as long as the debtor or the trustee has a legal, equitable, or possessory ownership interest in such unit, such corporation, or such lot.,*

but nothing in this paragraph shall except from discharge the debt of a debtor for a membership association fee or assessment for a period arising before entry of the order for relief in a pending or subsequent bankruptcy case;

(17) for a fee imposed by a court *on a prisoner by any court* for the filing of a case, motion, complaint, or appeal, or for other costs and expenses assessed with respect to such filing, regardless of an assertion of poverty by the debtor under section 1915(b) or (f) *subsection (b) or (f)(2) of section 1915* of title 28 *(or a similar non-Federal law),* or the debtor's status as a prisoner, as defined in section 1915(h) of title 28 *(or a similar non-Federal law);*

(18) owed to a pension, profit-sharing, stock bonus, or other plan established under section 401, 403, 408, 408A, 414, 457, or 501(c) of the Internal Revenue Code of 1986, under—

(A) a loan permitted under section 408(b)(1) of the Employee Retirement Income Security Act of 1974, or subject to section 72(p) of the Internal Revenue Code of 1986; or

(B) a loan from a thrift savings plan permitted under subchapter III of chapter 84 of title 5, that satisfies the requirements of section 8433(g) of such title;

but nothing in this paragraph may be construed to provide that any loan made under a governmental plan under section 414(d), or a contract or account under section 403(b), of the Internal Revenue Code of 1986 constitutes a claim or a debt under this title; or

(18) owed under State law to a State or municipality that is—

(A) in the nature of support, and

(B) enforceable under part D of title IV of the Social Security Act (42 U.S.C. 601 et seq.); or

(19) that—

(A) is for—

(i) the violation of any of the Federal securities laws (as that term is defined in section 3(a)(47) of the Securities Exchange Act of 1934), any of the State securities laws, or any regulation or order issued under such Federal or State securities laws; or

(ii) common law fraud, deceit, or manipulation in connection with the purchase or sale of any security; and

(B) results*, before, on, or after the date on which the petition was filed,* from—

(i) any judgment, order, consent order, or decree entered in any Federal or State judicial or administrative proceeding;

(ii) any settlement agreement entered into by the debtor; or

(iii) any court or administrative order for any damages, fine, penalty, citation, restitutionary payment, disgorgement payment, attorney fee, cost, or other payment owed by the debtor.

For purposes of this subsection, the term 'return' means a return that satisfies the requirements of applicable nonbankruptcy law (including applicable filing requirements). Such term includes a return prepared pursuant to section 6020(a) of the Internal Revenue Code of 1986, or similar State or local law, or a written stipulation to a judgment or a final order entered by a nonbankruptcy tribunal, but does not include a return made pursuant to section 6020(b) of the Internal Revenue Code of 1986, or a similar State or local law.

 (b) Notwithstanding subsection (a) of this section, a debt that was excepted from discharge under subsection (a)(1), (a)(3), or (a)(8) of this section, under section 17a(1), 17a(3), or 17a(5) of the Bankruptcy Act, under section 439A of the Higher Education Act of 1965, or under section 733(g) of the Public Health Service Act in a prior case concerning the debtor under this title, or under the Bankruptcy Act, is dischargeable in a case under this title unless, by the terms of subsection (a) of this section, such debt is not dischargeable in the case under this title.

 (c)(1) Except as provided in subsection (a)(3)(B) of this section, the debtor shall be discharged from a debt of a kind specified in paragraph (2), (4), (6), or (15)*or (6)* of subsection (a) of this section, unless, on request of the creditor to whom such debt is owed, and after notice and a hearing, the court determines such debt to be excepted from discharge under paragraph (2), (4), ~~(6), or (15)~~*or (6)*, as the case may be, of subsection (a) of this section.

(2) Paragraph (1) shall not apply in the case of a Federal depository institutions regulatory agency seeking, in its capacity as conservator, receiver, or liquidating agent for an insured depository institution, to recover a debt described in subsection (a)(2), (a)(4), (a)(6), or (a)(11) owed to such institution by an institution-affiliated party unless the receiver, conservator, or liquidating agent was appointed in time to reasonably comply, or for a Federal depository institutions regulatory agency acting in its corporate capacity as a successor to such receiver, conservator, or liquidating agent to reasonably comply, with subsection (a)(3)(B) as a creditor of such institution-affiliated party with respect to such debt.

(d) If a creditor requests a determination of dischargeability of a consumer debt under subsection (a)(2) of this section, and such debt is discharged, the court shall grant judgment in favor of the debtor for the costs of, and a reasonable attorney's fee for, the proceeding if the court finds that the position of the creditor was not substantially justified, except that the court shall not award such costs and fees if special circumstances would make the award unjust.

(e) Any institution-affiliated party of an insured depository institution shall be considered to be acting in a fiduciary capacity with respect to the purposes of subsection (a)(4) or (11).

§ 524. Effect of discharge

(a) A discharge in a case under this title—

(1) voids any judgment at any time obtained, to the extent that such judgment is a determination of the personal liability of the debtor with respect to any debt discharged under section 727, 944, 1141, 1228, or 1328 of this title, whether or not discharge of such debt is waived;

(2) operates as an injunction against the commencement or continuation of an action, the employment of process, or an act, to collect, recover or offset any such debt as a personal liability of the debtor, whether or not discharge of such debt is waived; and

(3) operates as an injunction against the commencement or continuation of an action, the employment of process, or an act, to collect or recover from, or off-set against, property of the debtor of the kind specified in section 541(a)(2) of this title that is acquired after the commencement of the case, on account of any allowable community claim, except a community claim that is excepted from discharge under ~~section 523, 1228(a)(1), or 1328(a)(1) of this title, or that~~ *section 523, 1228(a)(1), or 1328(a)(1), or that* would be so excepted, determined in accordance with the provisions of sections 523(c) and 523(d) of this title, in a case concerning the debtor's spouse commenced on the date of the filing of the petition in the case concerning the debtor, whether or not discharge of the debt based on such community claim is waived.

(b) Subsection (a)(3) of this section does not apply if—

(1)(A) the debtor's spouse is a debtor in a case under this title, or a bankrupt or a debtor in a case under the Bankruptcy Act, commenced within six years of the date of the filing of the petition in the case concerning the debtor; and

2005 Bꜱᴋᴘᴛᴄʏ Rᴇꜰᴏʀᴍ Lᴇɢɪꜱʟᴀᴛɪᴏɴ ᴡɪᴛʜ Aɴᴀʟʏꜱɪꜱ

(B) the court does not grant the debtor's spouse a discharge in such case concerning the debtor's spouse; or

(2)(A) the court would not grant the debtor's spouse a discharge in a case under chapter 7 of this title concerning such spouse commenced on the date of the filing of the petition in the case concerning the debtor; and

(B) a determination that the court would not so grant such discharge is made by the bankruptcy court within the time and in the manner provided for a determination under section 727 of this title of whether a debtor is granted a discharge.

(c) An agreement between a holder of a claim and the debtor, the consideration for which, in whole or in part, is based on a debt that is dischargeable in a case under this title is enforceable only to any extent enforceable under applicable non-bankruptcy law, whether or not discharge of such debt is waived, only if—

(1) such agreement was made before the granting of the discharge under section 727, 1141, 1228, or 1328 of this title;

~~(2)(A) such agreement contains a clear and conspicuous statement which advises the debtor that the agreement may be rescinded at any time prior to discharge or within sixty days after such agreement is filed with the court, whichever occurs later, by giving notice of rescission to the holder of such claim; and~~

~~(B) such agreement contains a clear and conspicuous statement which advises the debtor that such agreement is not required under this title, under nonbankruptcy law, or under any agreement not in accordance with the provisions of this subsection;~~

(2) the debtor received the disclosures described in subsection (k) at or before the time at which the debtor signed the agreement;

(3) such agreement has been filed with the court and, if applicable, accompanied by a declaration or an affidavit of the attorney that represented the debtor during the course of negotiating an agreement under this subsection, which states that—

(A) such agreement represents a fully informed and voluntary agreement by the debtor;

(B) such agreement does not impose an undue hardship on the debtor or a dependent of the debtor; and

(C) the attorney fully advised the debtor of the legal effect and consequences of—

(i) an agreement of the kind specified in this subsection; and

(ii) any default under such an agreement;

(4) the debtor has not rescinded such agreement at any time prior to discharge or within sixty days after such agreement is filed with the court, whichever occurs later, by giving notice of rescission to the holder of such claim;

(5) the provisions of subsection (d) of this section have been complied with; and

(6)(A) in a case concerning an individual who was not represented by an attorney during the course of negotiating an agreement under this subsection, the court approves such agreement as—

(i) not imposing an undue hardship on the debtor or a dependent of the debtor; and

(ii) in the best interest of the debtor.

(B) Subparagraph (A) shall not apply to the extent that such debt is a consumer debt secured by real property.

(d) In a case concerning an individual, when the court has determined whether to grant or not to grant a discharge under section 727, 1141, 1228, or 1328 of this title, the court may hold a hearing at which the debtor shall appear in person. At any such hearing, the court shall inform the debtor that a discharge has been granted or the reason why a discharge has not been granted. If a discharge has been granted and if the debtor desires to make an agreement of the kind specified in subsection (c) of this section and was not represented by an attorney during the course of negotiating such agreement, then the court shall hold a hearing at which the debtor shall appear in person and at such hearing the court shall—

(1) inform the debtor—

(A) that such an agreement is not required under this title, under nonbankruptcy law, or under any agreement not made in accordance with the provisions of subsection (c) of this section; and

(B) of the legal effect and consequences of—

(i) an agreement of the kind specified in subsection (c) of this section; and

(ii) a default under such an agreement; and

(2) determine whether the agreement that the debtor desires to make complies with the requirements of subsection (c)(6) of this section, if the consideration for such agreement is based in whole or in part on a consumer debt that is not secured by real property of the debtor.

(e) Except as provided in subsection (a)(3) of this section, discharge of a debt of the debtor does not affect the liability of any other entity on, or the property of any other entity for, such debt.

(f) Nothing contained in subsection (c) or (d) of this section prevents a debtor from voluntarily repaying any debt.

(g)(1)(A) After notice and hearing, a court that enters an order confirming a plan of reorganization under chapter 11 may issue, in connection with such order, an injunction in accordance with this subsection to supplement the injunctive effect of a discharge under this section.

(B) An injunction may be issued under subparagraph (A) to enjoin entities from taking legal action for the purpose of directly or indirectly collecting, recovering, or receiving payment or recovery with respect to any claim or demand that, under a plan of reorganization, is to be paid in whole or in part by a trust described in paragraph (2)(B)(i), except such legal actions as are expressly allowed by the injunction, the confirmation order, or the plan of reorganization.

(2)(A) Subject to subsection (h), if the requirements of subparagraph (B) are met at the time an injunction described in paragraph (1) is entered, then after entry of such injunction, any proceeding that involves the validity, application, construction, or modification of such injunction, or of this subsection with respect to such injunction, may be commenced only in the district court in which such injunction was entered, and such court shall have exclusive jurisdiction over any such proceeding without regard to the amount in controversy.

(B) The requirements of this subparagraph are that—

(i) the injunction is to be implemented in connection with a trust that, pursuant to the plan of reorganization—

(I) is to assume the liabilities of a debtor which at the time of entry of the order for relief has been named as a defendant in personal injury, wrongful death, or property-damage actions seeking recovery for damages allegedly caused by the presence of, or exposure to, asbestos or asbestos-containing products;

(II) is to be funded in whole or in part by the securities of 1 or more debtors involved in such plan and by the obligation of such debtor or debtors to make future payments, including dividends;

(III) is to own, or by the exercise of rights granted under such plan would be entitled to own if specified contingencies occur, a majority of the voting shares of—

(aa) each such debtor;

(bb) the parent corporation of each such debtor; or

(cc) a subsidiary of each such debtor that is also a debtor; and

(IV) is to use its assets or income to pay claims and demands; and

(ii) subject to subsection (h), the court determines that—

(I) the debtor is likely to be subject to substantial future demands for payment arising out of the same or similar conduct or events that gave rise to the claims that are addressed by the injunction;

(II) the actual amounts, numbers, and timing of such future demands cannot be determined;

(III) pursuit of such demands outside the procedures prescribed by such plan is likely to threaten the plan's purpose to deal equitably with claims and future demands;

(IV) as part of the process of seeking confirmation of such plan—

(aa) the terms of the injunction proposed to be issued under paragraph (1)(A), including any provisions barring actions against third parties pursuant to paragraph (4)(A), are set out in such plan and in any disclosure statement supporting the plan; and

(bb) a separate class or classes of the claimants whose claims are to be addressed by a trust described in clause (i) is established and votes, by at least 75 percent of those voting, in favor of the plan; and

(V) subject to subsection (h), pursuant to court orders or otherwise, the trust will operate through mechanisms such as structured, periodic, or supplemental payments, pro rata distributions, matrices, or periodic review of estimates of the numbers and values of present claims and future demands, or other comparable mechanisms, that provide reasonable assurance that the trust will value, and be in a financial position to pay, present claims and future demands that involve similar claims in substantially the same manner.

(3)(A) If the requirements of paragraph (2)(B) are met and the order confirming the plan of reorganization was issued or affirmed by the district court that has jurisdiction over the reorganization case, then after the time for appeal of the order that issues or affirms the plan—

(i) the injunction shall be valid and enforceable and may not be revoked or modified by any court except through appeal in accordance with paragraph (6);

(ii) no entity that pursuant to such plan or thereafter becomes a direct or indirect transferee of, or successor to any assets of, a debtor or trust that is the subject of the injunction shall be liable with respect to any claim or demand made against such entity by reason of its becoming such a transferee or successor; and

(iii) no entity that pursuant to such plan or thereafter makes a loan to such a debtor or trust or to such a successor or transferee shall, by reason of making the loan, be liable with respect to any claim or demand made against such entity, nor shall any pledge of assets made in connection with such a loan be upset or impaired for that reason;

(B) Subparagraph (A) shall not be construed to—

(i) imply that an entity described in subparagraph (A)(ii) or (iii) would, if this paragraph were not applicable, necessarily be liable to any entity by reason of any of the acts described in subparagraph (A);

(ii) relieve any such entity of the duty to comply with, or of liability under, any Federal or State law regarding the making of a fraudulent conveyance in a transaction described in subparagraph (A)(ii) or (iii); or

(iii) relieve a debtor of the debtor's obligation to comply with the terms of the plan of reorganization, or affect the power of the court to exercise its authority under sections 1141 and 1142 to compel the debtor to do so.

(4)(A)(i) Subject to subparagraph (B), an injunction described in paragraph (1) shall be valid and enforceable against all entities that it addresses.

(ii) Notwithstanding the provisions of section 524(e), such an injunction may bar any action directed against a third party who is identifiable from the terms of such injunction (by name or as part of an identifiable group) and is alleged to be directly or indirectly liable for the conduct of, claims against, or demands on the debtor to the extent such alleged liability of such third party arises by reason of—

(I) the third party's ownership of a financial interest in the debtor, a past or present affiliate of the debtor, or a predecessor in interest of the debtor;

(II) the third party's involvement in the management of the debtor or a predecessor in interest of the debtor, or service as an officer, director or employee of the debtor or a related party;

(III) the third party's provision of insurance to the debtor or a related party; or

(IV) the third party's involvement in a transaction changing the corporate structure, or in a loan or other financial transaction affecting the financial condition, of the debtor or a related party, including but not limited to—

(aa) involvement in providing financing (debt or equity), or advice to an entity involved in such a transaction; or

(bb) acquiring or selling a financial interest in an entity as part of such a transaction.

(iii) As used in this subparagraph, the term "related party" means—

(I) a past or present affiliate of the debtor;

(II) a predecessor in interest of the debtor; or

(III) any entity that owned a financial interest in—

(aa) the debtor;

(bb) a past or present affiliate of the debtor; or

(cc) a predecessor in interest of the debtor.

(B) Subject to subsection (h), if, under a plan of reorganization, a kind of demand described in such plan is to be paid in whole or in part by a trust described in paragraph (2)(B)(i) in connection with which an injunction described in paragraph (1) is to be implemented, then such injunction shall be valid and enforceable with respect to a demand of such kind made, after such plan is confirmed, against the debtor or debtors involved, or against a third party described in subparagraph (A)(ii), if—

(i) as part of the proceedings leading to issuance of such injunction, the court appoints a legal representative for the purpose of protecting the rights of persons that might subsequently assert demands of such kind, and

(ii) the court determines, before entering the order confirming such plan, that identifying such debtor or debtors, or such third party (by name or as part of an identifiable group), in such injunction with respect to such demands for purposes of this subparagraph is fair and equitable with respect to the persons that might subsequently assert such demands, in light of the benefits provided, or to be provided, to such trust on behalf of such debtor or debtors or such third party.

(5) In this subsection, the term "demand" means a demand for payment, present or future, that—

(A) was not a claim during the proceedings leading to the confirmation of a plan of reorganization;

(B) arises out of the same or similar conduct or events that gave rise to the claims addressed by the injunction issued under paragraph (1); and

(C) pursuant to the plan, is to be paid by a trust described in paragraph (2)(B)(i).

(6) Paragraph (3)(A)(i) does not bar an action taken by or at the direction of an appellate court on appeal of an injunction issued under paragraph (1) or of the order of confirmation that relates to the injunction.

(7) This subsection does not affect the operation of section 1144 or the power of the district court to refer a proceeding under section 157 of title 28 or any reference of a proceeding made prior to the date of the enactment of this subsection.

(h) Application to existing injunctions.—For purposes of subsection (g)—

(1) subject to paragraph (2), if an injunction of the kind described in subsection (g)(1)(B) was issued before the date of the enactment of this Act, as part of a plan of reorganization confirmed by an order entered before such date, then the injunction shall be considered to meet the requirements of subsection (g)(2)(B) for purposes of subsection (g)(2)(A), and to satisfy subsection (g)(4)(A)(ii), if—

(A) the court determined at the time the plan was confirmed that the plan was fair and equitable in accordance with the requirements of section 1129(b);

(B) as part of the proceedings leading to issuance of such injunction and confirmation of such plan, the court had appointed a legal representative for the purpose of protecting the rights of persons that might subsequently assert demands described in subsection (g)(4)(B) with respect to such plan; and

(C) such legal representative did not object to confirmation of such plan or issuance of such injunction; and

(2) for purposes of paragraph (1), if a trust described in subsection (g)(2)(B)(i) is subject to a court order on the date of the enactment of this Act staying such trust from settling or paying further claims—

(A) the requirements of subsection (g)(2)(B)(ii)(V) shall not apply with respect to such trust until such stay is lifted or dissolved; and

(B) if such trust meets such requirements on the date such stay is lifted or dissolved, such trust shall be considered to have met such requirements continuously from the date of the enactment of this Act.

(i) The willful failure of a creditor to credit payments received under a plan confirmed under this title, unless the order confirming the plan is revoked, the plan is in default, or the creditor has not received payments required to be made under the plan in the manner required by the plan (including crediting the amounts required under the plan), shall constitute a violation of an injunction under subsection (a)(2) if the act of the creditor to collect and failure to credit payments in the manner required by the plan caused material injury to the debtor.

(j) Subsection (a)(2) does not operate as an injunction against an act by a creditor that is the holder of a secured claim, if—

(1) such creditor retains a security interest in real property that is the principal residence of the debtor;

(2) such act is in the ordinary course of business between the creditor and the debtor; and

(3) such act is limited to seeking or obtaining periodic payments associated with a valid security interest in lieu of pursuit of in rem relief to enforce the lien.

(k)(1) The disclosures required under subsection (c)(2) shall consist of the disclosure statement described in paragraph (3), completed as required in that paragraph, together with the agreement specified in subsection (c), statement, declaration, motion and order described, respectively, in paragraphs (4) through (8), and shall be the only disclosures required in connection with entering into such agreement.

(2) Disclosures made under paragraph (1) shall be made clearly and conspicuously and in writing. The terms 'Amount Reaffirmed' and 'Annual Percentage Rate' shall be disclosed more conspicuously than other terms, data or informa-

tion provided in connection with this disclosure, except that the phrases 'Before agreeing to reaffirm a debt, review these important disclosures' and 'Summary of Reaffirmation Agreement' may be equally conspicuous. Disclosures may be made in a different order and may use terminology different from that set forth in paragraphs (2) through (8), except that the terms 'Amount Reaffirmed' and 'Annual Percentage Rate' must be used where indicated.

(3) The disclosure statement required under this paragraph shall consist of the following:

(A) The statement: 'Part A: Before agreeing to reaffirm a debt, review these important disclosures:';

(B) Under the heading 'Summary of Reaffirmation Agreement', the statement: 'This Summary is made pursuant to the requirements of the Bankruptcy Code';

(C) The 'Amount Reaffirmed', using that term, which shall be—

(i) the total amount of debt that the debtor agrees to reaffirm by entering into an agreement of the kind specified in subsection (c), and

(ii) the total of any fees and costs accrued as of the date of the disclosure statement, related to such total amount.

(D) In conjunction with the disclosure of the 'Amount Reaffirmed', the statements—

(i) 'The amount of debt you have agreed to reaffirm'; and

(ii) 'Your credit agreement may obligate you to pay additional amounts which may come due after the date of this disclosure. Consult your credit agreement.'.

(E) The 'Annual Percentage Rate', using that term, which shall be disclosed as—

(i) if, at the time the petition is filed, the debt is an extension of credit under an open end credit plan, as the terms 'credit' and 'open end credit plan' are defined in section 103 of the Truth in Lending Act, then—

(I) the annual percentage rate determined under paragraphs (5) and (6) of section 127(b) of the Truth in Lending Act, as applicable, as disclosed to the debtor in the most recent periodic statement prior to entering into an agreement of the kind specified in subsection (c) or, if no such periodic statement has been given to the debtor during the prior 6 months, the annual percentage rate as it would have been so disclosed at the time the disclosure statement is given to the debtor, or to the extent this annual percentage rate is not readily available or not applicable, then

(II) the simple interest rate applicable to the amount reaffirmed as of the date the disclosure statement is given to the debtor, or if different simple interest rates apply to different balances, the simple interest rate applicable to each such balance, identifying the amount of each such balance included in the amount reaffirmed, or

(III) if the entity making the disclosure elects, to disclose the annual percentage rate under subclause (I) and the simple interest rate under subclause (II); or

(ii) if, at the time the petition is filed, the debt is an extension of credit other than under an open end credit plan, as the terms 'credit' and 'open end credit plan' are defined in section 103 of the Truth in Lending Act, then—

(I) the annual percentage rate under section 128(a)(4) of the Truth in Lending Act, as disclosed to the debtor in the most recent disclosure statement given to the debtor prior to the entering into an agreement of the kind specified in subsection (c) with respect to the debt, or, if no such disclosure statement was given to the debtor, the annual percentage rate as it would have been so disclosed at the time the disclosure statement is given to the debtor, or to the extent this annual percentage rate is not readily available or not applicable, then

(II) the simple interest rate applicable to the amount reaffirmed as of the date the disclosure statement is given to the debtor, or if different simple interest rates apply to different balances, the simple interest rate applicable to each such balance, identifying the amount of such balance included in the amount reaffirmed, or

(III) if the entity making the disclosure elects, to disclose the annual percentage rate under (I) and the simple interest rate under (II).

(F) If the underlying debt transaction was disclosed as a variable rate transaction on the most recent disclosure given under the Truth in Lending Act, by stating 'The interest rate on your loan may be a variable interest rate which changes from time to time, so that the annual percentage rate disclosed here may be higher or lower.'.

(G) If the debt is secured by a security interest which has not been waived in whole or in part or determined to be void by a final order of the court at the time of the disclosure, by disclosing that a security interest or lien in goods or property is asserted over some or all of the debts the debtor is reaffirming and listing the items and their original purchase price that are subject to the asserted security interest, or if not a purchase-money security interest then listing by items or types and the original amount of the loan.

(H) At the election of the creditor, a statement of the repayment schedule using 1 or a combination of the following—

(i) by making the statement: 'Your first payment in the amount of $XXX is due on XXX but the future payment amount may be different. Consult your reaffirmation agreement or credit agreement, as applicable.', and stating the amount of the first payment and the due date of that payment in the places provided;

(ii) by making the statement: 'Your payment schedule will be:', and describing the repayment schedule with the number, amount, and due dates or period of payments scheduled to repay the debts reaffirmed to the extent then known by the disclosing party; or

(iii) by describing the debtor's repayment obligations with reasonable specificity to the extent then known by the disclosing party.

(I) The following statement: 'Note: When this disclosure refers to what a creditor 'may' do, it does not use the word 'may' to give the creditor specific permission. The word 'may' is used to tell you what might occur if the law permits the creditor to take the action. If you have questions about your reaffirming a debt or what the law requires, consult with the attorney who

helped you negotiate this agreement reaffirming a debt. If you don't have an attorney helping you, the judge will explain the effect of your reaffirming a debt when the hearing on the reaffirmation agreement is held.'.

(J)(i) The following additional statements:

Reaffirming a debt is a serious financial decision. The law requires you to take certain steps to make sure the decision is in your best interest. If these steps are not completed, the reaffirmation agreement is not effective, even though you have signed it.

1. Read the disclosures in this Part A carefully. Consider the decision to reaffirm carefully. Then, if you want to reaffirm, sign the reaffirmation agreement in Part B (or you may use a separate agreement you and your creditor agree on).

2. Complete and sign Part D and be sure you can afford to make the payments you are agreeing to make and have received a copy of the disclosure statement and a completed and signed reaffirmation agreement.

3. If you were represented by an attorney during the negotiation of your reaffirmation agreement, the attorney must have signed the certification in Part C.

4. If you were not represented by an attorney during the negotiation of your reaffirmation agreement, you must have completed and signed Part E.

5. The original of this disclosure must be filed with the court by you or your creditor. If a separate reaffirmation agreement (other than the one in Part B) has been signed, it must be attached.

6. If you were represented by an attorney during the negotiation of your reaffirmation agreement, your reaffirmation agreement becomes effective upon filing with the court unless the reaffirmation is presumed to be an undue hardship as explained in Part D.

7. If you were not represented by an attorney during the negotiation of your reaffirmation agreement, it will not be effective unless the court approves it. The court will notify you of the hearing on your reaffirmation agreement. You must attend this hearing in bankruptcy court where the judge will review your reaffirmation agreement. The bankruptcy court must approve your reaffirmation agreement as consistent with your best interests, except that no court approval is required if your reaffirmation agreement is for a consumer debt secured by a mortgage, deed of trust, security deed, or other lien on your real property, like your home.

Your right to rescind (cancel) your reaffirmation agreement. You may rescind (cancel) your reaffirmation agreement at any time before the bankruptcy court enters a discharge order, or before the expiration of the 60-day period that begins on the date your reaffirmation agreement is filed with the court, whichever occurs later. To rescind (cancel) your reaffirmation agreement, you must notify the creditor that your reaffirmation agreement is rescinded (or canceled).

What are your obligations if you reaffirm the debt? A reaffirmed debt remains your personal legal obligation. It is not discharged in your bankruptcy case. That means that if you default on your reaffirmed debt after your bankruptcy case is over, your creditor may be able to take your property or your wages. Otherwise, your obligations will be determined by the reaffirmation agreement which may have changed the terms of the original agreement. For example, if you are reaffirming an open end credit agreement, the creditor may be permitted by that agreement or applicable law to change the terms of that agreement in the future under certain conditions.

Are you required to enter into a reaffirmation agreement by any law? No, you are not required to reaffirm a debt by any law. Only agree to reaffirm a debt if it is in your best interest. Be sure you can afford the payments you agree to make.

What if your creditor has a security interest or lien? Your bankruptcy discharge does not eliminate any lien on your property. A 'lien' is often referred to as a security interest, deed of trust, mortgage or security deed. Even if you do not reaffirm and your personal liability on the debt is discharged, because of the lien your creditor may still have the right to take the security property if you do not pay the debt or default on it. If the lien is on an item of personal property that is exempt under your State's law or that the trustee has abandoned, you may be able to redeem the item rather than reaffirm the debt. To redeem, you make a single payment to the creditor equal to the current value of the security property, as agreed by the parties or determined by the court.

(ii) In the case of a reaffirmation under subsection (m)(2), numbered paragraph 6 in the disclosures required by clause (i) of this subparagraph shall read as follows:

6. If you were represented by an attorney during the negotiation of your reaffirmation agreement, your reaffirmation agreement becomes effective upon filing with the court.

(4) The form of such agreement required under this paragraph shall consist of the following:

Part B: Reaffirmation Agreement. I (we) agree to reaffirm the debts arising under the credit agreement described below.

Brief description of credit agreement:

Description of any changes to the credit agreement made as part of this reaffirmation agreement:

Signature: Date:

Borrower:

Co-borrower, if also reaffirming these debts:

Accepted by creditor:

Date of creditor acceptance:.

(5) The declaration shall consist of the following:

(A) The following certification:

Part C: Certification by Debtor's Attorney (If Any).

I hereby certify that (1) this agreement represents a fully informed and voluntary agreement by the debtor; (2) this agreement does not impose an undue hardship on the debtor or any dependent of the debtor; and (3) I have fully advised the debtor of the legal effect and consequences of this agreement and any default under this agreement.

Signature of Debtor's Attorney: Date:.

(B) If a presumption of undue hardship has been established with respect to such agreement, such certification shall state that in the opinion of the attorney, the debtor is able to make the payment.

(C) In the case of a reaffirmation agreement under subsection (m)(2), subparagraph (B) is not applicable.

(6)(A) The statement in support of such agreement, which the debtor shall sign and date prior to filing with the court, shall consist of the following:

Part D: Debtor's Statement in Support of Reaffirmation Agreement.

1. I believe this reaffirmation agreement will not impose an undue hardship on my dependents or me. I can afford to make the payments on the reaffirmed debt because my monthly income (take home pay plus any other income received) is $XXX, and my actual current monthly expenses including monthly payments on post-bankruptcy debt and other reaffirmation agreements total $XXX, leaving $XXXX to make the required payments on this reaffirmed debt. I understand that if my income less my monthly expenses does not leave enough to make the payments, this reaffirmation agreement is presumed to be an undue hardship on me and must be reviewed by the court. However, this presumption may be overcome if I explain to the satisfaction of the court how I can afford to make the payments here: XXX.

2. I received a copy of the Reaffirmation Disclosure Statement in Part A and a completed and signed reaffirmation agreement.

(B) Where the debtor is represented by an attorney and is reaffirming a debt owed to a creditor defined in section 19(b)(1)(A)(iv) of the Federal Reserve Act, the statement of support of the reaffirmation agreement, which the debtor shall sign and date prior to filing with the court, shall consist of the following:

I believe this reaffirmation agreement is in my financial interest. I can afford to make the payments on the reaffirmed debt. I received a copy of the Reaffirmation Disclosure Statement in Part A and a completed and signed reaffirmation agreement.

(7) The motion that may be used if approval of such agreement by the court is required in order for it to be effective, shall be signed and dated by the movant and shall consist of the following:

Part E: Motion for Court Approval (To be completed only if the debtor is not represented by an attorney.). I (we), the debtor(s), affirm the following to be true and correct:

I am not represented by an attorney in connection with this reaffirmation agreement.

I believe this reaffirmation agreement is in my best interest based on the income and expenses I have disclosed in my Statement in Support of this reaffirmation agreement, and because (provide any additional relevant reasons the court should consider):

Therefore, I ask the court for an order approving this reaffirmation agreement.'.

(8) The court order, which may be used to approve such agreement, shall consist of the following:

Court Order: The court grants the debtor's motion and approves the reaffirmation agreement described above.

(l) Notwithstanding any other provision of this title the following shall apply:

(1) A creditor may accept payments from a debtor before and after the filing of an agreement of the kind specified in subsection (c) with the court.

(2) A creditor may accept payments from a debtor under such agreement that the creditor believes in good faith to be effective.

(3) The requirements of subsections (c)(2) and (k) shall be satisfied if disclosures required under those subsections are given in good faith.

(m)(1) Until 60 days after an agreement of the kind specified in subsection (c) is filed with the court (or such additional period as the court, after notice and a hearing and for cause, orders before the expiration of such period), it shall be presumed that such agreement is an undue hardship on the debtor if the debtor's monthly income less the debtor's monthly expenses as shown on the debtor's completed and signed statement in support of such agreement required under subsection (k)(6)(A) is less than the scheduled payments on the reaffirmed debt. This presumption shall be reviewed by the court. The presumption may be rebutted in writing by the debtor if the statement includes an explanation that identifies additional sources of funds to make the payments as agreed upon under the terms of such agreement. If the presumption is not rebutted to the satisfaction of the court, the court may disapprove such agreement. No agreement shall be disapproved without notice and a hearing to the debtor and creditor, and such hearing shall be concluded before the entry of the debtor's discharge.

(2) This subsection does not apply to reaffirmation agreements where the creditor is a credit union, as defined in section 19(b)(1)(A)(iv) of the Federal Reserve Act.

§ 525. Protection against discriminatory treatment

(a) Except as provided in the Perishable Agricultural Commodities Act, 1930, the Packers and Stockyards Act, 1921, and section 1 of the Act entitled "An Act making appropriations for the Department of Agriculture for the fiscal year ending June 30, 1944, and for other purposes," approved July 12, 1943, a governmental unit may not deny, revoke, suspend, or refuse to renew a license, permit, charter, franchise, or other similar grant to, condition such a grant to, discriminate with respect to such a grant against, deny employment to, terminate the employment of, or discriminate with respect to employment against, a person that is or has been a debtor under this title or a bankrupt or a debtor under the Bankruptcy Act, or another person with whom such bankrupt or debtor has been associated, solely because such bankrupt or debtor is or has been a debtor under this title or a bankrupt or debtor under the Bankruptcy Act, has been insolvent before the commencement of the case under this title, or during the case but before the debtor is granted or denied a discharge, or has not paid a debt that is dischargeable in the case under this title or that was discharged under the Bankruptcy Act.

(b) No private employer may terminate the employment of, or discriminate with respect to employment against, an individual who is or has been a debtor under this title, a debtor or bankrupt under the Bankruptcy Act, or an individual associated with such debtor or bankrupt, solely because such debtor or bankrupt—

(1) is or has been a debtor under this title or a debtor or bankrupt under the Bankruptcy Act;

(2) has been insolvent before the commencement of a case under this title or during the case but before the grant or denial of a discharge; or

(3) has not paid a debt that is dischargeable in a case under this title or that was discharged under the Bankruptcy Act.

(c)(1) A governmental unit that operates a student grant or loan program and a person engaged in a business that includes the making of loans guaranteed or insured under a student loan program may not deny a student grant, loan, loan guarantee, or loan insurance to a person that is or has been a debtor under this title or a bankrupt or debtor under the Bankruptcy Act, or another person with whom the debtor or bankrupt has been associated, because the debtor or bankrupt is or has been a debtor under this title or a bankrupt or debtor under the Bankruptcy Act, has been insolvent before the commencement of a case under this title or during the pendency of the case but before the debtor is granted or denied a discharge, or has not paid a debt that is dischargeable in the case under this title or that was discharged under the Bankruptcy Act.

(2) In this section, "student loan program" means ~~the program operated under part B, D, or E of~~ *any program operated under* title IV of the Higher Education Act of 1965 or a similar program operated under State or local law.

§ 526. Restrictions on debt relief agencies

(a) A debt relief agency shall not—

(1) fail to perform any service that such agency informed an assisted person or prospective assisted person it would provide in connection with a case or proceeding under this title;

(2) make any statement, or counsel or advise any assisted person or prospective assisted person to make a statement in a document filed in a case or proceeding under this title, that is untrue and misleading, or that upon the exercise of reasonable care, should have been known by such agency to be untrue or misleading;

(3) misrepresent to any assisted person or prospective assisted person, directly or indirectly, affirmatively or by material omission, with respect to—

(A) the services that such agency will provide to such person; or

(B) the benefits and risks that may result if such person becomes a debtor in a case under this title; or

(4) advise an assisted person or prospective assisted person to incur more debt in contemplation of such person filing a case under this title or to pay an attorney or bankruptcy petition preparer fee or charge for services performed as part of preparing for or representing a debtor in a case under this title.

(b) Any waiver by any assisted person of any protection or right provided under this section shall not be enforceable against the debtor by any Federal or State court or any other person, but may be enforced against a debt relief agency.

(c)(1) Any contract for bankruptcy assistance between a debt relief agency and an assisted person that does not comply with the material requirements of this section, section 527, or section 528 shall be void and may not be enforced by any Federal or State court or by any other person, other than such assisted person.

(2) Any debt relief agency shall be liable to an assisted person in the amount of any fees or charges in connection with providing bankruptcy assistance to such person that such debt relief agency has received, for actual damages, and for reasonable attorneys' fees and costs if such agency is found, after notice and a hearing, to have—

(A) intentionally or negligently failed to comply with any provision of this section, section 527, or section 528 with respect to a case or proceeding under this title for such assisted person;

(B) provided bankruptcy assistance to an assisted person in a case or proceeding under this title that is dismissed or converted to a case under another chapter of this title because of such agency's intentional or negligent failure to file any required document including those specified in section 521; or

(C) intentionally or negligently disregarded the material requirements of this title or the Federal Rules of Bankruptcy Procedure applicable to such agency.

(3) In addition to such other remedies as are provided under State law, whenever the chief law enforcement officer of a State, or an official or agency designated by a State, has reason to believe that any person has violated or is violating this section, the State—

(A) may bring an action to enjoin such violation;

(B) may bring an action on behalf of its residents to recover the actual damages of assisted persons arising from such violation, including any liability under paragraph (2); and

(C) in the case of any successful action under subparagraph (A) or (B), shall be awarded the costs of the action and reasonable attorneys' fees as determined by the court.

(4) The district courts of the United States for districts located in the State shall have concurrent jurisdiction of any action under subparagraph (A) or (B) of paragraph (3).

(5) Notwithstanding any other provision of Federal law and in addition to any other remedy provided under Federal or State law, if the court, on its own motion or on the motion of the United States trustee or the debtor, finds that a person intentionally violated this section, or engaged in a clear and consistent pattern or practice of violating this section, the court may—

(A) enjoin the violation of such section; or

(B) impose an appropriate civil penalty against such person.

(d) No provision of this section, section 527, or section 528 shall—

(1) annul, alter, affect, or exempt any person subject to such sections from complying with any law of any State except to the extent that such law is inconsistent with those sections, and then only to the extent of the inconsistency; or

(2) be deemed to limit or curtail the authority or ability—

(A) of a State or subdivision or instrumentality thereof, to determine and enforce qualifications for the practice of law under the laws of that State; or

(B) of a Federal court to determine and enforce the qualifications for the practice of law before that court.

§ 527. Disclosures

(a) A debt relief agency providing bankruptcy assistance to an assisted person shall provide—

(1) the written notice required under section 342(b)(1); and

(2) to the extent not covered in the written notice described in paragraph (1), and not later than 3 business days after the first date on which a debt relief agency first offers to provide any bankruptcy assistance services to an assisted person, a clear and conspicuous written notice advising assisted persons that—

(A) all information that the assisted person is required to provide with a petition and thereafter during a case under this title is required to be complete, accurate, and truthful;

(B) all assets and all liabilities are required to be completely and accurately disclosed in the documents filed to commence the case, and the replacement value of each asset as defined in section 506 must be stated in those documents where requested after reasonable inquiry to establish such value;

(C) current monthly income, the amounts specified in section 707(b)(2), and, in a case under chapter 13 of this title, disposable income (determined in accordance with section 707(b)(2)), are required to be stated after reasonable inquiry; and

(D) information that an assisted person provides during their case may be audited pursuant to this title, and that failure to provide such information may result in dismissal of the case under this title or other sanction, including a criminal sanction.

(b) A debt relief agency providing bankruptcy assistance to an assisted person shall provide each assisted person at the same time as the notices required under subsection (a)(1) the following statement, to the extent applicable, or one substantially similar. The statement shall be clear and conspicuous and shall be in a single document separate from other documents or notices provided to the assisted person:

IMPORTANT INFORMATION ABOUT BANKRUPTCY ASSISTANCE SERVICES FROM AN ATTORNEY OR BANKRUPTCY PETITION PREPARER.

If you decide to seek bankruptcy relief, you can represent yourself, you can hire an attorney to represent you, or you can get help in some localities from a bankruptcy petition preparer who is not an attorney. THE LAW REQUIRES AN ATTORNEY OR BANKRUPTCY PETITION PREPARER TO GIVE YOU A WRITTEN CONTRACT SPECIFYING WHAT THE ATTORNEY OR BANKRUPTCY PETITION PREPARER WILL DO FOR YOU AND HOW MUCH IT WILL COST. Ask to see the contract before you hire anyone.

The following information helps you understand what must be done in a routine bankruptcy case to help you evaluate how much service you need. Although bankruptcy can be complex, many cases are routine.

Before filing a bankruptcy case, either you or your attorney should analyze your eligibility for different forms of debt relief available under the Bankruptcy Code and which form of relief is most likely to be beneficial for you. Be sure you understand the relief you can obtain and its limitations. To file a bankruptcy case, documents called a Petition, Schedules and Statement of Financial Affairs, as well as in some cases a Statement of Intention need to be prepared correctly and filed with the bankruptcy court. You will have to pay a filing fee to the bankruptcy court. Once your case starts, you will have to attend the required first meeting of creditors where you may be questioned by a court official called a 'trustee' and by creditors.

If you choose to file a chapter 7 case, you may be asked by a creditor to reaffirm a debt. You may want help deciding whether to do so. A creditor is not permitted to coerce you into reaffirming your debts.

If you choose to file a chapter 13 case in which you repay your creditors what you can afford over 3 to 5 years, you may also want help with preparing your chapter 13 plan and with the confirmation hearing on your plan which will be before a bankruptcy judge.

If you select another type of relief under the Bankruptcy Code other than chapter 7 or chapter 13, you will want to find out what should be done from someone familiar with that type of relief.

Your bankruptcy case may also involve litigation. You are generally permitted to represent yourself in litigation in bankruptcy court, but only attorneys, not bankruptcy petition preparers, can give you legal advice.

(c) Except to the extent the debt relief agency provides the required information itself after reasonably diligent inquiry of the assisted person or others so as to obtain such information reasonably accurately for inclusion on the petition, schedules or statement of financial affairs, a debt relief agency providing bankruptcy assistance to an assisted person, to the extent permitted by nonbankruptcy law, shall provide each assisted person at the time required for the notice required under subsection (a)(1) reasonably sufficient information (which shall be provided in a clear and conspicuous writing) to the assisted person on how to provide all the information the assisted person is required to provide under this title pursuant to section 521, including—

(1) how to value assets at replacement value, determine current monthly income, the amounts specified in section 707(b)(2) and, in a chapter 13 case, how to determine disposable income in accordance with section 707(b)(2) and related calculations;

(2) how to complete the list of creditors, including how to determine what amount is owed and what address for the creditor should be shown; and

(3) how to determine what property is exempt and how to value exempt property at replacement value as defined in section 506.

(d) A debt relief agency shall maintain a copy of the notices required under subsection (a) of this section for 2 years after the date on which the notice is given the assisted person.

§ 528. Requirements for debt relief agencies

(a) A debt relief agency shall—

(1) not later than 5 business days after the first date on which such agency provides any bankruptcy assistance services to an assisted person, but prior to such assisted person's petition under this title being filed, execute a written contract with such assisted person that explains clearly and conspicuously—

(A) the services such agency will provide to such assisted person; and

(B) the fees or charges for such services, and the terms of payment;

(2) provide the assisted person with a copy of the fully executed and completed contract;

(3) clearly and conspicuously disclose in any advertisement of bankruptcy assistance services or of the benefits of bankruptcy directed to the general public (whether in general media, seminars or specific mailings, telephonic or electronic messages, or otherwise) that the services or benefits are with respect to bankruptcy relief under this title; and

(4) clearly and conspicuously use the following statement in such advertisement: 'We are a debt relief agency. We help people file for bankruptcy relief under the Bankruptcy Code.' or a substantially similar statement.

(b)(1) An advertisement of bankruptcy assistance services or of the benefits of bankruptcy directed to the general public includes—

(A) descriptions of bankruptcy assistance in connection with a chapter 13 plan whether or not chapter 13 is specifically mentioned in such advertisement; and

(B) statements such as 'federally supervised repayment plan' or 'Federal debt restructuring help' or other similar statements that could lead a reasonable consumer to believe that debt counseling was being offered when in fact the services were directed to providing bankruptcy assistance with a chapter 13 plan or other form of bankruptcy relief under this title.

(2) An advertisement, directed to the general public, indicating that the debt relief agency provides assistance with respect to credit defaults, mortgage foreclosures, eviction proceedings, excessive debt, debt collection pressure, or inability to pay any consumer debt shall—

(A) disclose clearly and conspicuously in such advertisement that the assistance may involve bankruptcy relief under this title; and

(B) include the following statement: 'We are a debt relief agency. We help people file for bankruptcy relief under the Bankruptcy Code.' or a substantially similar statement.

SUBCHAPTER III—THE ESTATE

§ 541. Property of the estate

(a) The commencement of a case under section 301, 302, or 303 of this title creates an estate. Such estate is comprised of all the following property, wherever located and by whomever held:

(1) Except as provided in subsections (b) and (c)(2) of this section, all legal or equitable interests of the debtor in property as of the commencement of the case.

(2) All interests of the debtor and the debtor's spouse in community property as of the commencement of the case that is—

(A) under the sole, equal, or joint management and control of the debtor; or

(B) liable for an allowable claim against the debtor, or for both an allowable claim against the debtor and an allowable claim against the debtor's spouse, to the extent that such interest is so liable.

(3) Any interest in property that the trustee recovers under section 329(b), 363(n), 543, 550, 553, or 723 of this title.

(4) Any interest in property preserved for the benefit of or ordered transferred to the estate under section 510(c) or 551 of this title.

(5) Any interest in property that would have been property of the estate if such interest had been an interest of the debtor on the date of the filing of the petition, and that the debtor acquires or becomes entitled to acquire within 180 days after such date—

    (A) by bequest, devise, or inheritance;

    (B) as a result of a property settlement agreement with the debtor's spouse, or of an interlocutory or final divorce decree; or

    (C) as a beneficiary of a life insurance policy or of a death benefit plan.

(6) Proceeds, product, offspring, rents, or profits of or from property of the estate, except such as are earnings from services performed by an individual debtor after the commencement of the case.

(7) Any interest in property that the estate acquires after the commencement of the case.

(b) Property of the estate does not include—

(1) any power that the debtor may exercise solely for the benefit of an entity other than the debtor;

(2) any interest of the debtor as a lessee under a lease of nonresidential real property that has terminated at the expiration of the stated term of such lease before the commencement of the case under this title, and ceases to include any interest of the debtor as a lessee under a lease of nonresidential real property that has terminated at the expiration of the stated term of such lease during the case;

(3) any eligibility of the debtor to participate in programs authorized under the Higher Education Act of 1965 (20 U.S.C. 1001 et seq.; 42 U.S.C. 2751 et seq.), or any accreditation status or State licensure of the debtor as an educational institution;

(4) any interest of the debtor in liquid or gaseous hydrocarbons to the extent that—

    (A)(i) the debtor has transferred or has agreed to transfer such interest pursuant to a farmout agreement or any written agreement directly related to a farmout agreement; and

    (ii) but for the operation of this paragraph, the estate could include the interest referred to in clause (i) only by virtue of section 365 or 544(a)(3) of this title; or

    (B)(i) the debtor has transferred such interest pursuant to a written conveyance of a production payment to an entity that does not participate in the operation of the property from which such production payment is transferred; and

    (ii) but for the operation of this paragraph, the estate could include the interest referred to in clause (i) only by virtue of section *365 or* 542 of this title; or

(5) *funds placed in an education individual retirement account (as defined in section 530(b)(1) of the Internal Revenue Code of 1986) not later than 365 days before the date of the filing of the petition in a case under this title, but—*

 (A) only if the designated beneficiary of such account was a child, stepchild, grandchild, or stepgrandchild of the debtor for the taxable year for which funds were placed in such account;

 (B) only to the extent that such funds—

  (i) are not pledged or promised to any entity in connection with any extension of credit; and

  (ii) are not excess contributions (as described in section 4973(e) of the Internal Revenue Code of 1986); and

 (C) in the case of funds placed in all such accounts having the same designated beneficiary not earlier than 720 days nor later than 365 days before such date, only so much of such funds as does not exceed $5,000;

(6) *funds used to purchase a tuition credit or certificate or contributed to an account in accordance with section 529(b)(1)(A) of the Internal Revenue Code of 1986 under a qualified State tuition program (as defined in section 529(b)(1) of such Code) not later than 365 days before the date of the filing of the petition in a case under this title, but—*

 (A) only if the designated beneficiary of the amounts paid or contributed to such tuition program was a child, stepchild, grandchild, or stepgrandchild of the debtor for the taxable year for which funds were paid or contributed;

 (B) with respect to the aggregate amount paid or contributed to such program having the same designated beneficiary, only so much of such amount as does not exceed the total contributions permitted under section 529(b)(7) of such Code with respect to such beneficiary, as adjusted beginning on the date of the filing of the petition in a case under this title by the annual increase or decrease (rounded to the nearest tenth of 1 percent) in the education expenditure category of the Consumer Price Index prepared by the Department of Labor; and

 (C) in the case of funds paid or contributed to such program having the same designated beneficiary not earlier than 720 days nor later than 365 days before such date, only so much of such funds as does not exceed $5,000;

(7) *any amount—*

 (A) withheld by an employer from the wages of employees for payment as contributions—

  (i) to—

   (I) an employee benefit plan that is subject to title I of the Employee Retirement Income Security Act of 1974 or under an employee benefit plan which is a governmental plan under section 414(d) of the Internal Revenue Code of 1986;

   (II) a deferred compensation plan under section 457 of the Internal Revenue Code of 1986; or

   (III) a tax-deferred annuity under section 403(b) of the Internal Revenue Code of 1986;

except that such amount under this subparagraph shall not constitute disposable income as defined in section 1325(b)(2); or

 (ii) to a health insurance plan regulated by State law whether or not subject to such title; or

 (B) received by an employer from employees for payment as contributions—

  (i) to—

   (I) an employee benefit plan that is subject to title I of the Employee Retirement Income Security Act of 1974 or under an employee benefit plan which is a governmental plan under section 414(d) of the Internal Revenue Code of 1986;

   (II) a deferred compensation plan under section 457 of the Internal Revenue Code of 1986; or

   (III) a tax-deferred annuity under section 403(b) of the Internal Revenue Code of 1986;

 except that such amount under this subparagraph shall not constitute disposable income, as defined in section 1325(b)(2); or

  (ii) to a health insurance plan regulated by State law whether or not subject to such title;

(8) subject to subchapter III of chapter 5, any interest of the debtor in property where the debtor pledged or sold tangible personal property (other than securities or written or printed evidences of indebtedness or title) as collateral for a loan or advance of money given by a person licensed under law to make such loans or advances, where—

 (A) the tangible personal property is in the possession of the pledgee or transferee;

 (B) the debtor has no obligation to repay the money, redeem the collateral, or buy back the property at a stipulated price; and

 (C) neither the debtor nor the trustee have exercised any right to redeem provided under the contract or State law, in a timely manner as provided under State law and section 108(b); or

(~~5~~9) any interest in cash or cash equivalents that constitute proceeds of a sale by the debtor of a money order that is made—

 (A) on or after the date that is 14 days prior to the date on which the petition is filed; and

 (B) under an agreement with a money order issuer that prohibits the commingling of such proceeds with property of the debtor (notwithstanding that, contrary to the agreement, the proceeds may have been commingled with property of the debtor),

unless the money order issuer had not taken action, prior to the filing of the petition, to require compliance with the prohibition.

Paragraph (4) shall not be construed to exclude from the estate any consideration the debtor retains, receives, or is entitled to receive for transferring an interest in liquid or gaseous hydrocarbons pursuant to a farmout agreement.

(c)(1) Except as provided in paragraph (2) of this subsection, an interest of the debtor in property becomes property of the estate under subsection (a)(1), (a)(2), or (a)(5) of this section notwithstanding any provision in an agreement, transfer instrument, or applicable nonbankruptcy law—

(A) that restricts or conditions transfer of such interest by the debtor; or

(B) that is conditioned on the insolvency or financial condition of the debtor, on the commencement of a case under this title, or on the appointment of or taking possession by a trustee in a case under this title or a custodian before such commencement, and that effects or gives an option to effect a forfeiture, modification, or termination of the debtor's interest in property.

(2) A restriction on the transfer of a beneficial interest of the debtor in a trust that is enforceable under applicable nonbankruptcy law is enforceable in a case under this title.

(d) Property in which the debtor holds, as of the commencement of the case, only legal title and not an equitable interest, such as a mortgage secured by real property, or an interest in such a mortgage, sold by the debtor but as to which the debtor retains legal title to service or supervise the servicing of such mortgage or interest, becomes property of the estate under subsection (a)(1) or (2) of this section only to the extent of the debtor's legal title to such property, but not to the extent of any equitable interest in such property that the debtor does not hold.

(e) In determining whether any of the relationships specified in paragraph (5)(A) or (6)(A) of subsection (b) exists, a legally adopted child of an individual (and a child who is a member of an individual's household, if placed with such individual by an authorized placement agency for legal adoption by such individual), or a foster child of an individual (if such child has as the child's principal place of abode the home of the debtor and is a member of the debtor's household) shall be treated as a child of such individual by blood.

(f) Notwithstanding any other provision of this title, property that is held by a debtor that is a corporation described in section 501(c)(3) of the Internal Revenue Code of 1986 and exempt from tax under section 501(a) of such Code may be transferred to an entity that is not such a corporation, but only under the same conditions as would apply if the debtor had not filed a case under this title.

§ 542. Turnover of property to the estate

(a) Except as provided in subsection (c) or (d) of this section, an entity, other than a custodian, in possession, custody, or control, during the case, of property that the trustee may use, sell, or lease under section 363 of this title, or that the debtor may exempt under section 522 of this title, shall deliver to the trustee, and account for, such property or the value of such property, unless such property is of inconsequential value or benefit to the estate.

(b) Except as provided in subsection (c) or (d) of this section, an entity that owes a debt that is property of the estate and that is matured, payable on demand, or payable on order, shall pay such debt to, or on the order of, the trustee, except to the extent that such debt may be offset under section 553 of this title against a claim against the debtor.

(c) Except as provided in section 362(a)(7) of this title, an entity that has neither actual notice nor actual knowledge of the commencement of the case concerning the debtor may transfer property of the estate, or pay a debt owing to the debtor, in good faith and other than in the manner specified in subsection (d) of this section, to an entity other than the trustee, with the same effect as to the entity making such transfer or payment as if the case under this title concerning the debtor had not been commenced.

(d) A life insurance company may transfer property of the estate or property of the debtor to such company in good faith, with the same effect with respect to such company as if the case under this title concerning the debtor had not been commenced, if such transfer is to pay a premium or to carry out a nonforfeiture insurance option, and is required to be made automatically, under a life insurance contract with such company that was entered into before the date of the filing of the petition and that is property of the estate.

(e) Subject to any applicable privilege, after notice and a hearing, the court may order an attorney, accountant, or other person that holds recorded information, including books, documents, records, and papers, relating to the debtor's property or financial affairs, to turn over or disclose such recorded information to the trustee.

§ 543. Turnover of property by a custodian

(a) A custodian with knowledge of the commencement of a case under this title concerning the debtor may not make any disbursement from, or take any action in the administration of, property of the debtor, proceeds, product, offspring, rents, or profits of such property, or property of the estate, in the possession, custody, or control of such custodian, except such action as is necessary to preserve such property.

(b) A custodian shall—

(1) deliver to the trustee any property of the debtor held by or transferred to such custodian, or proceeds, product, offspring, rents, or profits of such property, that is in such custodian's possession, custody, or control on the date that such custodian acquires knowledge of the commencement of the case; and

(2) file an accounting of any property of the debtor, or proceeds, product, offspring, rents, or profits of such property, that, at any time, came into the possession, custody, or control of such custodian.

(c) The court, after notice and a hearing, shall—

(1) protect all entities to which a custodian has become obligated with respect to such property or proceeds, product, offspring, rents, or profits of such property;

(2) provide for the payment of reasonable compensation for services rendered and costs and expenses incurred by such custodian; and

(3) surcharge such custodian, other than an assignee for the benefit of the debtor's creditors that was appointed or took possession more than 120 days before the date of the filing of the petition, for any improper or excessive disbursement, other than a disbursement that has been made in accordance with applicable law or that has been approved, after notice and a hearing, by a court of competent jurisdiction before the commencement of the case under this title.

(d) After notice and hearing, the bankruptcy court—

(1) may excuse compliance with subsection (a), (b), or (c) of this section if the interests of creditors and, if the debtor is not insolvent, of equity security holders would be better served by permitting a custodian to continue in possession, custody, or control of such property, and

251

(2) shall excuse compliance with subsections (a) and (b)(1) of this section if the custodian is an assignee for the benefit of the debtor's creditors that was appointed or took possession more than 120 days before the date of the filing of the petition, unless compliance with such subsections is necessary to prevent fraud or injustice.

§ 544. Trustee as lien creditor and as successor to certain creditors and purchasers

(a) The trustee shall have, as of the commencement of the case, and without regard to any knowledge of the trustee or of any creditor, the rights and powers of, or may avoid any transfer of property of the debtor or any obligation incurred by the debtor that is voidable by—

(1) a creditor that extends credit to the debtor at the time of the commencement of the case, and that obtains, at such time and with respect to such credit, a judicial lien on all property on which a creditor on a simple contract could have obtained such a judicial lien, whether or not such a creditor exists;

(2) a creditor that extends credit to the debtor at the time of the commencement of the case, and obtains, at such time and with respect to such credit, an execution against the debtor that is returned unsatisfied at such time, whether or not such a creditor exists; or

(3) a bona fide purchaser of real property, other than fixtures, from the debtor, against whom applicable law permits such transfer to be perfected, that obtains the status of a bona fide purchaser and has perfected such transfer at the time of the commencement of the case, whether or not such a purchaser exists.

(b)(1) Except as provided in paragraph (2), the trustee may avoid any transfer of an interest of the debtor in property or any obligation incurred by the debtor that is voidable under applicable law by a creditor holding an unsecured claim that is allowable under section 502 of this title or that is not allowable only under section 502(e) of this title.

(2) Paragraph (1) shall not apply to a transfer of a charitable contribution (as that term is defined in section 548(d)(3)) that is not covered under section 548(a)(1)(B), by reason of section 548(a)(2). Any claim by any person to recover a transferred contribution described in the preceding sentence under Federal or State law in a Federal or State court shall be preempted by the commencement of the case.

§ 545. Statutory liens

The trustee may avoid the fixing of a statutory lien on property of the debtor to the extent that such lien—

(1) first becomes effective against the debtor—

(A) when a case under this title concerning the debtor is commenced;

(B) when an insolvency proceeding other than under this title concerning the debtor is commenced;

(C) when a custodian is appointed or authorized to take or takes possession;

(D) when the debtor becomes insolvent;

(E) when the debtor's financial condition fails to meet a specified standard; or

(F) at the time of an execution against property of the debtor levied at the instance of an entity other than the holder of such statutory lien;

(2) is not perfected or enforceable at the time of the commencement of the case against a bona fide purchaser that purchases such property at the time of the commencement of the case, whether or not such a purchaser exists, *except in any case in which a purchaser is a purchaser described in section 6323 of the Internal Revenue Code of 1986, or in any other similar provision of State or local law;*

(3) is for rent; or

(4) is a lien of distress for rent.

§ 546. Limitations on avoiding powers

(a) An action or proceeding under section 544, 545, 547, 548, or 553 of this title may not be commenced after the earlier of—

(1) the later of—

(A) 2 years after the entry of the order for relief; or

(B) 1 year after the appointment or election of the first trustee under section 702, 1104, 1163, 1202, or 1302 of this title if such appointment or such election occurs before the expiration of the period specified in subparagraph (A); or

(2) the time the case is closed or dismissed.

(b)(1) The rights and powers of a trustee under sections 544, 545, and 549 of this title are subject to any generally applicable law that—

(A) permits perfection of an interest in property to be effective against an entity that acquires rights in such property before the date of perfection; or

(B) provides for the maintenance or continuation of perfection of an interest in property to be effective against an entity that acquires rights in such property before the date on which action is taken to effect such maintenance or continuation.

(2) If—

(A) a law described in paragraph (1) requires seizure of such property or commencement of an action to accomplish such perfection, or maintenance or continuation of perfection of an interest in property; and

(B) such property has not been seized or such an action has not been commenced before the date of the filing of the petition;

such interest in such property shall be perfected, or perfection of such interest shall be maintained or continued, by giving notice within the time fixed by such law for such seizure or such commencement.

(c) Except as provided in subsection (d) of this section, the rights and powers of a trustee under sections 544(a), 545, 547, and 549 of this title are subject to any statutory or common-law right of a seller of goods that has sold goods to the debtor, in the ordinary course of such seller's business, to reclaim such goods if the debtor has received such goods while insolvent, but—

(1) such a seller may not reclaim any such goods unless such seller demands in writing reclamation of such goods—

(A) before 10 days after receipt of such goods by the debtor; or

(B) if such 10-day period expires after the commencement of the case, before 20 days after receipt of such goods by the debtor; and

(2) the court may deny reclamation to a seller with such a right of reclamation that has made such a demand only if the court—

(A) grants the claim of such a seller priority as a claim of a kind specified in section 503(b) of this title; or

(B) secures such claim by a lien.

(c)(1) Except as provided in subsection (d) of this section and in section 507(c), and subject to the prior rights of a holder of a security interest in such goods or the proceeds thereof, the rights and powers of the trustee under sections 544(a), 545, 547, and 549 are subject to the right of a seller of goods that has sold goods to the debtor, in the ordinary course of such seller's business, to reclaim such goods if the debtor has received such goods while insolvent, within 45 days before the date of the commencement of a case under this title, but such seller may not reclaim such goods unless such seller demands in writing reclamation of such goods—

(A) not later than 45 days after the date of receipt of such goods by the debtor; or

(B) not later than 20 days after the date of commencement of the case, if the 45-day period expires after the commencement of the case.

(2) If a seller of goods fails to provide notice in the manner described in paragraph (1), the seller still may assert the rights contained in section 503(b)(9).

(d) In the case of a seller who is a producer of grain sold to a grain storage facility, owned or operated by the debtor, in the ordinary course of such seller's business (as such terms are defined in section 557 of this title) or in the case of a United States fisherman who has caught fish sold to a fish processing facility owned or operated by the debtor in the ordinary course of such fisherman's business, the rights and powers of the trustee under sections 544(a), 545, 547, and 549 of this title are subject to any statutory or common law right of such producer or fisherman to reclaim such grain or fish if the debtor has received such grain or fish while insolvent, but—

(1) such producer or fisherman may not reclaim any grain or fish unless such producer or fisherman demands, in writing, reclamation of such grain or fish before ten days after receipt thereof by the debtor; and

(2) the court may deny reclamation to such a producer or fisherman with a right of reclamation that has made such a demand only if the court secures such claim by a lien.

(e) Notwithstanding sections 544, 545, 547, 548(a)(1)(B), and 548(b) of this title, the trustee may not avoid a transfer that is a margin payment, as defined in section 101, 741, or 761 of this title, or settlement payment, as defined in section 101 or 741 of this title, made by or to a commodity broker, forward contract merchant, stockbroker, financial institution, financial participant, or securities clearing agency, that is made before the commencement of the case, except under section 548(a)(1)(A) of this title.

(f) Notwithstanding sections 544, 545, 547, 548(a)(1)(B), and 548(b) of this title, the trustee may not avoid a transfer that is a margin payment, as defined in section 741 or 761 of this title, or settlement payment, as defined in section 741 of this title, made by or to a repo participant, in connection with a repurchase agreement and that is made before the commencement of the case, except under section 548(a)(1)(A) of this title.

(g) Notwithstanding sections 544, 545, 547, 548(a)(1)(B) and 548(b) of this title, the trustee may not avoid a transfer ~~under a swap agreement~~, made by or to a swap participant *or financial participant,* ~~in connection with a swap agreement~~ *under or in connection with any swap agreement* and that is made before the commencement of the case, except under section 548(a)(1)(A) of this title.

(~~g~~*h*) Notwithstanding the rights and powers of a trustee under sections 544(a), 545, 547, 549, and 553, if the court determines on a motion by the trustee made not later than 120 days after the date of the order for relief in a case under chapter 11 of this title and after notice and a hearing, that a return is in the best interests of the estate, the debtor, with the consent of a creditor *and subject to the prior rights of holders of security interests in such goods or the proceeds of such goods*, may return goods shipped to the debtor by the creditor before the commencement of the case, and the creditor may offset the purchase price of such goods against any claim of the creditor against the debtor that arose before the commencement of the case.

(i)(1) Notwithstanding paragraphs (2) and (3) of section 545, the trustee may not avoid a warehouseman's lien for storage, transportation, or other costs incidental to the storage and handling of goods.

(2) The prohibition under paragraph (1) shall be applied in a manner consistent with any State statute applicable to such lien that is similar to section 7-209 of the Uniform Commercial Code, as in effect on the date of enactment of the Bankruptcy Abuse Prevention and Consumer Protection Act of 2005, or any successor to such section 7-209.

(j) Notwithstanding sections 544, 545, 547, 548(a)(1)(B), and 548(b) the trustee may not avoid a transfer made by or to a master netting agreement participant under or in connection with any master netting agreement or any individual contract covered thereby that is made before the commencement of the case, except under section 548(a)(1)(A) and except to the extent that the trustee could otherwise avoid such a transfer made under an individual contract covered by such master netting agreement.

§ 547. Preferences

(a) In this section—

(1) "inventory" means personal property leased or furnished, held for sale or lease, or to be furnished under a contract for service, raw materials, work in process, or materials used or consumed in a business, including farm products such as crops or livestock, held for sale or lease;

(2) "new value" means money or money's worth in goods, services, or new credit, or release by a transferee of property previously transferred to such transferee in a transaction that is neither void nor voidable by the debtor or the trustee under any applicable law, including proceeds of such property, but does not include an obligation substituted for an existing obligation;

(3) "receivable" means right to payment, whether or not such right has been earned by performance; and

(4) a debt for a tax is incurred on the day when such tax is last payable without penalty, including any extension.

(b) Except as provided in subsections (c) *and (i)* of this section, the trustee may avoid any transfer of an interest of the debtor in property—

(1) to or for the benefit of a creditor;

(2) for or on account of an antecedent debt owed by the debtor before such transfer was made;

(3) made while the debtor was insolvent;

(4) made—

(A) on or within 90 days before the date of the filing of the petition; or

(B) between ninety days and one year before the date of the filing of the petition, if such creditor at the time of such transfer was an insider; and

(5) that enables such creditor to receive more than such creditor would receive if—

(A) the case were a case under chapter 7 of this title;

(B) the transfer had not been made; and

(C) such creditor received payment of such debt to the extent provided by the provisions of this title.

(c) The trustee may not avoid under this section a transfer—

(1) to the extent that such transfer was—

(A) intended by the debtor and the creditor to or for whose benefit such transfer was made to be a contemporaneous exchange for new value given to the debtor; and

(B) in fact a substantially contemporaneous exchange;

(2) ~~to the extent that such transfer was—~~

~~(A) in payment of a debt incurred by the debtor in the ordinary course of business or financial affairs of the debtor and the transferee;~~

~~(B) made in the ordinary course of business or financial affairs of the debtor and the transferee; and~~

~~(C) made according to ordinary business terms;~~ *to the extent that such transfer was in payment of a debt incurred by the debtor in the ordinary course of business or financial affairs of the debtor and the transferee, and such transfer was—*

(A) made in the ordinary course of business or financial affairs of the debtor and the transferee; or

(B) made according to ordinary business terms;

(3) that creates a security interest in property acquired by the debtor—

(A) to the extent such security interest secures new value that was—

(i) given at or after the signing of a security agreement that contains a description of such property as collateral;

(ii) given by or on behalf of the secured party under such agreement;

(iii) given to enable the debtor to acquire such property; and

(iv) in fact used by the debtor to acquire such property; and

(B) that is perfected on or before ~~20~~30 days after the debtor receives possession of such property;

(4) to or for the benefit of a creditor, to the extent that, after such transfer, such creditor gave new value to or for the benefit of the debtor—

(A) not secured by an otherwise unavoidable security interest; and

(B) on account of which new value the debtor did not make an otherwise unavoidable transfer to or for the benefit of such creditor;

(5) that creates a perfected security interest in inventory or a receivable or the proceeds of either, except to the extent that the aggregate of all such transfers to the transferee caused a reduction, as of the date of the filing of the petition and to the prejudice of other creditors holding unsecured claims, of any amount by which the debt secured by such security interest exceeded the value of all security interests for such debt on the later of—

(A)(i) with respect to a transfer to which subsection (b)(4)(A) of this section applies, 90 days before the date of the filing of the petition; or

(ii) with respect to a transfer to which subsection (b)(4)(B) of this section applies, one year before the date of the filing of the petition; or

(B) the date on which new value was first given under the security agreement creating such security interest;

(6) that is the fixing of a statutory lien that is not avoidable under section 545 of this title;

(7) to the extent such transfer was a bona fide payment of a debt *for a domestic support obligation;* ~~to a spouse, former spouse, or child of the debtor, for alimony to, maintenance for, or support of such spouse or child, in connection with a separation agreement, divorce decree or other order of a court of record, determination made in accordance with State or territorial law by a governmental unit, or property settlement agreement, but not to the extent that such debt—~~

(A) is assigned to another entity, voluntarily, by operation of law, or otherwise; or

(B) includes a liability designated as alimony, maintenance, or support, unless such liability is actually in the nature of alimony, maintenance or support; or

(8) if, in a case filed by an individual debtor whose debts are primarily consumer debts, the aggregate value of all property that constitutes or is affected by such transfer is less than $600~~.~~; or

(9) *if, in a case filed by a debtor whose debts are not primarily consumer debts, the aggregate value of all property that constitutes or is affected by such transfer is less than $5,000.*

(d) The trustee may avoid a transfer of an interest in property of the debtor transferred to or for the benefit of a surety to secure reimbursement of such a surety that furnished a bond or other obligation to dissolve a judicial lien that would have been avoidable by the trustee under subsection (b) of this section. The liability of such surety under such bond or obligation shall be discharged to the extent of the value of such property recovered by the trustee or the amount paid to the trustee.

(e)(1) For the purposes of this section—

(A) a transfer of real property other than fixtures, but including the interest of a seller or purchaser under a contract for the sale of real property, is perfected when a bona fide purchaser of such property from the debtor against whom applicable law permits such transfer to be perfected cannot acquire an interest that is superior to the interest of the transferee; and

(B) a transfer of a fixture or property other than real property is perfected when a creditor on a simple contract cannot acquire a judicial lien that is superior to the interest of the transferee.

(2) For the purposes of this section, except as provided in paragraph (3) of this subsection, a transfer is made—

(A) at the time such transfer takes effect between the transferor and the transferee, if such transfer is perfected at, or within ~~10~~*30* days after, such time, except as provided in subsection (c)(3)(B);

(B) at the time such transfer is perfected, if such transfer is perfected after such ~~10~~*-30* days; or

(C) immediately before the date of the filing of the petition, if such transfer is not perfected at the later of—

(i) the commencement of the case; or

(ii) ~~10~~*-30* days after such transfer takes effect between the transferor and the transferee.

(3) For the purposes of this section, a transfer is not made until the debtor has acquired rights in the property transferred.

(f) For the purposes of this section, the debtor is presumed to have been insolvent on and during the 90 days immediately preceding the date of the filing of the petition.

(g) For the purposes of this section, the trustee has the burden of proving the avoidability of a transfer under subsection (b) of this section, and the creditor or party in interest against whom recovery or avoidance is sought has the burden of proving the nonavoidability of a transfer under subsection (c) of this section.

(h) The trustee may not avoid a transfer if such transfer was made as a part of an alternative repayment schedule between the debtor and any creditor of the debtor created by an approved nonprofit budget and credit counseling agency.

(i) If the trustee avoids under subsection (b) a transfer made between 90 days and 1 year before the date of the filing of the petition, by the debtor to an entity that is not an insider for the benefit of a creditor that is an insider, such transfer shall be considered to be avoided under this section only with respect to the creditor that is an insider.

§ 548. Fraudulent transfers and obligations

(a)(1) The trustee may avoid any transfer *(including any transfer to or for the benefit of an insider under the employment contract)* of an interest of the debtor in property, or any obligation *(including any obligation to or for the benefit of an insider under an employment contract)* incurred by the debtor, that was made or incurred on or within ~~one year~~*2 years* before the date of the filing of the petition, if the debtor voluntarily or involuntarily—

(A) made such transfer or incurred such obligation with actual intent to hinder, delay, or defraud any entity to which the debtor was or became, on or after the date that such transfer was made or such obligation was incurred, indebted; or

(B)(i) received less than a reasonably equivalent value in exchange for such transfer or obligation; and

(ii)(I) was insolvent on the date that such transfer was made or such obligation was incurred, or became insolvent as a result of such transfer or obligation;

(II) was engaged in business or a transaction, or was about to engage in business or a transaction, for which any property remaining with the debtor was an unreasonably small capital; ~~or~~

(III) intended to incur, or believed that the debtor would incur, debts that would be beyond the debtor's ability to pay as such debts matured~~.~~*; or*

(IV) made such transfer to or for the benefit of an insider, or incurred such obligation to or for the benefit of an insider, under an employment contract and not in the ordinary course of business.

(2) A transfer of a charitable contribution to a qualified religious or charitable entity or organization shall not be considered to be a transfer covered under paragraph (1)(B) in any case in which.—

(A) the amount of that contribution does not exceed 15 percent of the gross annual income of the debtor for the year in which the transfer of the contribution is made; or

(B) the contribution made by a debtor exceeded the percentage amount of gross annual income specified in subparagraph (A), if the transfer was consistent with the practices of the debtor in making charitable contributions.

(b) The trustee of a partnership debtor may avoid any transfer of an interest of the debtor in property, or any obligation incurred by the debtor, that was made or incurred on or within ~~one year~~*2 years* before the date of the filing of the petition, to a general partner in the debtor, if the debtor was insolvent on the date such transfer was made or such obligation was incurred, or became insolvent as a result of such transfer or obligation.

(c) Except to the extent that a transfer or obligation voidable under this section is voidable under section 544, 545, or 547 of this title, a transferee or obligee of such a transfer or obligation that takes for value and in good faith has a lien on or may retain any interest transferred or may enforce any obligation incurred, as the case may be, to the extent that such transferee or obligee gave value to the debtor in exchange for such transfer or obligation.

(d)(1) For the purposes of this section, a transfer is made when such transfer is so perfected that a bona fide purchaser from the debtor against whom applicable law permits such transfer to be perfected cannot acquire an interest in the property transferred that is superior to the interest in such property of the transferee, but if such transfer is not so perfected before the commencement of the case, such transfer is made immediately before the date of the filing of the petition.

(2) In this section—

(A) "value" means property, or satisfaction or securing of a present or antecedent debt of the debtor, but does not include an unperformed promise to furnish support to the debtor or to a relative of the debtor;

(B) a commodity broker, forward contract merchant, stockbroker, financial institution, *financial participant,* or securities clearing agency that receives a margin payment, as defined in section 101, 741, or 761 of this title, or settlement payment, as defined in section 101 or 741 of this title, takes for value to the extent of such payment;

(C) a repo participant *or financial participant* that receives a margin payment, as defined in section 741 or 761 of this title, or settlement payment, as defined in section 741 of this title, in connection with a repurchase agreement, takes for value to the extent of such payment; ~~and~~

(D) a swap participant *or financial participant* that receives a transfer in connection with a swap agreement takes for value to the extent of such trans-fe~~r.~~*; and*

(E) a master netting agreement participant that receives a transfer in connection with a master netting agreement or any individual contract covered thereby takes for value to the extent of such transfer, except that, with respect to a transfer under any individual contract covered thereby, to the extent that such master netting agreement participant otherwise did not take (or is otherwise not deemed to have taken) such transfer for value.

(3) In this section, the term "charitable contribution" means a charitable contribution, as that term is defined in section 170(c) of the Internal Revenue Code of 1986, if that contribution—

(A) is made by a natural person; and

(B) consists of.—

(i) a financial instrument (as that term is defined in section 731(c)(2)(C) of the Internal Revenue Code of 1986); or

(ii) cash.

(4) In this section, the term "qualified religious or charitable entity or organization" means—

(A) an entity described in section 170(c)(1) of the Internal Revenue Code of 1986; or

(B) an entity or organization described in section 170(c)(2) of the Internal Revenue Code of 1986.

(e)(1) In addition to any transfer that the trustee may otherwise avoid, the trustee may avoid any transfer of an interest of the debtor in property that was made on or within 10 years before the date of the filing of the petition, if—

(A) such transfer was made to a self-settled trust or similar device;

(B) such transfer was by the debtor;

(C) the debtor is a beneficiary of such trust or similar device; and

(D) the debtor made such transfer with actual intent to hinder, delay, or defraud any entity to which the debtor was or became, on or after the date that such transfer was made, indebted.

(2) For the purposes of this subsection, a transfer includes a transfer made in anticipation of any money judgment, settlement, civil penalty, equitable order, or criminal fine incurred by, or which the debtor believed would be incurred by—

(A) any violation of the securities laws (as defined in section 3(a)(47) of the Securities Exchange Act of 1934 (15 U.S.C. 78c(a)(47))), any State securities laws, or any regulation or order issued under Federal securities laws or State securities laws; or

(B) fraud, deceit, or manipulation in a fiduciary capacity or in connection with the purchase or sale of any security registered under section 12 or 15(d) of the Securities Exchange Act of 1934 (15 U.S.C. 78l and 78o(d)) or under section 6 of the Securities Act of 1933 (15 U.S.C. 77f).

§ 549. Postpetition transactions

(a) Except as provided in subsection (b) or (c) of this section, the trustee may avoid a transfer of property of the estate—

(1) that occurs after the commencement of the case; and

(2)(A) that is authorized only under section 303(f) or 542(c) of this title; or

(B) that is not authorized under this title or by the court.

(b) In an involuntary case, the trustee may not avoid under subsection (a) of this section a transfer made after the commencement of such case but before the order for relief to the extent any value, including services, but not including satisfaction or securing of a debt that arose before the commencement of the case, is given after the commencement of the case in exchange for such transfer, notwithstanding any notice or knowledge of the case that the transferee has.

(c) The trustee may not avoid under subsection (a) of this section a transfer of *an interest in* real property to a good faith purchaser without knowledge of the commencement of the case and for present fair equivalent value unless a copy or notice of the petition was filed, where a transfer of *an interest in* such real property may be recorded to perfect such transfer, before such transfer is so perfected that a bona fide purchaser of such *real* property, against whom applicable law permits such transfer to be perfected, could not acquire an interest that is superior to *such* the-interest of such good faith purchaser. A good faith purchaser without knowledge of the commencement of the case and for less than present fair equivalent value has a lien on the property transferred to the extent of any present value given, unless a copy or notice of the petition was so filed before such transfer was so perfected.

(d) An action or proceeding under this section may not be commenced after the earlier of—

(1) two years after the date of the transfer sought to be avoided; or

(2) the time the case is closed or dismissed.

§ 550. Liability of transferee of avoided transfer

(a) Except as otherwise provided in this section, to the extent that a transfer is avoided under section 544, 545, 547, 548, 549, 553(b), or 724(a) of this title, the trustee may recover, for the benefit of the estate, the property transferred, or, if the court so orders, the value of such property, from—

(1) the initial transferee of such transfer or the entity for whose benefit such transfer was made; or

(2) any immediate or mediate transferee of such initial transferee.

(b) The trustee may not recover under section (a)(2) of this section from—

(1) a transferee that takes for value, including satisfaction or securing of a present or antecedent debt, in good faith, and without knowledge of the voidability of the transfer avoided; or

(2) any immediate or mediate good faith transferee of such transferee.

(c) If a transfer made between 90 days and one year before the filing of the petition—

(1) is avoided under section 547(b) of this title; and

(2) was made for the benefit of a creditor that at the time of such transfer was an insider;

the trustee may not recover under subsection (a) from a transferee that is not an insider.

(d) The trustee is entitled to only a single satisfaction under subsection (a) of this section.

(e)(1) A good faith transferee from whom the trustee may recover under subsection (a) of this section has a lien on the property recovered to secure the lesser of—

(A) the cost, to such transferee, of any improvement made after the transfer, less the amount of any profit realized by or accruing to such transferee from such property; and

(B) any increase in the value of such property as a result of such improvement, of the property transferred.

(2) In this subsection, "improvement" includes—

(A) physical additions or changes to the property transferred;

(B) repairs to such property;

(C) payment of any tax on such property;

(D) payment of any debt secured by a lien on such property that is superior or equal to the rights of the trustee; and

(E) preservation of such property.

(f) An action or proceeding under this section may not be commenced after the earlier of—

(1) one year after the avoidance of the transfer on account of which recovery under this section is sought; or

(2) the time the case is closed or dismissed.

§ 551. Automatic preservation of avoided transfer

Any transfer avoided under section 522, 544, 545, 547, 548, 549, or 724(a) of this title, or any lien void under section 506(d) of this title, is preserved for the benefit of the estate but only with respect to property of the estate.

§ 552. Postpetition effect of security interest

(a) Except as provided in subsection (b) of this section, property acquired by the estate or by the debtor after the commencement of the case is not subject to any lien resulting from any security agreement entered into by the debtor before the commencement of the case.

(b)(1) Except as provided in sections 363, 506(c), 522, 544, 545, 547, and 548 of this title, if the debtor and an entity entered into a security agreement before the commencement of the case and if the security interest created by such security agreement extends to property of the debtor acquired before the commencement of the case and to proceeds, ~~product~~*products*, offspring, or profits of such property, then such security interest extends to such proceeds, ~~product~~*products*, offspring, or profits acquired by the estate after the commencement of the case to the extent provided by such security agreement and by applicable nonbankruptcy law, except to any extent that the court, after notice and a hearing and based on the equities of the case, orders otherwise.

(2) Except as provided in sections 363, 506(c), 522, 544, 545, 547, and 548 of this title, and notwithstanding section 546(b) of this title, if the debtor and an entity entered into a security agreement before the commencement of the case and if the security interest created by such security agreement extends to property of the debtor acquired before the commencement of the case and to amounts paid as rents of such property or the fees, charges, accounts, or other payments for the use or occupancy of rooms and other public facilities in hotels, motels, or other lodging properties, then such security interest extends to such rents and such fees, charges, accounts, or other payments acquired by the estate after the commencement of the case to the extent provided in such security agreement, except to any extent that the court, after notice and a hearing and based on the equities of the case, orders otherwise.

§ 553. Setoff

(a) Except as otherwise provided in this section and in sections 362 and 363 of this title, this title does not affect any right of a creditor to offset a mutual debt owing by such creditor to the debtor that arose before the commencement of the case under this title against a claim of such creditor against the debtor that arose before the commencement of the case, except to the extent that—

(1) the claim of such creditor against the debtor is disallowed;

(2) such claim was transferred, by an entity other than the debtor, to such creditor—

(A) after the commencement of the case; or

(B)(i) after 90 days before the date of the filing of the petition; and

(ii) while the debtor was insolvent *(except for a setoff of a kind described in section 362(b)(6), 362(b)(7), 362(b)(17), 362(b)(27), 555, 556, 559, 560, or 561)*; or

(3) the debt owed to the debtor by such creditor was incurred by such creditor—

(A) after 90 days before the date of the filing of the petition;

(B) while the debtor was insolvent; and

(C) for the purpose of obtaining a right of setoff against the debtor *(except for a setoff of a kind described in section 362(b)(6), 362(b)(7), 362(b)(17), 362(b)(27), 555, 556, 559, 560, or 561)*.

(b)(1) Except with respect to a setoff of a kind described in section 362(b)(6), 362(b)(7), ~~362(b)(14)~~ *362(b)(17), 362(b)(27), 555, 556, 559, 560, 561*,~~;~~ 365(h), 546(h), or 365(i)(2) of this title, if a creditor offsets a mutual debt owing to the debtor against a claim against the debtor on or within 90 days before the date of the filing of the petition, then the trustee may recover from such creditor the amount so offset to the extent that any insufficiency on the date of such setoff is less than the insufficiency on the later of—

   (A) 90 days before the date of the filing of the petition; and

   (B) the first date during the 90 days immediately preceding the date of the filing of the petition on which there is an insufficiency.

   (2) In this subsection, "insufficiency" means amount, if any, by which a claim against the debtor exceeds a mutual debt owing to the debtor by the holder of such claim.

 (c) For the purposes of this section, the debtor is presumed to have been insolvent on and during the 90 days immediately preceding the date of the filing of the petition.

§ 554. Abandonment of property of the estate

 (a) After notice and a hearing, the trustee may abandon any property of the estate that is burdensome to the estate or that is of inconsequential value and benefit to the estate.

 (b) On request of a party in interest and after notice and a hearing, the court may order the trustee to abandon any property of the estate that is burdensome to the estate or that is of inconsequential value and benefit to the estate.

 (c) Unless the court orders otherwise, any property scheduled under section 521(1) of this title not otherwise administered at the time of the closing of a case is abandoned to the debtor and administered for purposes of section 350 of this title.

 (d) Unless the court orders otherwise, property of the estate that is not abandoned under this section and that is not administered in the case remains property of the estate.

§ ~~555. Contractual right to liquidate a securities contract~~*555. Contractual right to liquidate, terminate, or accelerate a securities contract*

The exercise of a contractual right of a stockbroker, financial institution, *financial participant,* or securities clearing agency to cause the ~~liquidation~~*liquidation, termination, or acceleration* of a securities contract, as defined in section 741 of this title, because of a condition of the kind specified in section 365(e)(1) of this title shall not be stayed, avoided, or otherwise limited by operation of any provision of this title or by order of a court or administrative agency in any proceeding under this title unless such order is authorized under the provisions of the Securities Investor Protection Act of 1970 or any statute administered by the Securities and Exchange Commission. ~~As used in this section, the term "contractual right" includes a right set forth in a rule or bylaw of a national securities exchange, a national securities association, or a securities clearing agency.~~ *As used in this section, the term 'contractual right' includes a right set forth in a rule or bylaw of a derivatives clearing organization (as defined in the Commodity Exchange Act), a multilateral clearing organization (as defined in the Federal Deposit Insurance Corporation Improvement Act of 1991), a national securities exchange, a national securities association, a securities clearing agency, a contract market designated under the Commodity Exchange Act, a derivatives transaction execution facility registered under the Commodity Exchange Act, or a board of trade (as defined in the Commodity Exchange Act), or in a resolution of the governing board thereof, and a right, whether or not in writing, arising under common law, under law merchant, or by reason of normal business practice.*

§ 556. ~~Contractual right to liquidate a commodities contract or forward contract~~ *Contractual right to liquidate, terminate, or accelerate a commodities contract or forward contract*

The contractual right of a commodity broker, *financial participant,* or forward contract merchant to cause the ~~liquidation~~ *liquidation, termination, or acceleration* of a commodity contract, as defined in section 761 of this title, or forward contract because of a condition of the kind specified in section 365(e)(1) of this title, and the right to a variation or maintenance margin payment received from a trustee with respect to open commodity contracts or forward contracts, shall not be stayed, avoided, or otherwise limited by operation of any provision of this title or by the order of a court in any proceeding under this title. ~~As used in this section, the term "contractual right" includes a right set forth in a rule or bylaw of a clearing organization or contract market or in a resolution of the governing board thereof and a right,~~ *As used in this section, the term 'contractual right' includes a right set forth in a rule or bylaw of a derivatives clearing organization (as defined in the Commodity Exchange Act), a multilateral clearing organization (as defined in the Federal Deposit Insurance Corporation Improvement Act of 1991), a national securities exchange, a national securities association, a securities clearing agency, a contract market designated under the Commodity Exchange Act, a derivatives transaction execution facility registered under the Commodity Exchange Act, or a board of trade (as defined in the Commodity Exchange Act) or in a resolution of the governing board thereof and a right,* whether or not evidenced in writing, arising under common law, under law merchant or by reason of normal business practice.

§ 557. Expedited determination of interests in, and abandonment or other disposition of grain assets

(a) This section applies only in a case concerning a debtor that owns or operates a grain storage facility and only with respect to grain and the proceeds of grain. This section does not affect the application of any other section of this title to property other than grain and proceeds of grain.

(b) In this section—

(1) "grain" means wheat, corn, flaxseed, grain sorghum, barley, oats, rye, soybeans, other dry edible beans, or rice;

(2) "grain storage facility" means a site or physical structure regularly used to store grain for producers, or to store grain acquired from producers for resale; and

(3) "producer" means an entity which engages in the growing of grain.

(c)(1) Notwithstanding sections 362, 363, 365, and 554 of this title, on the court's own motion the court may, and on the request of the trustee or an entity that claims an interest in grain or the proceeds of grain the court shall, expedite the procedures for the determination of interests in and the disposition of grain and the proceeds of grain, by shortening to the greatest extent feasible such time periods as are otherwise applicable for such procedures and by establishing, by order, a timetable having a duration of not to exceed 120 days for the completion of the applicable procedure specified in subsection (d) of this section. Such time periods and such timetable may be modified by the court, for cause, in accordance with subsection (f) of this section.

(2) The court shall determine the extent to which such time periods shall be shortened, based upon—

(A) any need of an entity claiming an interest in such grain or the proceeds of grain for a prompt determination of such interest;

(B) any need of such entity for a prompt disposition of such grain;

(C) the market for such grain;

(D) the conditions under which such grain is stored;

(E) the costs of continued storage or disposition of such grain;

(F) the orderly administration of the estate;

(G) the appropriate opportunity for an entity to assert an interest in such grain; and

(H) such other considerations as are relevant to the need to expedite such procedures in the case.

(d) The procedures that may be expedited under subsection (c) of this section include—

(1) the filing of and response to—

(A) a claim of ownership;

(B) a proof of claim;

(C) a request for abandonment;

(D) a request for relief from the stay of action against property under section 362(a) of this title;

(E) a request for determination of secured status;

(F) a request for determination of whether such grain or the proceeds of grain—

(i) is property of the estate;

(ii) must be turned over to the estate; or

(iii) may be used, sold, or leased; and

(G) any other request for determination of an interest in such grain or the proceeds of grain;

(2) the disposition of such grain or the proceeds of grain, before or after determination of interests in such grain or the proceeds of grain, by way of—

(A) sale of such grain;

(B) abandonment;

(C) distribution; or

(D) such other method as is equitable in the case;

(3) subject to sections 701, 702, 703, 1104, 1202, and 1302 of this title, the appointment of a trustee or examiner and the retention and compensation of any professional person required to assist with respect to matters relevant to the determination of interests in or disposition of such grain or the proceeds of grain; and

(4) the determination of any dispute concerning a matter specified in paragraph (1), (2), or (3) of this subsection.

(e)(1) Any governmental unit that has regulatory jurisdiction over the operation or liquidation of the debtor or the debtor's business shall be given notice of any request made or order entered under subsection (c) of this section.

(2) Any such governmental unit may raise, and may appear and be heard on, any issue relating to grain or the proceeds of grain in a case in which a request is made, or an order is entered, under subsection (c) of this section.

(3) The trustee shall consult with such governmental unit before taking any action relating to the disposition of grain in the possession, custody, or control of the debtor or the estate.

(f) The court may extend the period for final disposition of grain or the proceeds of grain under this section beyond 120 days if the court finds that—

(1) the interests of justice so require in light of the complexity of the case; and

(2) the interests of those claimants entitled to distribution of grain or the proceeds of grain will not be materially injured by such additional delay.

(g) Unless an order establishing an expedited procedure under subsection (c) of this section, or determining any interest in or approving any disposition of grain or the proceeds of grain, is stayed pending appeal—

(1) the reversal or modification of such order on appeal does not affect the validity of any procedure, determination, or disposition that occurs before such reversal or modification, whether or not any entity knew of the pendency of the appeal; and

(2) neither the court nor the trustee may delay, due to the appeal of such order, any proceeding in the case in which such order is issued.

(h)(1) The trustee may recover from grain and the proceeds of grain the reasonable and necessary costs and expenses allowable under section 503(b) of this title attributable to preserving or disposing of grain or the proceeds of grain, but may not recover from such grain or the proceeds of grain any other costs or expenses.

(2) Notwithstanding section 326(a) of this title, the dollar amounts of money specified in such section include the value, as of the date of disposition, of any grain that the trustee distributes in kind.

(i) In all cases where the quantity of a specific type of grain held by a debtor operating a grain storage facility exceeds ten thousand bushels, such grain shall be sold by the trustee and the assets thereof distributed in accordance with the provisions of this section.

§ 558. Defenses of the estate

The estate shall have the benefit of any defense available to the debtor as against any entity other than the estate, including statutes of limitation, statutes of frauds, usury, and other personal defenses. A waiver of any such defense by the debtor after the commencement of the case does not bind the estate.

§ 559. ~~Contractual right to liquidate a repurchase agreement~~ *Contractual right to liquidate, terminate, or accelerate a repurchase agreement*

The exercise of a contractual right of a repo participant *or financial participant* to cause the ~~liquidation~~ *liquidation, termination, or acceleration* of a repurchase agreement because of a condition of the kind specified in section 365(e)(1) of this title shall not be stayed, avoided, or otherwise limited by operation of any provision of this title or by order of a court or administrative agency in any proceeding under this title, unless, where the debtor is a stockbroker or securities clearing agency, such order is authorized under the provisions of the Securities Investor Protection Act of 1970 or any statute administered by the Securities and Exchange Commission. In the event that a repo participant or financial participant liquidates one or more repurchase agreements with a debtor and under the terms of one or more such agreements has agreed to deliver assets subject to repurchase agreements to the debtor, any excess of the market prices received on liquidation of such assets (or if any such assets are not disposed of on the date of liquidation of such repurchase agreements, at the prices available at the time of liquidation of such repurchase agreements from a generally recognized source or the most recent closing bid quotation from such a source) over the sum of the stated repurchase prices and all expenses in connection with the liquidation of such repurchase agreements shall be deemed property of the estate, subject to the available rights of setoff. ~~As used in this section, the term "contractual right" includes a right set forth in a rule or bylaw, applicable to each party to the repurchase agreement, of a national securities exchange, a national securities association, or a securities clearing agency, and a right,~~ *As used in this section, the term ' contractual right' includes a right set forth in a rule or bylaw of a derivatives clearing organization (as defined in the Commodity Exchange Act), a multilateral clearing organization (as defined in the Federal Deposit Insurance Corporation Improvement Act of 1991), a national securities exchange, a national securities association, a securities clearing agency, a contract market designated under the Commodity Exchange Act, a derivatives transaction execution facility registered under the Commodity Exchange Act, or a board of trade (as defined in the Commodity Exchange Act) or in a resolution of the governing board thereof and a right,* whether or not evidenced in writing, arising under common law, under law merchant or by reason of normal business practice.

§ 560. *Contractual right to liquidate, terminate, or accelerate a swap agreement* ~~Contractual right to terminate a swap agreement~~

The exercise of any contractual right of any swap participant *or financial participant* to cause the ~~termination of a swap agreement~~ *liquidation, termination, or acceleration of one or more swap agreements* because of a condition of the kind specified in section 365(e)(1) of this title or to offset or net out any termination values or payment amounts arising under or ~~in connection with any swap agreement~~ *in connection with the termination, liquidation, or acceleration of one or more swap agreements* shall not be stayed, avoided, or otherwise limited by operation of any provision of this title or by order of a court or administrative agency in any proceeding under this title. ~~As used in this section, the term "contractual~~

~~right" includes a right,~~ *As used in this section, the term 'contractual right' includes a right set forth in a rule or bylaw of a derivatives clearing organization (as defined in the Commodity Exchange Act), a multilateral clearing organization (as defined in the Federal Deposit Insurance Corporation Improvement Act of 1991), a national securities exchange, a national securities association, a securities clearing agency, a contract market designated under the Commodity Exchange Act, a derivatives transaction execution facility registered under the Commodity Exchange Act, or a board of trade (as defined in the Commodity Exchange Act) or in a resolution of the governing board thereof and a right,* whether or not evidenced in writing, arising under common law, under law merchant, or by reason of normal business practice.

§ 561. Contractual right to terminate, liquidate, accelerate, or offset under a master netting agreement and across contracts; proceedings under chapter 15

 (a) Subject to subsection (b), the exercise of any contractual right, because of a condition of the kind specified in section 365(e)(1), to cause the termination, liquidation, or acceleration of or to offset or net termination values, payment amounts, or other transfer obligations arising under or in connection with one or more (or the termination, liquidation, or acceleration of one or more)—

 (1) securities contracts, as defined in section 741(7);

 (2) commodity contracts, as defined in section 761(4);

 (3) forward contracts;

 (4) repurchase agreements;

 (5) swap agreements; or

 (6) master netting agreements,

shall not be stayed, avoided, or otherwise limited by operation of any provision of this title or by any order of a court or administrative agency in any proceeding under this title.

 (b)(1) A party may exercise a contractual right described in subsection (a) to terminate, liquidate, or accelerate only to the extent that such party could exercise such a right under section 555, 556, 559, or 560 for each individual contract covered by the master netting agreement in issue.

 (2) If a debtor is a commodity broker subject to subchapter IV of chapter 7—

 (A) a party may not net or offset an obligation to the debtor arising under, or in connection with, a commodity contract traded on or subject to the rules of a contract market designated under the Commodity Exchange Act or a derivatives transaction execution facility registered under the Commodity Exchange Act against any claim arising under, or in connection with, other instruments, contracts, or agreements listed in subsection (a) except to the extent that the party has positive net equity in the commodity accounts at the debtor, as calculated under such subchapter; and

 (B) another commodity broker may not net or offset an obligation to the debtor arising under, or in connection with, a commodity contract entered into or held on behalf of a customer of the debtor and traded on or subject to the rules of a contract market designated under the Commodity Exchange Act or a derivatives transaction execution facility registered under the Com-

269

modity Exchange Act against any claim arising under, or in connection with, other instruments, contracts, or agreements listed in subsection (a).

(3) No provision of subparagraph (A) or (B) of paragraph (2) shall prohibit the offset of claims and obligations that arise under —

(A) a cross-margining agreement or similar arrangement that has been approved by the Commodity Futures Trading Commission or submitted to the Commodity Futures Trading Commission under paragraph (1) or (2) of section 5c(c) of the Commodity Exchange Act and has not been abrogated or rendered ineffective by the Commodity Futures Trading Commission; or

(B) any other netting agreement between a clearing organization (as defined in section 761) and another entity that has been approved by the Commodity Futures Trading Commission.

(c) As used in this section, the term 'contractual right' includes a right set forth in a rule or bylaw of a derivatives clearing organization (as defined in the Commodity Exchange Act), a multilateral clearing organization (as defined in the Federal Deposit Insurance Corporation Improvement Act of 1991), a national securities exchange, a national securities association, a securities clearing agency, a contract market designated under the Commodity Exchange Act, a derivatives transaction execution facility registered under the Commodity Exchange Act, or a board of trade (as defined in the Commodity Exchange Act) or in a resolution of the governing board thereof, and a right, whether or not evidenced in writing, arising under common law, under law merchant, or by reason of normal business practice.

(d) Any provisions of this title relating to securities contracts, commodity contracts, forward contracts, repurchase agreements, swap agreements, or master netting agreements shall apply in a case under chapter 15, so that enforcement of contractual provisions of such contracts and agreements in accordance with their terms will not be stayed or otherwise limited by operation of any provision of this title or by order of a court in any case under this title, and to limit avoidance powers to the same extent as in a proceeding under chapter 7 or 11 of this title (such enforcement not to be limited based on the presence or absence of assets of the debtor in the United States).

§ 562. Timing of damage measurement in connection with swap agreements, securities contracts, forward contracts, commodity contracts, repurchase agreements, and master netting agreements

(a) If the trustee rejects a swap agreement, securities contract (as defined in section 741), forward contract, commodity contract (as defined in section 761), repurchase agreement, or master netting agreement pursuant to section 365(a), or if a forward contract merchant, stockbroker, financial institution, securities clearing agency, repo participant, financial participant, master netting agreement participant, or swap participant liquidates, terminates, or accelerates such contract or agreement, damages shall be measured as of the earlier of—

(1) the date of such rejection; or

(2) the date or dates of such liquidation, termination, or acceleration.

(b) If there are not any commercially reasonable determinants of value as of any date referred to in paragraph (1) or (2) of subsection (a), damages shall be mea-

sured as of the earliest subsequent date or dates on which there are commercially reasonable determinants of value.

(c) For the purposes of subsection (b), if damages are not measured as of the date or dates of rejection, liquidation, termination, or acceleration, and the forward contract merchant, stockbroker, financial institution, securities clearing agency, repo participant, financial participant, master netting agreement participant, or swap participant or the trustee objects to the timing of the measurement of damages—

(1) the trustee, in the case of an objection by a forward contract merchant, stockbroker, financial institution, securities clearing agency, repo participant, financial participant, master netting agreement participant, or swap participant; or

(2) the forward contract merchant, stockbroker, financial institution, securities clearing agency, repo participant, financial participant, master netting agreement participant, or swap participant, in the case of an objection by the trustee,

has the burden of proving that there were no commercially reasonable determinants of value as of such date or dates.

CHAPTER 7—LIQUIDATION

SUBCHAPTER I—OFFICERS AND ADMINISTRATION

§ 701. Interim trustee

(a)(1) Promptly after the order for relief under this chapter, the United States trustee shall appoint one disinterested person that is a member of the panel of private trustees established under section 586(a)(1) of title 28 or that is serving as trustee in the case immediately before the order for relief under this chapter to serve as interim trustee in the case.

(2) If none of the members of such panel is willing to serve as interim trustee in the case, then the United States trustee may serve as interim trustee in the case.

(b) The service of an interim trustee under this section terminates when a trustee elected or designated under section 702 of this title to serve as trustee in the case qualifies under section 322 of this title.

(c) An interim trustee serving under this section is a trustee in a case under this title.

§ 702. Election of trustee

(a) A creditor may vote for a candidate for trustee only if such creditor—

(1) holds an allowable, undisputed, fixed, liquidated, unsecured claim of a kind entitled to distribution under section 726(a)(2), 726(a)(3), 726(a)(4), 752(a), 766(h), or 766(i) of this title;

(2) does not have an interest materially adverse, other than an equity interest that is not substantial in relation to such creditor's interest as a creditor, to the interest of creditors entitled to such distribution; and

(3) is not an insider.

(b) At the meeting of creditors held under section 341 of this title, creditors may elect one person to serve as trustee in the case if election of a trustee is requested by creditors that may vote under subsection (a) of this section, and that hold at least 20 percent in amount of the claims specified in subsection (a)(1) of this section that are held by creditors that may vote under subsection (a) of this section.

(c) A candidate for trustee is elected trustee if—

(1) creditors holding at least 20 percent in amount of the claims of a kind specified in subsection (a)(1) of this section that are held by creditors that may vote under subsection (a) of this section vote; and

(2) such candidate receives the votes of creditors holding a majority in amount of claims specified in subsection (a)(1) of this section that are held by creditors that vote for a trustee.

(d) If a trustee is not elected under this section, then the interim trustee shall serve as trustee in the case.

§ 703. Successor trustee

(a) If a trustee dies or resigns during a case, fails to qualify under section 322 of this title, or is removed under section 324 of this title, creditors may elect, in the manner specified in section 702 of this title, a person to fill the vacancy in the office of trustee.

(b) Pending election of a trustee under subsection (a) of this section, if necessary to preserve or prevent loss to the estate, the United States trustee may appoint an interim trustee in the manner specified in section 701(a).

(c) If creditors do not elect a successor trustee under subsection (a) of this section or if a trustee is needed in a case reopened under section 350 of this title, then the United States trustee—

(1) shall appoint one disinterested person that is a member of the panel of private trustees established under section 586(a)(1) of title 28 to serve as trustee in the case; or

(2) may, if none of the disinterested members of such panel is willing to serve as trustee, serve as trustee in the case.

§ 704. Duties of trustee

(a) The trustee shall—

(1) collect and reduce to money the property of the estate for which such trustee serves, and close such estate as expeditiously as is compatible with the best interests of parties in interest;

(2) be accountable for all property received;

(3) ensure that the debtor shall perform his intention as specified in section 521(2)(B) of this title;

(4) investigate the financial affairs of the debtor;

(5) if a purpose would be served, examine proofs of claims and object to the allowance of any claim that is improper;

(6) if advisable, oppose the discharge of the debtor;

(7) unless the court orders otherwise, furnish such information concerning the estate and the estate's administration as is requested by a party in interest;

(8) if the business of the debtor is authorized to be operated, file with the court, with the United States trustee, and with any governmental unit charged with responsibility for collection or determination of any tax arising out of such operation, periodic reports and summaries of the operation of such business, including a statement of receipts and disbursements, and such other information as the United States trustee or the court requires; and

(9) make a final report and file a final account of the administration of the estate with the court and with the United States trustee.

(b)(1) With respect to a debtor who is an individual in a case under this chapter

> *(A) the United States trustee (or the bankruptcy administrator, if any) shall review all materials filed by the debtor and, not later than 10 days after the date of the first meeting of creditors, file with the court a statement as to whether the debtor's case would be presumed to be an abuse under section 707(b); and*

> *(B) not later than 5 days after receiving a statement under subparagraph (A), the court shall provide a copy of the statement to all creditors.*

(2) The United States trustee (or bankruptcy administrator, if any) shall, not later than 30 days after the date of filing a statement under paragraph (1), either file a motion to dismiss or convert under section 707(b) or file a statement setting forth the reasons the United States trustee (or the bankruptcy administrator, if any) does not consider such a motion to be appropriate, if the United States trustee (or the bankruptcy administrator, if any) determines that the debtor's case should be presumed to be an abuse under section 707(b) and the product of the debtor's current monthly income, multiplied by 12 is not less than—

> *(A) in the case of a debtor in a household of 1 person, the median family income of the applicable State for 1 earner; or*

> *(B) in the case of a debtor in a household of 2 or more individuals, the highest median family income of the applicable State for a family of the same number or fewer individuals.*

(c)(1) In a case described in subsection (a)(10) to which subsection (a)(10) applies, the trustee shall—

> *(A)(i) provide written notice to the holder of the claim described in subsection (a)(10) of such claim and of the right of such holder to use the services of the State child support enforcement agency established under sections 464 and 466 of the Social Security Act for the State in which such holder resides, for assistance in collecting child support during and after the case under this title;*

> *(ii) include in the notice provided under clause (i) the address and telephone number of such State child support enforcement agency; and*

> *(iii) include in the notice provided under clause (i) an explanation of the rights of such holder to payment of such claim under this chapter;*

> *(B)(i) provide written notice to such State child support enforcement agency of such claim; and*

> *(ii) include in the notice provided under clause (i) the name, address, and telephone number of such holder; and*

(C) at such time as the debtor is granted a discharge under section 727, provide written notice to such holder and to such State child support enforcement agency of—

(i) the granting of the discharge;

(ii) the last recent known address of the debtor;

(iii) the last recent known name and address of the debtor's employer; and

(iv) the name of each creditor that holds a claim that—

(I) is not discharged under paragraph (2), (4), or (14A) of section 523(a); or

(II) was reaffirmed by the debtor under section 524(c).

(2)(A) The holder of a claim described in subsection (a)(10) or the State child support enforcement agency of the State in which such holder resides may request from a creditor described in paragraph (1)(C)(iv) the last known address of the debtor.

(B) Notwithstanding any other provision of law, a creditor that makes a disclosure of a last known address of a debtor in connection with a request made under subparagraph (A) shall not be liable by reason of making such disclosure.

§ 705. Creditors' committee

(a) At the meeting under section 341(a) of this title, creditors that may vote for a trustee under section 702(a) of this title may elect a committee of not fewer than three, and not more than eleven, creditors, each of whom holds an allowable unsecured claim of a kind entitled to distribution under section 726(a)(2) of this title.

(b) A committee elected under subsection (a) of this section may consult with the trustee or the United States trustee in connection with the administration of the estate, make recommendations to the trustee or the United States trustee respecting the performance of the trustee's duties, and submit to the court or the United States trustee any question affecting the administration of the estate.

§ 706. Conversion

(a) The debtor may convert a case under this chapter to a case under chapter 11, 12, or 13 of this title at any time, if the case has not been converted under section 1112, 1208, or 1307 of this title. Any waiver of the right to convert a case under this subsection is unenforceable.

(b) On request of a party in interest and after notice and a hearing, the court may convert a case under this chapter to a case under chapter 11 of this title at any time.

(c) The court may not convert a case under this chapter to a case under chapter 12 or 13 of this title unless the debtor requests or consents to such conversion.

(d) Notwithstanding any other provision of this section, a case may not be converted to a case under another chapter of this title unless the debtor may be a debtor under such chapter.

§ 707. Dismissal *of a case or conversion to a case under Chapter 11 or 13*

(a) The court may dismiss a case under this chapter only after notice and a hearing and only for cause, including—

(1) unreasonable delay by the debtor that is prejudicial to creditors;

(2) nonpayment of any fees or charges required under chapter 123 of title 28; and

(3) failure of the debtor in a voluntary case to file, within fifteen days or such additional time as the court may allow after the filing of the petition commencing such case, the information required by paragraph (1) of section 521, but only on a motion by the United States trustee.

(b)*(1)* After notice and a hearing, the court, on its own motion or on a motion by the United States trustee, ~~but not at the request or suggestion of~~ *trustee (or bankruptcy administrator, if any) or* any party in interest, may dismiss a case filed by an individual debtor under this chapter whose debts are primarily consumer debts*, or, with the debtor's consent, convert such a case to a case under chapter 11 or 13 of this title* if it finds that the granting of relief would be ~~a substantial abuse~~ *an abuse* of the provisions of this chapter. ~~There shall be a presumption in favor of granting the relief requested by the debtor.~~ In making a determination whether to dismiss a case under this section, the court may not take into consideration whether a debtor has made, or continues to make, charitable contributions (that meet the definition of "charitable contribution" under section 548(d)(3)) to any qualified religious or charitable entity or organization (as that term is defined in section 548(d)(4)).

(2)(A)(i) In considering under paragraph (1) whether the granting of relief would be an abuse of the provisions of this chapter, the court shall presume abuse exists if the debtor's current monthly income reduced by the amounts determined under clauses (ii), (iii), and (iv), and multiplied by 60 is not less than the lesser of—

(I) 25 percent of the debtor's nonpriority unsecured claims in the case, or $6,000, whichever is greater; or

(II) $10,000.

(ii)(I) The debtor's monthly expenses shall be the debtor's applicable monthly expense amounts specified under the National Standards and Local Standards, and the debtor's actual monthly expenses for the categories specified as Other Necessary Expenses issued by the Internal Revenue Service for the area in which the debtor resides, as in effect on the date of the order for relief, for the debtor, the dependents of the debtor, and the spouse of the debtor in a joint case, if the spouse is not otherwise a dependent. Such expenses shall include reasonably necessary health insurance, disability insurance, and health savings account expenses for the debtor, the spouse of the debtor, or the dependents of the debtor. Notwithstanding any other provision of this clause, the monthly expenses of the debtor shall not include any payments for debts. In addition, the debtor's monthly expenses shall include the debtor's reasonably necessary expenses incurred to maintain the safety of the debtor and the family of the debtor from family violence as identified under section 309 of the Family Violence Prevention and Services Act, or other applicable Federal law. The expenses included in the debtor's monthly expenses described in the preceding sentence shall be

kept confidential by the court. In addition, if it is demonstrated that it is reasonable and necessary, the debtor's monthly expenses may also include an additional allowance for food and clothing of up to 5 percent of the food and clothing categories as specified by the National Standards issued by the Internal Revenue Service.

(II) In addition, the debtor's monthly expenses may include, if applicable, the continuation of actual expenses paid by the debtor that are reasonable and necessary for care and support of an elderly, chronically ill, or disabled household member or member of the debtor's immediate family (including parents, grandparents, siblings, children, and grandchildren of the debtor, the dependents of the debtor, and the spouse of the debtor in a joint case who is not a dependent) and who is unable to pay for such reasonable and necessary expenses.

(III) In addition, for a debtor eligible for chapter 13, the debtor's monthly expenses may include the actual administrative expenses of administering a chapter 13 plan for the district in which the debtor resides, up to an amount of 10 percent of the projected plan payments, as determined under schedules issued by the Executive Office for United States Trustees.

(IV) In addition, the debtor's monthly expenses may include the actual expenses for each dependent child less than 18 years of age, not to exceed $1,500 per year per child, to attend a private or public elementary or secondary school if the debtor provides documentation of such expenses and a detailed explanation of why such expenses are reasonable and necessary, and why such expenses are not already accounted for in the National Standards, Local Standards, or Other Necessary Expenses referred to in subclause (I).

(V) In addition, the debtor's monthly expenses may include an allowance for housing and utilities, in excess of the allowance specified by the Local Standards for housing and utilities issued by the Internal Revenue Service, based on the actual expenses for home energy costs if the debtor provides documentation of such actual expenses and demonstrates that such actual expenses are reasonable and necessary.

(iii) The debtor's average monthly payments on account of secured debts shall be calculated as the sum of—

(I) the total of all amounts scheduled as contractually due to secured creditors in each month of the 60 months following the date of the petition; and

(II) any additional payments to secured creditors necessary for the debtor, in filing a plan under chapter 13 of this title, to maintain possession of the debtor's primary residence, motor vehicle, or other property necessary for the support of the debtor and the debtor's dependents, that serves as collateral for secured debts;

divided by 60.

(iv) The debtor's expenses for payment of all priority claims (including priority child support and alimony claims) shall be calculated as the total amount of debts entitled to priority, divided by 60.

(B)(i) In any proceeding brought under this subsection, the presumption of abuse may only be rebutted by demonstrating special circumstances,

such as a serious medical condition or a call or order to active duty in the Armed Forces, to the extent such special circumstances that justify additional expenses or adjustments of current monthly income for which there is no reasonable alternative.

(ii) In order to establish special circumstances, the debtor shall be required to itemize each additional expense or adjustment of income and to provide—

(I) documentation for such expense or adjustment to income; and

(II) a detailed explanation of the special circumstances that make such expenses or adjustment to income necessary and reasonable.

(iii) The debtor shall attest under oath to the accuracy of any information provided to demonstrate that additional expenses or adjustments to income are required.

(iv) The presumption of abuse may only be rebutted if the additional expenses or adjustments to income referred to in clause (i) cause the product of the debtor's current monthly income reduced by the amounts determined under clauses (ii), (iii), and (iv) of subparagraph (A) when multiplied by 60 to be less than the lesser of—

(I) 25 percent of the debtor's nonpriority unsecured claims, or $6,000, whichever is greater; or

(II) $10,000.

(C) As part of the schedule of current income and expenditures required under section 521, the debtor shall include a statement of the debtor's current monthly income, and the calculations that determine whether a presumption arises under subparagraph (A)(i), that show how each such amount is calculated.

(D) Subparagraphs (A) through (C) shall not apply, and the court may not dismiss or convert a case based on any form of means testing, if the debtor is a disabled veteran (as defined in section 3741(1) of title 38), and the indebtedness occurred primarily during a period during which he or she was—

(i) on active duty (as defined in section 101(d)(1) of title 10); or

(ii) performing a homeland defense activity (as defined in section 901(1) of title 32).

(3) In considering under paragraph (1) whether the granting of relief would be an abuse of the provisions of this chapter in a case in which the presumption in subparagraph (A)(i) of such paragraph does not arise or is rebutted, the court shall consider—

(A) whether the debtor filed the petition in bad faith; or

(B) the totality of the circumstances (including whether the debtor seeks to reject a personal services contract and the financial need for such rejection as sought by the debtor) of the debtor's financial situation demonstrates abuse.

(4)(A) The court, on its own initiative or on the motion of a party in interest, in accordance with the procedures described in rule 9011 of the Federal Rules of Bankruptcy Procedure, may order the attorney for the debtor to reimburse the trustee for all reasonable costs in prosecuting a motion filed under section 707(b), including reasonable attorneys' fees, if—

(i) a trustee files a motion for dismissal or conversion under this subsection; and

(ii) the court—

(I) grants such motion; and

(II) finds that the action of the attorney for the debtor in filing a case under this chapter violated rule 9011 of the Federal Rules of Bankruptcy Procedure.

(B) If the court finds that the attorney for the debtor violated rule 9011 of the Federal Rules of Bankruptcy Procedure, the court, on its own initiative or on the motion of a party in interest, in accordance with such procedures, may order—

(i) the assessment of an appropriate civil penalty against the attorney for the debtor; and

(ii) the payment of such civil penalty to the trustee, the United States trustee (or the bankruptcy administrator, if any).

(C) The signature of an attorney on a petition, pleading, or written motion shall constitute a certification that the attorney has—

(i) performed a reasonable investigation into the circumstances that gave rise to the petition, pleading, or written motion; and

(ii) determined that the petition, pleading, or written motion—

(I) is well grounded in fact; and

(II) is warranted by existing law or a good faith argument for the extension, modification, or reversal of existing law and does not constitute an abuse under paragraph (1).

(D) The signature of an attorney on the petition shall constitute a certification that the attorney has no knowledge after an inquiry that the information in the schedules filed with such petition is incorrect.

(5)(A) Except as provided in subparagraph (B) and subject to paragraph (6), the court, on its own initiative or on the motion of a party in interest, in accordance with the procedures described in rule 9011 of the Federal Rules of Bankruptcy Procedure, may award a debtor all reasonable costs (including reasonable attorneys' fees) in contesting a motion filed by a party in interest (other than a trustee or United States trustee (or bankruptcy administrator, if any)) under this subsection if—

(i) the court does not grant the motion; and

(ii) the court finds that—

(I) the position of the party that filed the motion violated rule 9011 of the Federal Rules of Bankruptcy Procedure; or

(II) the attorney (if any) who filed the motion did not comply with the requirements of clauses (i) and (ii) of paragraph (4)(C), and the motion was made solely for the purpose of coercing a debtor into waiving a right guaranteed to the debtor under this title.

(B) A small business that has a claim of an aggregate amount less than $1,000 shall not be subject to subparagraph (A)(ii)(I).

(C) For purposes of this paragraph—

(i) the term 'small business' means an unincorporated business, partnership, corporation, association, or organization that—

(I) has fewer than 25 full-time employees as determined on the date on which the motion is filed; and

(II) is engaged in commercial or business activity; and

(ii) the number of employees of a wholly owned subsidiary of a corporation includes the employees of—

(I) a parent corporation; and

(II) any other subsidiary corporation of the parent corporation.

(6) Only the judge or United States trustee (or bankruptcy administrator, if any) may file a motion under section 707(b), if the current monthly income of the debtor, or in a joint case, the debtor and the debtor's spouse, as of the date of the order for relief, when multiplied by 12, is equal to or less than—

(A) in the case of a debtor in a household of 1 person, the median family income of the applicable State for 1 earner;

(B) in the case of a debtor in a household of 2, 3, or 4 individuals, the highest median family income of the applicable State for a family of the same number or fewer individuals; or

(C) in the case of a debtor in a household exceeding 4 individuals, the highest median family income of the applicable State for a family of 4 or fewer individuals, plus $525 per month for each individual in excess of 4.

(7)(A) No judge, United States trustee (or bankruptcy administrator, if any), trustee, or other party in interest may file a motion under paragraph (2) if the current monthly income of the debtor, including a veteran (as that term is defined in section 101 of title 38), and the debtor's spouse combined, as of the date of the order for relief when multiplied by 12, is equal to or less than—

(i) in the case of a debtor in a household of 1 person, the median family income of the applicable State for 1 earner;

(ii) in the case of a debtor in a household of 2, 3, or 4 individuals, the highest median family income of the applicable State for a family of the same number or fewer individuals; or

(iii) in the case of a debtor in a household exceeding 4 individuals, the highest median family income of the applicable State for a family of 4 or fewer individuals, plus $525 per month for each individual in excess of 4.

(B) In a case that is not a joint case, current monthly income of the debtor's spouse shall not be considered for purposes of subparagraph (A) if—

(i)(I) the debtor and the debtor's spouse are separated under applicable nonbankruptcy law; or

(II) the debtor and the debtor's spouse are living separate and apart, other than for the purpose of evading subparagraph (A); and

(ii) the debtor files a statement under penalty of perjury—

(I) specifying that the debtor meets the requirement of subclause (I) or (II) of clause (i); and

(II) disclosing the aggregate, or best estimate of the aggregate, amount of any cash or money payments received from the debtor's spouse attributed to the debtor's current monthly income.

(c)(1) In this subsection—

(A) the term 'crime of violence' has the meaning given such term in section 16 of title 18; and

(B) the term 'drug trafficking crime' has the meaning given such term in section 924(c)(2) of title 18.

(2) Except as provided in paragraph (3), after notice and a hearing, the court, on a motion by the victim of a crime of violence or a drug trafficking crime, may when it is in the best interest of the victim dismiss a voluntary case filed under this chapter by a debtor who is an individual if such individual was convicted of such crime.

(3) The court may not dismiss a case under paragraph (2) if the debtor establishes by a preponderance of the evidence that the filing of a case under this chapter is necessary to satisfy a claim for a domestic support obligation.

SUBCHAPTER II—COLLECTION, LIQUIDATION, AND DISTRIBUTION OF THE ESTATE

§ 721. Authorization to operate business

The court may authorize the trustee to operate the business of the debtor for a limited period, if such operation is in the best interest of the estate and consistent with the orderly liquidation of the estate.

§ 722. Redemption

An individual debtor may, whether or not the debtor has waived the right to redeem under this section, redeem tangible personal property intended primarily for personal, family, or household use, from a lien securing a dischargeable consumer debt, if such property is exempted under section 522 of this title or has been abandoned under section 554 of this title, by paying the holder of such lien the amount of the allowed secured claim of such holder that is secured by such lien *in full at the time of redemption.*

§ 723. Rights of partnership trustee against general partners

(a) If there is a deficiency of property of the estate to pay in full all claims which are allowed in a case under this chapter concerning a partnership and with respect to which a general partner of the partnership is personally liable, the trustee shall have a claim against such general partner to the extent that under applicable nonbankruptcy law such general partner is personally liable for such deficiency.

(b) To the extent practicable, the trustee shall first seek recovery of such deficiency from any general partner in such partnership that is not a debtor in a case under this title. Pending determination of such deficiency, the court may order any such partner to provide the estate with indemnity for, or assurance of payment of, any deficiency recoverable from such partner, or not to dispose of property.

(c) Notwithstanding section 728(c) of this title, the trustee has a claim against the estate of each general partner in such partnership that is a debtor in a case under this title for the full amount of all claims of creditors allowed in the case concerning such partnership. Notwithstanding section 502 of this title, there shall not be allowed in such partner's case a claim against such partner on which both such partner and such partnership are liable, except to any extent that such claim is secured only by property of such partner and not by property of such partnership. The claim of the trustee under this subsection is entitled to distribution in such partner's case under section 726(a) of this title the same as any other claim of a kind specified in such section.

(d) If the aggregate that the trustee recovers from the estates of general partners under subsection (c) of this section is greater than any deficiency not recovered under subsection (b) of this section, the court, after notice and a hearing, shall determine an equitable distribution of the surplus so recovered, and the trustee shall distribute such surplus to the estates of the general partners in such partnership according to such determination.

§ 724. Treatment of certain liens

(a) The trustee may avoid a lien that secures a claim of a kind specified in section 726(a)(4) of this title.

(b) Property in which the estate has an interest and that is subject to a lien that is not avoidable under this title *(other than to the extent that there is a properly perfected unavoidable tax lien arising in connection with an ad valorem tax on real or personal property of the estate)* and that secures an allowed claim for a tax, or proceeds of such property, shall be distributed—

(1) first, to any holder of an allowed claim secured by a lien on such property that is not avoidable under this title and that is senior to such tax lien;

(2) second, to any holder of a claim of a kind specified in section 507(a)(1) *(except that such expenses, other than claims for wages, salaries, or commissions that arise after the date of the filing of the petition, shall be limited to expenses incurred under chapter 7 of this title and shall not include expenses incurred under chapter 11 of this title)*, 507(a)(2), 507(a)(3), 507(a)(4), 507(a)(5), 507(a)(6), or 507(a)(7) of this title, to the extent of the amount of such allowed tax claim that is secured by such tax lien;

(3) third, to the holder of such tax lien, to any extent that such holder's allowed tax claim that is secured by such tax lien exceeds any amount distributed under paragraph (2) of this subsection;

(4) fourth, to any holder of an allowed claim secured by a lien on such property that is not avoidable under this title and that is junior to such tax lien;

(5) fifth, to the holder of such tax lien, to the extent that such holder's allowed claim secured by such tax lien is not paid under paragraph (3) of this subsection; and

(6) sixth, to the estate.

(c) If more than one holder of a claim is entitled to distribution under a particular paragraph of subsection (b) of this section, distribution to such holders under such paragraph shall be in the same order as distribution to such holders would have been other than under this section.

(d) A statutory lien the priority of which is determined in the same manner as the priority of a tax lien under section 6323 of the Internal Revenue Code of 1986 shall be treated under subsection (b) of this section the same as if such lien were a tax lien.

(e) Before subordinating a tax lien on real or personal property of the estate, the trustee shall—

(1) exhaust the unencumbered assets of the estate; and

(2) in a manner consistent with section 506(c), recover from property securing an allowed secured claim the reasonable, necessary costs and expenses of preserving or disposing of such property.

(f) Notwithstanding the exclusion of ad valorem tax liens under this section and subject to the requirements of subsection (e), the following may be paid from property of the estate which secures a tax lien, or the proceeds of such property:

(1) Claims for wages, salaries, and commissions that are entitled to priority under section 507(a)(4).

(2) Claims for contributions to an employee benefit plan entitled to priority under section 507(a)(5).

§ 725. Disposition of certain property

After the commencement of a case under this chapter, but before final distribution of property of the estate under section 726 of this title, the trustee, after notice and a hearing, shall dispose of any property in which an entity other than the estate has an interest, such as a lien, and that has not been disposed of under another section of this title.

§ 726. Distribution of property of the estate

(a) Except as provided in section 510 of this title, property of the estate shall be distributed—

(1) first, in payment of claims of the kind specified in, and in the order specified in, section 507 of this title, proof of which is timely filed under section 501 of this title or tardily filed ~~before the date on which the trustee commences distribution under this section;~~ *on or before the earlier of—*

(A) the date that is 10 days after the mailing to creditors of the summary of the trustee's final report; or

(B) the date on which the trustee commences final distribution under this section;

(2) second, in payment of any allowed unsecured claim, other than a claim of a kind specified in paragraph (1), (3), or (4) of this subsection, proof of which is—

(A) timely filed under section 501(a) of this title;

(B) timely filed under section 501(b) or 501(c) of this title; or

(C) tardily filed under section 501(a) of this title, if—

(i) the creditor that holds such claim did not have notice or actual knowledge of the case in time for timely filing of a proof of such claim under section 501(a) of this title; and

(ii) proof of such claim is filed in time to permit payment of such claim;

(3) third, in payment of any allowed unsecured claim proof of which is tardily filed under section 501(a) of this title, other than a claim of the kind specified in paragraph (2)(C) of this subsection;

(4) fourth, in payment of any allowed claim, whether secured or unsecured, for any fine, penalty, or forfeiture, or for multiple, exemplary, or punitive damages, arising before the earlier of the order for relief or the appointment of a trustee, to the extent that such fine, penalty, forfeiture, or damages are not compensation for actual pecuniary loss suffered by the holder of such claim;

(5) fifth, in payment of interest at the legal rate from the date of the filing of the petition, on any claim paid under paragraph (1), (2), (3), or (4) of this subsection; and

(6) sixth, to the debtor.

(b) Payment on claims of a kind specified in paragraph (1), (2), (3), (4), (5), (6), (7), or (8) of section 507(a) of this title, or in paragraph (2), (3), (4), or (5) of subsection (a) of this section, shall be made pro rata among claims of the kind specified in each such particular paragraph, except that in a case that has been converted to this chapter under section ~~1009,~~ 1112, 1208, or 1307 of this title, a claim allowed under section 503(b) of this title incurred under this chapter after such conversion has priority over a claim allowed under section 503(b) of this title incurred under any other chapter of this title or under this chapter before such conversion and over any expenses of a custodian superseded under section 543 of this title.

(c) Notwithstanding subsections (a) and (b) of this section, if there is property of the kind specified in section 541(a)(2) of this title, or proceeds of such property, in the estate, such property or proceeds shall be segregated from other property of the estate, and such property or proceeds and other property of the estate shall be distributed as follows:

(1) Claims allowed under section 503 of this title shall be paid either from property of the kind specified in section 541(a)(2) of this title, or from other property of the estate, as the interest of justice requires.

(2) Allowed claims, other than claims allowed under section 503 of this title, shall be paid in the order specified in subsection (a) of this section, and, with respect to claims of a kind specified in a particular paragraph of section 507 of this title or subsection (a) of this section, in the following order and manner:

(A) First, community claims against the debtor or the debtor's spouse shall be paid from property of the kind specified in section 541(a)(2) of this title, except to the extent that such property is solely liable for debts of the debtor.

(B) Second, to the extent that community claims against the debtor are not paid under subparagraph (A) of this paragraph, such community claims shall be paid from property of the kind specified in section 541(a)(2) of this title that is solely liable for debts of the debtor.

(C) Third, to the extent that all claims against the debtor including community claims against the debtor are not paid under subparagraph (A) or (B) of this paragraph such claims shall be paid from property of the estate other than property of the kind specified in section 541(a)(2) of this title.

(D) Fourth, to the extent that community claims against the debtor or the debtor's spouse are not paid under subparagraph (A), (B), or (C) of this paragraph, such claims shall be paid from all remaining property of the estate.

§ 727. Discharge

(a) The court shall grant the debtor a discharge, unless—

(1) the debtor is not an individual;

(2) the debtor, with intent to hinder, delay, or defraud a creditor or an officer of the estate charged with custody of property under this title, has transferred, removed, destroyed, mutilated, or concealed, or has permitted to be transferred, removed, destroyed, mutilated, or concealed—

(A) property of the debtor, within one year before the date of the filing of the petition; or

(B) property of the estate, after the date of the filing of the petition;

(3) the debtor has concealed, destroyed, mutilated, falsified, or failed to keep or preserve any recorded information, including books, documents, records, and papers, from which the debtor's financial condition or business transactions might be ascertained, unless such act or failure to act was justified under all of the circumstances of the case;

(4) the debtor knowingly and fraudulently, in or in connection with the case—

(A) made a false oath or account;

(B) presented or used a false claim;

(C) gave, offered, received, or attempted to obtain money, property, or advantage, or a promise of money, property, or advantage, for acting or forbearing to act; or

(D) withheld from an officer of the estate entitled to possession under this title, any recorded information, including books, documents, records, and papers, relating to the debtor's property or financial affairs;

(5) the debtor has failed to explain satisfactorily, before determination of denial of discharge under this paragraph, any loss of assets or deficiency of assets to meet the debtor's liabilities;

(6) the debtor has refused, in the case—

(A) to obey any lawful order of the court, other than an order to respond to a material question or to testify;

(B) on the ground of privilege against self-incrimination, to respond to a material question approved by the court or to testify, after the debtor has been granted immunity with respect to the matter concerning which such privilege was invoked; or

(C) on a ground other than the properly invoked privilege against self-incrimination, to respond to a material question approved by the court or to testify;

(7) the debtor has committed any act specified in paragraph (2), (3), (4), (5), or (6) of this subsection, on or within one year before the date of the filing of the petition, or during the case, in connection with another case, under this title or under the Bankruptcy Act, concerning an insider;

(8) the debtor has been granted a discharge under this section, under section 1141 of this title, or under section 14, 371, or 476 of the Bankruptcy Act, in a case commenced within six-8 years before the date of the filing of the petition;

(9) the debtor has been granted a discharge under section 1228 or 1328 of this title, or under section 660 or 661 of the Bankruptcy Act, in a case commenced within six years before the date of the filing of the petition, unless payments under the plan in such case totaled at least—

(A) 100 percent of the allowed unsecured claims in such case; or

(B)(i) 70 percent of such claims; and

(ii) the plan was proposed by the debtor in good faith, and was the debtor's best effort;—or

(10) the court approves a written waiver of discharge executed by the debtor after the order for relief under this chapter.

(11) after filing the petition, the debtor failed to complete an instructional course concerning personal financial management described in section 111, except that this paragraph shall not apply with respect to a debtor who is a person described in section 109(h)(4) or who resides in a district for which the United States trustee (or the bankruptcy administrator, if any) determines that the approved instructional courses are not adequate to service the additional individuals who would otherwise be required to complete such instructional courses under this section (The United States trustee (or the bankruptcy administrator, if any) who makes a determination described in this paragraph shall review such determination not later than 1 year after the date of such determination, and not less frequently than annually thereafter.); or

(12) the court after notice and a hearing held not more than 10 days before the date of the entry of the order granting the discharge finds that there is reasonable cause to believe that—

(A) section 522(q)(1) may be applicable to the debtor; and

(B) there is pending any proceeding in which the debtor may be found guilty of a felony of the kind described in section 522(q)(1)(A) or liable for a debt of the kind described in section 522(q)(1)(B).

(b) Except as provided in section 523 of this title, a discharge under subsection (a) of this section discharges the debtor from all debts that arose before the date of the order for relief under this chapter, and any liability on a claim that is determined under section 502 of this title as if such claim had arisen before the commencement of the case, whether or not a proof of claim based on any such debt or liability is filed under section 501 of this title, and whether or not a claim based on any such debt or liability is allowed under section 502 of this title.

(c)(1) The trustee, a creditor, or the United States trustee may object to the granting of a discharge under subsection (a) of this section.

(2) On request of a party in interest, the court may order the trustee to examine the acts and conduct of the debtor to determine whether a ground exists for denial of discharge.

(d) On request of the trustee, a creditor, or the United States trustee, and after notice and a hearing, the court shall revoke a discharge granted under subsection (a) of this section if—

(1) such discharge was obtained through the fraud of the debtor, and the requesting party did not know of such fraud until after the granting of such discharge;

(2) the debtor acquired property that is property of the estate, or became entitled to acquire property that would be property of the estate, and knowingly and fraudulently failed to report the acquisition of or entitlement to such property, or to deliver or surrender such property to the trustee;

(3) the debtor committed an act specified in subsection (a)(6) of this section; *or*

(4) the debtor has failed to explain satisfactorily—

(A) a material misstatement in an audit referred to in section 586(f) of title 28; or

(B) a failure to make available for inspection all necessary accounts, papers, documents, financial records, files, and all other papers, things, or property belonging to the debtor that are requested for an audit referred to in section 586(f) of title 28.

(e) The trustee, a creditor, or the United States trustee may request a revocation of a discharge—

(1) under subsection (d)(1) of this section within one year after such discharge is granted; or

(2) under subsection (d)(2) or (d)(3) of this section before the later of—

(A) one year after the granting of such discharge; and

(B) the date the case is closed.

§ 728. Special tax provisions

~~(a) For the purposes of any State or local law imposing a tax on or measured by income, the taxable period of a debtor that is an individual shall terminate on the date of the order for relief under this chapter, unless the case was converted under section 1112 or 1208 of this title.~~

~~(b) Notwithstanding any State or local law imposing a tax on or measured by income, the trustee shall make tax returns of income for the estate of an individual debtor in a case under this chapter or for a debtor that is a corporation in a case under this chapter only if such estate or corporation has net taxable income for the entire period after the order for relief under this chapter during which the case is pending. If such entity has such income, or if the debtor is a partnership, then the trustee shall make and file a return of income for each taxable period during which the case was pending after the order for relief under this chapter.~~

~~(c) If there are pending a case under this chapter concerning a partnership and a case under this chapter concerning a partner in such partnership, a governmental unit's claim for any unpaid liability of such partner for a State or local tax on or measured by income, to the extent that such liability arose from the inclusion in such partner's taxable income of earnings of such partnership that were not withdrawn by such partner, is a claim only against such partnership.~~

~~(d) Notwithstanding section 541 of this title, if there are pending a case under this chapter concerning a partnership and a case under this chapter concerning a partner in such partnership, then any State or local tax refund or reduction of tax of such partner that would have otherwise been property of the estate of such partner under section 541 of this title—~~

~~(1) is property of the estate of such partnership to the extent that such tax refund or reduction of tax is fairly apportionable to losses sustained by such partnership and not reimbursed by such partner; and~~

~~(2) is otherwise property of the estate of such partner.~~

SUBCHAPTER III—STOCKBROKER LIQUIDATION

§ 741. Definitions for this subchapter

In this subchapter—

(1) "Commission" means Securities and Exchange Commission;

(2) "customer" includes—

(A) entity with whom a person deals as principal or agent and that has a claim against such person on account of a security received, acquired, or held by such person in the ordinary course of such person's business as a stockbroker, from or for the securities account or accounts of such entity—

(i) for safekeeping;

(ii) with a view to sale;

(iii) to cover a consummated sale;

(iv) pursuant to a purchase;

(v) as collateral under a security agreement; or

(vi) for the purpose of effecting registration of transfer; and

(B) entity that has a claim against a person arising out of—

(i) a sale or conversion of a security received, acquired, or held as specified in subparagraph (A) of this paragraph; or

(ii) a deposit of cash, a security, or other property with such person for the purpose of purchasing or selling a security;

(3) "customer name security" means security—

(A) held for the account of a customer on the date of the filing of the petition by or on behalf of the debtor;

(B) registered in such customer's name on such date or in the process of being so registered under instructions from the debtor; and

(C) not in a form transferable by delivery on such date;

(4) "customer property" means cash, security, or other property, and proceeds of such cash, security, or property, received, acquired, or held by or for the account of the debtor, from or for the securities account of a customer—

(A) including—

(i) property that was unlawfully converted from and that is the lawful property of the estate;

(ii) a security held as property of the debtor to the extent such security is necessary to meet a net equity claim of a customer based on a security of the same class and series of an issuer;

(iii) resources provided through the use or realization of a customer's debit cash balance or a debit item includible in the Formula for Determination of Reserve Requirement for Brokers and Dealers as promulgated by the Commission under the Securities Exchange Act of 1934; and

(iv) other property of the debtor that any applicable law, rule, or regulation requires to be set aside or held for the benefit of a customer, unless including such property as customer property would not significantly increase customer property; but

(B) not including—

(i) a customer name security delivered to or reclaimed by a customer under section 751 of this title; or

(ii) property to the extent that a customer does not have a claim against the debtor based on such property;

(5) "margin payment" means payment or deposit of cash, a security, or other property, that is commonly known to the securities trade as original margin, initial margin, maintenance margin, or variation margin, or as a mark-to-market payment, or that secures an obligation of a participant in a securities clearing agency;

(6) "net equity" means, with respect to all accounts of a customer that such customer has in the same capacity—

(A)(i) aggregate dollar balance that would remain in such accounts after the liquidation, by sale or purchase, at the time of the filing of the petition, of all securities positions in all such accounts, except any customer name securities of such customer; minus

(ii) any claim of the debtor against such customer in such capacity that would have been owing immediately after such liquidation; plus

(B) any payment by such customer to the trustee, within 60 days after notice under section 342 of this title, of any business related claim of the debtor against such customer in such capacity;

~~(7) "securities contract" means contract for the purchase, sale, or loan of a security, including an option for the purchase or sale of a security, certificate of deposit, or group or index of securities (including any interest therein or based on the value thereof), or any option entered into on a national securities exchange relating to foreign currencies, or the guarantee of any settlement of cash or securities by or to a securities clearing agency;~~ *(7) 'securities contract'—*

(A) means—

(i) a contract for the purchase, sale, or loan of a security, a certificate of deposit, a mortgage loan or any interest in a mortgage loan, a group or index of securities, certificates of deposit, or mortgage loans or interests therein (including an interest therein or based on the value thereof), or option on any of the foregoing, including an option to purchase or sell any such security, certificate of deposit, mortgage loan, interest, group or index, or option, and including any repurchase or reverse repurchase transaction on any such security, certificate of deposit, mortgage loan, interest, group or index, or option;

(ii) any option entered into on a national securities exchange relating to foreign currencies;

(iii) the guarantee by or to any securities clearing agency of a settlement of cash, securities, certificates of deposit, mortgage loans or interests

therein, group or index of securities, or mortgage loans or interests therein (including any interest therein or based on the value thereof), or option on any of the foregoing, including an option to purchase or sell any such security, certificate of deposit, mortgage loan, interest, group or index, or option;

(iv) any margin loan;

(v) any other agreement or transaction that is similar to an agreement or transaction referred to in this subparagraph;

(vi) any combination of the agreements or transactions referred to in this subparagraph;

(vii) any option to enter into any agreement or transaction referred to in this subparagraph;

(viii) a master agreement that provides for an agreement or transaction referred to in clause (i), (ii), (iii), (iv), (v), (vi), or (vii), together with all supplements to any such master agreement, without regard to whether the master agreement provides for an agreement or transaction that is not a securities contract under this subparagraph, except that such master agreement shall be considered to be a securities contract under this sub-paragraph only with respect to each agreement or transaction under such master agreement that is referred to in clause (i), (ii), (iii), (iv), (v), (vi), or (vii); or

(ix) any security agreement or arrangement or other credit enhancement related to any agreement or transaction referred to in this subparagraph, including any guarantee or reimbursement obligation by or to a stockbroker, securities clearing agency, financial institution, or financial participant in connection with any agreement or transaction referred to in this subparagraph, but not to exceed the damages in connection with any such agreement or transaction, measured in accordance with section 562; and

(B) does not include any purchase, sale, or repurchase obligation under a participation in a commercial mortgage loan;

(8) "settlement payment" means a preliminary settlement payment, a partial settlement payment, an interim settlement payment, a settlement payment on account, a final settlement payment, or any other similar payment commonly used in the securities trade; and

(9) "SIPC" means Securities Investor Protection Corporation.

§ 742. Effect of section 362 of this title in this subchapter

Notwithstanding section 362 of this title, SIPC may file an application for a protective decree under the Securities Investor Protection Act of 1970. The filing of such application stays all proceedings in the case under this title unless and until such application is dismissed. If SIPC completes the liquidation of the debtor, then the court shall dismiss the case.

§ 743. Notice

The clerk shall give the notice required by section 342 of this title to SIPC and to the Commission.

§ 744. Executory contracts

Notwithstanding section 365(d) (1) of this title, the trustee shall assume or reject, under section 365 of this title, any executory contract of the debtor for the purchase or sale of a security in the ordinary course of the debtor's business, within a reasonable time after the date of the order for relief, but not to exceed 30 days. If the trustee does not assume such a contract within such time, such contract is rejected.

§ 745. Treatment of accounts

(a) Accounts held by the debtor for a particular customer in separate capacities shall be treated as accounts of separate customers.

(b) If a stockbroker or a bank holds a customer net equity claim against the debtor that arose out of a transaction for a customer of such stockbroker or bank, each such customer of such stockbroker or bank shall be treated as a separate customer of the debtor.

(c) Each trustee's account specified as such on the debtor's books, and supported by a trust deed filed with, and qualified as such by, the Internal Revenue Service, and under the Internal Revenue Code of 1986, shall be treated as a separate customer account for each beneficiary under such trustee account.

§ 746. Extent of customer claims

(a) If, after the date of the filing of the petition, an entity enters into a transaction with the debtor, in a manner that would have made such entity a customer had such transaction occurred before the date of the filing of the petition, and such transaction was entered into by such entity in good faith and before the qualification under section 322 of this title of a trustee, such entity shall be deemed a customer, and the date of such transaction shall be deemed to be the date of the filing of the petition for the purpose of determining such entity's net equity.

(b) An entity does not have a claim as a customer to the extent that such entity transferred to the debtor cash or a security that, by contract, agreement, understanding, or operation of law, is—

(1) part of the capital of the debtor; or

(2) subordinated to the claims of any or all creditors.

§ 747. Subordination of certain customer claims

Except as provided in section 510 of this title, unless all other customer net equity claims have been paid in full, the trustee may not pay in full or pay in part, directly or indirectly, any net equity claim of a customer that was, on the date the transaction giving rise to such claim occurred—

(1) an insider;

(2) a beneficial owner of at least five percent of any class of equity securities of the debtor, other than—

(A) nonconvertible stock having fixed preferential dividend and liquidation rights; or

(B) interests of limited partners in a limited partnership;

(3) a limited partner with a participation of at least five percent in the net assets or net profits of the debtor; or

(4) an entity that, directly or indirectly, through agreement or otherwise, exercised or had the power to exercise control over the management or policies of the debtor.

§ 748. Reduction of securities to money

As soon as practicable after the date of the order for relief, the trustee shall reduce to money, consistent with good market practice, all securities held as property of the estate, except for customer name securities delivered or reclaimed under section 751 of this title.

§ 749. Voidable transfers

(a) Except as otherwise provided in this section, any transfer of property that, but for such transfer, would have been customer property, may be avoided by the trustee, and such property shall be treated as customer property, if and to the extent that the trustee avoids such transfer under section 544, 545, 547, 548, or 549 of this title. For the purpose of such sections, the property so transferred shall be deemed to have been property of the debtor and, if such transfer was made to a customer or for a customer's benefit, such customer shall be deemed, for the purposes of this section, to have been a creditor.

(b) Notwithstanding sections 544, 545, 547, 548, and 549 of this title, the trustee may not avoid a transfer made before five days after the order for relief if such transfer is approved by the Commission by rule or order, either before or after such transfer, and if such transfer is—

(1) a transfer of a securities contract entered into or carried by or through the debtor on behalf of a customer, and of any cash, security, or other property margining or securing such securities contract; or

(2) the liquidation of a securities contract entered into or carried by or through the debtor on behalf of a customer.

§ 750. Distribution of securities

The trustee may not distribute a security except under section 751 of this title.

§ 751. Customer name securities

The trustee shall deliver any customer name security to or on behalf of the customer entitled to such security, unless such customer has a negative net equity. With the approval of the trustee, a customer may reclaim a customer name security after payment to the trustee, within such period as the trustee allows, of any claim of the debtor against such customer to the extent that such customer will not have a negative net equity after such payment.

§ 752. Customer property

(a) The trustee shall distribute customer property ratably to customers on the basis and to the extent of such customers' allowed net equity claims and in priority to all other claims, except claims of the kind specified in section 507(a)(~~1~~2) of this title that are attributable to the administration of such customer property.

(b)(1) The trustee shall distribute customer property in excess of that distributed under subsection (a) of this section in accordance with section 726 of this title.

(2) Except as provided in section 510 of this title, if a customer is not paid the full amount of such customer's allowed net equity claim from customer property, the unpaid portion of such claim is a claim entitled to distribution under section 726 of this title.

(c) Any cash or security remaining after the liquidation of a security interest created under a security agreement made by the debtor, excluding property excluded under section 741(4)(B) of this title, shall be apportioned between the general estate and customer property in the same proportion as the general estate of the debtor and customer property were subject to such security interest.

§ 753. Stockbroker liquidation and forward contract merchants, commodity brokers, stockbrokers, financial institutions, financial participants, securities clearing agencies, swap participants, repo participants, and master netting agreement participants

Notwithstanding any other provision of this title, the exercise of rights by a forward contract merchant, commodity broker, stockbroker, financial institution, financial participant, securities clearing agency, swap participant, repo participant, or master netting agreement participant under this title shall not affect the priority of any unsecured claim it may have after the exercise of such rights.

SUBCHAPTER IV—COMMODITY BROKER LIQUIDATION

§ 761. Definitions for this subchapter

In this subchapter—

(1) "Act" means Commodity Exchange Act;

(2) "clearing organization" means a derivatives clearing organization registered under the Act;

(3) "Commission" means Commodity Futures Trading Commission;

(4) "commodity contract" means—

(A) with respect to a futures commission merchant, contract for the purchase or sale of a commodity for future delivery on, or subject to the rules of, a contract market or board of trade;

(B) with respect to a foreign futures commission merchant, foreign future;

(C) with respect to a leverage transaction merchant, leverage transaction;

(D) with respect to a clearing organization, contract for the purchase or sale of a commodity for future delivery on, or subject to the rules of, a contract market or board of trade that is cleared by such clearing organization, or commodity option traded on, or subject to the rules of, a contract market or board of trade that is cleared by such clearing organization; ~~or~~

(E) with respect to a commodity options dealer, commodity option;

(F) any other agreement or transaction that is similar to an agreement or transaction referred to in this paragraph;

(G) any combination of the agreements or transactions referred to in this paragraph;

(H) any option to enter into an agreement or transaction referred to in this paragraph;

(I) a master agreement that provides for an agreement or transaction referred to in subparagraph (A), (B), (C), (D), (E), (F), (G), or (H), together with all supplements to such master agreement, without regard to whether the master agreement provides for an agreement or transaction that is not a commodity contract under this paragraph, except that the master agreement shall be considered to be a commodity contract under this paragraph only with respect to each agreement or transaction under the master agreement that is referred to in subparagraph (A), (B), (C), (D), (E), (F), (G), or (H); or

(J) any security agreement or arrangement or other credit enhancement related to any agreement or transaction referred to in this paragraph, including any guarantee or reimbursement obligation by or to a commodity broker or financial participant in connection with any agreement or transaction referred to in this paragraph, but not to exceed the damages in connection with any such agreement or transaction, measured in accordance with section 562;

(5) "commodity option" means agreement or transaction subject to regulation under section 4c(b) of the Act;

(6) "commodity options dealer" means person that extends credit to, or that accepts cash, a security, or other property from, a customer of such person for the purchase or sale of an interest in a commodity option;

(7) "contract market" means a registered entity;

(8) "contract of sale", "commodity", "derivatives clearing organization" , "future delivery", "board of trade", "registered entity", and "futures commission merchant" have the meanings assigned to those terms in the Act;

(9) "customer" means—

(A) with respect to a futures commission merchant—

(i) entity for or with whom such futures commission merchant deals and that holds a claim against such futures commission merchant on account of a commodity contract made, received, acquired, or held by or through such futures commission merchant in the ordinary course of such futures commission merchant's business as a futures commission merchant from or for the commodity futures account of such entity; or

(ii) entity that holds a claim against such futures commission merchant arising out of—

(I) the making, liquidation, or change in the value of a commodity contract of a kind specified in clause (i) of this subparagraph;

(II) a deposit or payment of cash, a security, or other property with such futures commission merchant for the purpose of making or margining such a commodity contract; or

(III) the making or taking of delivery on such a commodity contract;

(B) with respect to a foreign futures commission merchant—

(i) entity for or with whom such foreign futures commission merchant deals and that holds a claim against such foreign futures commission merchant on account of a commodity contract made, received, acquired, or held by or through such foreign futures commission merchant in the ordinary course of such foreign futures commission merchant's business as a foreign futures commission merchant from or for the foreign futures account of such entity; or

(ii) entity that holds a claim against such foreign futures commission merchant arising out of—

(I) the making, liquidation, or change in value of a commodity contract of a kind specified in clause (i) of this subparagraph;

(II) a deposit or payment of cash, a security, or other property with such foreign futures commission merchant for the purpose of making or margining such a commodity contract; or

(III) the making or taking of delivery on such a commodity contract;

(C) with respect to a leverage transaction merchant—

(i) entity for or with whom such leverage transaction merchant deals and that holds a claim against such leverage transaction merchant on account of a commodity contract engaged in by or with such leverage transaction merchant in the ordinary course of such leverage transaction merchant's business as a leverage transaction merchant from or for the leverage account of such entity; or

(ii) entity that holds a claim against such leverage transaction merchant arising out of—

(I) the making, liquidation, or change in value of a commodity contract of a kind specified in clause (i) of this subparagraph;

(II) a deposit or payment of cash, a security, or other property with such leverage transaction merchant for the purpose of entering into or margining such a commodity contract; or

(III) the making or taking of delivery on such a commodity contract;

(D) with respect to a clearing organization, clearing member of such clearing organization with whom such clearing organization deals and that holds a claim against such clearing organization on account of cash, a security, or other property received by such clearing organization to margin, guarantee, or secure a commodity contract in such clearing member's proprietary account or customers' account; or

(E) with respect to a commodity options dealer—

(i) entity for or with whom such commodity options dealer deals and that holds a claim on account of a commodity contract made, received, acquired, or held by or through such commodity options dealer in the ordinary course of such commodity options dealer's business as a commodity options dealer from or for the commodity options account of such entity; or

(ii) entity that holds a claim against such commodity options dealer arising out of—

(I) the making of, liquidation of, exercise of, or a change in value of, a commodity contract of a kind specified in clause (i) of this subparagraph; or

(II) a deposit or payment of cash, a security, or other property with such commodity options dealer for the purpose of making, exercising, or margining such a commodity contract;

(10) "customer property" means cash, a security, or other property, or proceeds of such cash, security, or property, received, acquired, or held by or for the account of the debtor, from or for the account of a customer—

(A) including—

(i) property received, acquired, or held to margin, guarantee, secure, purchase, or sell a commodity contract;

(ii) profits or contractual or other rights accruing to a customer as a result of a commodity contract;

(iii) an open commodity contract;

(iv) specifically identifiable customer property;

(v) warehouse receipt or other document held by the debtor evidencing ownership of or title to property to be delivered to fulfill a commodity contract from or for the account of a customer;

(vi) cash, a security, or other property received by the debtor as payment for a commodity to be delivered to fulfill a commodity contract from or for the account of a customer;

(vii) a security held as property of the debtor to the extent such security is necessary to meet a net equity claim based on a security of the same class and series of an issuer;

(viii) property that was unlawfully converted from and that is the lawful property of the estate; and

(ix) other property of the debtor that any applicable law, rule, or regulation requires to be set aside or held for the benefit of a customer, unless including such property as customer property would not significantly increase customer property; but

(B) not including property to the extent that a customer does not have a claim against the debtor based on such property;

(11) "foreign future" means contract for the purchase or sale of a commodity for future delivery on, or subject to the rules of, a board of trade outside the United States;

(12) "foreign futures commission merchant" means entity engaged in soliciting or accepting orders for the purchase or sale of a foreign future or that, in connection with such a solicitation or acceptance, accepts cash, a security, or other property, or extends credit to margin, guarantee, or secure any trade or contract that results from such a solicitation or acceptance;

(13) "leverage transaction" means agreement that is subject to regulation under section 19 of the Commodity Exchange Act, and that is commonly known to the commodities trade as a margin account, margin contract, leverage account, or leverage contract;

(14) "leverage transaction merchant" means person in the business of engaging in leverage transactions;

(15) "margin payment" means payment or deposit of cash, a security, or other property, that is commonly known to the commodities trade as original margin, initial margin, maintenance margin, or variation margin, including mark-to-market payments, settlement payments, variation payments, daily settlement payments, and final settlement payments made as adjustments to settlement prices;

(16) "member property" means customer property received, acquired, or held by or for the account of a debtor that is a clearing organization, from or for the proprietary account of a customer that is a clearing member of the debtor; and

(17) "net equity" means, subject to such rules and regulations as the Commission promulgates under the Act, with respect to the aggregate of all of a customer's accounts that such customer has in the same capacity—

(A) the balance remaining in such customer's accounts immediately after—

(i) all commodity contracts of such customer have been transferred, liquidated, or become identified for delivery; and

(ii) all obligations of such customer in such capacity to the debtor have been offset; plus

(B) the value, as of the date of return under section 766 of this title, of any specifically identifiable customer property actually returned to such customer before the date specified in subparagraph (A) of this paragraph; plus

(C) the value, as of the date of transfer, of—

(i) any commodity contract to which such customer is entitled that is transferred to another person under section 766 of this title; and

(ii) any cash, security, or other property of such customer transferred to such other person under section 766 of this title to margin or secure such transferred commodity contract.

§ 762. Notice to the Commission and right to be heard

(a) The clerk shall give the notice required by section 342 of this title to the Commission.

(b) The Commission may raise and may appear and be heard on any issue in a case under this chapter.

§ 763. Treatment of accounts

(a) Accounts held by the debtor for a particular customer in separate capacities shall be treated as accounts of separate customers.

(b) A member of a clearing organization shall be deemed to hold such member's proprietary account in a separate capacity from such member's customers' account.

(c) The net equity in a customer's account may not be offset against the net equity in the account of any other customer.

§ 764. Voidable transfers

(a) Except as otherwise provided in this section, any transfer by the debtor of property that, but for such transfer, would have been customer property, may be avoided by the trustee, and such property shall be treated as customer property, if and to the extent that the trustee avoids such transfer under section 544, 545, 547, 548, 549, or 724(a) of this title. For the purpose of such sections, the property so transferred shall be deemed to have been property of the debtor, and, if such transfer was made to a customer or for a customer's benefit, such customer shall be deemed, for the purposes of this section, to have been a creditor.

(b) Notwithstanding sections 544, 545, 547, 548, 549, and 724(a) of this title, the trustee may not avoid a transfer made before five days after the order for relief, if such transfer is approved by the Commission by rule or order, either before or after such transfer, and if such transfer is—

(1) a transfer of a commodity contract entered into or carried by or through the debtor on behalf of a customer, and of any cash, securities, or other property margining or securing such commodity contract; or

(2) the liquidation of a commodity contract entered into or carried by or through the debtor on behalf of a customer.

§ 765. Customer instructions

(a) The notice required by section 342 of this title to customers shall instruct each customer—

(1) to file a proof of such customer's claim promptly, and to specify in such claim any specifically identifiable security, property, or commodity contract; and

(2) to instruct the trustee of such customer's desired disposition, including transfer under section 766 of this title or liquidation, of any commodity contract specifically identified to such customer.

(b) The trustee shall comply, to the extent practicable, with any instruction received from a customer regarding such customer's desired disposition of any commodity contract specifically identified to such customer. If the trustee has transferred, under section 766 of this title, such a commodity contract, the trustee shall transmit any such instruction to the commodity broker to whom such commodity contract was so transferred.

§ 766. Treatment of customer property

(a) The trustee shall answer all margin calls with respect to a specifically identifiable commodity contract of a customer until such time as the trustee returns or transfers such commodity contract, but the trustee may not make a margin payment that has the effect of a distribution to such customer of more than that to which such customer is entitled under subsection (h) or (i) of this section.

(b) The trustee shall prevent any open commodity contract from remaining open after the last day of trading in such commodity contract, or into the first day on which notice of intent to deliver on such commodity contract may be tendered, whichever occurs first. With respect to any commodity contract that has remained open after the last day of trading in such commodity contract or with respect to which delivery must be made or accepted under the rules of the contract market on which such commodity contract was made, the trustee may operate the business of the debtor for the purpose of—

(1) accepting or making tender of notice of intent to deliver the physical commodity underlying such commodity contract;

(2) facilitating delivery of such commodity; or

(3) disposing of such commodity if a party to such commodity contract defaults.

(c) The trustee shall return promptly to a customer any specifically identifiable security, property, or commodity contract to which such customer is entitled, or shall transfer, on such customer's behalf, such security, property, or commodity contract to a commodity broker that is not a debtor under this title, subject to such rules or regulations as the Commission may prescribe, to the extent that the value of such security, property, or commodity contract does not exceed the amount to which such customer would be entitled under subsection (h) or (i) of this section if such security, property, or commodity contract were not returned or transferred under this subsection.

(d) If the value of a specifically identifiable security, property, or commodity contract exceeds the amount to which the customer of the debtor is entitled under subsection (h) or (i) of this section, then such customer to whom such security, property, or commodity contract is specifically identified may deposit cash with the trustee equal to the difference between the value of such security, property, or commodity contract and such amount, and the trustee then shall—

(1) return promptly such security, property, or commodity contract to such customer; or

(2) transfer, on such customer's behalf, such security, property, or commodity contract to a commodity broker that is not a debtor under this title, subject to such rules or regulations as the Commission may prescribe.

(e) Subject to subsection (b) of this section, the trustee shall liquidate any commodity contract that—

(1) is identified to a particular customer and with respect to which such customer has not timely instructed the trustee as to the desired disposition of such commodity contract;

(2) cannot be transferred under subsection (c) of this section; or

(3) cannot be identified to a particular customer.

(f) As soon as practicable after the commencement of the case, the trustee shall reduce to money, consistent with good market practice, all securities and other property, other than commodity contracts, held as property of the estate, except for specifically identifiable securities or property distributable under subsection (h) or (i) of this section.

(g) The trustee may not distribute a security or other property except under subsection (h) or (i) of this section.

(h) Except as provided in subsection (b) of this section, the trustee shall distribute customer property ratably to customers on the basis and to the extent of such customers' allowed net equity claims, and in priority to all other claims, except claims of a kind specified in section 507(a)(2+) of this title that are attributable to the administration of customer property. Such distribution shall be in the form of—

(1) cash;

(2) the return or transfer, under subsection (c) or (d) of this section, of specifically identifiable customer securities, property, or commodity contracts; or

(3) payment of margin calls under subsection (a) of this section.

Notwithstanding any other provision of this subsection, a customer net equity claim based on a proprietary account, as defined by Commission rule, regulation, or order, may not be paid either in whole or in part, directly or indirectly, out of customer property unless all other customer net equity claims have been paid in full.

(i) If the debtor is a clearing organization, the trustee shall distribute—

(1) customer property, other than member property, ratably to customers on the basis and to the extent of such customers' allowed net equity claims based on such customers' accounts other than proprietary accounts, and in priority to all other claims, except claims of a kind specified in section 507(a)(2‡) of this title that are attributable to the administration of such customer property; and

(2) member property ratably to customers on the basis and to the extent of such customers' allowed net equity claims based on such customers' proprietary accounts, and in priority to all other claims, except claims of a kind specified in section 507(a)(2‡) of this title that are attributable to the administration of member property or customer property.

(j)(1) The trustee shall distribute customer property in excess of that distributed under subsection (h) or (i) of this section in accordance with section 726 of this title.

(2) Except as provided in section 510 of this title, if a customer is not paid the full amount of such customer's allowed net equity claim from customer property, the unpaid portion of such claim is a claim entitled to distribution under section 726 of this title.

§ 767. Commodity broker liquidation and forward contract merchants, commodity brokers, stockbrokers, financial institutions, financial participants, securities clearing agencies, swap participants, repo participants, and master netting agreement participants

Notwithstanding any other provision of this title, the exercise of rights by a forward contract merchant, commodity broker, stockbroker, financial institution, financial participant, securities clearing agency, swap participant, repo participant, or master netting agreement participant under this title shall not affect the priority of any unsecured claim it may have after the exercise of such rights.

SUBCHAPTER V—CLEARING BANK LIQUIDATION

§ 781. Definitions

For purposes of this subchapter, the following definitions shall apply:

(1) Board.—The term "Board" means the Board of Governors of the Federal Reserve System.

(2) Depository institution.—The term "depository institution" has the same meaning as in section 3 of the Federal Deposit Insurance Act.

(3) Clearing bank.—The term "clearing bank" means an uninsured State member bank, or a corporation organized under section 25A of the Federal Reserve Act, which operates, or operates as, a multilateral clearing organization pursuant to section 409 of the Federal Deposit Insurance Corporation Improvement Act of 1991.

§ 782. Selection of trustee

(a) In general.—

(1) Appointment.—Notwithstanding any other provision of this title, the conservator or receiver who files the petition shall be the trustee under this chapter, unless the Board designates an alternative trustee.

(2) Successor.—The Board may designate a successor trustee if required.

(b) Authority of trustee.—Whenever the Board appoints or designates a trustee, chapter 3 and sections 704 and 705 of this title shall apply to the Board in the same way and to the same extent that they apply to a United States trustee.

§ 783. Additional powers of trustee

(a) Distribution of property not of the estate.—The trustee under this subchapter has power to distribute property not of the estate, including distributions to customers that are mandated by subchapters III and IV of this chapter.

(b) Disposition of institution.—The trustee under this subchapter may, after notice and a hearing—

(1) sell the clearing bank to a depository institution or consortium of depository institutions (which consortium may agree on the allocation of the clearing bank among the consortium);

(2) merge the clearing bank with a depository institution;

(3) transfer contracts to the same extent as could a receiver for a depository institution under paragraphs (9) and (10) of section 11(e) of the Federal Deposit Insurance Act;

(4) transfer assets or liabilities to a depository institution; and

(5) transfer assets and liabilities to a bridge bank as provided in paragraphs (1), (3)(A), (5), and (6) of section 11(n) of the Federal Deposit Insurance Act, paragraphs (9) through (13) of such section, and subparagraphs (A) through (H) and subparagraph (K) of paragraph (4) of such section 11(n), except that—

(A) the bridge bank to which such assets or liabilities are transferred shall be treated as a clearing bank for the purpose of this subsection; and

(B) any references in any such provision of law to the Federal Deposit Insurance Corporation shall be construed to be references to the appointing agency and that references to deposit insurance shall be omitted.

(c) Certain transfers included.—Any reference in this section to transfers of liabilities includes a ratable transfer of liabilities within a priority class.

§ 784. Right to be heard

The Board or a Federal reserve bank (in the case of a clearing bank that is a member of that bank) may raise and may appear and be heard on any issue in a case under this subchapter.

CHAPTER 9—ADJUSTMENT OF DEBTS OF A MUNICIPALITY

SUBCHAPTER I—GENERAL PROVISIONS

§ 901. Applicability of other sections of this title

 (a) Sections 301, 344, 347(b), 349, 350(b), 361, 362, 364(c), 364(d), 364(e), 364(f), 365, 366, 501, 502, 503, 504, 506, 507(a)(2+), 509, 510, 524(a)(1), 524(a)(2), 544, 545, 546, 547, 548, 549(a), 549(c), 549(d), 550, 551, 552, 553, 555, 556, 557, 559, 560, 561, 562, 1102, 1103, 1109, 1111(b), 1122, 1123(a)(1), 1123(a)(2), 1123(a)(3), 1123(a)(4), 1123(a)(5), 1123(b), 1123(d), 1124, 1125, 1126(a), 1126(b), 1126(c), 1126(e), 1126(f), 1126(g), 1127(d), 1128, 1129(a)(2), 1129(a)(3), 1129(a)(6), 1129(a)(8), 1129(a)(10), 1129(b)(1), 1129(b)(2)(A), 1129(b)(2)(B), 1142(b), 1143, 1144, and 1145 of this title apply in a case under this chapter.

 (b) A term used in a section of this title made applicable in a case under this chapter by subsection (a) of this section or section 103(e) of this title has the meaning defined for such term for the purpose of such applicable section, unless such term is otherwise defined in section 902 of this title.

 (c) A section made applicable in a case under this chapter by subsection (a) of this section that is operative if the business of the debtor is authorized to be operated is operative in a case under this chapter.

§ 902. Definitions for this chapter

In this chapter—

 (1) "property of the estate", when used in a section that is made applicable in a case under this chapter by section 103(e) or 901 of this title, means property of the debtor;

 (2) "special revenues" means—

   (A) receipts derived from the ownership, operation, or disposition of projects or systems of the debtor that are primarily used or intended to be used primarily to provide transportation, utility, or other services, including the proceeds of borrowings to finance the projects or systems;

   (B) special excise taxes imposed on particular activities or transactions;

   (C) incremental tax receipts from the benefited area in the case of tax-increment financing;

   (D) other revenues or receipts derived from particular functions of the debtor, whether or not the debtor has other functions; or

   (E) taxes specifically levied to finance one or more projects or systems, excluding receipts from general property, sales, or income taxes (other than tax-increment financing) levied to finance the general purposes of the debtor;

(3) "special tax payer" means record owner or holder of legal or equitable title to real property against which a special assessment or special tax has been levied the proceeds of which are the sole source of payment of an obligation issued by the debtor to defray the cost of an improvement relating to such real property;

(4) "special tax payer affected by the plan" means special tax payer with respect to whose real property the plan proposes to increase the proportion of special assessments or special taxes referred to in paragraph (2) of this section assessed against such real property; and

(5) "trustee", when used in a section that is made applicable in a case under this chapter by section 103(e) or 901 of this title, means debtor, except as provided in section 926 of this title.

§ 903. Reservation of State power to control municipalities

This chapter does not limit or impair the power of a State to control, by legislation or otherwise, a municipality of or in such State in the exercise of the political or governmental powers of such municipality, including expenditures for such exercise, but—

(1) a State law prescribing a method of composition of indebtedness of such municipality may not bind any creditor that does not consent to such composition; and

(2) a judgment entered under such a law may not bind a creditor that does not consent to such composition.

§ 904. Limitation on jurisdiction and powers of court

Notwithstanding any power of the court, unless the debtor consents or the plan so provides, the court may not, by any stay, order, or decree, in the case or otherwise, interfere with—

(1) any of the political or governmental powers of the debtor;

(2) any of the property or revenues of the debtor; or

(3) the debtor's use or enjoyment of any income-producing property.

SUBCHAPTER II—ADMINISTRATION

§ 921. Petition and proceedings relating to petition

(a) Notwithstanding sections 109(d) and 301 of this title, a case under this chapter concerning an unincorporated tax or special assessment district that does not have such district's own officials is commenced by the filing under section 301 of this title of a petition under this chapter by such district's governing authority or the board or body having authority to levy taxes or assessments to meet the obligations of such district.

(b) The chief judge of the court of appeals for the circuit embracing the district in which the case is commenced shall designate the bankruptcy judge to conduct the case.

(c) After any objection to the petition, the court, after notice and a hearing, may dismiss the petition if the debtor did not file the petition in good faith or if the petition does not meet the requirements of this title.

(d) If the petition is not dismissed under subsection (c) of this section, the court shall order relief under this chapter *notwithstanding section 301(b)*.

(e) The court may not, on account of an appeal from an order for relief, delay any proceeding under this chapter in the case in which the appeal is being taken; nor shall any court order a stay of such proceeding pending such appeal. The reversal on appeal of a finding of jurisdiction does not affect the validity of any debt incurred that is authorized by the court under section 364(c) or 364(d) of this title.

§ 922. Automatic stay of enforcement of claims against the debtor

(a) A petition filed under this chapter operates as a stay, in addition to the stay provided by section 362 of this title, applicable to all entities, of—

(1) the commencement or continuation, including the issuance or employment of process, of a judicial, administrative, or other action or proceeding against an officer or inhabitant of the debtor that seeks to enforce a claim against the debtor; and

(2) the enforcement of a lien on or arising out of taxes or assessments owed to the debtor.

(b) Subsections (c), (d), (e), (f), and (g) of section 362 of this title apply to a stay under subsection (a) of this section the same as such subsections apply to a stay under section 362(a) of this title.

(c) If the debtor provides, under section 362, 364, or 922 of this title, adequate protection of the interest of the holder of a claim secured by a lien on property of the debtor and if, notwithstanding such protection such creditor has a claim arising from the stay of action against such property under section 362 or 922 of this title or from the granting of a lien under section 364(d) of this title, then such claim shall be allowable as an administrative expense under section 503(b) of this title.

(d) Notwithstanding section 362 of this title and subsection (a) of this section, a petition filed under this chapter does not operate as a stay of application of pledged special revenues in a manner consistent with section 927 of this title to payment of indebtedness secured by such revenues.

§ 923. NOTICE

There shall be given notice of the commencement of a case under this chapter, notice of an order for relief under this chapter, and notice of the dismissal of a case under this chapter. Such notice shall also be published at least once a week for three successive weeks in at least one newspaper of general circulation published within the district in which the case is commenced, and in such other newspaper having a general circulation among bond dealers and bondholders as the court designates.

§ 924. List of creditors

The debtor shall file a list of creditors.

§ 925. Effect of list of claims

A proof of claim is deemed filed under section 501 of this title for any claim that appears in the list filed under section 924 of this title, except a claim that is listed as disputed, contingent, or unliquidated.

§ 926. Avoiding powers

(a) If the debtor refuses to pursue a cause of action under section 544, 545, 547, 548, 549(a), or 550 of this title, then on request of a creditor, the court may appoint a trustee to pursue such cause of action.

(b) A transfer of property of the debtor to or for the benefit of any holder of a bond or note, on account of such bond or note, may not be avoided under section 547 of this title.

§ 927. Limitation on recourse

The holder of a claim payable solely from special revenues of the debtor under applicable nonbankruptcy law shall not be treated as having recourse against the debtor on account of such claim pursuant to section 1111(b) of this title.

§ 928. Post petition effect of security interest

(a) Notwithstanding section 552(a) of this title and subject to subsection (b) of this section, special revenues acquired by the debtor after the commencement of the case shall remain subject to any lien resulting from any security agreement entered into by the debtor before the commencement of the case.

(b) Any such lien on special revenues, other than municipal betterment assessments, derived from a project or system shall be subject to the necessary operating expenses of such project or system, as the case may be.

§ 929. Municipal leases

A lease to a municipality shall not be treated as an executory contract or unexpired lease for the purposes of section 365 or 502(b)(6) of this title solely by reason of its being subject to termination in the event the debtor fails to appropriate rent.

§ 930. Dismissal

(a) After notice and a hearing, the court may dismiss a case under this chapter for cause, including—

(1) want of prosecution;

(2) unreasonable delay by the debtor that is prejudicial to creditors;

(3) failure to propose a plan within the time fixed under section 941 of this title;

(4) if a plan is not accepted within any time fixed by the court;

(5) denial of confirmation of a plan under section 943(b) of this title and denial of additional time for filing another plan or a modification of a plan; or

(6) if the court has retained jurisdiction after confirmation of a plan—

(A) material default by the debtor with respect to a term of such plan; or

(B) termination of such plan by reason of the occurrence of a condition specified in such plan.

(b) The court shall dismiss a case under this chapter if confirmation of a plan under this chapter is refused.

SUBCHAPTER III—THE PLAN

§ 941. Filing of plan

The debtor shall file a plan for the adjustment of the debtor's debts. If such a plan is not filed with the petition, the debtor shall file such a plan at such later time as the court fixes.

§ 942. Modification of plan

The debtor may modify the plan at any time before confirmation, but may not modify the plan so that the plan as modified fails to meet the requirements of this chapter. After the debtor files a modification, the plan as modified becomes the plan.

§ 943. Confirmation

(a) A special tax payer may object to confirmation of a plan.

(b) The court shall confirm the plan if—

(1) the plan complies with the provisions of this title made applicable by sections 103(e) and 901 of this title;

(2) the plan complies with the provisions of this chapter;

(3) all amounts to be paid by the debtor or by any person for services or expenses in the case or incident to the plan have been fully disclosed and are reasonable;

(4) the debtor is not prohibited by law from taking any action necessary to carry out the plan;

(5) except to the extent that the holder of a particular claim has agreed to a different treatment of such claim, the plan provides that on the effective date of the plan each holder of a claim of a kind specified in section 507(a)(2+) of this title will receive on account of such claim cash equal to the allowed amount of such claim;

(6) any regulatory or electoral approval necessary under applicable nonbankruptcy law in order to carry out any provision of the plan has been obtained, or such provision is expressly conditioned on such approval; and

(7) the plan is in the best interests of creditors and is feasible.

§ 944. Effect of confirmation

(a) The provisions of a confirmed plan bind the debtor and any creditor, whether or not—

(1) a proof of such creditor's claim is filed or deemed filed under section 501 of this title;

(2) such claim is allowed under section 502 of this title; or

(3) such creditor has accepted the plan.

(b) Except as provided in subsection (c) of this section, the debtor is discharged from all debts as of the time when—

(1) the plan is confirmed;

(2) the debtor deposits any consideration to be distributed under the plan with a disbursing agent appointed by the court; and

(3) the court has determined—

(A) that any security so deposited will constitute, after distribution, a valid legal obligation of the debtor; and

(B) that any provision made to pay or secure payment of such obligation is valid.

(c) The debtor is not discharged under subsection (b) of this section from any debt—

(1) excepted from discharge by the plan or order confirming the plan; or

(2) owed to an entity that, before confirmation of the plan, had neither notice nor actual knowledge of the case.

§ 945. Continuing jurisdiction and closing of the case

(a) The court may retain jurisdiction over the case for such period of time as is necessary for the successful implementation of the plan.

(b) Except as provided in subsection (a) of this section, the court shall close the case when administration of the case has been completed.

§ 946. Effect of exchange of securities before the date of the filing of the petition

The exchange of a new security under the plan for a claim covered by the plan, whether such exchange occurred before or after the date of the filing of the petition, does not limit or impair the effectiveness of the plan or of any provision of this chapter. The amount and number specified in section 1126(c) of this title include the amount and number of claims formerly held by a creditor that has participated in any such exchange.

CHAPTER 11—REORGANIZATION

SUBCHAPTER I—OFFICERS AND ADMINISTRATION

§ 1101. Definitions for this chapter

In this chapter—

(1) "debtor in possession" means debtor except when a person that has qualified under section 322 of this title is serving as trustee in the case;

(2) "substantial consummation" means—

(A) transfer of all or substantially all of the property proposed by the plan to be transferred;

(B) assumption by the debtor or by the successor to the debtor under the plan of the business or of the management of all or substantially all of the property dealt with by the plan; and

(C) commencement of distribution under the plan.

§ 1102. Creditors' and equity security holders' committees

(a)(1) Except as provided in paragraph (3), as soon as practicable after the order for relief under chapter 11 of this title, the United States trustee shall appoint a committee of creditors holding unsecured claims and may appoint additional committees of creditors or of equity security holders as the United States trustee deems appropriate.

(2) On request of a party in interest, the court may order the appointment of additional committees of creditors or of equity security holders if necessary to assure adequate representation of creditors or of equity security holders. The United States trustee shall appoint any such committee.

(3) On request of a party in interest in a case in which the debtor is a small business *debtor* and for cause, the court may order that a committee of creditors not be appointed.

(4) On request of a party in interest and after notice and a hearing, the court may order theUnited States trustee to change the membership of a committee appointed under this subsection, if the court determines that the change is necessary to ensure adequate representation of creditors or equity security holders. The court may order the United States trustee to increase the number of members of a committee to include a creditor that is a small business concern (as described in section 3(a)(1) of the Small Business Act), if the court determines that the creditor holds claims (of the kind represented by the committee) the aggregate amount of which, in comparison to the annual gross revenue of that creditor, is disproportionately large.

(b)(1) A committee of creditors appointed under subsection (a) of this section shall ordinarily consist of the persons, willing to serve, that hold the seven largest claims against the debtor of the kinds represented on such committee, or of the members of a committee organized by creditors before the commencement of the case under this chapter, if such committee was fairly chosen and is representative of the different kinds of claims to be represented.

(2) A committee of equity security holders appointed under subsection (a)(2) of this section shall ordinarily consist of the persons, willing to serve, that hold the seven largest amounts of equity securities of the debtor of the kinds represented on such committee.

(3) A committee appointed under subsection (a) shall—

(A) provide access to information for creditors who—

(i) hold claims of the kind represented by that committee; and

(ii) are not appointed to the committee;

(B) solicit and receive comments from the creditors described in subparagraph (A); and

(C) be subject to a court order that compels any additional report or disclosure to be made to the creditors described in subparagraph (A).

§ 1103. Powers and duties of committees

(a) At a scheduled meeting of a committee appointed under section 1102 of this title, at which a majority of the members of such committee are present, and with the court's approval, such committee may select and authorize the employment by such committee of one or more attorneys, accountants, or other agents, to represent or perform services for such committee.

(b) An attorney or accountant employed to represent a committee appointed under section 1102 of this title may not, while employed by such committee, represent any other entity having an adverse interest in connection with the case. Representation of one or more creditors of the same class as represented by the committee shall not per se constitute the representation of an adverse interest.

(c) A committee appointed under section 1102 of this title may—

(1) consult with the trustee or debtor in possession concerning the administration of the case;

(2) investigate the acts, conduct, assets, liabilities, and financial condition of the debtor, the operation of the debtor's business and the desirability of the continuance of such business, and any other matter relevant to the case or to the formulation of a plan;

(3) participate in the formulation of a plan, advise those represented by such committee of such committee's determinations as to any plan formulated, and collect and file with the court acceptances or rejections of a plan;

(4) request the appointment of a trustee or examiner under section 1104 of this title; and

(5) perform such other services as are in the interest of those represented.

(d) As soon as practicable after the appointment of a committee under section 1102 of this title, the trustee shall meet with such committee to transact such business as may be necessary and proper.

§ 1104. Appointment of trustee or examiner

(a) At any time after the commencement of the case but before confirmation of a plan, on request of a party in interest or the United States trustee, and after notice and a hearing, the court shall order the appointment of a trustee—

(1) for cause, including fraud, dishonesty, incompetence, or gross mismanagement of the affairs of the debtor by current management, either before or after the commencement of the case, or similar cause, but not including the number of holders of securities of the debtor or the amount of assets or liabilities of the debtor; or

(2) if such appointment is in the interests of creditors, any equity security holders, and other interests of the estate, without regard to the number of holders of securities of the debtor or the amount of assets or liabilities of the debtor.; or

(3) if grounds exist to convert or dismiss the case under section 1112, but the court determines that the appointment of a trustee or an examiner is in the best interests of creditors and the estate.

CHAPTER 11—REORGANIZATION

(b)*(1)* Except as provided in section 1163 of this title, on the request of a party in interest made not later than 30 days after the court orders the appointment of a trustee under subsection (a), the United States trustee shall convene a meeting of creditors for the purpose of electing one disinterested person to serve as trustee in the case. The election of a trustee shall be conducted in the manner provided in subsections (a), (b), and (c) of section 702 of this title.

(2)(A) If an eligible, disinterested trustee is elected at a meeting of creditors under paragraph (1), the United States trustee shall file a report certifying that election.

(B) Upon the filing of a report under subparagraph (A)—

(i) the trustee elected under paragraph (1) shall be considered to have been selected and appointed for purposes of this section; and

(ii) the service of any trustee appointed under subsection (d) shall terminate.

(C) The court shall resolve any dispute arising out of an election described in subparagraph (A).

(c) If the court does not order the appointment of a trustee under this section, then at any time before the confirmation of a plan, on request of a party in interest or the United States trustee, and after notice and a hearing, the court shall order the appointment of an examiner to conduct such an investigation of the debtor as is appropriate, including an investigation of any allegations of fraud, dishonesty, incompetence, misconduct, mismanagement, or irregularity in the management of the affairs of the debtor of or by current or former management of the debtor, if—

(1) such appointment is in the interests of creditors, any equity security holders, and other interests of the estate; or

(2) the debtor's fixed, liquidated, unsecured debts, other than debts for goods, services, or taxes, or owing to an insider, exceed $5,000,000.

(d) If the court orders the appointment of a trustee or an examiner, if a trustee or an examiner dies or resigns during the case or is removed under section 324 of this title, or if a trustee fails to qualify under section 322 of this title, then the United States trustee, after consultation with parties in interest, shall appoint, subject to the court's approval, one disinterested person other than the United States trustee to serve as trustee or examiner, as the case may be, in the case.

(e) The United States trustee shall move for the appointment of a trustee under subsection (a) if there are reasonable grounds to suspect that current members of the governing body of the debtor, the debtor's chief executive or chief financial officer, or members of the governing body who selected the debtor's chief executive or chief financial officer, participated in actual fraud, dishonesty, or criminal conduct in the management of the debtor or the debtor's public financial reporting.

§ 1105. Termination of trustee's appointment

At any time before confirmation of a plan, on request of a party in interest or the United States trustee, and after notice and a hearing, the court may terminate the trustee's appointment and restore the debtor to possession and management of the property of the estate and of the operation of the debtor's business.

§ 1106. Duties of trustee and examiner

(a) A trustee shall—

(1) perform the duties of *the* ~~a~~ trustee, *as* specified in *paragraphs* ~~sections~~*(2), (5), (7), (8), (9), (10), (11), and (12)* of section 704~~(2), 704(5), 704(7), 704(8), and 704(9) of this title~~;

(2) if the debtor has not done so, file the list, schedule, and statement required under section 521(1) of this title;

(3) except to the extent that the court orders otherwise, investigate the acts, conduct, assets, liabilities, and financial condition of the debtor, the operation of the debtor's business and the desirability of the continuance of such business, and any other matter relevant to the case or to the formulation of a plan;

(4) as soon as practicable—

(A) file a statement of any investigation conducted under paragraph (3) of this subsection, including any fact ascertained pertaining to fraud, dishonesty, incompetence, misconduct, mismanagement, or irregularity in the management of the affairs of the debtor, or to a cause of action available to the estate; and

(B) transmit a copy or a summary of any such statement to any creditors' committee or equity security holders' committee, to any indenture trustee, and to such other entity as the court designates;

(5) as soon as practicable, file a plan under section 1121 of this title, file a report of why the trustee will not file a plan, or recommend conversion of the case to a case under chapter 7, 12, or 13 of this title or dismissal of the case;

(6) for any year for which the debtor has not filed a tax return required by law, furnish, without personal liability, such information as may be required by the governmental unit with which such tax return was to be filed, in light of the condition of the debtor's books and records and the availability of such information; ~~and~~

(7) after confirmation of a plan, file such reports as are necessary or as the court orders~~.~~*; and*

(8) *if with respect to the debtor there is a claim for a domestic support obligation, provide the applicable notice specified in subsection (c).*

(b) An examiner appointed under section 1104(d) of this title shall perform the duties specified in paragraphs (3) and (4) of subsection (a) of this section, and, except to the extent that the court orders otherwise, any other duties of the trustee that the court orders the debtor in possession not to perform.

(c)(1) In a case described in subsection (a)(8) to which subsection (a)(8) applies, the trustee shall—

(A)(i) provide written notice to the holder of the claim described in subsection (a)(8) of such claim and of the right of such holder to use the services of the State child support enforcement agency established under sections 464 and 466 of the Social Security Act for the State in which such holder resides, for assistance in collecting child support during and after the case under this title; and

(ii) include in the notice required by clause (i) the address and telephone number of such State child support enforcement agency;

(B)(i) provide written notice to such State child support enforcement agency of such claim; and

(ii) include in the notice required by clause (i) the name, address, and telephone number of such holder; and

(C) at such time as the debtor is granted a discharge under section 1141, provide written notice to such holder and to such State child support enforcement agency of—

(i) the granting of the discharge;

(ii) the last recent known address of the debtor;

(iii) the last recent known name and address of the debtor's employer; and

(iv) the name of each creditor that holds a claim that—

(I) is not discharged under paragraph (2), (4), or (14A) of section 523(a); or

(II) was reaffirmed by the debtor under section 524(c).

(2)(A) The holder of a claim described in subsection (a)(8) or the State child enforcement support agency of the State in which such holder resides may request from a creditor described in paragraph (1)(C)(iv) the last known address of the debtor.

(B) Notwithstanding any other provision of law, a creditor that makes a disclosure of a last known address of a debtor in connection with a request made under subparagraph (A) shall not be liable by reason of making such disclosure.

§ 1107. Rights, powers, and duties of debtor in possession

(a) Subject to any limitations on a trustee serving in a case under this chapter, and to such limitations or conditions as the court prescribes, a debtor in possession shall have all the rights, other than the right to compensation under section 330 of this title, and powers, and shall perform all the functions and duties, except the duties specified in sections 1106(a)(2), (3), and (4) of this title, of a trustee serving in a case under this chapter.

(b) Notwithstanding section 327(a) of this title, a person is not disqualified for employment under section 327 of this title by a debtor in possession solely because of such person's employment by or representation of the debtor before the commencement of the case.

§ 1108. Authorization to operate business

Unless the court, on request of a party in interest and after notice and a hearing, orders otherwise, the trustee may operate the debtor's business.

§ 1109. Right to be heard

(a) The Securities and Exchange Commission may raise and may appear and be heard on any issue in a case under this chapter, but the Securities and Exchange Commission may not appeal from any judgment, order, or decree entered in the case.

(b) A party in interest, including the debtor, the trustee, a creditors' committee, an equity security holders' committee, a creditor, an equity security holder, or any indenture trustee, may raise and may appear and be heard on any issue in a case under this chapter.

§ 1110. Aircraft equipment and vessels

(a)(1) Except as provided in paragraph (2) and subject to subsection (b), the right of a secured party with a security interest in equipment described in paragraph (3), or of a lessor or conditional vendor of such equipment, to take possession of such equipment in compliance with a security agreement, lease, or conditional sale contract, and to enforce any of its other rights or remedies, under such security agreement, lease, or conditional sale contract, to sell, lease, or otherwise retain or dispose of such equipment, is not limited or otherwise affected by any other provision of this title or by any power of the court.

(2) The right to take possession and to enforce the other rights and remedies described in paragraph (1) shall be subject to section 362 if—

(A) before the date that is 60 days after the date of the order for relief under this chapter, the trustee, subject to the approval of the court, agrees to perform all obligations of the debtor under such security agreement, lease, or conditional sale contract; and

(B) any default, other than a default of a kind specified in section 365(b)(2), under such security agreement, lease, or conditional sale contract—

(i) that occurs before the date of the order is cured before the expiration of such 60-day period;

(ii) that occurs after the date of the order and before the expiration of such 60-day period is cured before the later of—

(I) the date that is 30 days after the date of the default; or

(II) the expiration of such 60-day period; and

(iii) that occurs on or after the expiration of such 60-day period is cured in compliance with the terms of such security agreement, lease, or conditional sale contract, if a cure is permitted under that agreement, lease, or contract.

(3) The equipment described in this paragraph—

(A) is—

(i) an aircraft, aircraft engine, propeller, appliance, or spare part (as defined in section 40102 of title 49) that is subject to a security interest granted by, leased to, or conditionally sold to a debtor that, at the time such transaction is entered into, holds an air carrier operating certificate issued pursuant to chapter 447 of title 49 for aircraft capable of carrying 10 or more individuals or 6,000 pounds or more of cargo; or

(ii) a documented vessel (as defined in section 30101(1) of title 46) that is subject to a security interest granted by, leased to, or conditionally sold to a debtor that is a water carrier that, at the time such transaction is entered into, holds a certificate of public convenience and necessity or permit issued by the Department of Transportation; and

(B) includes all records and documents relating to such equipment that are required, under the terms of the security agreement, lease, or conditional sale contract, to be surrendered or returned by the debtor in connection with the surrender or return of such equipment.

(4) Paragraph (1) applies to a secured party, lessor, or conditional vendor acting in its own behalf or acting as trustee or otherwise in behalf of another party.

(b) The trustee and the secured party, lessor, or conditional vendor whose right to take possession is protected under subsection (a) may agree, subject to the approval of the court, to extend the 60-day period specified in subsection (a)(1).

(c)(1) In any case under this chapter, the trustee shall immediately surrender and return to a secured party, lessor, or conditional vendor, described in subsection (a)(1), equipment described in subsection (a)(3), if at any time after the date of the order for relief under this chapter such secured party, lessor, or conditional vendor is entitled pursuant to subsection (a)(1) to take possession of such equipment and makes a written demand for such possession to the trustee.

(2) At such time as the trustee is required under paragraph (1) to surrender and return equipment described in subsection (a)(3), any lease of such equipment, and any security agreement or conditional sale contract relating to such equipment, if such security agreement or conditional sale contract is an executory contract, shall be deemed rejected.

(d) With respect to equipment first placed in service on or before October 22, 1994, for purposes of this section—

(1) the term 'lease' includes any written agreement with respect to which the lessor and the debtor, as lessee, have expressed in the agreement or in a substantially contemporaneous writing that the agreement is to be treated as a lease for Federal income tax purposes; and

(2) the term "security interest" means a purchase- money equipment security interest.

§ 1111. Claims and interests

(a) A proof of claim or interest is deemed filed under section 501 of this title for any claim or interest that appears in the schedules filed under section 521(1) or 1106(a)(2) of this title, except a claim or interest that is scheduled as disputed, contingent, or unliquidated.

(b)(1)(A) A claim secured by a lien on property of the estate shall be allowed or disallowed under section 502 of this title the same as if the holder of such claim had recourse against the debtor on account of such claim, whether or not such holder has such recourse, unless—

(i) the class of which such claim is a part elects, by at least two-thirds in amount and more than half in number of allowed claims of such class, application of paragraph (2) of this subsection; or

(ii) such holder does not have such recourse and such property is sold under section 363 of this title or is to be sold under the plan.

(B) A class of claims may not elect application of paragraph (2) of this subsection if—

(i) the interest on account of such claims of the holders of such claims in such property is of inconsequential value; or

(ii) the holder of a claim of such class has recourse against the debtor on account of such claim and such property is sold under section 363 of this title or is to be sold under the plan.

(2) If such an election is made, then notwithstanding section 506(a) of this title, such claim is a secured claim to the extent that such claim is allowed.

§ 1112. Conversion or dismissal

(a) The debtor may convert a case under this chapter to a case under chapter 7 of this title unless—

(1) the debtor is not a debtor in possession;

(2) the case originally was commenced as an involuntary case under this chapter; or

(3) the case was converted to a case under this chapter other than on the debtor's request.

(b)(1) Except as provided in paragraph (2) of this subsection, subsection (c) of this section, and section 1104(a)(3), on request of a party in interest, and after notice and a hearing, absent unusual circumstances specifically identified by the court that establish that the requested conversion or dismissal is not in the best interests of creditors and the estate, the court shall convert a case under this chapter to a case under chapter 7 or dismiss a case under this chapter, whichever is in the best interests of creditors and the estate, if the movant establishes cause.

(2) The relief provided in paragraph (1) shall not be granted absent unusual circumstances specifically identified by the court that establish that such relief is not in the best interests of creditors and the estate, if the debtor or another party in interest objects and establishes that—

(A) there is a reasonable likelihood that a plan will be confirmed within the timeframes established in sections 1121(e) and 1129(e) of this title, or if such sections do not apply, within a reasonable period of time; and

(B) the grounds for granting such relief include an act or omission of the debtor other than under paragraph (4)(A)—

(i) for which there exists a reasonable justification for the act or omission; and

(ii) that will be cured within a reasonable period of time fixed by the court.

(3) The court shall commence the hearing on a motion under this subsection not later than 30 days after filing of the motion, and shall decide the motion not later than 15 days after commencement of such hearing, unless the movant expressly consents to a continuance for a specific period of time or compelling circumstances prevent the court from meeting the time limits established by this paragraph.

(4) For purposes of this subsection, the term 'cause' includes—

(A) substantial or continuing loss to or diminution of the estate and the absence of a reasonable likelihood of rehabilitation;

(B) gross mismanagement of the estate;

(C) failure to maintain appropriate insurance that poses a risk to the estate or to the public;

(D) unauthorized use of cash collateral substantially harmful to 1 or more creditors;

(E) failure to comply with an order of the court;

(F) unexcused failure to satisfy timely any filing or reporting requirement established by this title or by any rule applicable to a case under this chapter;

(G) failure to attend the meeting of creditors convened under section 341(a) or an examination ordered under rule 2004 of the Federal Rules of Bankruptcy Procedure without good cause shown by the debtor;

(H) failure timely to provide information or attend meetings reasonably requested by the United States trustee (or the bankruptcy administrator, if any);

(I) failure timely to pay taxes owed after the date of the order for relief or to file tax returns due after the date of the order for relief;

(J) failure to file a disclosure statement, or to file or confirm a plan, within the time fixed by this title or by order of the court;

(K) failure to pay any fees or charges required under chapter 123 of title 28;

(L) revocation of an order of confirmation under section 1144;

(M) inability to effectuate substantial consummation of a confirmed plan;

(N) material default by the debtor with respect to a confirmed plan;

(O) termination of a confirmed plan by reason of the occurrence of a condition specified in the plan; and

(P) failure of the debtor to pay any domestic support obligation that first becomes payable after the date of the filing of the petition.

(c) The court may not convert a case under this chapter to a case under chapter 7 of this title if the debtor is a farmer or a corporation that is not a moneyed, business, or commercial corporation, unless the debtor requests such conversion.

(d) The court may convert a case under this chapter to a case under chapter 12 or 13 of this title only if—

(1) the debtor requests such conversion;

(2) the debtor has not been discharged under section 1141(d) of this title; and

(3) if the debtor requests conversion to chapter 12 of this title, such conversion is equitable.

(e) Except as provided in subsections (c) and (f), the court, on request of the United States trustee, may convert a case under this chapter to a case under chapter 7 of this title or may dismiss a case under this chapter, whichever is in the best interest of creditors and the estate if the debtor in a voluntary case fails to file, within fifteen days after the filing of the petition commencing such case or such additional time as the court may allow, the information required by paragraph (1) of section 521, including a list containing the names and addresses of the holders of the twenty largest unsecured claims (or of all unsecured claims if there are fewer than twenty unsecured claims), and the approximate dollar amounts of each of such claims.

(f) Notwithstanding any other provision of this section, a case may not be converted to a case under another chapter of this title unless the debtor may be a debtor under such chapter.

§ 1113. Rejection of collective bargaining agreements

(a) The debtor in possession, or the trustee if one has been appointed under the provisions of this chapter, other than a trustee in a case covered by subchapter IV of this chapter and by title I of the Railway Labor Act, may assume or reject a collective bargaining agreement only in accordance with the provisions of this section.

(b)(1) Subsequent to filing a petition and prior to filing an application seeking rejection of a collective bargaining agreement, the debtor in possession or trustee (hereinafter in this section "trustee" shall include a debtor in possession), shall—

(A) make a proposal to the authorized representative of the employees covered by such agreement, based on the most complete and reliable information available at the time of such proposal, which provides for those necessary modifications in the employees benefits and protections that are necessary to permit the reorganization of the debtor and assures that all creditors, the debtor and all of the affected parties are treated fairly and equitably; and

(B) provide, subject to subsection (d)(3), the representative of the employees with such relevant information as is necessary to evaluate the proposal.

(2) During the period beginning on the date of the making of a proposal provided for in paragraph (1) and ending on the date of the hearing provided for in subsection (d)(1), the trustee shall meet, at reasonable times, with the authorized representative to confer in good faith in attempting to reach mutually satisfactory modifications of such agreement.

(c) The court shall approve an application for rejection of a collective bargaining agreement only if the court finds that—

(1) the trustee has, prior to the hearing, made a proposal that fulfills the requirements of subsection (b)(1);

(2) the authorized representative of the employees has refused to accept such proposal without good cause; and

(3) the balance of the equities clearly favors rejection of such agreement.

(d)(1) Upon the filing of an application for rejection the court shall schedule a hearing to be held not later than fourteen days after the date of the filing of such application. All interested parties may appear and be heard at such hearing. Adequate notice shall be provided to such parties at least ten days before the date of such hearing. The court may extend the time for the commencement of such hearing for a period not exceeding seven days where the circumstances of the case, and the interests of justice require such extension, or for additional periods of time to which the trustee and representative agree.

(2) The court shall rule on such application for rejection within thirty days after the date of the commencement of the hearing. In the interests of justice, the court may extend such time for ruling for such additional period as the trustee and the employees' representative may agree to. If the court does not rule on such application within thirty days after the date of the commencement

of the hearing, or within such additional time as the trustee and the employees' representative may agree to, the trustee may terminate or alter any provisions of the collective bargaining agreement pending the ruling of the court on such application.

(3) The court may enter such protective orders, consistent with the need of the authorized representative of the employee to evaluate the trustee's proposal and the application for rejection, as may be necessary to prevent disclosure of information provided to such representative where such disclosure could compromise the position of the debtor with respect to its competitors in the industry in which it is engaged.

(e) If during a period when the collective bargaining agreement continues in effect, and if essential to the continuation of the debtor's business, or in order to avoid irreparable damage to the estate, the court, after notice and a hearing, may authorize the trustee to implement interim changes in the terms, conditions, wages, benefits, or work rules provided by a collective bargaining agreement. Any hearing under this paragraph shall be scheduled in accordance with the needs of the trustee. The implementation of such interim changes shall not render the application for rejection moot.

(f) No provision of this title shall be construed to permit a trustee to unilaterally terminate or alter any provisions of a collective bargaining agreement prior to compliance with the provisions of this section.

§ 1114. Payment of insurance benefits to retired employees

(a) For purposes of this section, the term "retiree benefits" means payments to any entity or person for the purpose of providing or reimbursing payments for retired employees and their spouses and dependents, for medical, surgical, or hospital care benefits, or benefits in the event of sickness, accident, disability, or death under any plan, fund, or program (through the purchase of insurance or otherwise) maintained or established in whole or in part by the debtor prior to filing a petition commencing a case under this title.

(b)(1) For purposes of this section, the term "authorized representative" means the authorized representative designated pursuant to subsection (c) for persons receiving any retiree benefits covered by a collective bargaining agreement or subsection (d) in the case of persons receiving retiree benefits not covered by such an agreement.

(2) Committees of retired employees appointed by the court pursuant to this section shall have the same rights, powers, and duties as committees appointed under sections 1102 and 1103 of this title for the purpose of carrying out the purposes of sections 1114 and 1129(a)(13) and, as permitted by the court, shall have the power to enforce the rights of persons under this title as they relate to retiree benefits.

(c)(1) A labor organization shall be, for purposes of this section, the authorized representative of those persons receiving any retiree benefits covered by any collective bargaining agreement to which that labor organization is signatory, unless (A) such labor organization elects not to serve as the authorized representative of such persons, or (B) the court, upon a motion by any party in interest, after notice and hearing, determines that different representation of such persons is appropriate.

(2) In cases where the labor organization referred to in paragraph (1) elects not to serve as the authorized representative of those persons receiving any retiree benefits covered by any collective bargaining agreement to which that labor organization is signatory, or in cases where the court, pursuant to paragraph (1) finds different representation of such persons appropriate, the court, upon a motion by any party in interest, and after notice and a hearing, shall appoint a committee of retired employees if the debtor seeks to modify or not pay the retiree benefits or if the court otherwise determines that it is appropriate, from among such persons, to serve as the authorized representative of such persons under this section.

(d) The court, upon a motion by any party in interest, and after notice and a hearing, shall *order the* appoint*ment of* a committee of retired employees if the debtor seeks to modify or not pay the retiree benefits or if the court otherwise determines that it is appropriate, to serve as the authorized representative, under this section, of those persons receiving any retiree benefits not covered by a collective bargaining agreement. *The United States trustee shall appoint any such committee.*

(e)(1) Notwithstanding any other provision of this title, the debtor in possession, or the trustee if one has been appointed under the provisions of this chapter (hereinafter in this section "trustee" shall include a debtor in possession), shall timely pay and shall not modify any retiree benefits, except that—

(A) the court, on motion of the trustee or authorized representative, and after notice and a hearing, may order modification of such payments, pursuant to the provisions of subsections (g) and (h) of this section, or

(B) the trustee and the authorized representative of the recipients of those benefits may agree to modification of such payments, after which such benefits as modified shall continue to be paid by the trustee.

(2) Any payment for retiree benefits required to be made before a plan confirmed under section 1129 of this title is effective has the status of an allowed administrative expense as provided in section 503 of this title.

(f)(1) Subsequent to filing a petition and prior to filing an application seeking modification of the retiree benefits, the trustee shall—

(A) make a proposal to the authorized representative of the retirees, based on the most complete and reliable information available at the time of such proposal, which provides for those necessary modifications in the retiree benefits that are necessary to permit the reorganization of the debtor and assures that all creditors, the debtor and all of the affected parties are treated fairly and equitably; and

(B) provide, subject to subsection (k)(3), the representative of the retirees with such relevant information as is necessary to evaluate the proposal.

(2) During the period beginning on the date of the making of a proposal provided for in paragraph (1), and ending on the date of the hearing provided for in subsection (k)(1), the trustee shall meet, at reasonable times, with the authorized representative to confer in good faith in attempting to reach mutually satisfactory modifications of such retiree benefits.

(g) The court shall enter an order providing for modification in the payment of retiree benefits if the court finds that—

(1) the trustee has, prior to the hearing, made a proposal that fulfills the requirements of subsection (f);

(2) the authorized representative of the retirees has refused to accept such proposal without good cause; and

(3) such modification is necessary to permit the reorganization of the debtor and assures that all creditors, the debtor, and all of the affected parties are treated fairly and equitably, and is clearly favored by the balance of the equities; except that in no case shall the court enter an order providing for such modification which provides for a modification to a level lower than that proposed by the trustee in the proposal found by the court to have complied with the requirements of this subsection and subsection (f): Provided, however, That at any time after an order is entered providing for modification in the payment of retiree benefits, or at any time after an agreement modifying such benefits is made between the trustee and the authorized representative of the recipients of such benefits, the authorized representative may apply to the court for an order increasing those benefits which order shall be granted if the increase in retiree benefits sought is consistent with the standard set forth in paragraph (3): Provided further, That neither the trustee nor the authorized representative is precluded from making more than one motion for a modification order governed by this subsection.

(h)(1) Prior to a court issuing a final order under subsection (g) of this section, if essential to the continuation of the debtor's business, or in order to avoid irreparable damage to the estate, the court, after notice and a hearing, may authorize the trustee to implement interim modifications in retiree benefits.

(2) Any hearing under this subsection shall be scheduled in accordance with the needs of the trustee.

(3) The implementation of such interim changes does not render the motion for modification moot.

(i) No retiree benefits paid between the filing of the petition and the time a plan confirmed under section 1129 of this title becomes effective shall be deducted or offset from the amounts allowed as claims for any benefits which remain unpaid, or from the amounts to be paid under the plan with respect to such claims for unpaid benefits, whether such claims for unpaid benefits are based upon or arise from a right to future unpaid benefits or from any benefits not paid as a result of modifications allowed pursuant to this section.

(j) No claim for retiree benefits shall be limited by section 502(b)(7) of this title.

(k)(1) Upon the filing of an application for modifying retiree benefits, the court shall schedule a hearing to be held not later than fourteen days after the date of the filing of such application. All interested parties may appear and be heard at such hearing. Adequate notice shall be provided to such parties at least ten days before the date of such hearing. The court may extend the time for the commencement of such hearing for a period not exceeding seven days where the circumstances of the case, and the interests of justice require such extension, or for additional periods of time to which the trustee and the authorized representative agree.

(2) The court shall rule on such application for modification within ninety days after the date of the commencement of the hearing. In the interests of justice, the court may extend such time for ruling for such additional period as the trustee and the authorized representative may agree to. If the court does not rule on such application within ninety days after the date of the commencement of the hearing, or within such additional time as the trustee and the authorized

representative may agree to, the trustee may implement the proposed modifications pending the ruling of the court on such application.

(3) The court may enter such protective orders, consistent with the need of the authorized representative of the retirees to evaluate the trustee's proposal and the application for modification, as may be necessary to prevent disclosure of information provided to such representative where such disclosure could compromise the position of the debtor with respect to its competitors in the industry in which it is engaged.

(l) If the debtor, during the 180-day period ending on the date of the filing of the petition—

(1) modified retiree benefits; and

(2) was insolvent on the date such benefits were modified; the court, on motion of a party in interest, and after notice and a hearing, shall issue an order reinstating as of the date the modification was made, such benefits as in effect immediately before such date unless the court finds that the balance of the equities clearly favors such modification.

(~~l~~*m*) This section shall not apply to any retiree, or the spouse or dependents of such retiree, if such retiree's gross income for the twelve months preceding the filing of the bankruptcy petition equals or exceeds $250,000, unless such retiree can demonstrate to the satisfaction of the court that he is unable to obtain health, medical, life, and disability coverage for himself, his spouse, and his dependents who would otherwise be covered by the employer's insurance plan, comparable to the coverage provided by the employer on the day before the filing of a petition under this title.

§ 1115. Property of the estate

(a) In a case in which the debtor is an individual, property of the estate includes, in addition to the property specified in section 541—

(1) all property of the kind specified in section 541 that the debtor acquires after the commencement of the case but before the case is closed, dismissed, or converted to a case under chapter 7, 12, or 13, whichever occurs first; and

(2) earnings from services performed by the debtor after the commencement of the case but before the case is closed, dismissed, or converted to a case under chapter 7, 12, or 13, whichever occurs first.

(b) Except as provided in section 1104 or a confirmed plan or order confirming a plan, the debtor shall remain in possession of all property of the estate.

§ 1116. Duties of trustee or debtor in possession in small business cases

In a small business case, a trustee or the debtor in possession, in addition to the duties provided in this title and as otherwise required by law, shall—

(1) append to the voluntary petition or, in an involuntary case, file not later than 7 days after the date of the order for relief—

(A) its most recent balance sheet, statement of operations, cash-flow statement, and Federal income tax return; or

(B) a statement made under penalty of perjury that no balance sheet, statement of operations, or cash-flow statement has been prepared and no Federal tax return has been filed;

(2) attend, through its senior management personnel and counsel, meetings scheduled by the court or the United States trustee, including initial debtor interviews, scheduling conferences, and meetings of creditors convened under section 341 unless the court, after notice and a hearing, waives that requirement upon a finding of extraordinary and compelling circumstances;

(3) timely file all schedules and statements of financial affairs, unless the court, after notice and a hearing, grants an extension, which shall not extend such time period to a date later than 30 days after the date of the order for relief, absent extraordinary and compelling circumstances;

(4) file all postpetition financial and other reports required by the Federal Rules of Bankruptcy Procedure or by local rule of the district court;

(5) subject to section 363(c)(2), maintain insurance customary and appropriate to the industry;

(6)(A) timely file tax returns and other required government filings; and

(B) subject to section 363(c)(2), timely pay all taxes entitled to administrative expense priority except those being contested by appropriate proceedings being diligently prosecuted; and

(7) allow the United States trustee, or a designated representative of the United States trustee, to inspect the debtor's business premises, books, and records at reasonable times, after reasonable prior written notice, unless notice is waived by the debtor.

SUBCHAPTER II—THE PLAN

§ 1121. Who may file a plan

(a) The debtor may file a plan with a petition commencing a voluntary case, or at any time in a voluntary case or an involuntary case.

(b) Except as otherwise provided in this section, only the debtor may file a plan until after 120 days after the date of the order for relief under this chapter.

(c) Any party in interest, including the debtor, the trustee, a creditors' committee, an equity security holders' committee, a creditor, an equity security holder, or any indenture trustee, may file a plan if and only if—

(1) a trustee has been appointed under this chapter;

(2) the debtor has not filed a plan before 120 days after the date of the order for relief under this chapter; or

(3) the debtor has not filed a plan that has been accepted, before 180 days after the date of the order for relief under this chapter, by each class of claims or interests that is impaired under the plan.

(d)*(1) Subject to paragraph (2), on* On request of a party in interest made within the respective periods specified in subsections (b) and (c) of this section and after notice and a hearing, the court may for cause reduce or increase the 120-day period or the 180-day period referred to in this section.

(2)(A) The 120-day period specified in paragraph (1) may not be extended beyond a date that is 18 months after the date of the order for relief under this chapter.

(B) The 180-day period specified in paragraph (1) may not be extended beyond a date that is 20 months after the date of the order for relief under this chapter.

(c) In a case in which the debtor is a small business and elects to be considered a small business—

(1) only the debtor may file a plan until after 100 days after the date of the order for relief under this chapter;

(2) all plans shall be filed within 160 days after the date of the order for relief; and

(3) on request of a party in interest made within the respective periods specified in paragraphs (1) and (2) and after notice and a hearing, the court may—

(A) reduce the 100-day period or the 160-day period specified in paragraph (1) or (2) for cause; and

(B) increase the 100-day period specified in paragraph (1) if the debtor shows that the need for an increase is caused by circumstances for which the debtor should not be held accountable.

(e) In a small business case—

(1) only the debtor may file a plan until after 180 days after the date of the order for relief, unless that period is—

(A) extended as provided by this subsection, after notice and a hearing; or

(B) the court, for cause, orders otherwise;

(2) the plan and a disclosure statement (if any) shall be filed not later than 300 days after the date of the order for relief; and

(3) the time periods specified in paragraphs (1) and (2), and the time fixed in section 1129(e) within which the plan shall be confirmed, may be extended only if—

(A) the debtor, after providing notice to parties in interest (including the United States trustee), demonstrates by a preponderance of the evidence that it is more likely than not that the court will confirm a plan within a reasonable period of time;

(B) a new deadline is imposed at the time the extension is granted; and

(C) the order extending time is signed before the existing deadline has expired.

§ 1122. Classification of claims or interests

(a) Except as provided in subsection (b) of this section, a plan may place a claim or an interest in a particular class only if such claim or interest is substantially similar to the other claims or interests of such class.

(b) A plan may designate a separate class of claims consisting only of every unsecured claim that is less than or reduced to an amount that the court approves as reasonable and necessary for administrative convenience.

§ 1123. Contents of plan

(a) Notwithstanding any otherwise applicable nonbankruptcy law, a plan shall—

(1) designate, subject to section 1122 of this title, classes of claims, other than claims of a kind specified in section 507(a)(2̶1̶), 507(a)(3̶2̶), or 507(a)(8) of this title, and classes of interests;

(2) specify any class of claims or interests that is not impaired under the plan;

(3) specify the treatment of any class of claims or interests that is impaired under the plan;

(4) provide the same treatment for each claim or interest of a particular class, unless the holder of a particular claim or interest agrees to a less favorable treatment of such particular claim or interest;

(5) provide adequate means for the plan's implementation, such as—

(A) retention by the debtor of all or any part of the property of the estate;

(B) transfer of all or any part of the property of the estate to one or more entities, whether organized before or after the confirmation of such plan;

(C) merger or consolidation of the debtor with one or more persons;

(D) sale of all or any part of the property of the estate, either subject to or free of any lien, or the distribution of all or any part of the property of the estate among those having an interest in such property of the estate;

(E) satisfaction or modification of any lien;

(F) cancellation or modification of any indenture or similar instrument;

(G) curing or waiving of any default;

(H) extension of a maturity date or a change in an interest rate or other term of outstanding securities;

(I) amendment of the debtor's charter; or

(J) issuance of securities of the debtor, or of any entity referred to in subparagraph (B) or (C) of this paragraph, for cash, for property, for existing securities, or in exchange for claims or interests, or for any other appropriate purpose;

(6) provide for the inclusion in the charter of the debtor, if the debtor is a corporation, or of any corporation referred to in paragraph (5)(B) or (5)(C) of this subsection, of a provision prohibiting the issuance of nonvoting equity securities, and providing, as to the several classes of securities possessing voting power, an appropriate distribution of such power among such classes, including, in the case of any class of equity securities having a preference over another class of equity securities with respect to dividends, adequate provisions for the election of directors representing such preferred class in the event of default in the payment of such dividends; a̶n̶d̶

(7) contain only provisions that are consistent with the interests of creditors and equity security holders and with public policy with respect to the manner of selection of any officer, director, or trustee under the plan and any successor to such officer, director, or trustee̶.̶; and

(8) in a case in which the debtor is an individual, provide for the payment to creditors under the plan of all or such portion of earnings from personal services performed by the debtor after the commencement of the case or other future income of the debtor as is necessary for the execution of the plan.

(b) Subject to subsection (a) of this section, a plan may—

(1) impair or leave unimpaired any class of claims, secured or unsecured, or of interests;

(2) subject to section 365 of this title, provide for the assumption, rejection, or assignment of any executory contract or unexpired lease of the debtor not previously rejected under such section;

(3) provide for—

(A) the settlement or adjustment of any claim or interest belonging to the debtor or to the estate; or

(B) the retention and enforcement by the debtor, by the trustee, or by a representative of the estate appointed for such purpose, of any such claim or interest;

(4) provide for the sale of all or substantially all of the property of the estate, and the distribution of the proceeds of such sale among holders of claims or interests;

(5) modify the rights of holders of secured claims, other than a claim secured only by a security interest in real property that is the debtor's principal residence, or of holders of unsecured claims, or leave unaffected the rights of holders of any class of claims; and

(6) include any other appropriate provision not inconsistent with the applicable provisions of this title.

(c) In a case concerning an individual, a plan proposed by an entity other than the debtor may not provide for the use, sale, or lease of property exempted under section 522 of this title, unless the debtor consents to such use, sale, or lease.

(d) Notwithstanding subsection (a) of this section and sections 506(b), 1129(a)(7), and 1129(b) of this title, if it is proposed in a plan to cure a default the amount necessary to cure the default shall be determined in accordance with the underlying agreement and applicable nonbankruptcy law.

§ 1124. Impairment of claims or interests

Except as provided in section 1123(a)(4) of this title, a class of claims or interests is impaired under a plan unless, with respect to each claim or interest of such class, the plan—

(1) leaves unaltered the legal, equitable, and contractual rights to which such claim or interest entitles the holder of such claim or interest; or

(2) notwithstanding any contractual provision or applicable law that entitles the holder of such claim or interest to demand or receive accelerated payment of such claim or interest after the occurrence of a default—

(A) cures any such default that occurred before or after the commencement of the case under this title, other than a default of a kind specified in section 365(b)(2) of this title *or of a kind that section 365(b)(2) expressly does not require to be cured*;

(B) reinstates the maturity of such claim or interest as such maturity existed before such default;

(C) compensates the holder of such claim or interest for any damages incurred as a result of any reasonable reliance by such holder on such contractual provision or such applicable law; and

(D) if such claim or such interest arises from any failure to perform a non-monetary obligation, other than a default arising from failure to operate a nonresidential real property lease subject to section 365(b)(1)(A), compensates the holder of such claim or such interest (other than the debtor or an insider) for any actual pecuniary loss incurred by such holder as a result of such failure; and

(~~D~~E) does not otherwise alter the legal, equitable, or contractual rights to which such claim or interest entitles the holder of such claim or interest.

§ 1125. Postpetition disclosure and solicitation

(a) In this section—

(1) "adequate information" means information of a kind, and in sufficient detail, as far as is reasonably practicable in light of the nature and history of the debtor and the condition of the debtor's books and records, *including a discussion of the potential material Federal tax consequences of the plan to the debtor, any successor to the debtor, and a hypothetical investor typical of the holders of claims or interests in the case,* that would enable ~~a hypothetical reasonable investor typical of holders of claims or interests~~*such a hypothetical investor* of the relevant class to make an informed judgment about the plan, but adequate information need not include such information about any other possible or proposed plan *and in determining whether a disclosure statement provides adequate information, the court shall consider the complexity of the case, the benefit of additional information to creditors and other parties in interest, and the cost of providing additional information*; and

(2) "investor typical of holders of claims or interests of the relevant class" means investor having—

(A) a claim or interest of the relevant class;

(B) such a relationship with the debtor as the holders of other claims or interests of such class generally have; and

(C) such ability to obtain such information from sources other than the disclosure required by this section as holders of claims or interests in such class generally have.

(b) An acceptance or rejection of a plan may not be solicited after the commencement of the case under this title from a holder of a claim or interest with respect to such claim or interest, unless, at the time of or before such solicitation, there is transmitted to such holder the plan or a summary of the plan, and a written disclosure statement approved, after notice and a hearing, by the court as containing adequate information. The court may approve a disclosure statement without a valuation of the debtor or an appraisal of the debtor's assets.

(c) The same disclosure statement shall be transmitted to each holder of a claim or interest of a particular class, but there may be transmitted different disclosure statements, differing in amount, detail, or kind of information, as between classes.

(d) Whether a disclosure statement required under subsection (b) of this section contains adequate information is not governed by any otherwise applicable non-bankruptcy law, rule, or regulation, but an agency or official whose duty is to administer or enforce such a law, rule, or regulation may be heard on the issue of whether a disclosure statement contains adequate information. Such an agency or official may not appeal from, or otherwise seek review of, an order approving a disclosure statement.

(e) A person that solicits acceptance or rejection of a plan, in good faith and in compliance with the applicable provisions of this title, or that participates, in good faith and in compliance with the applicable provisions of this title, in the offer, issuance, sale, or purchase of a security, offered or sold under the plan, of the debtor, of an affiliate participating in a joint plan with the debtor, or of a newly organized successor to the debtor under the plan, is not liable, on account of such solicitation or participation, for violation of any applicable law, rule, or regulation governing solicitation of acceptance or rejection of a plan or the offer, issuance, sale, or purchase of securities.

(f) Notwithstanding subsection (b), in a case in which the debtor has elected under section 1121(e) to be considered a small business—

(1) the court may conditionally approve a disclosure statement subject to final approval after notice and a hearing;

(2) acceptances and rejections of a plan may be solicited based on a conditionally approved disclosure statement as long as the debtor provides adequate information to each holder of a claim or interest that is solicited, but a conditionally approved disclosure statement shall be mailed at least 10 days prior to the date of the hearing on confirmation of the plan; and

(3) a hearing on the disclosure statement may be combined with a hearing on confirmation of a plan.

(f) Notwithstanding subsection (b), in a small business case—

(1) the court may determine that the plan itself provides adequate information and that a separate disclosure statement is not necessary;

(2) the court may approve a disclosure statement submitted on standard forms approved by the court or adopted under section 2075 of title 28; and

(3)(A) the court may conditionally approve a disclosure statement subject to final approval after notice and a hearing;

(B) acceptances and rejections of a plan may be solicited based on a conditionally approved disclosure statement if the debtor provides adequate information to each holder of a claim or interest that is solicited, but a conditionally approved disclosure statement shall be mailed not later than 25 days before the date of the hearing on confirmation of the plan; and

(C) the hearing on the disclosure statement may be combined with the hearing on confirmation of a plan.

(g) Notwithstanding subsection (b), an acceptance or rejection of the plan may be solicited from a holder of a claim or interest if such solicitation complies with applicable nonbankruptcy law and if such holder was solicited before the commencement of the case in a manner complying with applicable nonbankruptcy law.

§ 1126. Acceptance of plan

(a) The holder of a claim or interest allowed under section 502 of this title may accept or reject a plan. If the United States is a creditor or equity security holder, the Secretary of the Treasury may accept or reject the plan on behalf of the United States.

(b) For the purposes of subsections (c) and (d) of this section, a holder of a claim or interest that has accepted or rejected the plan before the commencement of the case under this title is deemed to have accepted or rejected such plan, as the case may be, if—

(1) the solicitation of such acceptance or rejection was in compliance with any applicable nonbankruptcy law, rule, or regulation governing the adequacy of disclosure in connection with such solicitation; or

(2) if there is not any such law, rule, or regulation, such acceptance or rejection was solicited after disclosure to such holder of adequate information, as defined in section 1125(a) of this title.

(c) A class of claims has accepted a plan if such plan has been accepted by creditors, other than any entity designated under subsection (e) of this section, that hold at least two-thirds in amount and more than one-half in number of the allowed claims of such class held by creditors, other than any entity designated under subsection (e) of this section, that have accepted or rejected such plan.

(d) A class of interests has accepted a plan if such plan has been accepted by holders of such interests, other than any entity designated under subsection (e) of this section, that hold at least two-thirds in amount of the allowed interests of such class held by holders of such interests, other than any entity designated under subsection (e) of this section, that have accepted or rejected such plan.

(e) On request of a party in interest, and after notice and a hearing, the court may designate any entity whose acceptance or rejection of such plan was not in good faith, or was not solicited or procured in good faith or in accordance with the provisions of this title.

(f) Notwithstanding any other provision of this section, a class that is not impaired under a plan, and each holder of a claim or interest of such class, are conclusively presumed to have accepted the plan, and solicitation of acceptances with respect to such class from the holders of claims or interests of such class is not required.

(g) Notwithstanding any other provision of this section, a class is deemed not to have accepted a plan if such plan provides that the claims or interests of such class do not entitle the holders of such claims or interests to receive or retain any property under the plan on account of such claims or interests.

§ 1127. Modification of plan

(a) The proponent of a plan may modify such plan at any time before confirmation, but may not modify such plan so that such plan as modified fails to meet the requirements of sections 1122 and 1123 of this title. After the proponent of a plan files a modification of such plan with the court, the plan as modified becomes the plan.

(b) The proponent of a plan or the reorganized debtor may modify such plan at any time after confirmation of such plan and before substantial consummation of such plan, but may not modify such plan so that such plan as modified fails to meet the requirements of sections 1122 and 1123 of this title. Such plan as modified under this subsection becomes the plan only if circumstances warrant such modification and the court, after notice and a hearing, confirms such plan as modified, under section 1129 of this title.

(c) The proponent of a modification shall comply with section 1125 of this title with respect to the plan as modified.

(d) Any holder of a claim or interest that has accepted or rejected a plan is deemed to have accepted or rejected, as the case may be, such plan as modified, unless, within the time fixed by the court, such holder changes such holder's previous acceptance or rejection.

(e) If the debtor is an individual, the plan may be modified at any time after confirmation of the plan but before the completion of payments under the plan, whether or not the plan has been substantially consummated, upon request of the debtor, the trustee, the United States trustee, or the holder of an allowed unsecured claim, to—

(1) increase or reduce the amount of payments on claims of a particular class provided for by the plan;

(2) extend or reduce the time period for such payments; or

(3) alter the amount of the distribution to a creditor whose claim is provided for by the plan to the extent necessary to take account of any payment of such claim made other than under the plan.

(f)(1) Sections 1121 through 1128 and the requirements of section 1129 apply to any modification under subsection (a).

(2) The plan, as modified, shall become the plan only after there has been disclosure under section 1125 as the court may direct, notice and a hearing, and such modification is approved.

§ 1128. Confirmation hearing

(a) After notice, the court shall hold a hearing on confirmation of a plan.

(b) A party in interest may object to confirmation of a plan.

§ 1129. Confirmation of plan

(a) The court shall confirm a plan only if all of the following requirements are met:

(1) The plan complies with the applicable provisions of this title.

(2) The proponent of the plan complies with the applicable provisions of this title.

(3) The plan has been proposed in good faith and not by any means forbidden by law.

(4) Any payment made or to be made by the proponent, by the debtor, or by a person issuing securities or acquiring property under the plan, for services or for costs and expenses in or in connection with the case, or in connection with the plan and incident to the case, has been approved by, or is subject to the approval of, the court as reasonable.

(5)(A)(i) The proponent of the plan has disclosed the identity and affiliations of any individual proposed to serve, after confirmation of the plan, as a director, officer, or voting trustee of the debtor, an affiliate of the debtor participating in a joint plan with the debtor, or a successor to the debtor under the plan; and

(ii) the appointment to, or continuance in, such office of such individual, is consistent with the interests of creditors and equity security holders and with public policy; and

(B) the proponent of the plan has disclosed the identity of any insider that will be employed or retained by the reorganized debtor, and the nature of any compensation for such insider.

(6) Any governmental regulatory commission with jurisdiction, after confirmation of the plan, over the rates of the debtor has approved any rate change provided for in the plan, or such rate change is expressly conditioned on such approval.

(7) With respect to each impaired class of claims or interests—

(A) each holder of a claim or interest of such class—

(i) has accepted the plan; or

(ii) will receive or retain under the plan on account of such claim or interest property of a value, as of the effective date of the plan, that is not less than the amount that such holder would so receive or retain if the debtor were liquidated under chapter 7 of this title on such date; or

(B) if section 1111(b)(2) of this title applies to the claims of such class, each holder of a claim of such class will receive or retain under the plan on account of such claim property of a value, as of the effective date of the plan, that is not less than the value of such holder's interest in the estate's interest in the property that secures such claims.

(8) With respect to each class of claims or interests—

(A) such class has accepted the plan; or

(B) such class is not impaired under the plan.

(9) Except to the extent that the holder of a particular claim has agreed to a different treatment of such claim, the plan provides that—

(A) with respect to a claim of a kind specified in section 507(a)(2̶1̶) or 507(a)(3̶2̶) of this title, on the effective date of the plan, the holder of such claim will receive on account of such claim cash equal to the allowed amount of such claim;

(B) with respect to a class of claims of a kind specified in section 507(a)(*1*3), 507(a)(4), 507(a)(5), 507(a)(6), or 507(a)(7) of this title, each holder of a claim of such class will receive—

(i) if such class has accepted the plan, deferred cash payments of a value, as of the effective date of the plan, equal to the allowed amount of such claim; or

(ii) if such class has not accepted the plan, cash on the effective date of the plan equal to the allowed amount of such claim; a̶n̶d̶

(C) with respect to a claim of a kind specified in section 507(a)(8) of this title, the holder of such claim will receive on account of such claim d̶e̶f̶e̶r̶r̶e̶d̶ c̶a̶s̶h̶ p̶a̶y̶m̶e̶n̶t̶s̶,̶ o̶v̶e̶r̶ a̶ p̶e̶r̶i̶o̶d̶ n̶o̶t̶ e̶x̶c̶e̶e̶d̶i̶n̶g̶ s̶i̶x̶ y̶e̶a̶r̶s̶ a̶f̶t̶e̶r̶ t̶h̶e̶ d̶a̶t̶e̶ o̶f̶ a̶s̶s̶e̶s̶s̶-̶ m̶e̶n̶t̶ o̶f̶ s̶u̶c̶h̶ c̶l̶a̶i̶m̶,̶ o̶f̶ a̶ v̶a̶l̶u̶e̶,̶ a̶s̶ o̶f̶ t̶h̶e̶ e̶f̶f̶e̶c̶t̶i̶v̶e̶ d̶a̶t̶e̶ o̶f̶ t̶h̶e̶ p̶l̶a̶n̶,̶ e̶q̶u̶a̶l̶ t̶o̶ t̶h̶e̶ a̶l̶l̶o̶w̶e̶d̶ a̶m̶o̶u̶n̶t̶ o̶f̶ s̶u̶c̶h̶ c̶l̶a̶i̶m̶.̶*regular installment payments in cash—*

(i) of a total value, as of the effective date of the plan, equal to the allowed amount of such claim;

(ii) over a period ending not later than 5 years after the date of the order for relief under section 301, 302, or 303; and

(iii) in a manner not less favorable than the most favored nonpriority unsecured claim provided for by the plan (other than cash payments made to a class of creditors under section 1122(b)); and

(D) with respect to a secured claim which would otherwise meet the description of an unsecured claim of a governmental unit under section 507(a)(8), but for the secured status of that claim, the holder of that claim will receive on account of that claim, cash payments, in the same manner and over the same period, as prescribed in subparagraph (C).

(10) If a class of claims is impaired under the plan, at least one class of claims that is impaired under the plan has accepted the plan, determined without including any acceptance of the plan by any insider.

(11) Confirmation of the plan is not likely to be followed by the liquidation, or the need for further financial reorganization, of the debtor or any successor to the debtor under the plan, unless such liquidation or reorganization is proposed in the plan.

(12) All fees payable under section 1930 of title 28, as determined by the court at the hearing on confirmation of the plan, have been paid or the plan provides for the payment of all such fees on the effective date of the plan.

(13) The plan provides for the continuation after its effective date of payment of all retiree benefits, as that term is defined in section 1114 of this title, at the level established pursuant to subsection (e)(1)(B) or (g) of section 1114 of this title, at any time prior to confirmation of the plan, for the duration of the period the debtor has obligated itself to provide such benefits.

(14) If the debtor is required by a judicial or administrative order, or by statute, to pay a domestic support obligation, the debtor has paid all amounts payable under such order or such statute for such obligation that first become payable after the date of the filing of the petition.

(15) In a case in which the debtor is an individual and in which the holder of an allowed unsecured claim objects to the confirmation of the plan—

(A) the value, as of the effective date of the plan, of the property to be distributed under the plan on account of such claim is not less than the amount of such claim; or

(B) the value of the property to be distributed under the plan is not less than the projected disposable income of the debtor (as defined in section 1325(b)(2)) to be received during the 5-year period beginning on the date that the first payment is due under the plan, or during the period for which the plan provides payments, whichever is longer.

(16) All transfers of property of the plan shall be made in accordance with any applicable provisions of nonbankruptcy law that govern the transfer of property by a corporation or trust that is not a moneyed, business, or commercial corporation or trust.

(b)(1) Notwithstanding section 510(a) of this title, if all of the applicable requirements of subsection (a) of this section other than paragraph (8) are met with respect to a plan, the court, on request of the proponent of the plan, shall confirm the plan notwithstanding the requirements of such paragraph if the plan does not discriminate unfairly, and is fair and equitable, with respect to each class of claims or interests that is impaired under, and has not accepted, the plan.

(2) For the purpose of this subsection, the condition that a plan be fair and equitable with respect to a class includes the following requirements:

(A) With respect to a class of secured claims, the plan provides—

(i)(I) that the holders of such claims retain the liens securing such claims, whether the property subject to such liens is retained by the debtor or transferred to another entity, to the extent of the allowed amount of such claims; and

(II) that each holder of a claim of such class receive on account of such claim deferred cash payments totaling at least the allowed amount of such claim, of a value, as of the effective date of the plan, of at least the value of such holder's interest in the estate's interest in such property;

(ii) for the sale, subject to section 363(k) of this title, of any property that is subject to the liens securing such claims, free and clear of such liens, with such liens to attach to the proceeds of such sale, and the treatment of such liens on proceeds under clause (i) or (iii) of this subparagraph; or

(iii) for the realization by such holders of the indubitable equivalent of such claims.

(B) With respect to a class of unsecured claims—

(i) the plan provides that each holder of a claim of such class receive or retain on account of such claim property of a value, as of the effective date of the plan, equal to the allowed amount of such claim; or

(ii) the holder of any claim or interest that is junior to the claims of such class will not receive or retain under the plan on account of such junior claim or interest any property, *except that in a case in which the debtor is an individual, the debtor may retain property included in the estate under section 1115, subject to the requirements of subsection (a)(14) of this section.*

(C) With respect to a class of interests—

(i) the plan provides that each holder of an interest of such class receive or retain on account of such interest property of a value, as of the effective date of the plan, equal to the greatest of the allowed amount of any fixed liquidation preference to which such holder is entitled, any fixed redemption price to which such holder is entitled, or the value of such interest; or

(ii) the holder of any interest that is junior to the interests of such class will not receive or retain under the plan on account of such junior interest any property.

(c) Notwithstanding subsections (a) and (b) of this section and except as provided in section 1127(b) of this title, the court may confirm only one plan, unless the order of confirmation in the case has been revoked under section 1144 of this title. If the requirements of subsections (a) and (b) of this section are met with respect to more than one plan, the court shall consider the preferences of creditors and equity security holders in determining which plan to confirm.

(d) Notwithstanding any other provision of this section, on request of a party in interest that is a governmental unit, the court may not confirm a plan if the principal purpose of the plan is the avoidance of taxes or the avoidance of the application of section 5 of the Securities Act of 1933. In any hearing under this subsection, the governmental unit has the burden of proof on the issue of avoidance.

(e) In a small business case, the court shall confirm a plan that complies with the applicable provisions of this title and that is filed in accordance with section 1121(e) not later than 45 days after the plan is filed unless the time for confirmation is extended in accordance with section 1121(e)(3).

SUBCHAPTER III—POSTCONFIRMATION MATTERS

§ 1141. Effect of confirmation

(a) Except as provided in subsections (d)(2) and (d)(3) of this section, the provisions of a confirmed plan bind the debtor, any entity issuing securities under the plan, any entity acquiring property under the plan, and any creditor, equity security holder, or general partner in the debtor, whether or not the claim or interest of such creditor, equity security holder, or general partner is impaired under the plan and whether or not such creditor, equity security holder, or general partner has accepted the plan.

(b) Except as otherwise provided in the plan or the order confirming the plan, the confirmation of a plan vests all of the property of the estate in the debtor.

(c) Except as provided in subsections (d)(2) and (d)(3) of this section and except as otherwise provided in the plan or in the order confirming the plan, after confirmation of a plan, the property dealt with by the plan is free and clear of all claims and interests of creditors, equity security holders, and of general partners in the debtor.

(d)(1) Except as otherwise provided in this subsection, in the plan, or in the order confirming the plan, the confirmation of a plan—

    (A) discharges the debtor from any debt that arose before the date of such confirmation, and any debt of a kind specified in section 502(g), 502(h), or 502(i) of this title, whether or not—

        (i) a proof of the claim based on such debt is filed or deemed filed under section 501 of this title;

        (ii) such claim is allowed under section 502 of this title; or

        (iii) the holder of such claim has accepted the plan; and

    (B) terminates all rights and interests of equity security holders and general partners provided for by the plan.

  (2) ~~The confirmation of a plan does not discharge an individual debtor.~~*A discharge under this chapter does not discharge a debtor who is an individual* from any debt excepted from discharge under section 523 of this title.

  (3) The confirmation of a plan does not discharge a debtor if—

    (A) the plan provides for the liquidation of all or substantially all of the property of the estate;

    (B) the debtor does not engage in business after consummation of the plan; and

    (C) the debtor would be denied a discharge under section 727(a) of this title if the case were a case under chapter 7 of this title.

    (4) The court may approve a written waiver of discharge executed by the debtor after the order for relief under this chapter.

  (5) In a case in which the debtor is an individual—

(A) unless after notice and a hearing the court orders otherwise for cause, confirmation of the plan does not discharge any debt provided for in the plan until the court grants a discharge on completion of all payments under the plan;

(B) at any time after the confirmation of the plan, and after notice and a hearing, the court may grant a discharge to the debtor who has not completed payments under the plan if—

(i) the value, as of the effective date of the plan, of property actually distributed under the plan on account of each allowed unsecured claim is not less than the amount that would have been paid on such claim if the estate of the debtor had been liquidated under chapter 7 on such date; and

(ii) modification of the plan under section 1127 is not practicable; and

(C) unless after notice and a hearing held not more than 10 days before the date of the entry of the order granting the discharge, the court finds that there is no reasonable cause to believe that—

(i) section 522(q)(1) may be applicable to the debtor; and

(ii) there is pending any proceeding in which the debtor may be found guilty of a felony of the kind described in section 522(q)(1)(A) or liable for a debt of the kind described in section 522(q)(1)(B).

(6) Notwithstanding paragraph (1), the confirmation of a plan does not discharge a debtor that is a corporation from any debt—

(A) of a kind specified in paragraph (2)(A) or (2)(B) of section 523(a) that is owed to a domestic governmental unit, or owed to a person as the result of an action filed under subchapter III of chapter 37 of title 31 or any similar State statute; or

(B) for a tax or customs duty with respect to which the debtor—

(i) made a fraudulent return; or

(ii) willfully attempted in any manner to evade or to defeat such tax or such customs duty.

§ 1142. Implementation of plan

(a) Notwithstanding any otherwise applicable nonbankruptcy law, rule, or regulation relating to financial condition, the debtor and any entity organized or to be organized for the purpose of carrying out the plan shall carry out the plan and shall comply with any orders of the court.

(b) The court may direct the debtor and any other necessary party to execute or deliver or to join in the execution or delivery of any instrument required to effect a transfer of property dealt with by a confirmed plan, and to perform any other act, including the satisfaction of any lien, that is necessary for the consummation of the plan.

§ 1143. Distribution

If a plan requires presentment or surrender of a security or the performance of any other act as a condition to participation in distribution under the plan, such action shall be taken not later than five years after the date of the entry of the order of confirmation. Any entity that has not within such time presented or surrendered such entity's security or taken any such other action that the plan requires may not participate in distribution under the plan.

§ 1144. Revocation of an order of confirmation

On request of a party in interest at any time before 180 days after the date of the entry of the order of confirmation, and after notice and a hearing, the court may revoke such order if and only if such order was procured by fraud. An order under this section revoking an order of confirmation shall—

(1) contain such provisions as are necessary to protect any entity acquiring rights in good faith reliance on the order of confirmation; and

(2) revoke the discharge of the debtor.

§ 1145. Exemption from securities laws

(a) Except with respect to an entity that is an underwriter as defined in subsection (b) of this section, section 5 of the Securities Act of 1933 and any State or local law requiring registration for offer or sale of a security or registration or licensing of an issuer of, underwriter of, or broker or dealer in, a security do not apply to—

(1) the offer or sale under a plan of a security of the debtor, of an affiliate participating in a joint plan with the debtor, or of a successor to the debtor under the plan—

(A) in exchange for a claim against, an interest in, or a claim for an administrative expense in the case concerning, the debtor or such affiliate; or

(B) principally in such exchange and partly for cash or property;

(2) the offer of a security through any warrant, option, right to subscribe, or conversion privilege that was sold in the manner specified in paragraph (1) of this subsection, or the sale of a security upon the exercise of such a warrant, option, right, or privilege;

(3) the offer or sale, other than under a plan, of a security of an issuer other than the debtor or an affiliate, if—

(A) such security was owned by the debtor on the date of the filing of the petition;

(B) the issuer of such security is—

(i) required to file reports under section 13 or 15(d) of the Securities Exchange Act of 1934; and

(ii) in compliance with the disclosure and reporting provision of such applicable section; and

(C) such offer or sale is of securities that do not exceed—

(i) during the two-year period immediately following the date of the filing of the petition, four percent of the securities of such class outstanding on such date; and

(ii) during any 180-day period following such two-year period, one percent of the securities outstanding at the beginning of such 180-day period; or

(4) a transaction by a stockbroker in a security that is executed after a transaction of a kind specified in paragraph (1) or (2) of this subsection in such secu-

rity and before the expiration of 40 days after the first date on which such security was bona fide offered to the public by the issuer or by or through an underwriter, if such stockbroker provides, at the time of or before such transaction by such stockbroker, a disclosure statement approved under section 1125 of this title, and, if the court orders, information supplementing such disclosure statement.

(b)(1) Except as provided in paragraph (2) of this subsection and except with respect to ordinary trading transactions of an entity that is not an issuer, an entity is an underwriter under section 2(11) of the Securities Act of 1933, if such entity—

(A) purchases a claim against, interest in, or claim for an administrative expense in the case concerning, the debtor, if such purchase is with a view to distribution of any security received or to be received in exchange for such a claim or interest;

(B) offers to sell securities offered or sold under the plan for the holders of such securities;

(C) offers to buy securities offered or sold under the plan from the holders of such securities, if such offer to buy is—

(i) with a view to distribution of such securities; and

(ii) under an agreement made in connection with the plan, with the consummation of the plan, or with the offer or sale of securities under the plan; or

(D) is an issuer, as used in such section 2(11), with respect to such securities.

(2) An entity is not an underwriter under section 2(11) of the Securities Act of 1933 or under paragraph (1) of this subsection with respect to an agreement that provides only for—

(A)(i) the matching or combining of fractional interests in securities offered or sold under the plan into whole interests; or

(ii) the purchase or sale of such fractional interests from or to entities receiving such fractional interests under the plan; or

(B) the purchase or sale for such entities of such fractional or whole interests as are necessary to adjust for any remaining fractional interests after such matching.

(3) An entity other than an entity of the kind specified in paragraph (1) of this subsection is not an underwriter under section 2(11) of the Securities Act of 1933 with respect to any securities offered or sold to such entity in the manner specified in subsection (a)(1) of this section.

(c) An offer or sale of securities of the kind and in the manner specified under subsection (a)(1) of this section is deemed to be a public offering.

(d) The Trust Indenture Act of 1939 does not apply to a note issued under the plan that matures not later than one year after the effective date of the plan.

§ 1146. Special tax provisions

(a) For the purposes of any State or local law imposing a tax on or measured by income, the taxable period of a debtor that is an individual shall terminate on the

~~date of the order for relief under this chapter, unless the case was converted under section 706 of this title.~~

~~(b) The trustee shall make a State or local tax return of income for the estate of an individual debtor in a case under this chapter for each taxable period after the order for relief under this chapter during which the case is pending.~~

(*a*~~e~~) The issuance, transfer, or exchange of a security, or the making or delivery of an instrument of transfer under a plan confirmed under section 1129 of this title, may not be taxed under any law imposing a stamp tax or similar tax.

(*b*~~d~~) The court may authorize the proponent of a plan to request a determination, limited to questions of law, by a State or local governmental unit charged with responsibility for collection or determination of a tax on or measured by income, of the tax effects, under section 346 of this title and under the law imposing such tax, of the plan. In the event of an actual controversy, the court may declare such effects after the earlier of—

(1) the date on which such governmental unit responds to the request under this subsection; or

(2) 270 days after such request.

SUBCHAPTER IV—RAILROAD REORGANIZATION

§ 1161. Inapplicability of other sections

Sections 341, 343, 1102(a)(1), 1104, 1105, 1107, 1129(a)(7), and 1129(c) of this title do not apply in a case concerning a railroad.

§ 1162. Definition

In this subchapter, "Board" means the "Surface Transportation Board".

§ 1163. Appointment of trustee

As soon as practicable after the order for relief the Secretary of Transportation shall submit a list of five disinterested persons that are qualified and willing to serve as trustees in the case. The United States trustee shall appoint one of such persons to serve as trustee in the case.

§ 1164. Right to be heard

The Board, the Department of Transportation, and any State or local commission having regulatory jurisdiction over the debtor may raise and may appear and be heard on any issue in a case under this chapter, but may not appeal from any judgment, order, or decree entered in the case.

§ 1165. Protection of the public interest

In applying sections 1166, 1167, 1169, 1170, 1171, 1172, 1173, and 1174 of this title, the court and the trustee shall consider the public interest in addition to the interests of the debtor, creditors, and equity security holders.

§ 1166. Effect of subtitle IV of title 49 and of Federal, State, or local regulations

Except with respect to abandonment under section 1170 of this title, or merger, modification of the financial structure of the debtor, or issuance or sale of securities under a plan, the trustee and the debtor are subject to the provisions of subtitle IV of title 49 that are applicable to railroads, and the trustee is subject to orders of any Federal, State, or local regulatory body to the same extent as the debtor would be if a petition commencing the case under this chapter had not been filed, but—

(1) any such order that would require the expenditure, or the incurring of an obligation for the expenditure, of money from the estate is not effective unless approved by the court; and

(2) the provisions of this chapter are subject to section 601(b) of the Regional Rail Reorganization Act of 1973.

§ 1167. Collective bargaining agreements

Notwithstanding section 365 of this title, neither the court nor the trustee may change the wages or working conditions of employees of the debtor established by a collective bargaining agreement that is subject to the Railway Labor Act except in accordance with section 6 of such Act.

§ 1168. Rolling stock equipment

(a)(1) The right of a secured party with a security interest in or of a lessor or conditional vendor of equipment described in paragraph (2) to take possession of such equipment in compliance with an equipment security agreement, lease, or conditional sale contract, and to enforce any of its other rights or remedies under such security agreement, lease, or conditional sale contract, to sell, lease, or otherwise retain or dispose of such equipment, is not limited or otherwise affected by any other provision of this title or by any power of the court, except that right to take possession and enforce those other rights and remedies shall be subject to section 362, if—

(A) before the date that is 60 days after the date of commencement of a case under this chapter, the trustee, subject to the court's approval, agrees to perform all obligations of the debtor under such security agreement, lease, or conditional sale contract; and

(B) any default, other than a default of a kind described in section 365(b)(2), under such security agreement, lease, or conditional sale contract—

(i) that occurs before the date of commencement of the case and is an event of default therewith is cured before the expiration of such 60-day period;

(ii) that occurs or becomes an event of default after the date of commencement of the case and before the expiration of such 60-day period is cured before the later of—

(I) the date that is 30 days after the date of the default or event of the default; or

(II) the expiration of such 60-day period; and

(iii) that occurs on or after the expiration of such 60-day period is cured in accordance with the terms of such security agreement, lease, or conditional sale contract, if cure is permitted under that agreement, lease, or conditional sale contract.

(2) The equipment described in this paragraph—

(A) is rolling stock equipment or accessories used on rolling stock equipment, including superstructures or racks, that is subject to a security interest granted by, leased to, or conditionally sold to a debtor; and

(B) includes all records and documents relating to such equipment that are required, under the terms of the security agreement, lease, or conditional sale contract, that is to be surrendered or returned by the debtor in connection with the surrender or return of such equipment.

(3) Paragraph (1) applies to a secured party, lessor, or conditional vendor acting in its own behalf or acting as trustee or otherwise in behalf of another party.

(b) The trustee and the secured party, lessor, or conditional vendor whose right to take possession is protected under subsection (a) may agree, subject to the court's approval, to extend the 60-day period specified in subsection (a)(1).

(c)(1) In any case under this chapter, the trustee shall immediately surrender and return to a secured party, lessor, or conditional vendor, described in subsection (a)(1), equipment described in subsection (a)(2), if at any time after the date of commencement of the case under this chapter such secured party, lessor, or conditional vendor is entitled pursuant to subsection (a)(1) to take possession of such equipment and makes a written demand for such possession of the trustee.

(2) At such time as the trustee is required under paragraph (1) to surrender and return equipment described in subsection (a)(2), any lease of such equipment, and any security agreement or conditional sale contract relating to such equipment, if such security agreement or conditional sale contract is an executory contract, shall be deemed rejected.

(d) With respect to equipment first placed in service on or prior to October 22, 1994, for purposes of this section—

(1) the term "lease" includes any written agreement with respect to which the lessor and the debtor, as lessee, have expressed in the agreement or in a substantially contemporaneous writing that the agreement is to be treated as a lease for Federal income tax purposes; and

(2) the term "security interest" means a purchase- money equipment security interest.

(e) With respect to equipment first placed in service after October 22, 1994, for purposes of this section, the term "rolling stock equipment" includes rolling stock equipment that is substantially rebuilt and accessories used on such equipment.

§ 1169. Effect of rejection of lease of railroad line

(a) Except as provided in subsection (b) of this section, if a lease of a line of railroad under which the debtor is the lessee is rejected under section 365 of this title, and if the trustee, within such time as the court fixes, and with the court's approval, elects not to operate the leased line, the lessor under such lease, after such approval, shall operate the line.

(b) If operation of such line by such lessor is impracticable or contrary to the public interest, the court, on request of such lessor, and after notice and a hearing, shall order the trustee to continue operation of such line for the account of such lessor until abandonment is ordered under section 1170 of this title, or until such operation is otherwise lawfully terminated, whichever occurs first.

(c) During any such operation, such lessor is deemed a carrier subject to the provisions of subtitle IV of title 49 that are applicable to railroads.

§ 1170. Abandonment of railroad line

(a) The court, after notice and a hearing, may authorize the abandonment of all or a portion of a railroad line if such abandonment is

(1)(A) in the best interest of the estate; or

(B) essential to the formulation of a plan; and

(2) consistent with the public interest.

(b) If, except for the pendency of the case under this chapter, such abandonment would require approval by the Board under a law of the United States, the trustee shall initiate an appropriate application for such abandonment with the Board. The court may fix a time within which the Board shall report to the court on such application.

(c) After the court receives the report of the Board, or the expiration of the time fixed under subsection (b) of this section, whichever occurs first, the court may authorize such abandonment, after notice to the Board, the Secretary of Transportation, the trustee, any party in interest that has requested notice, any affected shipper or community, and any other entity prescribed by the court, and a hearing.

(d)(1) Enforcement of an order authorizing such abandonment shall be stayed until the time for taking an appeal has expired, or, if an appeal is timely taken, until such order has become final.

(2) If an order authorizing such abandonment is appealed, the court, on request of a party in interest, may authorize suspension of service on a line or a portion of a line pending the determination of such appeal, after notice to the Board, the Secretary of Transportation, the trustee, any party in interest that has requested notice, any affected shipper or community, and any other entity prescribed by the court, and a hearing. An appellant may not obtain a stay of the enforcement of an order authorizing such suspension by the giving of a supersedeas bond or otherwise, during the pendency of such appeal.

(e)(1) In authorizing any abandonment of a railroad line under this section, the court shall require the rail carrier to provide a fair arrangement at least as protective of the interests of employees as that established under section 11347*11326(a)* of title 49.

(2) Nothing in this subsection shall be deemed to affect the priorities or timing of payment of employee protection which might have existed in the absence of this subsection.

§ 1171. Priority claims

(a) There shall be paid as an administrative expense any claim of an individual or of the personal representative of a deceased individual against the debtor or the estate, for personal injury to or death of such individual arising out of the operation of the debtor or the estate, whether such claim arose before or after the commencement of the case.

(b) Any unsecured claim against the debtor that would have been entitled to priority if a receiver in equity of the property of the debtor had been appointed by a Federal court on the date of the order for relief under this title shall be entitled to the same priority in the case under this chapter.

§ 1172. Contents of plan

(a) In addition to the provisions required or permitted under section 1123 of this title, a plan—

(1) shall specify the extent to and the means by which the debtor's rail service is proposed to be continued, and the extent to which any of the debtor's rail service is proposed to be terminated; and

(2) may include a provision for—

(A) the transfer of any or all of the operating railroad lines of the debtor to another operating railroad; or

(B) abandonment of any railroad line in accordance with section 1170 of this title.

(b) If, except for the pendency of the case under this chapter, transfer of, or operation of or over, any of the debtor's rail lines by an entity other than the debtor or a successor to the debtor under the plan would require approval by the Board under a law of the United States, then a plan may not propose such a transfer or such operation unless the proponent of the plan initiates an appropriate application for such a transfer or such operation with the Board and, within such time as the court may fix, not exceeding 180 days, the Board, with or without a hearing, as the Board may determine, and with or without modification or condition, approves such application, or does not act on such application. Any action or order of the Board approving, modifying, conditioning, or disapproving such application is subject to review by the court only under sections 706(2)(A), 706(2)(B), 706(2)(C), and 706(2)(D) of title 5.

(c)(1) In approving an application under subsection (b) of this section, the Board shall require the rail carrier to provide a fair arrangement at least as protective of the interests of employees as that established under section 11347*11326(a)*of title 49.

(2) Nothing in this subsection shall be deemed to affect the priorities or timing of payment of employee protection which might have existed in the absence of this subsection.

§ 1173. Confirmation of plan

(a) The court shall confirm a plan if—

(1) the applicable requirements of section 1129 of this title have been met;

(2) each creditor or equity security holder will receive or retain under the plan property of a value, as of the effective date of the plan, that is not less than the value of property that each such creditor or equity security holder would so receive or retain if all of the operating railroad lines of the debtor were sold, and the proceeds of such sale, and the other property of the estate, were distributed under chapter 7 of this title on such date;

(3) in light of the debtor's past earnings and the probable prospective earnings of the reorganized debtor, there will be adequate coverage by such prospective earnings of any fixed charges, such as interest on debt, amortization of funded debt, and rent for leased railroads, provided for by the plan; and

(4) the plan is consistent with the public interest.

(b) If the requirements of subsection (a) of this section are met with respect to more than one plan, the court shall confirm the plan that is most likely to maintain adequate rail service in the public interest.

§ 1174. Liquidation

On request of a party in interest and after notice and a hearing, the court may, or, if a plan has not been confirmed under section 1173 of this title before five years after the date of the order for relief, the court shall, order the trustee to cease the debtor's operation and to collect and reduce to money all of the property of the estate in the same manner as if the case were a case under chapter 7 of this title.

CHAPTER 12—ADJUSTMENT OF DEBTS OF A FAMILY FARMER OR FISHERMAN WITH REGULAR ANNUAL INCOME

SUBCHAPTER I—OFFICERS, ADMINISTRATION, AND THE ESTATE

§ 1201. Stay of action against codebtor

(a) Except as provided in subsections (b) and (c) of this section, after the order for relief under this chapter, a creditor may not act, or commence or continue any civil action, to collect all or any part of a consumer debt of the debtor from any individual that is liable on such debt with the debtor, or that secured such debt, unless—

(1) such individual became liable on or secured such debt in the ordinary course of such individual's business; or

(2) the case is closed, dismissed, or converted to a case under chapter 7 of this title.

(b) A creditor may present a negotiable instrument, and may give notice of dishonor of such an instrument.

(c) On request of a party in interest and after notice and a hearing, the court shall grant relief from the stay provided by subsection (a) of this section with respect to a creditor, to the extent that—

(1) as between the debtor and the individual protected under subsection (a) of this section, such individual received the consideration for the claim held by such creditor;

(2) the plan filed by the debtor proposes not to pay such claim; or

(3) such creditor's interest would be irreparably harmed by continuation of such stay.

(d) Twenty days after the filing of a request under subsection (c)(2) of this section for relief from the stay provided by subsection (a) of this section, such stay is terminated with respect to the party in interest making such request, unless the debtor or any individual that is liable on such debt with the debtor files and serves upon such party in interest a written objection to the taking of the proposed action.

§ 1202. Trustee

(a) If the United States trustee has appointed an individual under section 586(b) of title 28 to serve as standing trustee in cases under this chapter and if such individual qualifies as a trustee under section 322 of this title, then such individual shall serve as trustee in any case filed under this chapter. Otherwise, the United States trustee shall appoint one disinterested person to serve as trustee in the case or the United States trustee may serve as trustee in the case if necessary.

(b) The trustee shall—

(1) perform the duties specified in sections 704(2), 704(3), 704(5), 704(6), 704(7), and 704(9) of this title;

(2) perform the duties specified in section 1106(a)(3) and 1106(a)(4) of this title if the court, for cause and on request of a party in interest, the trustee, or the United States trustee, so orders;

(3) appear and be heard at any hearing that concerns—

(A) the value of property subject to a lien;

(B) confirmation of a plan;

(C) modification of the plan after confirmation; or

(D) the sale of property of the estate;

(4) ensure that the debtor commences making timely payments required by a confirmed plan; and

(5) if the debtor ceases to be a debtor in possession, perform the duties specified in sections 704(8), 1106(a)(1), 1106(a)(2), 1106(a)(6), 1106(a)(7), and 1203.; and

(6) if with respect to the debtor there is a claim for a domestic support obligation, provide the applicable notice specified in subsection (c).

(c)(1) In a case described in subsection (b)(6) to which subsection (b)(6) applies, the trustee shall—

(A)(i) provide written notice to the holder of the claim described in subsection (b)(6) of such claim and of the right of such holder to use the services of the State child support enforcement agency established under sections 464 and 466 of the Social Security Act for the State in which such holder resides, for assistance in collecting child support during and after the case under this title; and

(ii) include in the notice provided under clause (i) the address and telephone number of such State child support enforcement agency;

(B)(i) provide written notice to such State child support enforcement agency of such claim; and

(ii) include in the notice provided under clause (i) the name, address, and telephone number of such holder; and

(C) at such time as the debtor is granted a discharge under section 1228, provide written notice to such holder and to such State child support enforcement agency of—

(i) the granting of the discharge;

(ii) the last recent known address of the debtor;

(iii) the last recent known name and address of the debtor's employer; and

(iv) the name of each creditor that holds a claim that—

(I) is not discharged under paragraph (2), (4), or (14A) of section 523(a); or

(II) was reaffirmed by the debtor under section 524(c).

(2)(A) The holder of a claim described in subsection (b)(6) or the State child support enforcement agency of the State in which such holder resides may request from a creditor described in paragraph (1)(C)(iv) the last known address of the debtor.

(B) Notwithstanding any other provision of law, a creditor that makes a disclosure of a last known address of a debtor in connection with a request made under subparagraph (A) shall not be liable by reason of making that disclosure.

§ 1203. Rights and powers of debtor

Subject to such limitations as the court may prescribe, a debtor in possession shall have all the rights, other than the right to compensation under section 330, and powers, and shall perform all the functions and duties, except the duties specified in paragraphs (3) and (4) of section 1106(a), of a trustee serving in a case under chapter 11, including operating the debtor's farm *or commercial fishing operation.*

§ 1204. Removal of debtor as debtor in possession

(a) On request of a party in interest, and after notice and a hearing, the court shall order that the debtor shall not be a debtor in possession for cause, including fraud, dishonesty, incompetence, or gross mismanagement of the affairs of the debtor, either before or after the commencement of the case.

(b) On request of a party in interest, and after notice and a hearing, the court may reinstate the debtor in possession.

§ 1205. Adequate protection

(a) Section 361 does not apply in a case under this chapter.

(b) In a case under this chapter, when adequate protection is required under section 362, 363, or 364 of this title of an interest of an entity in property, such adequate protection may be provided by—

(1) requiring the trustee to make a cash payment or periodic cash payments to such entity, to the extent that the stay under section 362 of this title, use, sale, or lease under section 363 of this title, or any grant of a lien under section 364 of

this title results in a decrease in the value of property securing a claim or of an entity's ownership interest in property;

(2) providing to such entity an additional or replacement lien to the extent that such stay, use, sale, lease, or grant results in a decrease in the value of property securing a claim or of an entity's ownership interest in property;

(3) paying to such entity for the use of farmland the reasonable rent customary in the community where the property is located, based upon the rental value, net income, and earning capacity of the property; or

(4) granting such other relief, other than entitling such entity to compensation allowable under section 503(b)(1) of this title as an administrative expense, as will adequately protect the value of property securing a claim or of such entity's ownership interest in property.

§ 1206. Sales free of interests

After notice and a hearing, in addition to the authorization contained in section 363(f), the trustee in a case under this chapter may sell property under section 363(b) and (c) free and clear of any interest in such property of an entity other than the estate if the property is farmland or farm equipment*if the property is farmland, farm equipment, or property used to carry out a commercial fishing operation (including a commercial fishing vessel)*, except that the proceeds of such sale shall be subject to such interest.

§ 1207. Property of the estate

(a) Property of the estate includes, in addition to the property specified in section 541 of this title—

(1) all property of the kind specified in such section that the debtor acquires after the commencement of the case but before the case is closed, dismissed, or converted to a case under chapter 7 of this title, whichever occurs first; and

(2) earnings from services performed by the debtor after the commencement of the case but before the case is closed, dismissed, or converted to a case under chapter 7 of this title, whichever occurs first.

(b) Except as provided in section 1204, a confirmed plan, or an order confirming a plan, the debtor shall remain in possession of all property of the estate.

§ 1208. Conversion or dismissal

(a) The debtor may convert a case under this chapter to a case under chapter 7 of this title at any time. Any waiver of the right to convert under this subsection is unenforceable.

(b) On request of the debtor at any time, if the case has not been converted under section 706 or 1112 of this title, the court shall dismiss a case under this chapter. Any waiver of the right to dismiss under this subsection is unenforceable.

(c) On request of a party in interest, and after notice and a hearing, the court may dismiss a case under this chapter for cause, including—

(1) unreasonable delay, or gross mismanagement, by the debtor that is prejudicial to creditors;

(2) nonpayment of any fees and charges required under chapter 123 of title 28;

(3) failure to file a plan timely under section 1221 of this title;

(4) failure to commence making timely payments required by a confirmed plan;

(5) denial of confirmation of a plan under section 1225 of this title and denial of a request made for additional time for filing another plan or a modification of a plan;

(6) material default by the debtor with respect to a term of a confirmed plan;

(7) revocation of the order of confirmation under section 1230 of this title, and denial of confirmation of a modified plan under section 1229 of this title;

(8) termination of a confirmed plan by reason of the occurrence of a condition specified in the plan;~~ or~~

(9) continuing loss to or diminution of the estate and absence of a reasonable likelihood of rehabilitation~~.~~; *and*

(10) failure of the debtor to pay any domestic support obligation that first becomes payable after the date of the filing of the petition.

(d) On request of a party in interest, and after notice and a hearing, the court may dismiss a case under this chapter or convert a case under this chapter to a case under chapter 7 of this title upon a showing that the debtor has committed fraud in connection with the case.

(e) Notwithstanding any other provision of this section, a case may not be converted to a case under another chapter of this title unless the debtor may be a debtor under such chapter.

SUBCHAPTER II—THE PLAN

§ 1221. Filing of plan

The debtor shall file a plan not later than 90 days after the order for relief under this chapter, except that the court may extend such period if the need for an extension is attributable to circumstances for which the debtor should not justly be held accountable.

§ 1222. Contents of plan

(a) The plan shall—

(1) provide for the submission of all or such portion of future earnings or other future income of the debtor to the supervision and control of the trustee as is necessary for the execution of the plan;

(2) ~~provide for the full payment, in deferred cash payments, of all claims entitled to priority under section 507 of this title, unless the holder of a particular claim agrees to a different treatment of such claim; and~~ *provide for the full payment, in deferred cash payments, of all claims entitled to priority under section 507, unless—*

(A) the claim is a claim owed to a governmental unit that arises as a result of the sale, transfer, exchange, or other disposition of any farm asset used in the debtor's farming operation, in which case the claim

shall be treated as an unsecured claim that is not entitled to priority under section 507, but the debt shall be treated in such manner only if the debtor receives a discharge; or

(B) the holder of a particular claim agrees to a different treatment of that claim;

(3) if the plan classifies claims and interests, provide the same treatment for each claim or interest within a particular class unless the holder of a particular claim or interest agrees to less favorable treatment~;~ *and*

(4) notwithstanding any other provision of this section, a plan may provide for less than full payment of all amounts owed for a claim entitled to priority under section 507(a)(1)(B) only if the plan provides that all of the debtor's projected disposable income for a 5-year period beginning on the date that the first payment is due under the plan will be applied to make payments under the plan.

(b) Subject to subsections (a) and (c) of this section, the plan may—

(1) designate a class or classes of unsecured claims, as provided in section 1122 of this title, but may not discriminate unfairly against any class so designated; however, such plan may treat claims for a consumer debt of the debtor if an individual is liable on such consumer debt with the debtor differently than other unsecured claims;

(2) modify the rights of holders of secured claims, or of holders of unsecured claims, or leave unaffected the rights of holders of any class of claims;

(3) provide for the curing or waiving of any default;

(4) provide for payments on any unsecured claim to be made concurrently with payments on any secured claim or any other unsecured claim;

(5) provide for the curing of any default within a reasonable time and maintenance of payments while the case is pending on any unsecured claim or secured claim on which the last payment is due after the date on which the final payment under the plan is due;

(6) subject to section 365 of this title, provide for the assumption, rejection, or assignment of any executory contract or unexpired lease of the debtor not previously rejected under such section;

(7) provide for the payment of all or part of a claim against the debtor from property of the estate or property of the debtor;

(8) provide for the sale of all or any part of the property of the estate or the distribution of all or any part of the property of the estate among those having an interest in such property;

(9) provide for payment of allowed secured claims consistent with section 1225(a)(5) of this title, over a period exceeding the period permitted under section 1222(c);

(10) provide for the vesting of property of the estate, on confirmation of the plan or at a later time, in the debtor or in any other entity~; and~

(11) provide for the payment of interest accruing after the date of the filing of the petition on unsecured claims that are nondischargeable under

section 1228(a), except that such interest may be paid only to the extent that the debtor has disposable income available to pay such interest after making provision for full payment of all allowed claims; and

(12++) include any other appropriate provision not inconsistent with this title.

(c) Except as provided in subsections (b)(5) and (b)(9), the plan may not provide for payments over a period that is longer than three years unless the court for cause approves a longer period, but the court may not approve a period that is longer than five years.

(d) Notwithstanding subsection (b)(2) of this section and sections 506(b) and 1225(a)(5) of this title, if it is proposed in a plan to cure a default, the amount necessary to cure the default, shall be determined in accordance with the underlying agreement and applicable nonbankruptcy law.

§ 1223. Modification of plan before confirmation

(a) The debtor may modify the plan at any time before confirmation, but may not modify the plan so that the plan as modified fails to meet the requirements of section 1222 of this title.

(b) After the debtor files a modification under this section, the plan as modified becomes the plan.

(c) Any holder of a secured claim that has accepted or rejected the plan is deemed to have accepted or rejected, as the case may be, the plan as modified, unless the modification provides for a change in the rights of such holder from what such rights were under the plan before modification, and such holder changes such holder's previous acceptance or rejection.

§ 1224. Confirmation hearing

After expedited notice, the court shall hold a hearing on confirmation of the plan. A party in interest, the trustee, or the United States trustee may object to the confirmation of the plan. Except for cause, the hearing shall be concluded not later than 45 days after the filing of the plan.

§ 1225. Confirmation of plan

(a) Except as provided in subsection (b), the court shall confirm a plan if—

(1) the plan complies with the provisions of this chapter and with the other applicable provisions of this title;

(2) any fee, charge, or amount required under chapter 123 of title 28, or by the plan, to be paid before confirmation, has been paid;

(3) the plan has been proposed in good faith and not by any means forbidden by law;

(4) the value, as of the effective date of the plan, of property to be distributed under the plan on account of each allowed unsecured claim is not less than the amount that would be paid on such claim if the estate of the debtor were liquidated under chapter 7 of this title on such date;

(5) with respect to each allowed secured claim provided for by the plan—

(A) the holder of such claim has accepted the plan;

   (B)(i) the plan provides that the holder of such claim retain the lien securing such claim; and

   (ii) the value, as of the effective date of the plan, of property to be distributed by the trustee or the debtor under the plan on account of such claim is not less than the allowed amount of such claim; or

   (C) the debtor surrenders the property securing such claim to such holder; ~~and~~

 (6) the debtor will be able to make all payments under the plan and to comply with the plan~~.~~*; and*

 (7) the debtor has paid all amounts that are required to be paid under a domestic support obligation and that first become payable after the date of the filing of the petition if the debtor is required by a judicial or administrative order, or by statute, to pay such domestic support obligation.

(b)(1) If the trustee or the holder of an allowed unsecured claim objects to the confirmation of the plan, then the court may not approve the plan unless, as of the effective date of the plan—

   (A) the value of the property to be distributed under the plan on account of such claim is not less than the amount of such claim; ~~or~~

   (B) the plan provides that all of the debtor's projected disposable income to be received in the three-year period, or such longer period as the court may approve under section 1222(c), beginning on the date that the first payment is due under the plan will be applied to make payments under the plan*; or*~~.~~

   (C) the value of the property to be distributed under the plan in the 3-year period, or such longer period as the court may approve under section 1222(c), beginning on the date that the first distribution is due under the plan is not less than the debtor's projected disposable income for such period.

 (2) For purposes of this subsection, "disposable income" means income which is received by the debtor and which is not reasonably necessary to be expended—

   (A) for the maintenance or support of the debtor or a dependent of the debtor *or for a domestic support obligation that first becomes payable after the date of the filing of the petition*; or

   (B) for the payment of expenditures necessary for the continuation, preservation, and operation of the debtor's business.

 (c) After confirmation of a plan, the court may order any entity from whom the debtor receives income to pay all or any part of such income to the trustee.

§ 1226. Payments

 (a) Payments and funds received by the trustee shall be retained by the trustee until confirmation or denial of confirmation of a plan. If a plan is confirmed, the trustee shall distribute any such payment in accordance with the plan. If a plan is not confirmed, the trustee shall return any such payments to the debtor, after deducting—

(1) any unpaid claim allowed under section 503(b) of this title; and

(2) if a standing trustee is serving in the case, the percentage fee fixed for such standing trustee.

(b) Before or at the time of each payment to creditors under the plan, there shall be paid—

(1) any unpaid claim of the kind specified in section 507(a)(2+) of this title; and

(2) if a standing trustee appointed under section 1202(c) of this title is serving in the case, the percentage fee fixed for such standing trustee under section 1202(d) of this title.

(c) Except as otherwise provided in the plan or in the order confirming the plan, the trustee shall make payments to creditors under the plan.

§ 1227. Effect of confirmation

(a) Except as provided in section 1228(a) of this title, the provisions of a confirmed plan bind the debtor, each creditor, each equity security holder, and each general partner in the debtor, whether or not the claim of such creditor, such equity security holder, or such general partner in the debtor is provided for by the plan, and whether or not such creditor, such equity security holder, or such general partner in the debtor has objected to, has accepted, or has rejected the plan.

(b) Except as otherwise provided in the plan or the order confirming the plan, the confirmation of a plan vests all of the property of the estate in the debtor.

(c) Except as provided in section 1228(a) of this title and except as otherwise provided in the plan or in the order confirming the plan, the property vesting in the debtor under subsection (b) of this section is free and clear of any claim or interest of any creditor provided for by the plan.

§ 1228. Discharge

(a) As *Subject to subsection (d), as* soon as practicable after completion by the debtor of all payments under the plan, *and in the case of a debtor who is required by a judicial or administrative order, or by statute, to pay a domestic support obligation, after such debtor certifies that all amounts payable under such order or such statute that are due on or before the date of the certification (including amounts due before the petition was filed, but only to the extent provided for by the plan) have been paid,* other than payments to holders of allowed claims provided for under section 1222(b)(5) or 1222(b)(9) of this title, unless the court approves a written waiver of discharge executed by the debtor after the order for relief under this chapter, the court shall grant the debtor a discharge of all debts provided for by the plan allowed under section 503 of this title or disallowed under section 502 of this title, except any debt—

(1) provided for under section 1222(b)(5) or 1222(b)(9) of this title; or

(2) of the kind specified in section 523(a) of this title.

(b) At *Subject to subsection (d), at* any time after the confirmation of the plan and after notice and a hearing, the court may grant a discharge to a debtor that has not completed payments under the plan only if—

(1) the debtor's failure to complete such payments is due to circumstances for which the debtor should not justly be held accountable;

(2) the value, as of the effective date of the plan, of property actually distributed under the plan on account of each allowed unsecured claim is not less than the amount that would have been paid on such claim if the estate of the debtor had been liquidated under chapter 7 of this title on such date; and

(3) modification of the plan under section 1229 of this title is not practicable.

(c) A discharge granted under subsection (b) of this section discharges the debtor from all unsecured debts provided for by the plan or disallowed under section 502 of this title, except any debt—

(1) provided for under section 1222(b)(5) or 1222(b)(9) of this title; or

(2) of a kind specified in section 523(a) of this title.

(d) On request of a party in interest before one year after a discharge under this section is granted, and after notice and a hearing, the court may revoke such discharge only if—

(1) such discharge was obtained by the debtor through fraud; and

(2) the requesting party did not know of such fraud until after such discharge was granted.

(e) After the debtor is granted a discharge, the court shall terminate the services of any trustee serving in the case.

(f) The court may not grant a discharge under this chapter unless the court after notice and a hearing held not more than 10 days before the date of the entry of the order granting the discharge finds that there is no reasonable cause to believe that —

(1) section 522(q)(1) may be applicable to the debtor; and

(2) there is pending any proceeding in which the debtor may be found guilty of a felony of the kind described in section 522(q)(1)(A) or liable for a debt of the kind described in section 522(q)(1)(B).

§ 1229. Modification of plan after confirmation

(a) At any time after confirmation of the plan but before the completion of payments under such plan, the plan may be modified, on request of the debtor, the trustee, or the holder of an allowed unsecured claim, to—

(1) increase or reduce the amount of payments on claims of a particular class provided for by the plan;

(2) extend or reduce the time for such payments; or

(3) alter the amount of the distribution to a creditor whose claim is provided for by the plan to the extent necessary to take account of any payment of such claim other than under the plan.

(b)(1) Sections 1222(a), 1222(b), and 1223(c) of this title and the requirements of section 1225(a) of this title apply to any modification under subsection (a) of this section.

(2) The plan as modified becomes the plan unless, after notice and a hearing, such modification is disapproved.

(c) A plan modified under this section may not provide for payments over a period that expires after three years after the time that the first payment under the original confirmed plan was due, unless the court, for cause, approves a longer period, but the court may not approve a period that expires after five years after such time.

(d) A plan may not be modified under this section—

(1) to increase the amount of any payment due before the plan as modified becomes the plan;

(2) by anyone except the debtor, based on an increase in the debtor's disposable income, to increase the amount of payments to unsecured creditors required for a particular month so that the aggregate of such payments exceeds the debtor's disposable income for such month; or

(3) in the last year of the plan by anyone except the debtor, to require payments that would leave the debtor with insufficient funds to carry on the farming operation after the plan is completed.

§ 1230. Revocation of an order of confirmation

(a) On request of a party in interest at any time within 180 days after the date of the entry of an order of confirmation under section 1225 of this title, and after notice and a hearing, the court may revoke such order if such order was procured by fraud.

(b) If the court revokes an order of confirmation under subsection (a) of this section, the court shall dispose of the case under section 1207 of this title, unless, within the time fixed by the court, the debtor proposes and the court confirms a modification of the plan under section 1229 of this title.

§ 1231. Special tax provisions

~~(a) For the purpose of any State or local law imposing a tax on or measured by income, the taxable period of a debtor that is an individual shall terminate on the date of the order for relief under this chapter, unless the case was converted under section 706 of this title.~~

~~(b) The trustee shall make a State or local tax return of income for the estate of an individual debtor in a case under this chapter for each taxable period after the order for relief under this chapter during which the case is pending.~~

(*a*e) The issuance, transfer, or exchange of a security, or the making or delivery of an instrument of transfer under a plan confirmed under section 1225 of this title, may not be taxed under any law imposing a stamp tax or similar tax.

(*b*d) The court may authorize the proponent of a plan to request a determination, limited to questions of law, by ~~a State or local governmental unit~~ *any governmental unit* charged with responsibility for collection or determination of a tax on or measured by income, of the tax effects, under section 346 of this title and under the law imposing such tax, of the plan. In the event of an actual controversy, the court may declare such effects after the earlier of—

(1) the date on which such governmental unit responds to the request under this subsection; or

(2) 270 days after such request.

CHAPTER 13—ADJUSTMENT OF DEBTS OF AN INDIVIDUAL WITH REGULAR INCOME

SUBCHAPTER I—OFFICERS, ADMINISTRATION, AND THE ESTATE

§ 1301. Stay of action against codebtor

(a) Except as provided in subsections (b) and (c) of this section, after the order for relief under this chapter, a creditor may not act, or commence or continue any civil action, to collect all or any part of a consumer debt of the debtor from any individual that is liable on such debt with the debtor, or that secured such debt, unless—

(1) such individual became liable on or secured such debt in the ordinary course of such individual's business; or

(2) the case is closed, dismissed, or converted to a case under chapter 7 or 11 of this title.

(b) A creditor may present a negotiable instrument, and may give notice of dishonor of such an instrument.

(c) On request of a party in interest and after notice and a hearing, the court shall grant relief from the stay provided by subsection (a) of this section with respect to a creditor, to the extent that—

(1) as between the debtor and the individual protected under subsection (a) of this section, such individual received the consideration for the claim held by such creditor;

(2) the plan filed by the debtor proposes not to pay such claim; or

(3) such creditor's interest would be irreparably harmed by continuation of such stay.

(d) Twenty days after the filing of a request under subsection (c)(2) of this section for relief from the stay provided by subsection (a) of this section, such stay is terminated with respect to the party in interest making such request, unless the debtor or any individual that is liable on such debt with the debtor files and serves upon such party in interest a written objection to the taking of the proposed action.

§ 1302. Trustee

(a) If the United States trustee appoints an individual under section 586(b) of title 28 to serve as standing trustee in cases under this chapter and if such individual qualifies under section 322 of this title, then such individual shall serve as trustee in the case. Otherwise, the United States trustee shall appoint one disinterested person to serve as trustee in the case or the United States trustee may serve as a trustee in the case.

(b) The trustee shall—

(1) perform the duties specified in sections 704(2), 704(3), 704(4), 704(5), 704(6), 704(7), and 704(9) of this title;

(2) appear and be heard at any hearing that concerns—

(A) the value of property subject to a lien;

(B) confirmation of a plan; or

(C) modification of the plan after confirmation;

(3) dispose of, under regulations issued by the Director of the Administrative Office of the United States Courts, moneys received or to be received in a case under chapter XIII of the Bankruptcy Act;

(4) advise, other than on legal matters, and assist the debtor in performance under the plan;—and

(5) ensure that the debtor commences making timely payments under section 1326 of this title.; and

(6) if with respect to the debtor there is a claim for a domestic support obligation, provide the applicable notice specified in subsection (d).

(c) If the debtor is engaged in business, then in addition to the duties specified in subsection (b) of this section, the trustee shall perform the duties specified in sections 1106(a)(3) and 1106(a)(4) of this title.

(d)(1) In a case described in subsection (b)(6) to which subsection (b)(6) applies, the trustee shall—

(A)(i) provide written notice to the holder of the claim described in subsection (b)(6) of such claim and of the right of such holder to use the services of the State child support enforcement agency established under sections 464 and 466 of the Social Security Act for the State in which such holder resides, for assistance in collecting child support during and after the case under this title; and

(ii) include in the notice provided under clause (i) the address and telephone number of such State child support enforcement agency;

(B)(i) provide written notice to such State child support enforcement agency of such claim; and

(ii) include in the notice provided under clause (i) the name, address, and telephone number of such holder; and

(C) at such time as the debtor is granted a discharge under section 1328, provide written notice to such holder and to such State child support enforcement agency of—

(i) the granting of the discharge;

(ii) the last recent known address of the debtor;

(iii) the last recent known name and address of the debtor's employer; and

(iv) the name of each creditor that holds a claim that—

(I) is not discharged under paragraph (2) or (4) of section 523(a); or

(II) was reaffirmed by the debtor under section 524(c).

(2)(A) The holder of a claim described in subsection (b)(6) or the State child support enforcement agency of the State in which such holder resides may

request from a creditor described in paragraph (1)(C)(iv) the last known address of the debtor.

(B) Notwithstanding any other provision of law, a creditor that makes a disclosure of a last known address of a debtor in connection with a request made under subparagraph (A) shall not be liable by reason of making that disclosure.

§ 1303. Rights and powers of debtor

Subject to any limitations on a trustee under this chapter, the debtor shall have, exclusive of the trustee, the rights and powers of a trustee under sections 363(b), 363(d), 363(e), 363(f), and 363(l), of this title.

§ 1304. Debtor engaged in business

(a) A debtor that is self-employed and incurs trade credit in the production of income from such employment is engaged in business.

(b) Unless the court orders otherwise, a debtor engaged in business may operate the business of the debtor and, subject to any limitations on a trustee under sections 363(c) and 364 of this title and to such limitations or conditions as the court prescribes, shall have, exclusive of the trustee, the rights and powers of the trustee under such sections.

(c) A debtor engaged in business shall perform the duties of the trustee specified in section 704(8) of this title.

§ 1305. Filing and allowance of postpetition claims

(a) A proof of claim may be filed by any entity that holds a claim against the debtor—

(1) for taxes that become payable to a governmental unit while the case is pending; or

(2) that is a consumer debt, that arises after the date of the order for relief under this chapter, and that is for property or services necessary for the debtor's performance under the plan.

(b) Except as provided in subsection (c) of this section, a claim filed under subsection (a) of this section shall be allowed or disallowed under section 502 of this title, but shall be determined as of the date such claim arises, and shall be allowed under section 502(a), 502(b), or 502(c) of this title, or disallowed under section 502(d) or 502(e) of this title, the same as if such claim had arisen before the date of the filing of the petition.

(c) A claim filed under subsection (a)(2) of this section shall be disallowed if the holder of such claim knew or should have known that prior approval by the trustee of the debtor's incurring the obligation was practicable and was not obtained.

§ 1306. Property of the estate

(a) Property of the estate includes, in addition to the property specified in section 541 of this title—

(1) all property of the kind specified in such section that the debtor acquires after the commencement of the case but before the case is closed, dismissed, or

converted to a case under chapter 7, 11, or 12 of this title, whichever occurs first; and

(2) earnings from services performed by the debtor after the commencement of the case but before the case is closed, dismissed, or converted to a case under chapter 7, 11, or 12 of this title, whichever occurs first.

(b) Except as provided in a confirmed plan or order confirming a plan, the debtor shall remain in possession of all property of the estate.

§ 1307. Conversion or dismissal

(a) The debtor may convert a case under this chapter to a case under chapter 7 of this title at any time. Any waiver of the right to convert under this subsection is unenforceable.

(b) On request of the debtor at any time, if the case has not been converted under section 706, 1112, or 1208 of this title, the court shall dismiss a case under this chapter. Any waiver of the right to dismiss under this subsection is unenforceable.

(c) Except as provided in subsection (e) of this section, on request of a party in interest or the United States trustee and after notice and a hearing, the court may convert a case under this chapter to a case under chapter 7 of this title, or may dismiss a case under this chapter, whichever is in the best interests of creditors and the estate, for cause, including—

(1) unreasonable delay by the debtor that is prejudicial to creditors;

(2) nonpayment of any fees and charges required under chapter 123 of title 28;

(3) failure to file a plan timely under section 1321 of this title;

(4) failure to commence making timely payments under section 1326 of this title;

(5) denial of confirmation of a plan under section 1325 of this title and denial of a request made for additional time for filing another plan or a modification of a plan;

(6) material default by the debtor with respect to a term of a confirmed plan;

(7) revocation of the order of confirmation under section 1330 of this title, and denial of confirmation of a modified plan under section 1329 of this title;

(8) termination of a confirmed plan by reason of the occurrence of a condition specified in the plan other than completion of payments under the plan;

(9) only on request of the United States trustee, failure of the debtor to file, within fifteen days, or such additional time as the court may allow, after the filing of the petition commencing such case, the information required by paragraph (1) of section 521; or

(10) only on request of the United States trustee, failure to timely file the information required by paragraph (2) of section 521.; or

(11) failure of the debtor to pay any domestic support obligation that first becomes payable after the date of the filing of the petition.

(d) Except as provided in subsection (e) of this section, at any time before the confirmation of a plan under section 1325 of this title, on request of a party in interest or the United States trustee and after notice and a hearing, the court may convert a case under this chapter to a case under chapter 11 or 12 of this title.

(e) Upon the failure of the debtor to file a tax return under section 1308, on request of a party in interest or the United States trustee and after notice and a hearing, the court shall dismiss a case or convert a case under this chapter to a case under chapter 7 of this title, whichever is in the best interest of the creditors and the estate.

(e*f*) The court may not convert a case under this chapter to a case under chapter 7, 11, or 12 of this title if the debtor is a farmer, unless the debtor requests such conversion.

(f*g*) Notwithstanding any other provision of this section, a case may not be converted to a case under another chapter of this title unless the debtor may be a debtor under such chapter.

§ 1308. Filing of prepetition tax returns

(a) Not later than the day before the date on which the meeting of the creditors is first scheduled to be held under section 341(a), if the debtor was required to file a tax return under applicable nonbankruptcy law, the debtor shall file with appropriate tax authorities all tax returns for all taxable periods ending during the 4-year period ending on the date of the filing of the petition.

(b)(1) Subject to paragraph (2), if the tax returns required by subsection (a) have not been filed by the date on which the meeting of creditors is first scheduled to be held under section 341(a), the trustee may hold open that meeting for a reasonable period of time to allow the debtor an additional period of time to file any unfiled returns, but such additional period of time shall not extend beyond—

(A) for any return that is past due as of the date of the filing of the petition, the date that is 120 days after the date of that meeting; or

(B) for any return that is not past due as of the date of the filing of the petition, the later of—

(i) the date that is 120 days after the date of that meeting; or

(ii) the date on which the return is due under the last automatic extension of time for filing that return to which the debtor is entitled, and for which request is timely made, in accordance with applicable nonbankruptcy law.

(2) After notice and a hearing, and order entered before the tolling of any applicable filing period determined under this subsection, if the debtor demonstrates by a preponderance of the evidence that the failure to file a return as required under this subsection is attributable to circumstances beyond the control of the debtor, the court may extend the filing period established by the trustee under this subsection for—

(A) a period of not more than 30 days for returns described in paragraph (1); and

(B) a period not to extend after the applicable extended due date for a return described in paragraph (2).

(c) For purposes of this section, the term 'return' includes a return prepared pursuant to subsection (a) or (b) of section 6020 of the Internal Revenue Code of 1986, or a similar State or local law, or a written stipulation to a judgment or a final order entered by a nonbankruptcy tribunal.

SUBCHAPTER II—THE PLAN

§ 1321. Filing of plan

The debtor shall file a plan.

§ 1322. Contents of plan

(a) The plan shall—

(1) provide for the submission of all or such portion of future earnings or other future income of the debtor to the supervision and control of the trustee as is necessary for the execution of the plan;

(2) provide for the full payment, in deferred cash payments, of all claims entitled to priority under section 507 of this title, unless the holder of a particular claim agrees to a different treatment of such claim; and

(3) if the plan classifies claims, provide the same treatment for each claim within a particular class.; and

(4) *notwithstanding any other provision of this section, a plan may provide for less than full payment of all amounts owed for a claim entitled to priority under section 507(a)(1)(B) only if the plan provides that all of the debtor's projected disposable income for a 5-year period beginning on the date that the first payment is due under the plan will be applied to make payments under the plan.*

(b) Subject to subsections (a) and (c) of this section, the plan may—

(1) designate a class or classes of unsecured claims, as provided in section 1122 of this title, but may not discriminate unfairly against any class so designated; however, such plan may treat claims for a consumer debt of the debtor if an individual is liable on such consumer debt with the debtor differently than other unsecured claims;

(2) modify the rights of holders of secured claims, other than a claim secured only by a security interest in real property that is the debtor's principal residence, or of holders of unsecured claims, or leave unaffected the rights of holders of any class of claims;

(3) provide for the curing or waiving of any default;

(4) provide for payments on any unsecured claim to be made concurrently with payments on any secured claim or any other unsecured claim;

(5) notwithstanding paragraph (2) of this subsection, provide for the curing of any default within a reasonable time and maintenance of payments while the case is pending on any unsecured claim or secured claim on which the last payment is due after the date on which the final payment under the plan is due;

(6) provide for the payment of all or any part of any claim allowed under section 1305 of this title;

(7) subject to section 365 of this title, provide for the assumption, rejection, or assignment of any executory contract or unexpired lease of the debtor not previously rejected under such section;

(8) provide for the payment of all or part of a claim against the debtor from property of the estate or property of the debtor;

(9) provide for the vesting of property of the estate, on confirmation of the plan or at a later time, in the debtor or in any other entity; and

(10) provide for the payment of interest accruing after the date of the filing of the petition on unsecured claims that are nondischargeable under section 1328(a), except that such interest may be paid only to the extent that the debtor has disposable income available to pay such interest after making provision for full payment of all allowed claims; and

(11~~10~~) include any other appropriate provision not inconsistent with this title.

(c) Notwithstanding subsection (b)(2) and applicable nonbankruptcy law—

(1) a default with respect to, or that gave rise to, a lien on the debtor's principal residence may be cured under paragraph (3) or (5) of subsection (b) until such residence is sold at a foreclosure sale that is conducted in accordance with applicable nonbankruptcy law; and

(2) in a case in which the last payment on the original payment schedule for a claim secured only by a security interest in real property that is the debtor's principal residence is due before the date on which the final payment under the plan is due, the plan may provide for the payment of the claim as modified pursuant to section 1325(a)(5) of this title.

(d) ~~The plan may not provide for payments over a period that is longer than three years, unless the court, for cause, approves a longer period, but the court may not approve a period that is longer than five years.~~ *(1) If the current monthly income of the debtor and the debtor's spouse combined, when multiplied by 12, is not less than—*

(A) in the case of a debtor in a household of 1 person, the median family income of the applicable State for 1 earner;

(B) in the case of a debtor in a household of 2, 3, or 4 individuals, the highest median family income of the applicable State for a family of the same number or fewer individuals; or

(C) in the case of a debtor in a household exceeding 4 individuals, the highest median family income of the applicable State for a family of 4 or fewer individuals, plus $525 per month for each individual in excess of 4,

the plan may not provide for payments over a period that is longer than 5 years.

(2) If the current monthly income of the debtor and the debtor's spouse combined, when multiplied by 12, is less than—

(A) in the case of a debtor in a household of 1 person, the median family income of the applicable State for 1 earner;

(B) in the case of a debtor in a household of 2, 3, or 4 individuals, the highest median family income of the applicable State for a family of the same number or fewer individuals; or

(C) in the case of a debtor in a household exceeding 4 individuals, the highest median family income of the applicable State for a family of 4 or fewer individuals, plus $525 per month for each individual in excess of 4,

the plan may not provide for payments over a period that is longer than 3 years, unless the court, for cause, approves a longer period, but the court may not approve a period that is longer than 5 years.

(e) Notwithstanding subsection (b)(2) of this section and sections 506(b) and 1325(a)(5) of this title, if it is proposed in a plan to cure a default, the amount necessary to cure the default, shall be determined in accordance with the underlying agreement and applicable nonbankruptcy law.

(f) A plan may not materially alter the terms of a loan described in section 362(b)(19) and any amounts required to repay such loan shall not constitute 'disposable income' under section 1325.

§ 1323. Modification of plan before confirmation

(a) The debtor may modify the plan at any time before confirmation, but may not modify the plan so that the plan as modified fails to meet the requirements of section 1322 of this title.

(b) After the debtor files a modification under this section, the plan as modified becomes the plan.

(c) Any holder of a secured claim that has accepted or rejected the plan is deemed to have accepted or rejected, as the case may be, the plan as modified, unless the modification provides for a change in the rights of such holder from what such rights were under the plan before modification, and such holder changes such holder's previous acceptance or rejection.

§ 1324. Confirmation hearing

~~After~~ *(a) Except as provided in subsection (b) and after* notice, the court shall hold a hearing on confirmation of the plan. A party in interest may object to confirmation of the plan.

(b) The hearing on confirmation of the plan may be held not earlier than 20 days and not later than 45 days after the date of the meeting of creditors under section 341(a), unless the court determines that it would be in the best interests of the creditors and the estate to hold such hearing at an earlier date and there is no objection to such earlier date.

§ 1325. Confirmation of plan

(a) Except as provided in subsection (b), the court shall confirm a plan if—

(1) the plan complies with the provisions of this chapter and with the other applicable provisions of this title;

(2) any fee, charge, or amount required under chapter 123 of title 28, or by the plan, to be paid before confirmation, has been paid;

(3) the plan has been proposed in good faith and not by any means forbidden by law;

(4) the value, as of the effective date of the plan, of property to be distributed under the plan on account of each allowed unsecured claim is not less than the amount that would be paid on such claim if the estate of the debtor were liquidated under chapter 7 of this title on such date;

(5) with respect to each allowed secured claim provided for by the plan—

(A) the holder of such claim has accepted the plan;

(B)(i) ~~the plan provides that the holder of such claim retain the lien securing such claim; and~~*the plan provides that—*

(I) *the holder of such claim retain the lien securing such claim until the earlier of—*

(aa) the payment of the underlying debt determined under nonbankruptcy law; or

(bb) discharge under section 1328; and

(II) if the case under this chapter is dismissed or converted without completion of the plan, such lien shall also be retained by such holder to the extent recognized by applicable nonbankruptcy law;

(ii) the value, as of the effective date of the plan, of property to be distributed under the plan on account of such claim is not less than the allowed amount of such claim;—or *and*

(iii) if—

(I) property to be distributed pursuant to this subsection is in the form of periodic payments, such payments shall be in equal monthly amounts; and

(II) the holder of the claim is secured by personal property, the amount of such payments shall not be less than an amount sufficient to provide to the holder of such claim adequate protection during the period of the plan; or

(C) the debtor surrenders the property securing such claim to such holder; ~~and~~

(6) the debtor will be able to make all payments under the plan and to comply with the plan.~~;~~

(7) the action of the debtor in filing the petition was in good faith;

(8) the debtor has paid all amounts that are required to be paid under a domestic support obligation and that first become payable after the date of the filing of the petition if the debtor is required by a judicial or administrative order, or by statute, to pay such domestic support obligation; and

(9) the debtor has filed all applicable Federal, State, and local tax returns as required by section 1308.

For purposes of paragraph (5), section 506 shall not apply to a claim described in that paragraph if the creditor has a purchase money security interest securing the debt that is the subject of the claim, the debt was incurred within the 910-day preceding the date of the filing of the petition, and the collateral for that debt consists of a motor vehicle (as defined in section 30102 of title 49) acquired for the personal use of the debtor, or if collateral for that debt consists of any other thing of value, if the debt was incurred during the 1-year period preceding that filing.

(b)(1) If the trustee or the holder of an allowed unsecured claim objects to the confirmation of the plan, then the court may not approve the plan unless, as of the effective date of the plan—

(A) the value of the property to be distributed under the plan on account of such claim is not less than the amount of such claim; or

(B) the plan provides that all of the debtor's projected disposable income to be received in the ~~three-year period~~ *applicable commitment period* beginning on the date that the first payment is due under the plan will be applied to make payments *to unsecured creditors* under the plan.

~~(2) For purposes of this subsection, "disposable income" means income which is received by the debtor and which is not reasonably necessary to be expended——~~

~~(A) for the maintenance or support of the debtor or a dependent of the debtor, including charitable contributions (that meet the definition of "charitable contribution" under section 548(d)(3)) to a qualified religious or charitable entity or organization (as that term is defined in section 548(d)(4)) in an amount not to exceed 15 percent of the gross income of the debtor for the year in which the contributions are made; and~~

~~(B) if the debtor is engaged in business, for the payment of expenditures necessary for the continuation, preservation, and operation of such business.~~

(2) For purposes of this subsection, the term 'disposable income' means current monthly income received by the debtor (other than child support payments, foster care payments, or disability payments for a dependent child made in accordance with applicable nonbankruptcy law to the extent reasonably necessary to be expended for such child) less amounts reasonably necessary to be expended—

> *(A)(i) for the maintenance or support of the debtor or a dependent of the debtor, or for a domestic support obligation, that first becomes payable after the date the petition is filed; and*

> *(ii) for charitable contributions (that meet the definition of ' charitable contribution' under section 548(d)(3) to a qualified religious or charitable entity or organization (as defined in section 548(d)(4)) in an amount not to exceed 15 percent of gross income of the debtor for the year in which the contributions are made; and*

> *(B) if the debtor is engaged in business, for the payment of expenditures necessary for the continuation, preservation, and operation of such business.*

(3) Amounts reasonably necessary to be expended under paragraph (2) shall be determined in accordance with subparagraphs (A) and (B) of section 707(b)(2), if the debtor has current monthly income, when multiplied by 12, greater than—

> *(A) in the case of a debtor in a household of 1 person, the median family income of the applicable State for 1 earner;*

> *(B) in the case of a debtor in a household of 2, 3, or 4 individuals, the highest median family income of the applicable State for a family of the same number or fewer individuals; or*

> *(C) in the case of a debtor in a household exceeding 4 individuals, the highest median family income of the applicable State for a family of 4 or fewer individuals, plus $525 per month for each individual in excess of 4.*

(4) For purposes of this subsection, the 'applicable commitment period'—

> *(A) subject to subparagraph (B), shall be—*

>> *(i) 3 years; or*

>> *(ii) not less than 5 years, if the current monthly income of the debtor and the debtor's spouse combined, when multiplied by 12, is not less than—*

>>> *(I) in the case of a debtor in a household of 1 person, the median family income of the applicable State for 1 earner;*

>>> *(II) in the case of a debtor in a household of 2, 3, or 4 individuals, the highest median family income of the applicable State for a family of the same number or fewer individuals; or*

(III) in the case of a debtor in a household exceeding 4 individuals, the highest median family income of the applicable State for a family of 4 or fewer individuals, plus $525 per month for each individual in excess of 4; and

(B) may be less than 3 or 5 years, whichever is applicable under subparagraph (A), but only if the plan provides for payment in full of all allowed unsecured claims over a shorter period.

(c) After confirmation of a plan, the court may order any entity from whom the debtor receives income to pay all or any part of such income to the trustee.

§ 1326. Payments

(a)(1) ~~Unless the court orders otherwise, the debtor shall commence making the payments proposed by a plan within 30 days after the plan is filed.~~ *Unless the court orders otherwise, the debtor shall commence making payments not later than 30 days after the date of the filing of the plan or the order for relief, whichever is earlier, in the amount—*

(A) proposed by the plan to the trustee;

(B) scheduled in a lease of personal property directly to the lessor for that portion of the obligation that becomes due after the order for relief, reducing the payments under subparagraph (A) by the amount so paid and providing the trustee with evidence of such payment, including the amount and date of payment; and

(C) that provides adequate protection directly to a creditor holding an allowed claim secured by personal property to the extent the claim is attributable to the purchase of such property by the debtor for that portion of the obligation that becomes due after the order for relief, reducing the payments under subparagraph (A) by the amount so paid and providing the trustee with evidence of such payment, including the amount and date of payment.

~~(2) A payment made under this subsection shall be retained by the trustee until confirmation or denial of confirmation of a plan. If a plan is confirmed, the trustee shall distribute any such payment in accordance with the plan as soon as practicable. If a plan is not confirmed, the trustee shall return any such payment to the debtor, after deducting any unpaid claim allowed under section 503(b) of this title.~~

(2) A payment made under paragraph (1)(A) shall be retained by the trustee until confirmation or denial of confirmation. If a plan is confirmed, the trustee shall distribute any such payment in accordance with the plan as soon as is practicable. If a plan is not confirmed, the trustee shall return any such payments not previously paid and not yet due and owing to creditors pursuant to paragraph (3) to the debtor, after deducting any unpaid claim allowed under section 503(b).

(3) Subject to section 363, the court may, upon notice and a hearing, modify, increase, or reduce the payments required under this subsection pending confirmation of a plan.

(4) Not later than 60 days after the date of filing of a case under this chapter, a debtor retaining possession of personal property subject to a lease or securing a claim attributable in whole or in part to the purchase price of such property shall provide the lessor or secured creditor reasonable evidence of the mainte-

nance of any required insurance coverage with respect to the use or ownership of such property and continue to do so for so long as the debtor retains possession of such property.

(b) Before or at the time of each payment to creditors under the plan, there shall be paid—

(1) any unpaid claim of the kind specified in section 507(a)(2~~1~~) of this title; ~~and~~

(2) if a standing trustee appointed under section 586(b) of title 28 is serving in the case, the percentage fee fixed for such standing trustee under section 586(e)(1)(B) of title 28~~.~~*; and*

(3) if a chapter 7 trustee has been allowed compensation due to the conversion or dismissal of the debtor's prior case pursuant to section 707(b), and some portion of that compensation remains unpaid in a case converted to this chapter or in the case dismissed under section 707(b) and refiled under this chapter, the amount of any such unpaid compensation, which shall be paid monthly—

(A) by prorating such amount over the remaining duration of the plan; and

(B) by monthly payments not to exceed the greater of—

(i) $25; or

(ii) the amount payable to unsecured nonpriority creditors, as provided by the plan, multiplied by 5 percent, and the result divided by the number of months in the plan.

(c) Except as otherwise provided in the plan or in the order confirming the plan, the trustee shall make payments to creditors under the plan.

(d) Notwithstanding any other provision of this title—

(1) compensation referred to in subsection (b)(3) is payable and may be collected by the trustee under that paragraph, even if such amount has been discharged in a prior case under this title; and

(2) such compensation is payable in a case under this chapter only to the extent permitted by subsection (b)(3).

§ 1327. Effect of confirmation

(a) The provisions of a confirmed plan bind the debtor and each creditor, whether or not the claim of such creditor is provided for by the plan, and whether or not such creditor has objected to, has accepted, or has rejected the plan.

(b) Except as otherwise provided in the plan or the order confirming the plan, the confirmation of a plan vests all of the property of the estate in the debtor.

(c) Except as otherwise provided in the plan or in the order confirming the plan, the property vesting in the debtor under subsection (b) of this section is free and clear of any claim or interest of any creditor provided for by the plan.

§ 1328. Discharge

(a) ~~As~~ *Subject to subsection (d), as* soon as practicable after completion by the debtor of all payments under the plan*, and in the case of a debtor who is required by a judicial or administrative order, or by statute, to pay a domestic support obligation, after such debtor certifies that all amounts payable under such order or such statute that are due on or before the date of the certification (including* *amounts due before the petition was filed, but only to the extent provided for by the plan) have been paid*, unless the court approves a written waiver of discharge executed by the debtor after the order for relief under this chapter, the court shall grant the debtor a discharge of all debts provided for by the plan or disallowed under section 502 of this title, except any debt—

~~(1) provided for under section 1322(b)(5) of this title;~~

~~(2) of the kind specified in paragraph (5), (8), or (9) of section 523(a) of this title; or~~

~~(3) for restitution, or a criminal fine, included in a sentence on the debtor's conviction of a crime.~~ *(1) provided for under section 1322(b)(5);*

(2) of the kind specified in section 507(a)(8)(C) or in paragraph (1)(B), (1)(C), (2), (3), (4), (5), (8), or (9) of section 523(a);

(3) for restitution, or a criminal fine, included in a sentence on the debtor's conviction of a crime; or

(4) for restitution, or damages, awarded in a civil action against the debtor as a result of willful or malicious injury by the debtor that caused personal injury to an individual or the death of an individual.

(b) ~~At~~ *Subject to subsection (d), at* any time after the confirmation of the plan and after notice and a hearing, the court may grant a discharge to a debtor that has not completed payments under the plan only if—

(1) the debtor's failure to complete such payments is due to circumstances for which the debtor should not justly be held accountable;

(2) the value, as of the effective date of the plan, of property actually distributed under the plan on account of each allowed unsecured claim is not less than the amount that would have been paid on such claim if the estate of the debtor had been liquidated under chapter 7 of this title on such date; and

(3) modification of the plan under section 1329 of this title is not practicable.

(c) A discharge granted under subsection (b) of this section discharges the debtor from all unsecured debts provided for by the plan or disallowed under section 502 of this title, except any debt—

(1) provided for under section 1322(b)(5) of this title; or

(2) of a kind specified in section 523(a) of this title.

(d) Notwithstanding any other provision of this section, a discharge granted under this section does not discharge the debtor from any debt based on an allowed claim filed under section 1305(a)(2) of this title if prior approval by the trustee of the debtor's incurring such debt was practicable and was not obtained.

(e) On request of a party in interest before one year after a discharge under this section is granted, and after notice and a hearing, the court may revoke such discharge only if—

(1) such discharge was obtained by the debtor through fraud; and

(2) the requesting party did not know of such fraud until after such discharge was granted.

(f) Notwithstanding subsections (a) and (b), the court shall not grant a discharge of all debts provided for in the plan or disallowed under section 502, if the debtor has received a discharge—

(1) in a case filed under chapter 7, 11, or 12 of this title during the 4-year period preceding the date of the order for relief under this chapter; or

(2) in a case filed under chapter 13 of this title during the 2-year period preceding the date of such order.

(g)(1) The court shall not grant a discharge under this section to a debtor unless after filing a petition the debtor has completed an instructional course concerning personal financial management described in section 111.

(2) Paragraph (1) shall not apply with respect to a debtor who is a person described in section 109(h)(4) or who resides in a district for which the United States trustee (or the bankruptcy administrator, if any) determines that the approved instructional courses are not adequate to service the additional individuals who would otherwise be required to complete such instructional course by reason of the requirements of paragraph (1).

(3) The United States trustee (or the bankruptcy administrator, if any) who makes a determination described in paragraph (2) shall review such determination not later than 1 year after the date of such determination, and not less frequently than annually thereafter.

(h) The court may not grant a discharge under this chapter unless the court after notice and a hearing held not more than 10 days before the date of the entry of the order granting the discharge finds that there is no reasonable cause to believe that—

(1) section 522(q)(1) may be applicable to the debtor; and

(2) there is pending any proceeding in which the debtor may be found guilty of a felony of the kind described in section 522(q)(1)(A) or liable for a debt of the kind described in section 522(q)(1)(B).

§ 1329. Modification of plan after confirmation

(a) At any time after confirmation of the plan but before the completion of payments under such plan, the plan may be modified, upon request of the debtor, the trustee, or the holder of an allowed unsecured claim, to—

(1) increase or reduce the amount of payments on claims of a particular class provided for by the plan;

(2) extend or reduce the time for such payments; ~~or~~

(3) alter the amount of the distribution to a creditor whose claim is provided for by the plan to the extent necessary to take account of any payment of such claim other than under the plan~~.~~; or

(4) reduce amounts to be paid under the plan by the actual amount expended by the debtor to purchase health insurance for the debtor (and for any dependent of the debtor if such dependent does not otherwise have health insurance coverage) if the debtor documents the cost of such insurance and demonstrates that—

(A) such expenses are reasonable and necessary;

(B)(i) if the debtor previously paid for health insurance, the amount is not materially larger than the cost the debtor previously paid or the cost necessary to maintain the lapsed policy; or

(ii) if the debtor did not have health insurance, the amount is not materially larger than the reasonable cost that would be incurred by a debtor

who purchases health insurance, who has similar income, expenses, age, and health status, and who lives in the same geographical location with the same number of dependents who do not otherwise have health insurance coverage; and

(C) the amount is not otherwise allowed for purposes of determining disposable income under section 1325(b) of this title;

and upon request of any party in interest, files proof that a health insurance policy was purchased.

(b)(1) Sections 1322(a), 1322(b), and 1323(c) of this title and the requirements of section 1325(a) of this title apply to any modification under subsection (a) of this section.

(2) The plan as modified becomes the plan unless, after notice and a hearing, such modification is disapproved.

(c) A plan modified under this section may not provide for payments over a period that expires after ~~three years~~ *the applicable commitment period under section 1325(b)(1)(B)* after the time that the first payment under the original confirmed plan was due, unless the court, for cause, approves a longer period, but the court may not approve a period that expires after five years after such time.

§ 1330. Revocation of an order of confirmation

(a) On request of a party in interest at any time within 180 days after the date of the entry of an order of confirmation under section 1325 of this title, and after notice and a hearing, the court may revoke such order if such order was procured by fraud.

(b) If the court revokes an order of confirmation under subsection (a) of this section, the court shall dispose of the case under section 1307 of this title, unless, within the time fixed by the court, the debtor proposes and the court confirms a modification of the plan under section 1329 of this title.

CHAPTER 15
—REPEALED]

[§ § 1501 TO 151326. REPEALED. PUB.L. 99-554, TITLE II, § 231, OCT. 27, 1986, 100 STAT. 3103]*ANCILLARY AND OTHER CROSS-BORDER CASES*

§ 1501. Purpose and scope of application

(a) The purpose of this chapter is to incorporate the Model Law on Cross-Border Insolvency so as to provide effective mechanisms for dealing with cases of cross-border insolvency with the objectives of—

(1) cooperation between—

(A) courts of the United States, United States trustees, trustees, examiners, debtors, and debtors in possession; and

(B) the courts and other competent authorities of foreign countries involved in cross-border insolvency cases;

(2) greater legal certainty for trade and investment;

(3) fair and efficient administration of cross-border insolvencies that protects the interests of all creditors, and other interested entities, including the debtor;

(4) protection and maximization of the value of the debtor's assets; and

(5) facilitation of the rescue of financially troubled businesses, thereby protecting investment and preserving employment.

(b) This chapter applies where—

(1) assistance is sought in the United States by a foreign court or a foreign representative in connection with a foreign proceeding;

(2) assistance is sought in a foreign country in connection with a case under this title;

(3) a foreign proceeding and a case under this title with respect to the same debtor are pending concurrently; or

(4) creditors or other interested persons in a foreign country have an interest in requesting the commencement of, or participating in, a case or proceeding under this title.

(c) This chapter does not apply to—

(1) a proceeding concerning an entity, other than a foreign insurance company, identified by exclusion in section 109(b);

(2) an individual, or to an individual and such individual's spouse, who have debts within the limits specified in section 109(e) and who are citizens of the United States or aliens lawfully admitted for permanent residence in the United States; or

(3) an entity subject to a proceeding under the Securities Investor Protection Act of 1970, a stockbroker subject to subchapter III of chapter 7 of this title, or a commodity broker subject to subchapter IV of chapter 7 of this title.

(d) The court may not grant relief under this chapter with respect to any deposit, escrow, trust fund, or other security required or permitted under any applicable State insurance law or regulation for the benefit of claim holders in the United States.

§ 1502. Definitions

For the purposes of this chapter, the term—

(1) 'debtor' means an entity that is the subject of a foreign proceeding;

(2) 'establishment' means any place of operations where the debtor carries out a nontransitory economic activity;

(3) 'foreign court' means a judicial or other authority competent to control or supervise a foreign proceeding;

(4) 'foreign main proceeding' means a foreign proceeding pending in the country where the debtor has the center of its main interests;

(5) 'foreign nonmain proceeding' means a foreign proceeding, other than a foreign main proceeding, pending in a country where the debtor has an establishment;

(6) 'trustee' includes a trustee, a debtor in possession in a case under any chapter of this title, or a debtor under chapter 9 of this title;

(7) 'recognition' means the entry of an order granting recognition of a foreign main proceeding or foreign nonmain proceeding under this chapter; and

(8) 'within the territorial jurisdiction of the United States', when used with reference to property of a debtor, refers to tangible property located within the territory of the United States and intangible property deemed under applicable nonbankruptcy law to be located within that territory, including any property subject to attachment or garnishment that may properly be seized or garnished by an action in a Federal or State court in the United States.

§ 1503. International obligations of the United States

To the extent that this chapter conflicts with an obligation of the United States arising out of any treaty or other form of agreement to which it is a party with one or more other countries, the requirements of the treaty or agreement prevail.

§ 1504. Commencement of ancillary case

A case under this chapter is commenced by the filing of a petition for recognition of a foreign proceeding under section 1515.

§ 1505. Authorization to act in a foreign country

A trustee or another entity (including an examiner) may be authorized by the court to act in a foreign country on behalf of an estate created under section 541. An entity authorized to act under this section may act in any way permitted by the applicable foreign law.

§ 1506. Public policy exception

Nothing in this chapter prevents the court from refusing to take an action governed by this chapter if the action would be manifestly contrary to the public policy of the United States.

§ 1507. Additional assistance

(a) Subject to the specific limitations stated elsewhere in this chapter the court, if recognition is granted, may provide additional assistance to a foreign representative under this title or under other laws of the United States.

(b) In determining whether to provide additional assistance under this title or under other laws of the United States, the court shall consider whether such additional assistance, consistent with the principles of comity, will reasonably assure—

(1) just treatment of all holders of claims against or interests in the debtor's property;

(2) protection of claim holders in the United States against prejudice and inconvenience in the processing of claims in such foreign proceeding;

(3) prevention of preferential or fraudulent dispositions of property of the debtor;

(4) distribution of proceeds of the debtor's property substantially in accordance with the order prescribed by this title; and

(5) if appropriate, the provision of an opportunity for a fresh start for the individual that such foreign proceeding concerns.

§ 1508. Interpretation

In interpreting this chapter, the court shall consider its international origin, and the need to promote an application of this chapter that is consistent with the application of similar statutes adopted by foreign jurisdictions.

§ 1509. Right of direct access

(a) A foreign representative may commence a case under section 1504 by filing directly with the court a petition for recognition of a foreign proceeding under section 1515.

(b) If the court grants recognition under section 1517, and subject to any limitations that the court may impose consistent with the policy of this chapter—

(1) the foreign representative has the capacity to sue and be sued in a court in the United States;

(2) the foreign representative may apply directly to a court in the United States for appropriate relief in that court; and

(3) a court in the United States shall grant comity or cooperation to the foreign representative.

(c) A request for comity or cooperation by a foreign representative in a court in the United States other than the court which granted recognition shall be accompanied by a certified copy of an order granting recognition under section 1517.

(d) If the court denies recognition under this chapter, the court may issue any appropriate order necessary to prevent the foreign representative from obtaining comity or cooperation from courts in the United States.

(e) Whether or not the court grants recognition, and subject to sections 306 and 1510, a foreign representative is subject to applicable nonbankruptcy law.

(f) Notwithstanding any other provision of this section, the failure of a foreign representative to commence a case or to obtain recognition under this chapter does not affect any right the foreign representative may have to sue in a court in the United States to collect or recover a claim which is the property of the debtor.

§ 1510. Limited jurisdiction

The sole fact that a foreign representative files a petition under section 1515 does not subject the foreign representative to the jurisdiction of any court in the United States for any other purpose.

§ 1511. Commencement of case under section 301 or 303

(a) Upon recognition, a foreign representative may commence—

(1) an involuntary case under section 303; or

(2) a voluntary case under section 301 or 302, if the foreign proceeding is a foreign main proceeding.

(b) The petition commencing a case under subsection (a) must be accompanied by a certified copy of an order granting recognition. The court where the petition

for recognition has been filed must be advised of the foreign representative's intent to commence a case under subsection (a) prior to such commencement.

§ 1512. Participation of a foreign representative in a case under this title

Upon recognition of a foreign proceeding, the foreign representative in the recognized proceeding is entitled to participate as a party in interest in a case regarding the debtor under this title.

§ 1513. Access of foreign creditors to a case under this title

(a) Foreign creditors have the same rights regarding the commencement of, and participation in, a case under this title as domestic creditors.

(b)(1) Subsection (a) does not change or codify present law as to the priority of claims under section 507 or 726, except that the claim of a foreign creditor under those sections shall not be given a lower priority than that of general unsecured claims without priority solely because the holder of such claim is a foreign creditor.

(2)(A) Subsection (a) and paragraph (1) do not change or codify present law as to the allowability of foreign revenue claims or other foreign public law claims in a proceeding under this title.

(B) Allowance and priority as to a foreign tax claim or other foreign public law claim shall be governed by any applicable tax treaty of the United States, under the conditions and circumstances specified therein.

§ 1514. Notification to foreign creditors concerning a case under this title

(a) Whenever in a case under this title notice is to be given to creditors generally or to any class or category of creditors, such notice shall also be given to the known creditors generally, or to creditors in the notified class or category, that do not have addresses in the United States. The court may order that appropriate steps be taken with a view to notifying any creditor whose address is not yet known.

(b) Such notification to creditors with foreign addresses described in subsection (a) shall be given individually, unless the court considers that, under the circumstances, some other form of notification would be more appropriate. No letter or other formality is required.

(c) When a notification of commencement of a case is to be given to foreign creditors, such notification shall—

(1) indicate the time period for filing proofs of claim and specify the place for filing such proofs of claim;

(2) indicate whether secured creditors need to file proofs of claim; and

(3) contain any other information required to be included in such notification to creditors under this title and the orders of the court.

(d) Any rule of procedure or order of the court as to notice or the filing of a proof of claim shall provide such additional time to creditors with foreign addresses as is reasonable under the circumstances.

§ 1515. Application for recognition

(a) A foreign representative applies to the court for recognition of a foreign proceeding in which the foreign representative has been appointed by filing a petition for recognition.

(b) A petition for recognition shall be accompanied by—

(1) a certified copy of the decision commencing such foreign proceeding and appointing the foreign representative;

(2) a certificate from the foreign court affirming the existence of such foreign proceeding and of the appointment of the foreign representative; or

(3) in the absence of evidence referred to in paragraphs (1) and (2), any other evidence acceptable to the court of the existence of such foreign proceeding and of the appointment of the foreign representative.

(c) A petition for recognition shall also be accompanied by a statement identifying all foreign proceedings with respect to the debtor that are known to the foreign representative.

(d) The documents referred to in paragraphs (1) and (2) of subsection (b) shall be translated into English. The court may require a translation into English of additional documents.

§ 1516. Presumptions concerning recognition

(a) If the decision or certificate referred to in section 1515(b) indicates that the foreign proceeding is a foreign proceeding and that the person or body is a foreign representative, the court is entitled to so presume.

(b) The court is entitled to presume that documents submitted in support of the petition for recognition are authentic, whether or not they have been legalized.

(c) In the absence of evidence to the contrary, the debtor's registered office, or habitual residence in the case of an individual, is presumed to be the center of the debtor's main interests.

§ 1517. Order granting recognition

(a) Subject to section 1506, after notice and a hearing, an order recognizing a foreign proceeding shall be entered if—

(1) such foreign proceeding for which recognition is sought is a foreign main proceeding or foreign nonmain proceeding within the meaning of section 1502;

(2) the foreign representative applying for recognition is a person or body; and

(3) the petition meets the requirements of section 1515.

(b) Such foreign proceeding shall be recognized—

(1) as a foreign main proceeding if it is pending in the country where the debtor has the center of its main interests; or

(2) as a foreign nonmain proceeding if the debtor has an establishment within the meaning of section 1502 in the foreign country where the proceeding is pending.

(c) A petition for recognition of a foreign proceeding shall be decided upon at the earliest possible time. Entry of an order recognizing a foreign proceeding constitutes recognition under this chapter.

(d) The provisions of this subchapter do not prevent modification or termination of recognition if it is shown that the grounds for granting it were fully or partially lacking or have ceased to exist, but in considering such action the court shall give due weight to possible prejudice to parties that have relied upon the order granting recognition. A case under this chapter may be closed in the manner prescribed under section 350.

§ 1518. Subsequent information

From the time of filing the petition for recognition of a foreign proceeding, the foreign representative shall file with the court promptly a notice of change of status concerning—

(1) any substantial change in the status of such foreign proceeding or the status of the foreign representative's appointment; and

(2) any other foreign proceeding regarding the debtor that becomes known to the foreign representative.

§ 1519. Relief that may be granted upon filing petition for recognition

(a) From the time of filing a petition for recognition until the court rules on the petition, the court may, at the request of the foreign representative, where relief is urgently needed to protect the assets of the debtor or the interests of the creditors, grant relief of a provisional nature, including—

(1) staying execution against the debtor's assets;

(2) entrusting the administration or realization of all or part of the debtor's assets located in the United States to the foreign representative or another person authorized by the court, including an examiner, in order to protect and preserve the value of assets that, by their nature or because of other circumstances, are perishable, susceptible to devaluation or otherwise in jeopardy; and

(3) any relief referred to in paragraph (3), (4), or (7) of section 1521(a).

(b) Unless extended under section 1521(a)(6), the relief granted under this section terminates when the petition for recognition is granted.

(c) It is a ground for denial of relief under this section that such relief would interfere with the administration of a foreign main proceeding.

(d) The court may not enjoin a police or regulatory act of a governmental unit, including a criminal action or proceeding, under this section.

(e) The standards, procedures, and limitations applicable to an injunction shall apply to relief under this section.

(f) The exercise of rights not subject to the stay arising under section 362(a) pursuant to paragraph (6), (7), (17), or (27) of section 362(b) or pursuant to section 362(n) shall not be stayed by any order of a court or administrative agency in any proceeding under this chapter.

§ 1520. Effects of recognition of a foreign main proceeding

(a) Upon recognition of a foreign proceeding that is a foreign main proceeding—

(1) sections 361 and 362 apply with respect to the debtor and the property of the debtor that is within the territorial jurisdiction of the United States;

(2) sections 363, 549, and 552 apply to a transfer of an interest of the debtor in property that is within the territorial jurisdiction of the United States to the same extent that the sections would apply to property of an estate;

(3) unless the court orders otherwise, the foreign representative may operate the debtor's business and may exercise the rights and powers of a trustee under and to the extent provided by sections 363 and 552; and

(4) section 552 applies to property of the debtor that is within the territorial jurisdiction of the United States.

(b) Subsection (a) does not affect the right to commence an individual action or proceeding in a foreign country to the extent necessary to preserve a claim against the debtor.

(c) Subsection (a) does not affect the right of a foreign representative or an entity to file a petition commencing a case under this title or the right of any party to file claims or take other proper actions in such a case.

§ 1521. Relief that may be granted upon recognition

(a) Upon recognition of a foreign proceeding, whether main or nonmain, where necessary to effectuate the purpose of this chapter and to protect the assets of the debtor or the interests of the creditors, the court may, at the request of the foreign representative, grant any appropriate relief, including—

(1) staying the commencement or continuation of an individual action or pro-ceeding concerning the debtor's assets, rights, obligations or liabilities to the extent they have not been stayed under section 1520(a);

(2) staying execution against the debtor's assets to the extent it has not been stayed under section 1520(a);

(3) suspending the right to transfer, encumber or otherwise dispose of any assets of the debtor to the extent this right has not been suspended under sec-tion 1520(a);

(4) providing for the examination of witnesses, the taking of evidence or the delivery of information concerning the debtor's assets, affairs, rights, obliga-tions or liabilities;

(5) entrusting the administration or realization of all or part of the debtor's assets within the territorial jurisdiction of the United States to the foreign rep-resentative or another person, including an examiner, authorized by the court;

(6) extending relief granted under section 1519(a); and

(7) granting any additional relief that may be available to a trustee, except for relief available under sections 522, 544, 545, 547, 548, 550, and 724(a).

(b) Upon recognition of a foreign proceeding, whether main or nonmain, the court may, at the request of the foreign representative, entrust the distribution of all or part of the debtor's assets located in the United States to the foreign repre-sentative or another person, including an examiner, authorized by the court, pro-vided that the court is satisfied that the interests of creditors in the United States are sufficiently protected.

(c) In granting relief under this section to a representative of a foreign nonmain proceeding, the court must be satisfied that the relief relates to assets that, under the law of the United States, should be administered in the foreign nonmain pro-ceeding or concerns information required in that proceeding.

(d) The court may not enjoin a police or regulatory act of a governmental unit, including a criminal action or proceeding, under this section.

(e) The standards, procedures, and limitations applicable to an injunction shall apply to relief under paragraphs (1), (2), (3), and (6) of subsection (a).

(f) The exercise of rights not subject to the stay arising under section 362(a) pursuant to paragraph (6), (7), (17), or (27) of section 362(b) or pursuant to section 362(n) shall not be stayed by any order of a court or administrative agency in any proceeding under this chapter.

§ 1522. Protection of creditors and other interested persons

(a) The court may grant relief under section 1519 or 1521, or may modify or terminate relief under subsection (c), only if the interests of the creditors and other interested entities, including the debtor, are sufficiently protected.

(b) The court may subject relief granted under section 1519 or 1521, or the operation of the debtor's business under section 1520(a)(3), to conditions it considers appropriate, including the giving of security or the filing of a bond.

(c) The court may, at the request of the foreign representative or an entity affected by relief granted under section 1519 or 1521, or at its own motion, modify or terminate such relief.

(d) Section 1104(d) shall apply to the appointment of an examiner under this chapter. Any examiner shall comply with the qualification requirements imposed on a trustee by section 322.

§ 1523. Actions to avoid acts detrimental to creditors

(a) Upon recognition of a foreign proceeding, the foreign representative has standing in a case concerning the debtor pending under another chapter of this title to initiate actions under sections 522, 544, 545, 547, 548, 550, 553, and 724(a).

(b) When a foreign proceeding is a foreign nonmain proceeding, the court must be satisfied that an action under subsection (a) relates to assets that, under United States law, should be administered in the foreign nonmain proceeding.

§ 1524. Intervention by a foreign representative

Upon recognition of a foreign proceeding, the foreign representative may intervene in any proceedings in a State or Federal court in the United States in which the debtor is a party.

§ 1525. Cooperation and direct communication between the court and foreign courts or foreign representatives

(a) Consistent with section 1501, the court shall cooperate to the maximum extent possible with a foreign court or a foreign representative, either directly or through the trustee.

(b) The court is entitled to communicate directly with, or to request information or assistance directly from, a foreign court or a foreign representative, subject to the rights of a party in interest to notice and participation.

§ 1526. Cooperation and direct communication between the trustee and foreign courts or foreign representatives

(a) Consistent with section 1501, the trustee or other person, including an examiner, authorized by the court, shall, subject to the supervision of the court, cooperate to the maximum extent possible with a foreign court or a foreign representative.

(b) The trustee or other person, including an examiner, authorized by the court is entitled, subject to the supervision of the court, to communicate directly with a foreign court or a foreign representative.

§ 1527. Forms of cooperation

Cooperation referred to in sections 1525 and 1526 may be implemented by any appropriate means, including—

(1) appointment of a person or body, including an examiner, to act at the direction of the court;

(2) communication of information by any means considered appropriate by the court;

(3) coordination of the administration and supervision of the debtor's assets and affairs;

(4) approval or implementation of agreements concerning the coordination of proceedings; and

(5) coordination of concurrent proceedings regarding the same debtor.

§ 1528. Commencement of a case under this title after recognition of a foreign main proceeding

After recognition of a foreign main proceeding, a case under another chapter of this title may be commenced only if the debtor has assets in the United States. The effects of such case shall be restricted to the assets of the debtor that are within the territorial jurisdiction of the United States and, to the extent necessary to implement cooperation and coordination under sections 1525, 1526, and 1527, to other assets of the debtor that are within the jurisdiction of the court under sections 541(a) of this title, and 1334(e) of title 28, to the extent that such other assets are not subject to the jurisdiction and control of a foreign proceeding that has been recognized under this chapter.

§ 1529. Coordination of a case under this title and a foreign proceeding

If a foreign proceeding and a case under another chapter of this title are pending concurrently regarding the same debtor, the court shall seek cooperation and coordination under sections 1525, 1526, and 1527, and the following shall apply:

(1) If the case in the United States pending at the time the petition for recognition of such foreign proceeding is filed—

(A) any relief granted under section 1519 or 1521 must be consistent with the relief granted in the case in the United States; and

(B) section 1520 does not apply even if such foreign proceeding is recognized as a foreign main proceeding.

(2) If a case in the United States under this title commences after recognition, or after the date of the filing of the petition for recognition, of such foreign proceeding—

(A) any relief in effect under section 1519 or 1521 shall be reviewed by the court and shall be modified or terminated if inconsistent with the case in the United States; and

(B) if such foreign proceeding is a foreign main proceeding, the stay and suspension referred to in section 1520(a) shall be modified or terminated if inconsistent with the relief granted in the case in the United States.

(3) In granting, extending, or modifying relief granted to a representative of a foreign nonmain proceeding, the court must be satisfied that the relief relates to assets that, under the laws of the United States, should be administered in the foreign nonmain proceeding or concerns information required in that proceeding.

(4) In achieving cooperation and coordination under sections 1528 and 1529, the court may grant any of the relief authorized under section 305.

§ 1530. Coordination of more than 1 foreign proceeding

In matters referred to in section 1501, with respect to more than 1 foreign proceeding regarding the debtor, the court shall seek cooperation and coordination under sections 1525, 1526, and 1527, and the following shall apply:

(1) Any relief granted under section 1519 or 1521 to a representative of a foreign nonmain proceeding after recognition of a foreign main proceeding must be consistent with the foreign main proceeding.

(2) If a foreign main proceeding is recognized after recognition, or after the filing of a petition for recognition, of a foreign nonmain proceeding, any relief in effect under section 1519 or 1521 shall be reviewed by the court and shall be modified or terminated if inconsistent with the foreign main proceeding.

(3) If, after recognition of a foreign nonmain proceeding, another foreign nonmain proceeding is recognized, the court shall grant, modify, or terminate relief for the purpose of facilitating coordination of the proceedings.

§ 1531. Presumption of insolvency based on recognition of a foreign main proceeding

In the absence of evidence to the contrary, recognition of a foreign main proceeding is, for the purpose of commencing a proceeding under section 303, proof that the debtor is generally not paying its debts as such debts become due.

§ 1532. Rule of payment in concurrent proceedings

Without prejudice to secured claims or rights in rem, a creditor who has received payment with respect to its claim in a foreign proceeding pursuant to a law relating to insolvency may not receive a payment for the same claim in a case under any other chapter of this title regarding the debtor, so long as the payment to other creditors of the same class is proportionately less than the payment the creditor has already received.

TITLE 18 (SELECTED PROVISIONS)

PART I CRIMES

§ 156. Knowing disregard of bankruptcy law or rule

(a) Definitions- In this section—

(1) *the term* `bankruptcy petition preparer' means a person, other than the debtor's attorney or an employee of such an attorney, who prepares for compensation a document for filing ~;~ *and*

(2) *the term* `document for filing' means a petition or any other document prepared for filing by a debtor in a United States bankruptcy court or a United States district court in connection with a case under ~this title~*title 11*.

§ 157. Bankruptcy fraud

A person who, having devised or intending to devise a scheme or artifice to defraud and for the purpose of executing or concealing such a scheme or artifice or attempting to do so—

(1) files a petition under title 11, *including a fraudulent involuntary bankruptcy petition under section 303 of such title;*

(2) files a document in a proceeding under title 11, *including a fraudulent involuntary bankruptcy petition under section 303 of such title;* or

(3) makes a false or fraudulent representation, claim, or promise concerning or in relation to a proceeding under title 11, *including a fraudulent involuntary bankruptcy petition under section 303 of such title*, at any time before or after the filing of the petition, or in relation to a proceeding falsely asserted to be pending under such title, shall be fined under this title, imprisoned not more than 5 years, or both.

§ 158. Designation of United States attorneys and agents of the Federal Bureau of Investigation to address abusive reaffirmations of debt and materially fraudulent statements in bankruptcy schedules

(a) IN GENERAL- The Attorney General of the United States shall designate the individuals described in subsection (b) to have primary responsibility in carrying out enforcement activities in addressing violations of section 152 or 157 relating to abusive reaffirmations of debt. In addition to addressing the violations referred to in the preceding sentence, the individuals described under subsection (b) shall address violations of section 152 or 157 relating to materially fraudulent statements in bankruptcy schedules that are intentionally false or intentionally misleading.

(b) UNITED STATES ATTORNEYS AND AGENTS OF THE FEDERAL BUREAU OF INVESTIGATION- The individuals referred to in subsection (a) are—

(1) the United States attorney for each judicial district of the United States; and

(2) *an agent of the Federal Bureau of Investigation for each field office of the Federal Bureau of Investigation.*

(c) *BANKRUPTCY INVESTIGATIONS- Each United States attorney designated under this section shall, in addition to any other responsibilities, have primary responsibility for carrying out the duties of a United States attorney under section 3057.*

(d) *BANKRUPTCY PROCEDURES- The bankruptcy courts shall establish procedures for referring any case that may contain a materially fraudulent statement in a bankruptcy schedule to the individuals designated under this section.*

TITLE 28—UNITED STATES CODE (SELECTED PROVISIONS)

CHAPTER 6—BANKRUPTCY JUDGES

§ 152. Appointment of bankruptcy judges

(a)(1) The United States court of appeals for the circuit shall appoint bankruptcy judges for the judicial districts established in paragraph (2) in such numbers as are established in such paragraph. *Each bankruptcy judge to be appointed for a judicial district, as provided in paragraph (2), shall be appointed by the court of appeals of the United States for the circuit in which such district is located.* Such appointments shall be made after considering the recommendations of the Judicial Conference submitted pursuant to subsection (b). Each bankruptcy judge shall be appointed for a term of fourteen years, subject to the provisions of subsection (e). However, upon the expiration of the term, a bankruptcy judge may, with the approval of the judicial council of the circuit, continue to perform the duties of the office until the earlier of the date which is 180 days after the expiration of the term or the date of the appointment of a successor. Bankruptcy judges shall serve as judicial officers of the United States district court established under Article III of the Constitution.

(2) The bankruptcy judges appointed pursuant to this section shall be appointed for the several judicial districts as follows:

[New judges added are temporary and the list is omitted here]

§ 157. Procedures

(a) * * *

(b)(1) * * *

(2) Core proceedings include, but are not limited to—

(A) * * *

* * * * * * *

(N) orders approving the sale of property other than property resulting from claims brought by the estate against persons who have not filed claims against the estate; and

(O) other proceedings affecting the liquidation of the assets of the estate or the adjustment of the debtor-creditor or the equity security holder relationship, except personal injury tort or wrongful death claims -; *and*

(P) recognition of foreign proceedings and other matters under chapter 15 of title 11.

* * * * * * *

§ 158. Appeals

(a) * * *

* * * * * * *

(c)(1) ~~Subject to subsection (b),~~*Subject to subsections (b) and (d)(2),* each appeal under subsection (a) shall be heard by a 3-judge panel of the bankruptcy appellate panel service established under subsection (b)(1) unless —

    (A) * * *

* * * * * * *

(d)*(1)* The courts of appeals shall have jurisdiction of appeals from all final decisions, judgments, orders, and decrees entered under subsections (a) and (b) of this section.

    (2)(A) The appropriate court of appeals shall have jurisdiction of appeals described in the first sentence of subsection (a) if the bankruptcy court, the district court, or the bankruptcy appellate panel involved, acting on its own motion or on the request of a party to the judgment, order, or decree described in such first sentence, or all the appellants and appellees (if any) acting jointly, certify that

        (i) the judgment, order, or decree involves a question of law as to which there is no controlling decision of the court of appeals for the circuit or of the Supreme Court of the United States, or involves a matter of public importance;

        (ii) the judgment, order, or decree involves a question of law requiring resolution of conflicting decisions; or

        (iii) an immediate appeal from the judgment, order, or decree may materially advance the progress of the case or proceeding in which the appeal is taken; and if the court of appeals authorizes the direct appeal of the judgment, order, or decree.

    (B) If the bankruptcy court, the district court, or the bankruptcy appellate panel—

        (i) on its own motion or on the request of a party, determines that a circumstance specified in clause (i), (ii), or (iii) of subparagraph (A) exists; or

        (ii) receives a request made by a majority of the appellants and a majority of appellees (if any) to make the certification described in subparagraph (A); then the bankruptcy court, the district court, or the bankruptcy appellate panel shall make the certification described in subparagraph (A).

    (C) The parties may supplement the certification with a short statement of the basis for the certification.

    (D) An appeal under this paragraph does not stay any proceeding of the bankruptcy court, the district court, or the bankruptcy appellate panel from which the appeal is taken, unless the respective bankruptcy court, district

court, or bankruptcy appellate panel, or the court of appeals in which the appeal in pending, issues a stay of such proceeding pending the appeal.

(E) Any request under subparagraph (B) for certification shall be made not later than 60 days after the entry of the judgment, order, or decree.

§ 159. Bankruptcy statistics

(a) The clerk of the district court, or the clerk of the bankruptcy court if one is certified pursuant to section 156(b) of this title, shall collect statistics regarding debtors who are individuals with primarily consumer debts seeking relief under chapters 7, 11, and 13 of title 11. Those statistics shall be in a standardized format prescribed by the Director of the Administrative Office of the United States Courts (referred to in this section as the `Director').

(b) The Director shall—

(1) compile the statistics referred to in subsection (a);

(2) make the statistics available to the public; and

(3) not later than July 1, 2008, and annually thereafter, prepare, and submit to Congress a report concerning the information collected under subsection (a) that contains an analysis of the information.

(c) The compilation required under subsection (b) shall—

(1) be itemized, by chapter, with respect to title 11;

(2) be presented in the aggregate and for each district; and

(3) include information concerning—

(A) the total assets and total liabilities of the debtors described in subsection (a), and in each category of assets and liabilities, as reported in the schedules prescribed pursuant to section 2075 of this title and filed by debtors;

(B) the current monthly income, average income, and average expenses of debtors as reported on the schedules and statements that each such debtor files under sections 521 and 1322 of title 11;

(C) the aggregate amount of debt discharged in cases filed during the reporting period, determined as the difference between the total amount of debt and obligations of a debtor reported on the schedules and the amount of such debt reported in categories which are predominantly nondischargeable;

(D) the average period of time between the date of the filing of the petition and the closing of the case for cases closed during the reporting period;

(E) for cases closed during the reporting period—

(i) the number of cases in which a reaffirmation agreement was filed; and

(ii)(I) the total number of reaffirmation agreements filed;

(II) of those cases in which a reaffirmation agreement was filed, the number of cases in which the debtor was not represented by an attorney; and

(III) of those cases in which a reaffirmation agreement was filed, the number of cases in which the reaffirmation agreement was approved by the court;

(F) with respect to cases filed under chapter 13 of title 11, for the reporting period—

(i)(I) the number of cases in which a final order was entered determining the value of property securing a claim in an amount less than the amount of the claim; and

(II) the number of final orders entered determining the value of property securing a claim;

(ii) the number of cases dismissed, the number of cases dismissed for failure to make payments under the plan, the number of cases refiled after dismissal, and the number of cases in which the plan was completed, separately itemized with respect to the number of modifications made before completion of the plan, if any; and

(iii) the number of cases in which the debtor filed another case during the 6-year period preceding the filing;

(G) the number of cases in which creditors were fined for misconduct and any amount of punitive damages awarded by the court for creditor misconduct; and

(H) the number of cases in which sanctions under rule 9011 of the Federal Rules of Bankruptcy Procedure were imposed against debtor's attorney or damages awarded under such Rule.

* * * * * * *

CHAPTER 39—UNITED STATES TRUSTEES

§ 586. Duties; supervision by Attorney General

(a) Each United States trustee, within the region for which such United States trustee is appointed, shall—

(1) * * *

* * * * * * *

(3) supervise the administration of cases and trustees in cases under chapter 7, 11, 12, ~~or 13~~ *13, or 15* of title 11 by, whenever the United States trustee considers it to be appropriate—

(A) * * *

* * * * * * *

(G) monitoring the progress of cases under title 11 and taking such actions as the United States trustee deems to be appropriate to prevent undue delay in such progress; ~~and~~

(H) in small business cases (as defined in section 101 of title 11), performing the additional duties specified in title 11 pertaining to such cases; and

~~(H)~~ *(I)* monitoring applications filed under section 327 of title 11 and, whenever the United States trustee deems it to be appropriate, filing with the court comments with respect to the approval of such applications;

* * * * * * *

(5) perform the duties prescribed for the United States trustee under title 11 and this title, and such duties consistent with title 11 and this title as the Attorney General may prescribe; ~~and~~

~~(6) make such reports as the Attorney General directs.~~

(6) make such reports as the Attorney General directs, including the results of audits performed under section 603(a) of the Bankruptcy Abuse Prevention and Consumer Protection Act of 2005;

(7) in each of such small business cases—

(A) conduct an initial debtor interview as soon as practicable after the date of the order for relief but before the first meeting scheduled under section 341(a) of title 11, at which time the United States trustee shall—

(i) begin to investigate the debtor's viability;

(ii) inquire about the debtor's business plan;

(iii) explain the debtor's obligations to file monthly operating reports and other required reports;

(iv) attempt to develop an agreed scheduling order; and (v) inform the debtor of other obligations;

(B) if determined to be appropriate and advisable, visit the appropriate business premises of the debtor, ascertain the state of the debtor's books and records, and verify that the debtor has filed its tax returns; and

(C) review and monitor diligently the debtor's activities, to identify as promptly as possible whether the debtor will be unable to confirm a plan; and

(8) in any case in which the United States trustee finds material grounds for any relief under section 1112 of title 11, the United States trustee shall apply promptly after making that finding to the court for relief.

* * * * * * *

(d)*(1)* The Attorney General shall prescribe by rule qualifications for membership on the panels established by United States trustees under paragraph (a)(1) of this section, and qualifications for appointment under subsection (b) of this section to serve as standing trustee in cases under chapter 12 or 13 of title 11. The Attorney General may not require that an individual be an attorney in order to qualify for appointment under subsection (b) of this section to serve as standing trustee in cases under chapter 12 or 13 of title 11.

(2) A trustee whose appointment under subsection (a)(1) or under subsection (b) is terminated or who ceases to be assigned to cases filed under title 11, United States Code, may obtain judicial review of the final agency decision by commencing an action in the district court of the United States for the district for which the panel to which the trustee is appointed under subsection (a)(1), or in the district court of the United States for the district in which the trustee is appointed under subsection (b) resides, after first exhausting all available administrative remedies, which if the trustee so elects, shall also include an administrative hearing on the record. Unless the trustee elects to have an administrative hearing on the record, the trustee shall be deemed to have exhausted all administrative remedies for purposes of this paragraph if the agency fails to make a final agency decision within 90 days after the trustee requests administrative remedies. The Attorney General shall prescribe procedures to implement this paragraph. The decision of the agency shall be

affirmed by the district court unless it is unreasonable and without cause based on the administrative record before the agency.

(e)(1) * * *

* * * * * * *

(3) After first exhausting all available administrative remedies, an individual appointed under subsection (b) may obtain judicial review of final agency action to deny a claim of actual, necessary expenses under this subsection by commencing an action in the district court of the United States for the district where the individual resides. The decision of the agency shall be affirmed by the district court unless it is unreasonable and without cause based upon the administrative record before the agency.

(4) The Attorney General shall prescribe procedures to implement this subsection.

(f)(1) The United States trustee for each district is authorized to contract with auditors to perform audits in cases designated by the United States trustee, in accordance with the procedures established under section 603(a) of the Bankruptcy Abuse Prevention and Consumer Protection Act of 2005.

(2)(A) The report of each audit referred to in paragraph (1) shall be filed with the court and transmitted to the United States trustee. Each report shall clearly and conspicuously specify any material misstatement of income or expenditures or of assets identified by the person performing the audit. In any case in which a material misstatement of income or expenditures or of assets has been reported, the clerk of the district court (or the clerk of the bankruptcy court if one is certified under section 156(b) of this title) shall give notice of the misstatement to the creditors in the case.

(B) If a material misstatement of income or expenditures or of assets is reported, the United States trustee shall—

(i) report the material misstatement, if appropriate, to the United States Attorney pursuant to section 3057 of title 18; and

(ii) if advisable, take appropriate action, including but not limited to commencing an adversary proceeding to revoke the debtor's discharge pursuant to section 727(d) of title 11.

* * * * * * *

§ 589a. United States Trustee System Fund

(a) * * *

(b) For the purpose of recovering the cost of services of the United States Trustee System, there shall be deposited as offsetting collections to the appropriation `United States Trustee System Fund', to remain available until expended, the following—

(1) ~~27.42 percent of the fees collected under section 1930(a)(1) of this title;~~

(1)(A) 40.63 percent of the fees collected under section 1930(a)(1)(A) of this title; and

(B) 70.00 percent of the fees collected under section 1930(a)(1)(B);

(2) ~~one-half~~ *75 percent* of the fees collected under section 1930(a)(3) of this title;

* * * * * * *

(4) ~~one-half~~ *100 percent* of the fees collected under section 1930(a)(5) of this title;

* * * * * * *

§ 589b. Bankruptcy data

(a) RULES- The Attorney General shall, within a reasonable time after the effective date of this section, issue rules requiring uniform forms for (and from time to time thereafter to appropriately modify and approve)—

(1) final reports by trustees in cases under chapters 7, 12, and 13 of title 11; and

(2) periodic reports by debtors in possession or trustees in cases under chapter 11 of title 11.

(b) REPORTS- Each report referred to in subsection (a) shall be designed (and the requirements as to place and manner of filing shall be established) so as to facilitate compilation of data and maximum possible access of the public, both by physical inspection at one or more central filing locations, and by electronic access through the Internet or other appropriate media.

(c) REQUIRED INFORMATION- The information required to be filed in the reports referred to in subsection (b) shall be that which is in the best interests of debtors and creditors, and in the public interest in reasonable and adequate information to evaluate the efficiency and practicality of the Federal bankruptcy system. In issuing rules proposing the forms referred to in subsection (a), the Attorney General shall strike the best achievable practical balance between—

(1) the reasonable needs of the public for information about the operational results of the Federal bankruptcy system;

(2) economy, simplicity, and lack of undue burden on persons with a duty to file reports; and

(3) appropriate privacy concerns and safeguards.

(d) FINAL REPORTS- The uniform forms for final reports required under subsection (a) for use by trustees under chapters 7, 12, and 13 of title 11 shall, in addition to such other matters as are required by law or as the Attorney General in the discretion of the Attorney General shall propose, include with respect to a case under such title—

(1) information about the length of time the case was pending;

(2) assets abandoned;

(3) assets exempted;

(4) receipts and disbursements of the estate;

(5) expenses of administration, including for use under section 707(b), actual costs of administering cases under chapter 13 of title 11;

(6) claims asserted;

(7) claims allowed; and

(8) distributions to claimants and claims discharged without payment, in each case by appropriate category and, in cases under chapters 12 and 13 of title 11, date of confirmation of the plan, each modification thereto, and defaults by the debtor in performance under the plan.

(e) PERIODIC REPORTS- The uniform forms for periodic reports required under subsection (a) for use by trustees or debtors in possession under chapter 11 of title 11 shall, in addition to such other matters as are required by law or as the Attorney General in the discretion of the Attorney General shall propose, include—

(1) information about the industry classification, published by the Department of Commerce, for the businesses conducted by the debtor;

(2) length of time the case has been pending;

(3) number of full-time employees as of the date of the order for relief and at the end of each reporting period since the case was filed;

(4) cash receipts, cash disbursements and profitability of the debtor for the most recent period and cumulatively since the date of the order for relief;

(5) compliance with title 11, whether or not tax returns and tax payments since the date of the order for relief have been timely filed and made;

(6) all professional fees approved by the court in the case for the most recent period and cumulatively since the date of the order for relief (separately reported, for the professional fees incurred by or on behalf of the debtor, between those that would have been incurred absent a bankruptcy case and those not); and

(7) plans of reorganization filed and confirmed and, with respect thereto, by class, the recoveries of the holders, expressed in aggregate dollar values and, in the case of claims, as a percentage of total claims of the class allowed.

* * * * * * *

CHAPTER 57—GENERAL PROVISIONS APPLICABLE TO COURT OFFICERS AND EMPLOYEES

§ 960. Tax liability

(a) Any officers and agents conducting any business under authority of a United States court shall be subject to all Federal, State and local taxes applicable to such business to the same extent as if it were conducted by an individual or corporation.

(b) A tax under subsection (a) shall be paid on or before the due date of the tax under applicable nonbankruptcy law, unless—

(1) the tax is a property tax secured by a lien against property that is abandoned under section 554 of title 11, within a reasonable period of time after the lien attaches, by the trustee in a case under title 11; or

(2) payment of the tax is excused under a specific provision of title 11.

(c) In a case pending under chapter 7 of title 11, payment of a tax may be deferred until final distribution is made under section 726 of title 11, if—

(1) the tax was not incurred by a trustee duly appointed or elected under chapter 7 of title 11; or

(2) before the due date of the tax, an order of the court makes a finding of probable insufficiency of funds of the estate to pay in full the administrative expenses allowed under section 503(b) of title 11 that have the same priority in distribution under section 726(b) of title 11 as the priority of that tax.

* * * * * * *

CHAPTER 85—DISTRICT COURTS; JURISDICTION

§ 1334. Bankruptcy cases and proceedings

(a) * * *

(b) ~~Notwithstanding~~*Except as provided in subsection (e)(2), and notwithstanding* any Act of Congress that confers exclusive jurisdiction on a court or courts other than the district courts, the district courts shall have original but not exclusive jurisdiction of all civil proceedings arising under title 11, or arising in or related to cases under title 11.

(c)(1) ~~Nothing in~~*Except with respect to a case under chapter 15 of title 11, nothing in* this section prevents a district court in the interest of justice, or in the interest of comity with State courts or respect for State law, from abstaining from hearing a particular proceeding arising under title 11 or arising in or related to a case under title 11.

* * * * * * *

(d) Any decision to abstain or not to abstain ~~made under this subsection~~*made under subsection (c)* (other than a decision not to abstain in a proceeding described in subsection (c)(2)) is not reviewable by appeal or otherwise by the court of appeals under section 158(d), 1291, or 1292 of this title or by the Supreme Court of the United States under section 1254 of this title. ~~This subsection~~*Subsection (c) and this subsection* shall not be construed to limit the applicability of the stay provided for by section 362 of title 11, United States Code, as such section applies to an action affecting the property of the estate in bankruptcy.

~~(e) The district court in which a case under title 11 is commenced or is pending shall have exclusive jurisdiction of all of the property, wherever located, of the debtor as of the commencement of such case, and of property of the estate.~~

(e) The district court in which a case under title 11 is commenced or is pending shall have exclusive jurisdiction—

(1) of all the property, wherever located, of the debtor as of the commencement of such case, and of property of the estate; and

(2) over all claims or causes of action that involve construction of section 327 of title 11, United States Code, or rules relating to disclosure requirements under section 327.

* * * * * * *

CHAPTER 87—DISTRICT COURTS; VENUE

§ 1409. Venue of proceedings arising under title 11 or arising in or related to cases under title 11

(a) * * *

(b) Except as provided in subsection (d) of this section, a trustee in a case under title 11 may commence a proceeding arising in or related to such case to recover a money judgment of or property worth less than $1,000 or a consumer debt of less than ~~$5,000~~, *$15,000, or a debt (excluding a consumer debt) against a noninsider of less than $10,000,* only in the district court for the district in which the defendant resides.

§ 1410. Venue of cases ancillary to foreign proceedings

~~(a) A case under section 304 of title 11 to enjoin the commencement or continuation of an action or proceeding in a State or Federal court, or the enforcement of a judgment, may be commenced only in the district court for the district where the State or Federal court sits in which is pending the action or proceeding against which the injunction is sought.~~

~~(b) A case under section 304 of title 11 to enjoin the enforcement of a lien against a property, or to require the turnover of property of an estate, may be commenced only in the district court for the district in which such property is found.~~

~~(c) A case under section 304 of title 11, other than a case specified in subsection (a) or (b) of this~~ section, ~~may be commenced only in the district court for the district in which is located the principal place of business in the United States, or the principal assets in the United States, of the estate that is the subject of such case.~~

A case under chapter 15 of title 11 may be commenced in the district court of the United States for the district—

(1) in which the debtor has its principal place of business or principal assets in the United States;

(2) if the debtor does not have a place of business or assets in the United States, in which there is pending against the debtor an action or proceeding in a Federal or State court; or

(3) in a case other than those specified in paragraph (1) or (2), in which venue will be consistent with the interests of justice and the convenience of the parties, having regard to the relief sought by the foreign representative.

* * * * * * *

CHAPTER 123—FEES AND COSTS

§ 1930. Bankruptcy fees

(a) ~~Notwithstanding section 1915 of this title, the~~ *The* parties commencing a case under title 11 shall pay to the clerk of the district court or the clerk of the bankruptcy court, if one has been certified pursuant to section 156(b) of this title, the following filing fees:

~~(1) For a case commenced under chapter 7 or 13 of title 11, $155.~~

(1) For a case commenced under—

(A) chapter 7 of title 11, $200; and

(B) chapter 13 of title 11, $150.

* * * * * * *

(3) For a case commenced under chapter 11 of title 11 that does not concern a railroad, as defined in section 101 of title 11, ~~$800~~ *$1000*.

* * * * * * *

(f)(1) Under the procedures prescribed by the Judicial Conference of the United States, the district court or the bankruptcy court may waive the filing fee in a case under chapter 7 of title 11 for an individual if the court determines that such individual has income less than 150 percent of the income official poverty line (as defined by the Office of Management and Budget, and revised annually

in accordance with section 673(2) of the Omnibus Budget Reconciliation Act of 1981) applicable to a family of the size involved and is unable to pay that fee in installments. For purposes of this paragraph, the term `filing fee' means the filing fee required by subsection (a), or any other fee prescribed by the Judicial Conference under subsections (b) and (c) that is payable to the clerk upon the commencement of a case under chapter 7.

(2) The district court or the bankruptcy court may waive for such debtors other fees prescribed under subsections (b) and (c).

(3) This subsection does not restrict the district court or the bankruptcy court from waiving, in accordance with Judicial Conference policy, fees prescribed under this section for other debtors and creditors.

* * * * * * *

CHAPTER 131—RULES OF COURTS

§ 2075. Bankruptcy rules

The Supreme Court shall have the power to prescribe by general rules, the forms of process, writs, pleadings, and motions, and the practice and procedure in cases under title 11. Such rules shall not abridge, enlarge, or modify any substantive right. The Supreme Court shall transmit to Congress not later than May 1 of the year in which a rule prescribed under this section is to become effective a copy of the proposed rule. The rule shall take effect no earlier than December 1 of the year in which it is transmitted to Congress unless otherwise provided by law. *The bankruptcy rules promulgated under this section shall prescribe a form for the statement required under section 707(b)(2)(C) of title 11 and may provide general rules on the content of such statement.*

* * * * * * *

SECTION 406 OF THE JUDICIARY APPROPRIATIONS ACT, 1990

§ 406.

(a) * * * *

(b) All fees as shall be hereafter collected for any service not of a kind described in any of the items enumerated as items 1 through 7 and as items 9 through 18, as in effect on November 21, 1989, of the bankruptcy miscellaneous fee schedule prescribed by the Judicial Conference of the United States ~~pursuant to 28 U.S.C. section 1930(b) and 33.87 percent of the fees hereafter collected under 28 U.S.C. section 1930(a)(1) and 25 percent of the fees hereafter collected under 28 U.S.C. section 1930(a)(3) shall be deposited as offsetting receipts to the fund established under 28 U.S.C. section 1931~~*under section 1930(b) of title 28, United States Code, 31.25 of the fees collected under section 1930(a)(1)(A) of that title, 30.00 percent of the fees collected under section 1930(a)(1)(B) of that title, and 25 percent of the fees collected under section 1930(a)(3) of that title shall be deposited as offsetting receipts to the fund established under section 1931 of that title* and shall remain available to the Judiciary until expended to reimburse any appropriation for the amount paid out of such appropriation for expenses of the Courts of Appeals, District Courts, and other Judicial Services and the Administrative

SECTION 406 OF THE JUDICIARY APPROPRIATIONS ACT, 1990

Office of the United States Courts. The Judicial Conference shall report to the Committees on Appropriations of the House of Representatives and the Senate on a quarterly basis beginning on the first day of each fiscal year regarding the sums deposited in said fund.

* * * * * * *

APPENDIX: MEDIAN INCOME TABLES

PCT118. MEDIAN FAMILY INCOME IN 1999 (DOLLARS) BY FAMILY SIZE [7] -
Universe: Families
Universe: Total population
Data Set: Census 2000 Summary File 4 (SF 4) - Sample Data

NOTE: Data based on a sample. For information on confidentiality protection, sampling error, nonsampling error, and definitions see http://factfinder.census.gov/home/en/datanotes/expsf4.htm.

	Total	2-person families	3-person families	4-person families	5-person families	6-person families	7-or-more-person families
Alabama	41,657	37,497	42,624	48,701	45,789	43,686	39,534
Alaska	59,036	55,886	58,258	64,025	61,864	58,712	56,136
Arizona	46,723	44,056	47,637	52,432	47,963	46,157	44,277
Arkansas	38,663	35,285	39,910	45,065	41,243	40,346	38,185
California	53,025	50,574	53,424	60,251	52,907	49,707	50,936
Colorado	55,883	51,356	56,237	63,286	59,653	57,259	56,652
Connecticut	65,521	56,381	67,490	76,089	74,853	72,172	64,211
Delaware	55,257	48,699	56,479	64,672	62,350	61,431	59,905
District of Columbia	46,283	47,594	44,229	50,632	42,420	40,282	45,778
Florida	45,625	41,603	46,758	52,689	51,068	49,199	47,614
Georgia	49,280	44,592	49,271	56,029	52,460	50,966	51,021
Hawaii	56,961	49,052	58,160	62,143	61,548	65,738	82,425
Idaho	43,490	39,260	44,164	49,150	47,403	48,652	47,296
Illinois	55,545	48,479	56,621	64,042	62,156	59,606	57,449
Indiana	50,261	43,298	52,262	57,884	56,824	55,085	55,516
Iowa	48,005	42,158	50,359	55,878	54,865	52,345	50,786
Kansas	49,624	44,415	50,751	56,887	53,949	52,360	51,529
Kentucky	40,939	35,846	42,361	48,815	47,720	45,139	42,859
Louisiana	39,774	35,184	40,209	47,062	44,653	40,924	34,821
Maine	45,179	39,425	47,367	53,087	52,952	51,199	53,171
Maryland	61,876	54,579	61,880	71,825	70,126	67,194	68,245
Massachusetts	61,664	51,370	63,999	72,451	71,743	70,423	71,301
Michigan	53,457	45,957	55,795	62,812	61,752	58,840	52,109
Minnesota	56,874	48,994	60,037	66,652	65,340	60,200	52,961
Mississippi	37,406	34,001	37,768	43,074	40,920	36,745	34,142
Missouri	46,044	40,509	47,436	54,519	53,144	50,716	49,527
Montana	40,487	37,213	41,305	46,327	43,972	41,618	39,793
Nebraska	48,032	42,486	49,677	54,891	54,228	52,756	50,682
Nevada	50,849	46,883	51,484	56,081	54,344	54,644	56,478
New Hampshire	57,575	50,023	59,385	66,627	67,438	69,074	67,901
New Jersey	65,370	54,703	67,029	76,138	73,995	72,386	70,577
New Mexico	39,425	37,707	39,192	43,493	39,791	38,569	36,396
New York	51,691	44,921	52,389	60,671	58,531	56,714	54,683
North Carolina	46,335	42,120	47,498	53,481	50,170	47,413	44,811
North Dakota	43,654	37,769	45,925	51,297	50,969	47,435	42,790
Ohio	50,037	42,923	51,665	58,777	57,979	56,194	52,081
Oklahoma	40,709	37,210	41,738	46,351	43,818	41,931	41,202
Oregon	48,680	44,278	50,260	55,536	52,473	50,723	50,769
Pennsylvania	49,184	41,394	52,066	58,734	57,991	55,968	50,497
Rhode Island	52,781	44,899	54,935	62,731	60,706	62,018	54,129
South Carolina	44,227	40,325	44,724	51,163	48,108	44,450	43,491
South Dakota	43,237	38,596	45,538	50,596	48,528	45,301	33,005
Tennessee	43,517	38,858	45,002	50,776	49,990	46,962	46,082
Texas	45,861	43,483	45,999	51,607	45,712	41,819	41,957
Utah	51,022	42,497	50,002	55,411	58,452	61,603	63,208
Vermont	48,625	43,469	50,009	56,370	54,894	52,237	54,231
Virginia	54,169	49,211	53,951	61,387	60,653	60,556	61,464
Washington	53,760	49,542	54,622	61,389	58,078	54,680	53,094
West Virginia	36,484	32,722	39,022	42,290	40,601	38,659	37,287
Wisconsin	52,911	46,064	55,713	61,511	60,490	56,572	48,939
Wyoming	45,685	41,299	47,268	51,170	50,572	50,793	49,785
Puerto Rico	16,543	13,615	17,036	20,110	18,991	16,994	15,935

NOTE: When a race or ethnic group or an ancestry group is selected, the data in this table refer to the race, Hispanic or Latino origin, American Indian or Alaska Native tribe, or ancestry of the householder.
U.S. Census Bureau
Census 2000

PCT115. MEDIAN FAMILY INCOME IN 1999 (DOLLARS) BY NUMBER OF WORKERS IN FAMILY IN 1999 [5] - Universe: Families
Universe: Total population
Data Set: Census 2000 Summary File 4 (SF 4) - Sample Data

NOTE: Data based on a sample. For information on confidentiality protection, sampling error, nonsampling error, and definitions see http://factfinder.census.gov/home/en/datanotes/expsf4.htm.

	Total	No workers	1 worker	2 or more workers, husband and wife worked	2 or more workers, other
Alabama	41,657	18,205	29,791	59,524	42,689
Alaska	59,036	23,743	38,496	74,846	56,089
Arizona	46,723	29,580	32,428	65,376	45,879
Arkansas	30,663	19,900	27,086	53,173	38,905
California	53,025	24,074	36,617	76,285	52,424
Colorado	55,883	28,958	37,575	70,629	50,719
Connecticut	65,521	28,055	44,268	85,362	60,333
Delaware	55,257	29,436	37,510	74,389	51,582
District of Columbia	46,283	9,990	31,983	95,148	54,918
Florida	45,625	29,505	32,314	63,300	45,936
Georgia	49,280	19,042	31,912	67,353	47,109
Hawaii	56,961	27,873	37,397	73,103	65,759
Idaho	43,490	26,471	30,877	54,746	42,112
Illinois	55,545	24,981	37,861	73,666	54,196
Indiana	50,261	24,719	34,388	64,816	48,635
Iowa	48,005	26,645	31,769	59,280	43,159
Kansas	49,624	27,574	33,134	61,959	45,332
Kentucky	40,939	16,896	29,038	58,734	43,577
Louisiana	39,774	15,111	27,641	60,570	41,097
Maine	45,179	22,648	30,889	58,489	43,229
Maryland	61,876	28,467	40,256	82,212	57,912
Massachusetts	61,664	23,020	41,217	82,018	60,151
Michigan	53,457	26,524	37,553	72,382	53,302
Minnesota	56,874	28,390	36,807	69,668	51,818
Mississippi	37,406	14,450	25,733	56,188	38,754
Missouri	46,044	24,326	31,374	61,426	45,262
Montana	40,487	25,372	28,098	51,650	37,012
Nebraska	48,032	27,009	31,170	58,694	43,944
Nevada	50,849	29,009	35,726	66,666	52,420
New Hampshire	57,575	27,295	39,727	70,820	52,796
New Jersey	65,370	27,013	45,722	87,860	63,124
New Mexico	39,425	20,179	27,461	57,330	39,762
New York	51,691	18,896	36,095	76,479	56,127
North Carolina	46,335	21,609	30,677	61,909	43,674
North Dakota	43,654	24,193	28,212	53,825	39,462
Ohio	50,037	24,603	34,664	66,830	49,293
Oklahoma	40,709	22,037	28,433	55,745	39,715
Oregon	48,680	28,448	34,581	63,454	46,150
Pennsylvania	49,184	23,795	35,329	66,822	50,961
Rhode Island	52,781	20,533	35,608	71,127	53,192
South Carolina	44,227	20,421	29,551	61,115	42,635
South Dakota	43,237	23,196	27,586	53,446	38,017
Tennessee	43,517	19,036	30,446	59,410	44,672
Texas	45,861	20,192	30,636	64,735	43,606
Utah	51,022	30,373	37,494	60,537	54,119
Vermont	48,625	24,712	31,764	60,856	42,935
Virginia	54,169	26,245	35,960	71,063	50,520
Washington	53,760	30,971	38,445	69,955	50,636
West Virginia	36,484	19,704	29,041	53,549	41,797
Wisconsin	52,911	27,509	34,836	65,665	48,311
Wyoming	45,685	27,151	31,463	56,570	41,506
Puerto Rico	16,543	6,065	15,470	34,423	29,283

NOTE: When a race or ethnic group or an ancestry group is selected, the data in this table refer to the race, Hispanic or Latino origin, American Indian or Alaska Native tribe, or ancestry of the householder.
U.S. Census Bureau
Census 2000